Simon & Schuster's

SUPER
CROSTICS

Book #6

THOMAS H. MIDDLETON

Simon & Schuster's

SUPER CROSTICS

Book #6

A FIRESIDE BOOK
PUBLISHED BY SIMON & SCHUSTER

New York   London   Toronto   Sydney

FIRESIDE
Rockefeller Center
1230 Avenue of the Americas
New York, NY 10020

For information about special discounts for bulk purchases,
please contact Simon & Schuster Special Sales:
1-800-456-6798 or business@simonandschuster.com

Designed by Helen Barrow
Manufactured in the United States of America

5 7 9 10 8 6

ISBN 0-7432-3696-3
ISBN 978-0-7432-3696-6

This is a compilation of previously published puzzles.

FOREWORD

Welcome to the newest installment of *Super Crostics* from Simon & Schuster!

A well-constructed crostic is no mere word game or puzzle; it is preeminently a test of human will. Yet such a test need not be unpleasant or arduous. Indeed, when it comes to the splendid crostics of Thomas H. Middleton, the joy is in the doing. And in the newest giant collection of classic puzzles, there is a lot of doing to be done. In the following pages, you'll find 185 of the trickiest brain-busters ever created, all culled from the Middleton archives here in Rockefeller Center.

So don't just sit there. Test *your* will—and enjoy the results.

THE PUBLISHER

SPECIAL NOTE

For the convience of solvers who find it awkward to work Crostics in a paperback book, the pages are perforated along the spine edge. This makes for easy removal of a single leaf. If you prefer not to remove pages, open the book at several different places and press down gently from top to bottom along the bound edge. This will help the book lie flat.

COMPLETE ANSWERS WILL BE FOUND AT THE BACK.

IF YOU ENJOY OUR PUZZLES, HERE'S MORE TO EXPLORE.

Simon & Schuster has been publishing outstanding crossword puzzle books every year since 1924—a grand tradition that continues into the twenty-first century.

The world's first and longest-running crossword series continues its tradition of all brand-new and totally original puzzles, constructed by top experts in the field. Editor John M. Samson promises another year of prime cruciverbal wizardry that will keep your brow furrowed and your mind spinning.

So get out your pens or pencils, sharpen your wits, and get ready for months of brain-teasing fun!

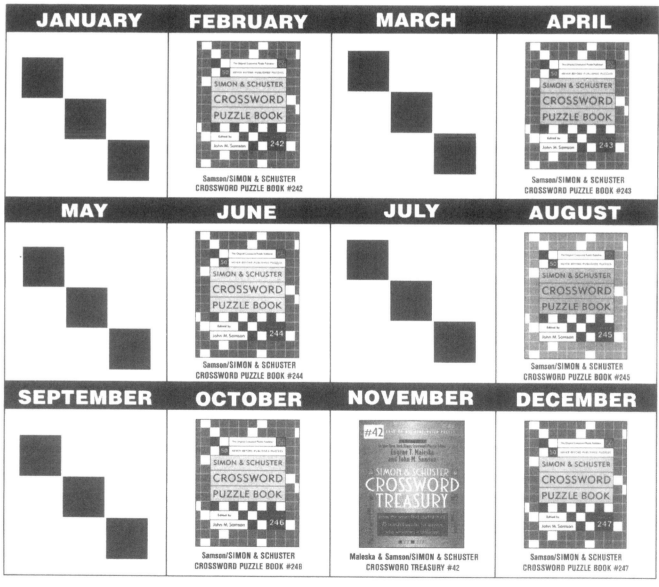

JANUARY   FEBRUARY   MARCH   APRIL

Samson/SIMON & SCHUSTER CROSSWORD PUZZLE BOOK #242

Samson/SIMON & SCHUSTER CROSSWORD PUZZLE BOOK #243

MAY   JUNE   JULY   AUGUST

Samson/SIMON & SCHUSTER CROSSWORD PUZZLE BOOK #244

Samson/SIMON & SCHUSTER CROSSWORD PUZZLE BOOK #245

SEPTEMBER   OCTOBER   NOVEMBER   DECEMBER

Samson/SIMON & SCHUSTER CROSSWORD PUZZLE BOOK #246

Maleska & Samson/SIMON & SCHUSTER CROSSWORD TREASURY #42

Samson/SIMON & SCHUSTER CROSSWORD PUZZLE BOOK #247

For Simon & Schuster's online crosswords,
visit us at www.simonsays.com.

1

CLUES

A Burlesque comic's expression of surprise, or whatever (3 wds.) · 166 96 145 38 4 177 175 75 150 36

B Not to be allowed · 180 57 43 14 230 79 49 32 197 99 76
(answer partly entered: F O R B I D — E N)

C Pharos · 221 226 106 19 72 192 140 89 37 129

D Former term for port at sea · 33 98 126 77 212 199 146 16

E Join (an organization, e.g.) surreptitiously · 142 31 224 70 90 1 78 23 21 218

F Fabled fabulist · 115 209 3 152 128

G "The gay ___ that people the sunbeams" (Milton, "Il Penseroso") · 104 184 208 64 169

H Minor prophet of the 6th cent. B.C. · 108 97 113 7 61 141 103 20 22

I Place into office · 52 118 62 74 87 211 163

J Milt Gross character who was praised for finishing his chicken soup (2 wds.) · 41 228 81 147 205 105 174 144

K Makes explosive popping or sizzling sounds · 69 164 137 148 95 50 39 181

L Caledonian · 231 6 219 191 161 30 122 139

M Intermissions · 25 59 173 160 156 227 194 193 201

N Harmonious relation · 85 107 131 196 159 210 189

O Burdensome, tyrannical · 195 220 153 27 158 204 188 24 66

P Summer resort-cum-naval base in Rhode Island · 86 133 176 217 223 15 60

Q Means · 13 124 5 68 121 187 134 138 162 229 132

R Daydream, visionary concept · 198 11 83 206 155 82

S Apprehensions, grasps · 54 110 157 34 186 149 207 17

T Gives rise to, initiates (2 wds.) · 63 26 100 213 171 111 12 119 225 94

U "He fell ___ / And saw heaven opened" (3 wds., Acts 10:10–11) · 109 56 18 8 2 151 183 45 135 88 222

V Cows, oxen · 71 84 172 179 10

W 1881 Ibsen play · 29 190 93 112 143 53

X Slogan · 182 214 35 51 44 123 73 168 47

Y Subject favored by John Le Carre · 125 117 48 28 58 46 91 42 67

Z Territory formerly governed by Ann Richards (3 wds. after the) · 216 130 102 167 200 120 136 92 116 170 178 203 80

Z₁ Song often lovingly destroyed on Jack Benny's violin (3 wds.) · 114 55 65 40 202 185 154 215 9 165 101

GRID

1	E2	U3	F4	A5	Q6							L
7	H8	U9	Z₁10	V11	R12	▓	13	Q14	B15	P16	D17	S
18	U19	C20	H21	▓	22	H23	E24	O25	▓	26		T
27	O28	Y29	W30	L31	▓	32	B33	D34	S35	X36	37	C
38	A39	K40	Z₁41	J42	Y43	B44	X	▓	45	U46	Y47	X
48	Y49	B50	K51	X52	I53	W54	S55	Z₁56	▓	57	B58	Y
59	M —		60	P61	H62	I63	T64	G	65	Z₁66	O67	Y68	Q
69	K	▓	70	E71	V72	C73	X	74	I75	A76	B	77	D
78	E79	B80	Z81	J82	R	83	R84	V85	N86	P87	I88	U
89	C90	E91	Y92	Z	93	W94	T	95	K96	A97	H	
98	D99	B100	T101	Z₁102	Z103	H	104	G105	J106	C107	N108	H
109	U110	S111	T112	W	113	H114	Z₁115	Z116	Y117	I118	I	
119	T120	Q121	L122	X123	Q124	Y125	D126	O127	F128	F		
129	C130	Z131	N132	Q133	▓	134	Q135	U	136	Z137	K138	Q
139	L140	H141	E142	W143	W144	J	145	A146	D147	J	148	K
149	S150	A151	U152	F153	O	154	Z₁155	R156	M157	S158	O	
159	N160	M161	L162	Q163	I	164	K165	Z₁166	A167	Z		
168	X169	G170	Z171	T172	V173	M174	J175	A176	P			
177	A178	Z179	V180	B181	K182	X183	U184	G185	Z₁186	S		
187	Q188	O189	N190	W191	L192	C193	M194	M195	O			
196	N197	B198	R199	D200	Z201	M202	Z₁203	Z204	O			
205	J206	R207	S208	G209	F210	N211	I212	D213	T214	X		
215	Z₁216	Z217	P218	E219	L220	C221	C222	U223	P224	E		
225	T226	C227	M228	J229	B230	B231	L					

2

Grid

■	■	■	■	1 D	2 R	3 L	4 Q	5 M	6 X	7 J
8 U	■	9 K	10 M	11 F	12 C	13 M	14 V	15 R	16 O	17 E
■	■	18 B	19 E	20 L	21 A	22 X	23 A	24 D	25 Y	26 Z
27 R	28 T	29 S	30 Q	31 P	32 O	33 B	34 L	35 K	36 N	37 I
■	38 S	39 W	40 A	41 Q	42 X	43 H	44 G	45 P	46 M	47 G
■	48 K	49 I	50 Q	51 E	52 O	53 P	54 Z	55 B	56 N	57 B
58 V	59 U	60 F	61 C	62 X	63 S	64 C	65 W	66 E	67 Z	68 U
■	■	69 P	70 Y	71 V	72 B	73 W	74 A	75 N	76 I	77 L
■	78 Q	79 N	80 L	81 W	82 Y	83 H	84 K	85 P	86 I	87 D
■	■	88 J	89 H	90 Q	91 R	92 M	93 J	94 B	95 W	96 O
■	97 U	98 I	99 C	100 D	101 X	102 W	103 U	104 Z	105 M	106 P
■	107 S	108 U	109 O	110 C	111 R	112 G	113 L	114 M	115 B	116 M
■	117 E	118 I	119 O	120 L	121 A	122 M	123 K	124 A	125 F	126 M
■	127 E	128 S	129 V	130 M	131 L	132 H	133 B	134 Y	135 T	136 Z
■	■	137 F	138 Q	139 P	140 I	141 Y	142 U	143 Y	144 M	145 F
■	146 Y	147 O	148 F	149 N	150 W	151 R	152 D	153 S	154 Z	155 A
■	■	156 P	157 Y	158 A	159 V	160 J	161 V	162 B	163 E	164 S
■	165 M	166 N	167 I	168 H	169 L	170 D	171 S	172 M	173 Q	174 N
■	175 G	176 L	177 V	178 C	179 J	180 U	181 X	182 O	183 B	184 D
■	185 J	186 G	187 E	188 I	189 S	190 T	191 C	192 U	193 A	194 F
■	■	■	■	■	195 H	196 U	197 W	198 R	199 D	200 P

CLUES

A. Casting out, denial

B. Wacky, screwball, unpredictable (3 wds.)

C. Crude, rude

D. Having a sense of the beautiful

E. Respite from impending punishment

F. First-rate (hyph., Brit. sl.)

G. Liquor bottle, perhaps

H. Am. writer (1923–: "The Naked and the Dead")

I. Callous, unsympathetic

J. 1775 Sheridan comedy (after "The")

K. Respect, veneration, awe

L. Professional murderer (2 wds.)

M. "___, and Pleasure at the helm" (4 wds.; Gray, "The Bard")

N. "Death, whene'er he call, / Must call ___" (2 wds.; Gilbert, "Yeomen of the Guard")

O. Portable cooking appliance (2 wds.)

P. Cilia

Q. 1940 Spencer Tracy film (2 wds.)

R. Survive

S. Highly desirable member of the opposite sex

T. Craving

U. Quality or article peculiar to a particular person, place, etc. (chiefly Brit.)

V. Out of favor (2 wds.)

W. What Lilli Marlene was standing underneath "by the barrack gate"

X. "___ shadows fly" (Shelley, "Adonais")

Y. Edward Lear's specialty

Z. Hand tool with a flat or scooplike blade

WORDS

A. 21 121 40 74 193 23 155 158 124

B. 72 162 18 133 55 57 115 183 33 94

C. 99 12 178 61 191 64 110

D. 170 184 199 24 100 152 87 1

E. 17 19 51 127 66 163 187 117

F. 125 194 11 145 148 137 60

G. 175 186 47 44 112

H. 195 132 43 83 89 168

I. 76 118 167 49 140 86 188 98 37

J. 7 179 88 93 160 185

K. 48 35 123 9 84

L. 131 20 80 176 120 169 77 34 113 3

M. 122 172 165 144 105 46 114 92 116 126 13 5 10 130

N. 166 79 75 149 56 174 36

O. 147 96 109 182 52 16 119 32

P. 200 45 106 69 85 139 31 53 156

Q. 90 41 50 173 4 138 30 78

R. 2 91 111 15 151 27 198

S. 171 29 128 153 38 164 63 107 189

T. 190 28 135

U. 192 196 103 180 142 68 108 97 59 8

V. 161 58 129 14 159 71 177

W. 197 39 73 65 150 81 95 102

X. 181 6 42 101 62 22

Y. 82 134 157 70 146 143 141 25

Z. 67 104 26 54 136 154

3

CLUES

A. Eng. philosopher (1861–1947) co-author with Bertrand Russell of "Principia Mathematica": 158 146 129 189 127 141 121 21 91

B. Meaningless; insincere: 171 212 70 108 56 198

C. Rashness; violence: 196 33 180 18 67 205 3 166 75 22 122

D. Drinking mugs featuring tricorns: 64 193 221 16 203 162

E. Portable writing surface: 124 95 161 217 209 194 61 133 73

F. Evil inclination inherent in human nature (2 wds.): 113 119 35 195 5 219 153 148 160 181 80

G. Demon; ogre; teratism: 216 82 137 100 112 13 52

H. Ball, feast, banquet, shindig: 19 207 118 176 89 25 138

I. Flaubert's Emma: 204 200 17 49 165 116

J. Came forth: 40 135 28 106 76 208 117

K. Plant of the mustard family; moolah, long green: 59 41 1 192 168 104 164

L. Show servile deference: 110 199 185 38 125 97

M. Vigorous attack: 24 103 120 71 58 134 11 31 184

N. In these times, currently: 90 215 101 66 29 43 211 14

O. Rudimentary, lacking order: 102 57 88 77 10 98 163 6

P. Indispensable: 44 136 26 87 144 46 177 39 220

Q. Antiquated; fanciful; barbarous; uneducated: 201 2 23 84 183 167

R. Food-storage areas: 213 74 157 197 62 32 99 86

S. 1925 Sinclair Lewis novel: 55 156 182 69 92 7 42 79 187 151

T. White hellebore (Veratrum album) of Europe: 109 132 214 174 145 85 47 96

U. Enjoyed: 68 175 140 53 15 190 152 155

V. Metal eyelet: 206 126 210 114 50 191 83

W. Feeling indignant displeasure at: 12 51 107 20 36 143 202 154 170

X. Arrange by clever planning: 93 9 54 188 105 131 78 178 34 81 63

Y. State of northern India; cap. Lucknow (2 wds.): 169 48 30 139 94 8 60 218 128 111 159 27

Z. Dusk to dawn: 130 186 4 65 172 150 142 115 149

Z₁. Stops, gives up: 45 72 37 147 179 173 123

WORDS

1	2	3	4	5	6	7	8	9	10	11	12	13
K1	Q2	C3	Z4	F5	O6	S7	Y8	■	X9	O10	M11	■
W12	G13	N14	U15	D16	I17	C18	■	H19	W20	A21	C22	■
Q23	M24	H25	P26	Y27	J28	N29	■	Y30	M31	R32	■	■
C33	X34	F35	W36	Z₁37	L38	P39	J40	K41	S42	■	■	■
N43	P44	Z₁45	P46	T47	Y48	■	I49	V50	W51	G52	■	■
U53	X54	S55	B56	O57	■	M58	■	K59	Y60	E61	■	■
R62	X63	D64	Z65	N66	C67	■	U68	S69	B70	M71	■	■
Z₁72	E73	R74	C75	J76	O77	X78	■	S79	F80	X81	■	■
G82	V83	Q84	T85	R86	P87	O88	H89	N90	A91	■	■	■
S92	X93	Y94	E95	T96	■	L97	O98	R99	G100	■	■	■
N101	O102	M103	K104	X105	J106	W107	■	B108	T109	■	■	■
L110	Y111	G112	F113	V114	Z115	I116	J117	H118	F119	M120	A121	■
C122	Z₁123	E124	L125	V126	A127	Y128	A129	Z130	X131	■	■	■
T132	E133	M134	J135	P136	G137	H138	Y139	U140	A141	Z142	■	■
W143	P144	T145	A146	Z₁147	F148	Z149	Z150	S151	U152	■	■	■
F153	W154	U155	S156	R157	A158	Y159	F160	E161	D162	■	■	■
O163	K164	I165	C166	Q167	K168	Y169	W170	B171	Z172	■	■	■
Z₁173	T174	U175	H176	P177	X178	Z₁179	C180	F181	S182	■	■	■
Q183	M184	L185	Z186	S187	X188	A189	U190	V191	■	■	■	■
K192	D193	E194	F195	C196	R197	B198	L199	I200	Q201	W202	■	■
D203	I204	C205	V206	H207	J208	E209	V210	N211	■	■	■	■
B212	R213	T214	N215	G216	E217	Y218	F219	P220	D221	■	■	■

4

Grid

■	■	■	1 W	2 E	3 C	4 O	5 M	6 J	7 U	8 E
9 B	10 C	11 S	12 R	13 O	14 Q	15 M	16 S	17 K	■	■
18 U	19 E	20 X	21 T	22 Y	23 W	24 B	25 H	26 U	27 Y	28 F
29 P	30 R	31 F	32 J	33 U	34 V	35 N	36 W	37 E	38 M	■
39 Q	40 E	41 T	42 X	43 E	44 B	45 S	46 W	47 I	48 V	49 R
50 K	51 O	52 D	53 N	54 B	55 J	56 W	57 S	58 R	59 G	■
60 Y	61 K	62 S	63 N	64 A	65 H	66 W	67 E	68 Q	69 B	70 T
71 V	72 X	73 L	74 U	75 J	76 V	77 H	78 G	79 P	80 T	■
81 H	82 J	83 Q	84 F	85 M	86 O	87 W	88 S	89 Y	90 L	■
91 V	92 U	93 J	94 I	95 X	96 M	97 T	98 F	99 F	100 S	■
101 X	102 K	103 S	104 O	105 B	106 I	107 F	108 N	109 M	■	■
110 I	111 R	112 S	113 R	114 V	115 O	116 I	117 U	118 U	■	■
119 U	120 V	121 L	122 C	123 H	124 I	125 D	126 G	127 B	128 H	■
129 J	130 O	131 Y	132 G	133 X	134 N	135 K	136 B	137 D	138 I	139 M
140 T	141 W	142 A	143 O	144 J	145 F	146 X	147 V	148 I	149 O	150 R
151 B	152 D	153 P	154 Y	155 L	156 K	157 F	158 X	159 T	160 S	■
161 Q	162 A	163 P	164 R	165 Y	166 Y	167 G	168 F	169 D	170 Y	■
171 U	172 V	173 X	174 D	175 N	176 E	177 H	178 A	179 T	180 J	181 G
182 F	183 X	184 Q	185 P	186 G	187 R	188 Y	189 T	190 U	■	■
191 N	192 A	193 B	194 F	195 T	196 K	197 A	198 H	199 X	200 Q	■
201 V	202 R	203 W	204 N	205 D	206 J	207 E	208 K	209 T	210 A	211 P
212 I	213 B	214 M	215 G	216 C	217 L	218 S	■	■	■	■

CLUES

WORDS

A. "Old Hickory" Andrew . . . . — 64 162 142 192 178 197 210

B. Conceitedly dogmatic . . . . — 127 136 193 44 151 69 213 24 9 105 54

C. Ger. poet and essayist (1797–1856, "Reisebilder") . . . . — 104 216 10 122 3

D. Colorless petroleum distillate used as a fuel, solvent, etc. . . . . — 152 52 174 137 205 125 169

E. No way! Forget it! (2 wds.) . . . . . . — 40 43 67 37 2 19 207 8 176

F. Lack of resolution . . . . — 157 98 28 168 31 145 182 84 107 194

G. "___ thought is slow and durable" (Browning, "Luria") . . . . — 181 186 132 59 215 126 167 78

H. Erotically suggestive . . . . — 25 65 99 81 123 198 77 128 177

I. Determine, settle, as a dispute . . . . . — 47 116 148 138 124 106 212 110 94

J. Path of a body moving under the action of given forces . . . . — 129 75 206 6 32 93 144 180 55 82

K. Provoked, chafed, nettled . . . . — 135 196 102 61 50 208 17 156

L. Drive off . . . . — 155 121 73 90 217

M. Loathed . . . . — 109 38 96 5 139 15 85 214

N. Samuel Johnson's "Prince of Abissinia" . . . . — 175 35 134 204 63 53 108 191

O. Improper, unfortunate . . . . — 149 86 51 13 130 143 4 115

P. Opening in the railing or bulwark of a ship . . . . — 118 29 163 211 153 79 185

Q. Vulture of southern Europe; monster with the head of an eagle and the body of a lion . . . . — 83 161 68 184 14 39 200

R. Shield; ornamental plate around a keyhole . . . . — 202 58 30 187 150 164 113 49 111 12

S. "The lady ___ too much," says Queen Gertrude (2 wds. "Hamlet") . . — 45 160 112 16 218 62 11 103 100 57 88

T. "The Lady with the Lamp" (1820–1910, last name) . . . . — 159 209 41 189 140 179 70 195 97 80 21

U. Baloney, bunk, hooey . . . . — 190 33 18 171 7 119 26 117 92 74

V. Ballerinas, e.g. (2 wds.) . . . . — 34 71 172 201 91 147 120 114 48 76

W. Cut off in mid-passage . . . . — 141 36 23 87 203 66 56 46 1

X. Organization formed by Frank Buchanan in 1921; predecessor to Moral Re-Armament (2 wds.) . . . . . . — 183 173 72 146 42 133 158 20 101 199 95

Y. He regretted that he had but one life to lose for his country (full name) . . . . — 22 131 188 89 154 27 60 166 170 165

5

CLUES

A. Bend easily to one's desires
(2 wds. followed by WORD B) . . .   59 22 53 148 89 163 15 105 138 170

B. See WORD A (2 wds.) 83 132 164 78 81 31 14 58 181 3

C. Gestures 63 125 45 12 147 103 115

D. Soil plot to be sown for
transplanting 48 169 184 38 55 72 112

E. One who frequents the tables of
others; parasite (2 wds.) 6 160 187 68 167 71 96 118 90 44 122 76 153 49

F. Son of Agamemnon and
Clytemnestra 87 24 33 144 173 159 5

G. Mackerel-like fish also called the
cero 196 47 40 149 137 4 86

H. Scottish-born U.S. detective,
1819–84 . . . .   27 157 37 154 189 77 62 2 66

I. Something added; consent 166 140 101 11 161 178 152 119 13

J. Limiting, confining 156 114 165 199 93 54 30 70 39 191 8

K. Documents containing detailed
information on a subject 186 135 51 34 111 17 28 121

L. Beat as if with a flail 35 60 110 197 133 95

M. Nag, plug, crowbait 151 65 98 104 172 10 136 21 176

N. Am. theologian and meta-
physician, 1703–58, "Freedom
of the Will" 129 146 155 25 168 139 188

O. Regularly recurring, cadenced . . .   193 75 82 182 141 97 134 117

P. "'Tis better to be vile than vile
_____," (contr.; Shakespeare,
"Sonnet 121") 192 32 19 194 92 126 108

Q. Thistle-like plant with an edible
flower 116 128 158 67 16 7 43 88 50

R. Inept sailor 107 61 57 177 85 100 109 171 131 190

S. 1965 Edward Albee play (2 wds.) . .   150 80 123 185 179 26 145 198 64

T. Clink, pokey, lockup, jug 130 175 99 195 29 69 79 1

U. Thereby (2 wds.) 106 127 120 73 42 162 52 23 143

V. Rembrandt's most famous group
painting, popularly (2 wds. after
The) 18 56 41 46 74 174 102 94 124 183

W. Type of security 113 84 36 180 142 20 91 9

Grid

1 T	2 H	3 B	4 G	5 F	6 E	7 Q	8 J	9 W	10 M	11 I	
12 C	13 I	14 B	15 A	16 Q	17 K	18 V	19 P	20 W	21 M		
22 A	23 U	24 F	25 N	26 S	■	27 H	28 K	29 T	30 J	31 B	32 P
33 F	■	34 K	35 L	36 W	37 H	38 D	39 J	40 G	41 V	42 U	
43 Q	44 E	45 C	46 V	47 G	48 D	■	49 E	50 Q	51 K	52 U	
53 A	54 J	55 D	56 V	57 R	58 B	■	59 A	60 L	61 R	62 H	
63 C	64 S	65 M	66 H	67 Q	68 E	69 T	70 J	71 E	72 D		
73 U	74 V	75 O	76 E	77 H	■	78 B	79 T	80 S	81 B		
82 O	83 B	84 W	■	85 R	86 G	87 F	88 Q	89 A	90 E	91 W	
92 P	93 J	94 V	95 L	96 E	97 O	98 M	99 T	100 R			
101 I	102 V	103 C	104 M	105 A	106 U	107 R	108 P	109 R	110 L		
111 K	112 D	113 W	114 J	115 C	■	116 Q	117 O	118 E	119 I	120 U	121 K
■	122 E	123 S	124 V	125 C	126 P	127 U	128 Q	129 N	130 T	131 R	132 B
133 L	134 O	135 K	136 M	■	137 G	138 A	139 N	140 I	141 O	142 W	
143 U	144 F	145 S	■	146 N	147 C	148 A	149 G	■	150 S	151 M	
152 I	153 E	154 H	155 N	156 J	157 H	158 Q	159 F	160 E	161 I		
162 U	163 A	164 B	165 J	166 I	167 E	168 N	169 D	170 A	171 R		
172 M	173 F	■	174 V	175 T	176 M	177 R	178 I	179 S	180 W	181 B	
182 O	183 V	184 D	185 S	186 K	187 E	188 N	189 H	190 R	191 J		
192 P	■	193 O	194 P	195 T	196 G	197 L	198 S	199 J			

6

CLUES

	Clue	Word numbers
A	Release tension, as by loud talking or violent activity (3 wds.)	13 102 203 28 189 162 180 88 94 157 4 17
B	Strike terror into	199 76 177 164 146 223 122 9
C	Tin Lizzie, bucket o' bolts	21 16 114 106 97 44 121 156 63 200
D	Youngest son of Jacob and Rachel (Gen. 35:18)	188 87 145 11 14 67 32 70
E	Eagerness	168 220 120 196 178 207 215
F	Nocturnal arboreal carnivore of North America: Var. sp.	86 150 205 193 216 185
G	Snacks for ladybugs	111 201 160 79 170 29
H	Disgust	61 35 73 8 105 52 51 128
I	Offensive	20 151 93 219 85 186
J	Gave utterance to	92 144 7 192 165 54
K	Nougat ingredient	30 195 183 66 137 173
L	O.K., legit	113 65 15 2 154 202
M	Cut for record-keeping	131 125 6 101 208 174 190
N	To the nth degree; thoroughly (3 wds.)	204 143 153 179 197 191 31 184 24
O	Follower of Aquinas	176 139 56 117 127 36 225
P	Not pure; bawdy	194 19 57 43 172 112 84 75
Q	Massage	124 213 96 55 142 34 104
R	Rough calculation	116 109 33 18 59 187 37 27
S	"Ye men of ___, I perceive that in all things ye are too superstitious," said Paul (Acts 17:22)	77 110 135 98 53 118
T	Refinements	222 26 78 46 23 108 136 50
U	Markedly, clearly	69 103 166 148 123 169 152 72 210 133
V	Chin, jaw, shoot the breeze (3 wds.)	141 107 68 134 41 149 115 217 71 159
W	Unprecedented (hyph.)	211 80 206 60 83 182 158 38 47
X	Wasting time	132 12 48 1 91 5 224 126 39
Y	Fawners, lickspittles	138 181 95 64 221 100 147
Z	Fruitless	58 90 214 198 119 155 45 99 175 82 81
Z₁	In 1906, he used the term "muckrake" in its modern journalistic sense	49 163 130 129 25 3 218 42
Z₂	Hands and feet, for instance	40 212 62 74 140 171 89 167 22 161 10

Diagram (cell number / clue letter)

1 X	2 L	3 Z₁	4 A	5 X	6 M	7 J	8 H	9 B	10 Z₂
11 D	12 X	13 A	14 D	15 L	16 C	17 A	18 R	19 P	
20 I	21 C	22 Z₂	23 T	24 N	25 Z₁	26 T	27 R	28 A	
29 G	30 K	31 N	32 D	33 R	34 Q	35 H	36 O	37 R	
38 W	39 X	40 Z₂	41 V	42 Z₁	43 P	44 C	45 Z	46 T	
47 W	48 X	49 Z₁	50 T	51 H	52 H	53 S	54 J	55 Q	56 O
57 P	58 Z	59 R	60 W	61 H	62 Z₂	63 C	64 Y	65 L	66 K
67 D	68 V	69 U	70 D	71 V	72 U	73 H	74 Z₂	75 P	76 B
77 S	78 T	79 G	80 W	81 Z	82 Z	83 W	84 P	85 I	86 F	87 D
88 A	89 Z₂	90 Z	91 X	92 J	93 I	94 A	95 Y	96 Q	97 C	98 S
99 Z	100 Y	101 M	102 A	103 U	104 Q	105 H	106 C	107 V	108 T
109 R	110 S	111 G	112 P	113 L	114 C	115 V	116 R	117 O	118 S
119 Z	120 E	121 C	122 B	123 U	124 Q	125 M	126 X	127 O	128 H
129 Z₁	130 Z₁	131 M	132 X	133 U	134 V	135 S	136 T	137 K	
138 Y	139 O	140 Z₂	141 V	142 Q	143 N	144 J	145 D	146 B	147 Y	148 U
149 V	150 F	151 I	152 U	153 N	154 L	155 Z	156 C	157 A	158 W
159 V	160 G	161 Z₂	162 A	163 Z₁	164 B	165 J	166 U	167 Z₂	
168 E	169 U	170 G	171 Z₂	172 P	173 K	174 M	175 Z	176 O	
177 B	178 E	179 N	180 A	181 Y	182 W	183 K	184 N	185 F	186 I
187 R	188 D	189 A	190 M	191 N	192 J	193 F	194 P	195 K	196 E
197 N	198 Z	199 B	200 C	201 G	202 L	203 A	204 N	205 F	206 W
207 E	208 M	209 Z₁	210 U	211 W	212 Z₂	213 Q	214 Z	215 E	
216 F	217 V	218 Z₁	219 I	220 E	221 Y	222 T	223 B	224 X	225 O

7

CLUES

A. Mrs. Shakespeare's maiden name . . . . `14 4 16 83 111 173 126 123`

B. Ger. physician, 1854–1915, Nobel Prize for Medicine, 1908, played in film by Edw. G. Robinson . . . . . . `146 53 105 161 41 86 26`

C. Snacked between meals . . . . . . `120 180 169 148 134 128`

D. Rank; despicable . . . . `20 102 147 175 37 28`

E. Lack of capacity or means . . . . . . `93 109 58 170 159 36 174 121 7`

F. Ger. novelist, 1875–1955, "Death in Venice" (full name) . . . . . `13 152 198 9 77 140 88 27 127 154`

G. Skiff, perhaps . . . . `196 165 142 117 122 72 172`

H. Thorough; unqualified (hyph.) . . . `44 199 52 6 40 63 54 168 151`

I. Boorish lout . . . . `76 34 47 61 29`

J. "The charmèd water burnt alway / A still and ___ red" (Coleridge, "The Ancient Mariner") . . . . . . `32 80 45 171 132`

K. "Towards the age of twenty-six, / ___ him into politics" (2 wds.; Belloc, "Lord Lundy") . . . . `18 182 104 137 112 178 82 164 186 85`

L. 1901 Justin McCarthy play about François Villon (4 wds.) . . . . `71 1 56 187 179 133 130 31 150 11 43`

M. Gives an improved appearance to; embellishes . . . . `116 50 101 23 155 94`

N. Astounded . . . . `135 99 19 33 163 191`

O. Family whose members include tobacco, potatoes, and tomatoes . . `35 107 12 156 177 79 185 38 162 66`

P. Also (2 wds.) . . . . `141 10 74 87 118 64`

Q. Salubrity . . . . `129 115 17 189 46 65`

R. Supplements (2 wds.) . . . . . . `192 25 145 70 75 125 60`

S. He shot Stanford White . . . . . `22 110 131 5`

T. She won the USLTA women's singles, 1975–78 . . . . `114 103 48 39 96`

U. Type of practice session . . . . . `3 89 81 24 139 184 21 100 160`

V. Irritate, annoy (4 wds.) . . . . . `119 195 113 90 138 157 149 51 143 59 108 158 2 197`

W. Turned upside down . . . . . . `98 73 57 106 78 181 15 136`

X. Clown, fool . . . . `49 166 30 55 153 91 42`

Y. Unstinted, generous . . . . . . `62 84 92 188 69 97`

Z. U.S. Secretary of War, 1899–1904, winner Nobel Peace Prize, 1912 (full name) . . . . . . `183 190 95 176 68 167 194 124 144`

Diagram (clue-letter for each numbered square)

1 L	2 V	3 U	4 A	5 S	6 H	7 E	8 ·	9 F	10 P
11 L	12 O	13 F	14 A	15 W	16 A	17 Q	18 K	19 N	20 D
21 U	22 S	23 M	24 U	25 R	26 B	27 F	28 D	29 I	30 X
31 L	32 J	33 N	34 I	35 O	36 E	37 D	38 O	39 T	40 H
41 B	42 ·	43 L	44 H	45 J	46 Q	47 I	48 T	49 X	50 M
51 V	52 H	53 B	54 H	55 ·	56 L	57 W	58 E	59 V	60 R
61 I	62 Y	63 H	64 P	65 Q	66 O	67 ·	68 Z	69 Y	70 R
71 L	72 G	73 W	74 P	75 R	76 I	77 F	78 W	79 O	80 J
81 U	82 K	83 A	84 Y	85 K	86 B	87 P	88 F	89 U	90 V
91 X	92 Y	93 E	94 M	95 Z	96 T	97 Y	98 W	99 N	100 U
101 M	102 D	103 T	104 K	105 B	106 W	107 O	108 V	109 E	110 S
111 A	112 K	113 V	114 T	115 Q	116 M	117 G	118 P	119 V	120 C
121 E	122 G	123 A	124 Z	125 R	126 A	127 F	128 C	129 Q	130 L
131 S	132 J	133 L	134 C	135 N	136 W	137 K	138 V	139 U	140 F
141 P	142 G	143 V	144 Z	145 R	146 B	147 D	148 C	149 V	150 L
151 H	152 F	153 X	154 F	155 M	156 O	157 V	158 V	159 E	160 U
161 B	162 O	163 N	164 O	165 G	166 X	167 Z	168 H	169 C	170 E
171 J	172 G	173 A	174 E	175 D	176 Z	177 O	178 K	179 L	180 C
181 W	182 K	183 Z	184 U	185 O	186 K	187 L	188 Y	189 Q	190 Z
191 N	192 R	193 ·	194 Z	195 V	196 G	197 V	198 F	199 H	

CLUES

A Articles of cowboy garb 86 116 93 163 103

B Yearns 130 179 32 19 47

C Lambskin with curled wool . . . 62 135 44 186 109 97 125 78 158

D Unreasoning 4 55 129 77 182 28 184 41 37

E Voracious reader 200 154 12 174 107 54 165 74

F Without delay (3 wds.) 112 208 16 121 87 161 148 35 197

G U.S. general who led the 82nd Airborne into Sicily, Italy, and France 171 18 95 57 115 120 204

H Rib 211 164 143 64 150 81

I "Life is good, and joy runs high / Between English ___" (3 wds.; Henley, "For England's Sake") 192 210 21 14 156 133 169 100 36 90 131

J In a fix (3 wds.) 84 159 76 194 190 167 155 101 124

K Coupling between rotating shafts set at an angle to each other (2 wds.) 206 63 98 29 49 153 188 73 202 127 43 168 94 53

L "The singing masons building ___" (3 wds., "Henry V") 31 181 138 207 111 160 102 42 15 7 83

M 2600-mile-long river emptying into the Gulf of Guinea 61 187 40 114 123

N Jaques says it is a stage (3 wds., "As You Like It") 106 27 119 70 178 152 136 20 205 203 144

O Strictly 118 69 170 2 166 151 183

P Time bomb, e.g. (2 wds.) 209 10 85 149 105 39 140 180 146 66 89 198 51 24 173

Q Type of sorcery 67 33 128 50 38 25

R Author of works on language and usage; chairman, American Heritage Usage Panel (full name) 122 193 26 46 52 72 3 34 139 9 99

S "He that will have a cake out of ___ must tarry the grinding" (2 wds., "Troilus and Cressida") 110 185 56 45 145 91 6 1

T "Pointedly foolish" literary device 23 162 176 113 30 80 59 142

U Polaris (2 wds.) 92 157 60 48 137 147 132 117 13

V Strong wind; noisy outburst 65 96 17 82

W Of an indefinitely large number in succession 201 175 11 5 126 195 191 104 58

X Fortress built c1000 at Koblenz, overlooking the Rhine 172 108 134 68 22 79 196 75 8 189 71 177 199 88 141

Diagram

1 S	2 O	3 R	4 D	5 W	6 S	7 L	8 X
9 R	10 P	11 W	12 E	13 U	14 I	15 L	16 F	17 V
18 G	19 B	20 N	21 I	22 X	23 T	24 P	25 Q	26 R	27 N
28 D	29 K	30 T	31 L	32 B	33 Q	34 R	35 F	36 I	37 D
38 Q	39 P	40 M	41 D	42 L	43 K	44 C	45 S	46 R	47 B
48 U	49 K	50 Q	51 P	52 R	53 K	54 E	55 D	56 S	57 G
58 W	59 T	60 U	61 M	62 C	63 K	64 H	65 V	66 P	67 Q
68 X	69 O	70 N	71 X	72 R	73 K	74 E	75 X	76 J
77 D	78 C	79 X	80 T	81 H	82 V	83 L	84 J	85 P
86 A	87 F	88 X	89 P	90 I	91 S	92 U	93 A	94 K	95 G
96 V	97 C	98 K	99 R	100 I	101 J	102 L	103 A
104 W	105 P	106 N	107 E	108 X	109 C	110 S	111 L	112 F	113 T
114 M	115 G	116 A	117 U	118 O	119 N	120 G	121 F	122 R	123 M
124 J	125 C	126 W	127 K	128 Q	129 D	130 B	131 I	132 U	133 I
134 X	135 C	136 N	137 U	138 L	139 R	140 P	141 X	142 T	143 H
144 N	145 S	146 P	147 U	148 F	149 P	150 H	151 O	152 N	153 K
154 E	155 J	156 I	157 U	158 C	159 J	160 L	161 F	162 T	163 A
164 H	165 E	166 O	167 J	168 K	169 I	170 O	171 G	172 X	173 P
174 E	175 W	176 T	177 X	178 N	179 B	180 P	181 L	182 D	183 O
184 D	185 S	186 C	187 M	188 K	189 X	190 J	191 W	192 I	193 R	194 J
195 W	196 X	197 F	198 P	199 X	200 E	201 W	202 K	203 N	204 G
205 N	206 K	207 L	208 F	209 P	210 I	211 H

9

CLUES

A Proclamation of intended marriage 113 27 192 30 151

B Searching for prey (3 wds.) 93 120 163 183 60 198 40 103 107 176

C Villainy of a lighter sort 187 108 57 196 11 16 19 84 50

D Pins, limbs 12 65 85 97

E Atonement 89 195 175 73 25 64 162 98 116

F Changed to a pulp by pounding . . . 49 9 63 190 95 67

G Afforded 166 191 70 158 123 129 167

H Glowing 94 157 141 43 125 186 5

I Toughen, temper 33 83 36 39 126 161

J Seams; fissures; streaks. 185 133 153 26 42

K Rosebay 55 34 152 135 131 90 169 3

L Prepared 102 122 45 88 35 197 21

M Insusceptible of change. 119 54 24 156 189 77 1 136 29

N Esau and Jacob, e.g. 142 180 62 14 114

O Build earthworks for defense . . . 82 61 100 47 76 137

P Hopeless; not reformable 181 7 132 111 92 72 146 28 201 80 22 115

Q 1935 Jeannette MacDonald–Nelson Eddy film (2 wds.) 87 112 150 74 59 182 188 174 53 32 160 17 37 68 204

R Swell, dandy, fine gent. 127 4 155 144

S Delight, bewitch. 184 205 58 145 164 66 178

T Beat, stung, flimflammed 165 2 140 18 179 104

U Dreams, goes woolgathering . . . 118 71 101 154 96

V County town of East Suffolk, England 75 203 81 8 105 172 128

W Swamp 110 78 173 56 193 148

X Train, retinue; ordered series of instrumental movements 202 41 86 124 138

Y Evergreen of Eurasia and northern Africa with upright branches and dark green foliage (2 wds.) . . . 44 99 6 147 69 23 194 134

Z 1922 D. W. Griffith film starring the Gish sisters (4 wds.) 149 168 91 38 79 20 10 130 52 15 200 31 109 206 143 48 159

Z_1 Settled down, took up residence . . 106 177 171 199 13 121

Z_2 Supports, bears 170 117 51 46 139 207

GRID

Row	Cells (number · letter)
1	1 M · 2 T · 3 K · 4 R · 5 H · 6 Y · 7 P · 8 V · 9 F
2	10 Z · 11 C · 12 D · 13 Z_1 · 14 N · 15 Z · 16 C · 17 Q · 18 T
3	19 C · 20 Z · 21 L · 22 P · 23 Y · 24 M · 25 E · 26 J · 27 A
4	28 P · 29 M · 30 A · 31 Z · 32 Q · 33 I · 34 K · 35 L · 36 I · 37 Q
5	38 Z · 39 I · 40 B · 41 X · 42 J · 43 H · 44 Y · 45 L · 46 Z_2 · 47 O
6	48 Z · 49 F · 50 C · 51 Z_2 · 52 Z · 53 Q · 54 M · 55 K · 56 W · 57 C
7	58 S · 59 Q · 60 B · 61 O · 62 N · 63 F · 64 E · 65 D · 66 S · 67 F
8	68 Q · 69 Y · 70 G · 71 U · 72 P · 73 E · 74 Q · 75 V · 76 O · 77 M
9	78 W · 79 Z · 80 P · 81 V · 82 O · 83 I · 84 C · 85 D · 86 X · 87 Q · 88 L
10	89 E · 90 K · 91 Z · 92 P · 93 B · 94 H · 95 F · 96 U · 97 D · 98 E · 99 Y
11	100 O · 101 U · 102 L · 103 B · 104 T · 105 V · 106 Z_1 · 107 B · 108 C · 109 Z
12	110 W · 111 P · 112 Q · 113 A · 114 N · 115 P · 116 E · 117 Z_2 · 118 U · 119 M
13	120 B · 121 Z_1 · 122 L · 123 G · 124 X · 125 H · 126 I · 127 R · 128 V · 129 G
14	130 Z · 131 K · 132 P · 133 J · 134 Y · 135 K · 136 M · 137 O · 138 X · 139 Z_2
15	140 T · 141 H · 142 N · 143 Z · 144 R · 145 S · 146 P · 147 Y
16	148 W · 149 Z · 150 Q · 151 A · 152 K · 153 J · 154 U · 155 R · 156 M · 157 H
17	158 G · 159 Z · 160 Q · 161 I · 162 E · 163 B · 164 S · 165 T · 166 G · 167 G
18	168 Z · 169 K · 170 Z_2 · 171 Z_1 · 172 V · 173 W · 174 Q · 175 E · 176 B · 177 Z_1 · 178 S
19	179 T · 180 N · 181 P · 182 Q · 183 B · 184 S · 185 J · 186 H · 187 C · 188 Q
20	189 M · 190 F · 191 G · 192 A · 193 W · 194 Y · 195 E · 196 C · 197 L · 198 B · 199 Z_1
21	200 Z · 201 P · 202 X · 203 V · 204 Q · 205 S · 206 Z · 207 Z_2

10

CLUES · **WORDS**

A. Make easier to endure 157 127 171 162 68 11 1 17 175

B. Baseball commissioner, 1921-44 . 170 77 4 74 36 22

C. Teeny (hyph.) 118 109 158 3 115 136 146 56

D. "See skulking Truth to her old ___ fled" (Pope, "The Dunciad") . . . 140 132 43 161 65 176 152

E. Authorize 130 164 101 21 148 44 141

F. Region of northern Scandinavia . . 70 57 138 80 91 120 54

G. Not scaly 105 12 32 169 106 14 165 49 46

H. Striker's bane 145 6 95 55

I. Harass; pester; tantalize 64 144 151 104 173

J. Worn out 27 30 100 53 39 82

K. Controlling power 51 73 122 35 26 92

L. Seize eagerly (2 wds.) 25 67 34 58 15 92

M. 1933 song by Jimmy Durante, Ben Ryan, and Harry Donnelly (3 wds.) . . . 50 166 153 93 62 75 41 81 160 108 99 147

N. Suburb of Mexico City, famous for canals and flowers 131 42 117 87 79 150 178 8 111 29

O. Escaped; avoided 37 103 78 16 90 180

P. Abnormal fear of red 66 94 113 134 135 163 102 20 59 168 18 89 126

Q. Stingy 76 85 10 96 110 159 156 128 167

R. Interested in and responsive to others 149 33 143 2 97 124 107 86

S. Wild; staunch; immoral; quick . . 177 142 48 112

T. Mollify 23 139 123 88 69 179

U. Manage 125 61 137 31

V. Mean 38 155 13 119 47 28

W. "___ no man's happiness" ("As You Like It") 5 172 45 40

X. Idea; caprice 98 9 121 154 71 83

Y. Fresh and bracing 133 52 63 116 72

Z. "Let's find out what ___ is doing" (Herbert, "Let's Stop Somebody") . . . 114 174 24 60 129 7 84 19

Diagram grid (cell number / clue letter)

1 A	2 R	3 C	4 B	5 B	6 W	7 Z	8 N	9 N	10 Q
11 A	12 G	13 V	■	14 R	15 L	16 O	17 A	18 P	19 Z
20 P	21 E	22 B	23 T	24 Z	25 L	26 K	27 J	28 V	29 N · 30 J
31 U	32 G	33 R	34 L	35 L	36 B	37 O	38 V	39 J	40 W
41 M	42 N	43 D	44 E	45 W	46 G	47 V	48 S	49 G	50 M
51 K	52 Y	53 J	54 F	55 H	56 C	57 F	58 L	59 P	60 Z
61 U	62 K	63 Y	64 I	65 D	66 P	67 L	68 A	69 T	70 F · 71 X
72 Y	73 K	74 B	75 M	76 Q	77 B	78 O	79 N	80 F	■
81 M	82 J	83 X	84 Z	85 Q	86 R	87 N	88 T	89 P	90 O
91 F	92 L	93 M	94 P	95 H	96 Q	97 R	98 X	99 M	100 J
101 E	102 P	103 O	104 I	105 G	106 G	107 R	108 M	109 C	■
110 Q	111 N	112 S	113 P	114 Z	115 C	116 Y	117 N	118 C	119 V
120 F	121 X	122 K	123 T	124 R	125 U	126 P	127 A	128 Q	129 Z · 130 E
131 N	132 D	133 Y	134 P	135 P	136 C	137 U	138 F	139 T	140 D · 141 E
142 S	143 R	144 I	145 H	146 C	147 M	148 E	149 R	150 N	151 I
152 D	153 M	154 X	155 V	156 Q	157 A	158 C	159 Q	160 M	161 D
162 A	163 P	164 E	165 G	166 M	167 Q	168 P	169 P	170 B	171 A
172 W	173 I	174 Z	175 A	176 D	177 S	178 N	179 T	180 O	■

11

CLUES

A Binge, tear, toot 53 128 207 184 153 25

B Swiss resort town on the Lake of
Constance 32 206 126 13 189 172 61 90 2

C Native 86 179 20 68 91 127 118 108

D Heed 169 51 122 178 115 1 193 103 66

E Oral; not written (esp. of a will) . 139 148 87 29 186 121 203 41 78 113 175

F Suddenly and unexpectedly
(4 wds.) 18 104 81 109 96 125 144 183 157 196 62 33

G Drugs 67 145 22 15 174

H Back of the head 131 200 72 191 165 31 7

I Ungues 42 160 98 70 46

J Derivation of mythology from
history 138 12 80 155 120 43 167 28 38 185

K Afr. cobra that squirts its venom . 182 50 105 88 188 95 77 6

L Ministers to 171 57 76 133 16

M Seaport of SW Eire 52 92 75 130 117 35

N Certify (2 wds.) 83 168 55 37 147 73 116 11

O "Through verdurous glooms and
winding _____ ways" (Keats,
"Ode to a Nightingale") 102 99 26 134 5

P Leader and bishop of the
Moravian Church in the U. S.
(1721–1802) 71 137 106 56 114 205 170

Q Negligent, careless 49 24 164 141 151 63

R Beginning; outset 10 154 187 181 23 30 45 166 40

S Mass of ice detached from an
iceberg 149 65 132 82

T Harmony 89 159 60 142 9 180

U Center of a large coal-mining area
in SE Australia 143 119 146 152 101 124 192 97 3

V Having no equal 161 48 140 194 150 202 112 34 94

W Acclaim 110 47 27 85 195 201 93 162

X Am. editor and author (1866–
1936; "Shame of the Cities") 74 204 158 69 19 64 176 17

Y "Repentance is but want of
power _____" (2 wds.; Dryden,
"Palamon and Arcite") 136 21 156 163 59

Z Slip by (of time) 8 84 135 198 107 58

Z₁ Memento 190 199 4 39 111 44 54 100

Z₂ Dark, gloomy; infernal 197 129 123 79 36 173 14

WORDS

(Grid)

	1	D2	B3	U	4	Z₅	O6	K7	H
8 Z	9 T	10 R	11 N	12 J	13 B	14 B	15 G	16 L	17 X	18 F
19 X	20 C	21 Y	22 G	23 R	24 Q	25 A	26 O	27 W	28 J
29 E	30 R	31 H	32 B	33 F	34 V	35 M	36 Z₂	37 J	38 J
39 Z₁	40 R	41 E	42 I	43 J	■	44 Z₁	45 R	46 I	47 W	48 V
49 Q	50 K	51 D	52 M	53 A	54 Z₁	55 N	56 P	57 L	58 Z	59 Y
60 T	61 B	62 F	63 Q	64 X	■	65 S	66 D	67 G	68 C
69 X	70 I	71 P	72 H	73 N	74 X	75 M	76 L	77 K	78 E	79 Z₂
80 J	81 F	82 S	83 N	84 Z	85 W	86 C	87 E	88 K	89 T
90 B	91 C	92 M	93 W	94 V	95 K	96 F	97 U	98 I	99 O
100 Z₁	101 U	102 O	103 D	104 F	105 K	106 P	107 Z	108 C	109 F
110 W	111 Z₁	112 V	113 E	114 P	115 D	116 N	117 M	118 C
119 U	120 J	121 E	122 D	123 Z₂	124 U	125 F	126 B	127 C	128 A
129 Z₂	130 M	131 H	132 S	133 L	134 O	135 Z	136 Y	137 P	138 J
139 E	140 V	141 Q	142 T	143 U	144 F	145 G	146 U	147 N	148 E
149 S	150 V	151 Q	152 U	153 A	154 R	155 J	156 Y	157 F	158 X
159 T	160 I	161 V	162 W	163 Y	164 Q	165 H	166 R	167 J	168 N	169 D
170 P	171 L	172 B	173 Z₂	174 G	175 E	176 X	177 M	178 D	179 C
180 T	181 R	182 K	183 F	184 A	185 J	186 E	187 R	188 K	189 B
190 Z₁	191 H	192 U	193 D	194 V	195 W	196 F	197 Z₂	198 Z	199 Z₁	200 H
201 W	202 V	203 E	204 X	205 P	206 B	207 A

CLUES

A. Residue of combustion — 144 54 60 200 79 188 172

B. Intoxicating; exhilarating — 150 97 183 192 132

C. Makes fine or slender — 146 12 75 166 47 180 159 105 71 145

D. 1938 Marx Brothers film (2 wds.) — 176 34 32 77 41 187 98 80 117 53 87

E. Sobriquet for Durocher — 103 155 129 167 136

F. Rapture; witchery — 119 72 154 58 67 184 91 140 181 7 193

G. Fresh, cheeky — 28 131 114 178 111

H. Devised, made up — 33 175 25 85 50 148

I. Coniferous non-evergreen with durable wood — 130 4 24 179 163

J. Talented; given — 18 147 38 164 173 102 44

K. Henry James's young Miss Farange — 49 14 168 36 11 23

L. Blennylike marine fish — 90 99 110 112 170 27 15

M. Bright, lustrous — 109 37 171 46 134

N. "Ask where's the North? at York, 'tis on ___" (2 wds.; Pope, "Essay on Man") — 116 96 191 62 3 70 59 185

O. Capuchin monkey — 22 93 149 20 10 113 43

P. "Still you keep o' the ___ side of the law" ("Twelfth Night") — 125 84 199 51 45

Q. Raise, increase, aggravate — 52 65 137 123 21 158 9 186 30

R. "All the gifts from all ___, your own, Love" (2 wds.; Browning, "One Word More") — 104 174 133 138 141 153 48 194 57 5

S. One who denies any real ground of truth — 35 89 66 1 122 100 152 162

T. Space in which to move freely — 78 169 135 64 73 127 121 108 94

U. Type of social gathering — 165 61 16 82 56 195

V. Sarah Kemble married him — 83 6 68 161 157 197 124

W. "I thought ___ to have deck'd, sweet maid" (wd. & hyph., "Hamlet") — 2 76 151 17 120 115 182 107 69 139 202

X. Arrogant; vain — 26 88 39 189 95 201 126 55 74 160 19

Y. Slight gust of wind, vapor, etc. — 196 106 190 8 101

Z. Genuine — 198 42 13 81 92 31 143 86

Z_1. Vituperated, berated — 156 177 118 63 29 128 142

13

	1	2	3	4	5	6	7	8	9
	1 Q		U3	N4	C5	O6	Q7	M8	E9	T
10 V	11 I	12 C	13	A14	15 V	16 V		17	U18	K
19 F	20 P	21 D	22 V	23 T	24 U	25 U	H26	R27	G29	A
30 N	31 I	32 D	33 D	34	M35	L36	A37	O38	K39	V
40 D	41 F	42 P	43 I	44 U	D46	W47		48	I49	C
50 Q	51 M	52 D	53 E	Q55	G56	57	V58			
59 W	60 R	61 M	L62	H63	B65	G66	S67	68	U69	P
70 M	71 D	B72	M74	75	M76	H77	W78	K79	J	
80 I	81 M	82	D83	84 S	85	L86	F	87	V88	A
89 U	90 A	91 I	92	93 G	94	J95	A96		97	O
98 F	99 I	100 E	101 A	102 N	103 M	104 J	105 R	106 P	107 D	108 G
109K	110 M	111 A	112 V	113 S	114 C	115 R	116 G	117 Q	118 L	
119 M	120 F	121 P	122 K	123 H	124 B	125 A	126 F	127 V		
128 W	129 M	130 K	131 D	132 H	133 R	134 J	135 U	136 V	137 T	
138 K	139 U	140 M	141 L	142 V	143 C	144 N	145 F	146 C		
147 W	148 T	149 H	150 E	151 R	152 L	153 M	154 V	155 S	156 Q	157 D
158 V	159 G	160 M	161 S	162 N	163 E	164 K	165 M			
166 W	167 V	168 E	169 P	170 M	171 D	172 F	173 O	174 H	175 N	176 E
177 A	178 C	179 S	180 B	181 W	182 S	183 B	184 A	185 T	186 E	
187 D	188 A	189 U	190 C	191 V	192 J	193 E	194 A	195 W	196 V	
197 S	198 D	199 V	200 R	201 M	202 W	203 O	204 V	205 G	206 W	
207 A	208 C	209 W	210 F	211 S	212 I	213 B	214 R			

14

Grid

1 A	2 Y	3 N	4 Q	5 L	6 J	7 E
8 B	9 S	10 C	11 S	12 L	13 R	14 D
15 Z	16 T	17 O	18 G	19 U	20 V	21 I
22 Y	23 U	24 J	25 M	26 H	27 U	28 R
29 E	30 A	31 S	32 H	33 P	34 P	35 L
36 W	37 N	38 D	39 K	40 B	41 Q	42 C
43 J	44 R	45 I	46 T	47 V	48 L	49 B
50 Y	51 A	52 Z	53 Q	54 N	55 G	56 W
57 Y	58 H	59 B	60 W	61 N	62 Z	63 D
64 L	65 C	66 X	67 M	68 S	69 U	70 N
71 F	72 K	73 C	74 P	75 B	76 N	77 Z
78 X	79 U	80 N	81 J	82 W	83 T	84 X
85 I	86 V	87 G	88 S	89 L	90 H	91 Q
92 G	93 T	94 D	95 K	96 X	97 A	98 I
99 T	100 C	101 W	102 Z	103 S	104 O	105 B
106 O	107 I	108 Z	109 M	110 K	111 Z	112 F
113 B	114 P	115 Z	116 N	117 N	118 M	119 K
120 W	121 L	122 H	123 Z	124 Y	125 O	126 R
127 X	128 A	129 M	130 X	131 O	132 Y	133 F
134 U	135 B	136 G	137 Q	138 A	139 Y	140 P
141 I	142 Q	143 J	144 A	145 U	146 D	147 B
148 U	149 T	150 X	151 S	152 E	153 H	154 V
155 Q	156 W	157 O	158 O	159 I	160 T	161 F
162 R	163 L	164 D	165 Q	166 E	167 C	168 D
169 P	170 M	171 U	172 B	173 V	174 U	175 B
176 O	177 T	178 N	179 J	180 V	181 L	182 D
183 I	184 F	185 D	186 O	187 X	188 A	189 T
190 E						

CLUES

WORDS

A Bran, e.g. 51 138 30 128 144 1 97 188

B Elaborated to excess 49 75 172 8 135 113 105 175 40 59 147

C Affording little space; confined .. 167 73 65 100 42 10

D Gr. goddess of love and beauty .. 182 63 14 146 185 168 38 94 164

E Receive enthusiastically (2 wds.) . 190 166 152 7 29

F Evidence 131 161 133 184 71 112

G Small, dark-colored goose 92 87 136 55 18

H Delitescent 122 32 26 153 90 58

I Persistent desire 85 98 159 45 21 107 141 183

J Waver 6 24 143 43 81 179

K Sharpens 95 119 39 110 72

L The Furies (after "the") 35 89 163 121 5 64 181 48 12

M Consume 25 109 129 157 118 170 67

N Averts (2 wds.) 117 76 54 116 80 70 178 3 61 37

O Gave umbrage 17 158 104 106 125 131 157 176 186

P U.S. lawyer and author (1857–1938; "Farmington") 74 140 33 34 114 169

Q "A Poetic Romance" by Keats . 4 165 91 137 53 155 142 41

R Follower of Zeno's school of philosophy 162 13 28 126 44

S Basis of a type of cookie; breakfast food 88 11 103 151 9 68 31

T Explode 177 93 83 160 46 16 189 99 149

U "Clean bomb," "underachiever," and "disadvantaged," e.g. 145 79 27 148 171 134 19 174 23 69

V Dealer 47 20 173 86 180 154

W Universal medicine 82 156 120 36 56 60 101

X Flood 150 127 96 130 187 84 78 66

Y U.S. composer ("Slaughter on Tenth Avenue") 50 132 2 124 57 139 22

Z Conveying waste 15 62 115 77 102 108 52 111 123

15

CLUES

A. Am. actor, star of "The Great White Hope," 1968 (full name) — 118 59 48 180 3 112 142 124 102 44 56 16 185 31

B. Nickname of baseball's William Joseph Skowron — 18 9 29 176 79

C. Wrongs; hurts — 131 55 179 74 23 1 63 164

D. Heaps — 110 156 47 25

E. German-born U.S. composer ("The Tempest," "The Prairie") — 160 40 207 95

F. On the fritz, not working (3 wds.) — 73 11 28 167 122 32 129 192 69 101 58

G. Buttercup genus — 171 15 146 206 66 181 116 42 195 82

H. Misrepresent; pervert — 27 153 204 70 89 14 196

I. Assign; consecrate — 43 209 147 163 67 85

J. Rise — 109 150 104 170 133 193

K. Not habitual — 81 155 39 123 126 65 169

L. Plaster of Paris — 13 175 86 115 6

M. Simple knot tied around an object (hyph.) — 141 135 52 10 4 203 106 91 71

N. Frugality — 121 162 139 49 190 111

O. Purify — 198 184 128 92 120 45 134 114 35 22

P. Eng. author (1689–1761; "Pamela") — 149 88 205 21 77 113 51 62 34 174

Q. Disseminated, spread seed — 183 145 96 138 202

R. Ballet pose — 68 38 99 194 72 94 83 61 158

S. Third eyelid, developed in birds, etc. (2 wds.) — 90 125 144 182 46 136 93 161 54 157 78 64 5 108 117 168 30 7 191

T. Loony, bonkers, off one's nut — 100 132 152 87 53

U. Indirect — 76 154 41 143 17 105 178 159 57 130

V. Shifty, slippery — 37 188 84 208 173 199 26

W. Artillery unit — 166 151 75 127 165 201 189

X. Stipend — 186 60 80 172 24 33 8 197 20

Y. 1900 opera by Charpentier — 50 19 177 103 98 148

Z. Deep-bodied, black-banded food fish of the U.S. Atlantic coast — 12 36 107 119 187 2 137 200 97 210

Grid

1 C	2 Z	3 A	4 M	5 S	6 L	7 S	8 X	9 B		
10 M	11 F	12 Z	13 L	14 H	15 G	16 A	17 U	18 B	19 Y	
20 X	21 P	22 O	23 C	24 X	25 D	26 V	27 H	28 F	29 B	
30 S	31 A	32 F	33 X	34 P	35 O	36 Z	37 V	38 R		
39 K	40 E	41 U	42 G	43 I	44 A	45 O	46 S	47 D	48 A	
49 N	50 Y	51 P	52 M	53 T	54 S	55 C	56 A	57 U	58 F	
59 A	60 X	61 R	62 P	63 C	64 S	65 K	66 G	67 I	68 R	
69 F	70 H	71 M	72 R	73 F	74 C	75 W	76 U	77 P	78 S	
79 B	80 X	81 K	82 G	83 R	84 V	85 I	86 L	87 T	88 P	89 H
90 S	91 M	92 O	93 S	94 R	95 E	96 Q	97 Z	98 Y		
99 R	100 T	101 F	102 A	103 Y	104 J	105 U	106 M	107 Z	108 S	
109 J	110 D	111 N	112 A	113 P	114 O	115 L	116 G	117 S	118 A	
119 Z	120 O	121 N	122 F	123 K	124 A	125 S	126 K	127 W	128 O	
129 F	130 U	131 C	132 T	133 J	134 O	135 M	136 S	137 Z	138 Q	139 N
140 K	141 M	142 A	143 U	144 S	145 Q	146 G	147 I	148 Y	149 P	
150 J	151 W	152 T	153 H	154 U	155 K	156 D	157 S	158 R	159 U	
160 E	161 S	162 N	163 I	164 C	165 W	166 W	167 F	168 S	169 K	
170 J	171 G	172 X	173 V	174 P	175 L	176 B	177 Y	178 U	179 C	180 A
181 G	182 S	183 Q	184 O	185 A	186 X	187 Z	188 V	189 W	190 N	
191 S	192 F	193 J	194 R	195 G	196 H	197 X	198 O	199 V	200 Z	
201 W	202 Q	203 M	204 H	205 P	206 G	207 E	208 V	209 I	210 Z	

Grid

1 T	2 J	3 N	4 E	5 Z	6 L	7 Z₁	8 O	9 H	10 C	11 A	12 P
13 U	14 P	15 Y	16 N	17 I	18 X	19 V	20 F	21 U	22 R		
23 C	24 U	25 X	26 N	27 Q	28 Q	29 E	30 C				
31 S	32 F	33 V	34 O	35 K	36 O	37 P	38 Q	39 L	40 D		
41 Z	42 V	43 G	44 E	45 R	46 Q	47 R	48 Q				
49 L	50 J	51 X	52 N	53 N	54 D	55 O	56 F	57 J	58 Z₁		
59 Z	60 N	61 Y	62 N	63 X	64 W	65 T	66 U	67 G			
68 M	69 A	70 W	71 Q	72 E	73 L	74 D	75 X	76 Y	77 J	78 P	
79 Z	80 G	81 T	82 Q	83 Y	84 L	85 P	86 Z₁	87 H	88 O		
89 E	90 Q	91 J	92 H	93 Y	94 E	95 Y	96 T	97 N	98 C		
99 J	100 U	101 C	102 R	103 R	104 N	105 T	106 N	107 K			
108 C	109 Y	110 M	111 Z	112 J	113 Z	114 Z	115 X	116 V			
117 N	118 A	119 I	120 F	121 J	122 Y	123 U	124 Q	125 O	126 J		
127 F	128 X	129 X	130 K	131 A	132 Z₁	133 V	134 G	135 B	136 C	137 R	
138 M	139 W	140 J	141 F	142 Z₁	143 R	144 J	145 H	146 Q			
147 S	148 R	149 L	150 Z₁	151 A	152 Z	153 N	154 Y	155 Z	156 W		
157 K	158 Q	159 U	160 I	161 J	162 D	163 V	164 G	165 A	166 N		
167 A	168 B	169 O	170 L	171 Z	172 Z	173 J	174 E	175 J	176 G		
177 D	178 R	179 V	180 Z₁	181 H	182 B	183 M	184 G	185 M			
186 P	187 X	188 J	189 R	190 Z₁	191 X	192 F	193 Y	194 V	195 K		
196 N	197 Q	198 W	199 M	200 I	201 T	202 R	203 K	204 B	205 V		
206 S	207 F	208 W	209 Z	210 W	211 S	212 R	213 H	214 Z			

CLUES

WORDS

A Drum 167 151 118 131 11 69 165

B Weight 168 135 182 204

C Musical sweet potato 108 98 101 136 10 23 30

D Live-bearing fresh-water fish often kept in aquariums 177 162 74 54 40

E Long diatribe 89 72 4 28 174 44

F River flowing from Angola to Bechuanaland 120 32 192 56 127 141 20 207 94

G Excess, overabundance . . . 43 176 67 184 164 134 80

H N American elk 92 145 87 213 9 181

I Cannabis sativa; rope material 17 200 160 119

J Father of Olwen (Welsh legend; full name) 77 121 2 140 188 175 126 57 173 161 53 50 99 112 144 91

K Culmination; peak 107 35 203 130 195 157

L Pelagic 49 6 149 73 39 170 84

M Engaged, as gear teeth . . . 68 110 185 199 183 138

N Former coins of Spain and Sp. America, often mentioned in pirate stories (3 wds.) 3 62 106 16 153 166 117 60 26 97 196 52 104

O Harbach-Hammerstein song from "The Desert Song" (2 wds.) 36 29 55 8 34 88 125 169

P Mitigate, mollify, allay . . . 78 85 37 186 14 12

Q She marries Clym Yeobright in Hardy's "The Return of the Native" (full name) . . 197 82 48 46 38 158 71 124 27 146 90

R Ability or disposition to laugh 202 189 212 45 148 47 143 103 102 178 137 22

S "Washed by the rivers, blest by ___ of home" (Brooke, "The Soldier") . . 147 211 206 31

T Burrowing, herbivorous marsupial of Australia . . . 201 81 65 105 1 96

U Given to unrestrained revelry; boisterous 123 21 159 13 24 66 100

V Belonging to a thing by its very nature 33 19 133 194 205 179 163 42 116

W British privates 198 208 210 139 64 156 70

X Annihilation 129 115 25 75 63 191 51 18 187 128

Y Settles, as by strenuous or repeated effort; pounds or hits forcefully (2 wds.) . . . 93 15 61 109 122 83 95 154 193 76

Z Nuts, loony, bonkers (3 wds.) 172 155 209 113 5 111 152 79 214 41 114 171

Z₁ Red Sox outfielder who batted .406 in 1941 . . . . . 150 7 58 180 132 142 86 190

17

CLUES

A Inflexible; unbreakable 189 84 174 166 55 182 111 17

B Greed; great eagerness 65 37 137 185 128 171 48 155

C Improving, getting better (3 wds.) . 30 99 63 2 136 169 14 110

D Recidivists and six-shooters, e.g. . 39 10 73 91 62 135 132 161 6

E Unmasking 75 140 61 183 164 96 125 109 15

F City in SE Suffolk, England 191 138 58 153 162 26 86

G Castigates, disciplines. 126 78 95 107 45 85 134 24

H Eng. philosopher, 1588–1679; "Leviathan" 12 101 188 115 83 123

I Sticky 87 190 180 16 76 149 9 47

J Street urchins, perhaps. 51 187 5 154 28 151 103 38 104 57 70

K Crazy 42 72 102 117

L "Be not severe; / So save a ——" (2 wds.; Gay, "The Beggar's Opera") 186 139 168 119 11 82 90 20 179 3 94 178

M Comforters of a sort 43 98 143 34 167 113 150 69 175 88

N Shreds 163 41 77 22 68 60 156

O Sesame-honey confection 7 18 46 146 157 33

P High-spirited 40 131 116 97 184 165 50 172 124

Q Fortified places 160 170 114 81 122 56 192 152

R An incarnation of Vishnu 148 13 35 93

S Concentrated; earnestly emotional 64 105 32 142 145 106 74

T Violent or boisterous women 49 66 44 29 108 59 25 130 1 127

U Negligence 133 31 129 121 80 193 19 176 144 54 158

V Scrophulariaceous plants cultivated for showy flowers . . . 173 4 120 71 159 112 79 100 27 92 52

W Dwellings 177 147 89 21 141 8 53 23 181 67 118

Grid (cell number · clue letter):

8 W	9	10 D				7 O
18 O	19 U	20 L	21	22 N	23 W	24 G	25 T
26 F	27 V	28 V	29 J	30	31 U	32 S	33 O	34 M	35 R	36 C
37 B	38 J	39	40 P	41 P	42 K	43 M	44 T	45 G
46 O	47 I	48 B	49	50	51 P	52 V	53 W	54 U	55 A
56 Q	57 J	58	59 F	60	61	62	63 D	64 S	65 S	66 T
67 W	68 N	69 M	70	71 I	72 K	73 D	74 D	75 S	76 E	77 N
78 G	79 V	80 U	81	82	83 L	84 H	85 A	86 F	87 I
88 M	89 W	90 L	91	92 V	93 R	94 L	95 G	96 G
97 P	98 M	99 M	100 V	101 H	102 K	103 K	104 J	105 J	106 S
107 G	108 T	109 E	110 C	111 A	112	113 V	114 Q	115 H	116 P	117 K
118 W	119 L	120 V	121 U	122 Q	123 H	124	125 E	126	127 T
128 B	129 U	130 T	131 P	132 D	133	134 G	135 D	136 C	137 B
138 F	139 L	140 E	141 W	142 S	143 M	144 U	145 S	146 O	147 W
148 R	149 I	150 M	151 J	152 Q	153 F	154 J	155 B	156	157 O
158 U	159 V	160 Q	161 D	162 F	163 N	164 E	165 P	166 A	167 M
168 L	169 C	170 Q	171 B	172 P	173 V	174 A	175 M	176 U	177 W
178 L	179 L	180 I	181 W	182 A	183 E	184 P	185 B	186	187 L
188 H	189 A	190 I	191 F	192 Q	193 T					

CLUES

WORDS

A	Scold vigorously	39	46	3	124	75	66				
B	Patron saint of shoemakers	35	30	10	33	89	127	62			
C	Suddenly and unexpectedly (4 wds.)	52	110	94	5	171	88	25	168	79	103 29 17
D	Companions; equals; pairs	31	73	45	43	69					
E	Temperament, spirit	136	38	147	27	7	82				
F	Poisonous evergreen having rose-colored or white flowers . .	28	81	36	15	161	109	130	153		
G	Monodon . . .	20	152	121	99	134	1	57			
H	"Arise, fair sun, and kill the ——," says Romeo (2 wds.) . .	160	116	60	155	50	175	14	18	98	32 125
I	Mohammedan month of fasting by day	113	41	65	122	129	104	156			
J	Worn out, having lost novelty and interest . .	112	23	2	144	64					
K	Visits frequently; resorts . . .	48	91	8	119	68	111				
L	Conceivably possible in the world . .	154	58	16	170	84	150	114			
M	Signify secondarily	63	165	12	105	137	70	159			
N	Timber or stone over a doorway or window . .	90	115	108	9	149	51				
O	Mystic; oracular	78	164	4	95	19	55				
P	Regular; calm	148	24	87	61	44	145				
Q	Great English architect, 1573–1652 (full name)	143	67	13	53	76	86	11	141	135	178
R	Egyptian personification of femininity; mother of Ra . .	169	131	146	34	71					
S	"More laud than —— o'er-dusted" ("Troilus and Cressida") . .	117	173	6	42						
T	Pressed into folds . . .	142	101	54	167	102	118	126			
U	Deduced by logical conclusion . .	80	49	151	85	140	96	166	157	107	26 37
V	Excessive bureaucratic routine (2 wds.) . . .	40	177	132	133	56	97	72			
W	Disorderly heap or assemblage . .	47	123	74	106	83	93	176			
X	Whitewashed	174	163	77	22	138					
Y	Impartial, equitable (hyph.)	120	162	139	128	158	172	92	59	100	21

19

CLUES

A. Kill by incantations, as rats were supposed to be killed in Ireland (3 wds.)
B. Norse explorer, fl. 880
C. Plunder
D. Elevates; cops
E. Dexterous
F. "The time has been my senses would have cool'd / To hear a ___" (hyph., "Macbeth")
G. The little one includes Polaris
H. Directive; earnest request
I. Elkton, Md., and Gretna Green used to be famous for these
J. Island of the central New Hebrides
K. Withdrew; escorted (2 wds.)
L. Tolkien creation
M. Carrion; rubbish
N. Noxious or disgusting animals or people
O. Ample scope for action
P. Aphra Behn and Herman Melville, e.g.
Q. Disengage oneself from; discharge; cast aside (2 wds.)
R. Hortatory discourses
S. Cast a shadow on; obscure; surpass
T. Public good
U. Disorder; agitate
V. Racing-shell crews, perhaps
W. Give satisfaction; make up for deficiencies
X. "In Cliveden's proud alcove / ___ of wanton Shrewsbury and love" (2 wds.; Pope, "Moral Essays, Epistle iii")
Y. Pertaining to the eye
Z. In all directions (3 wds.)

WORDS

Clue	Numbers
A	62 128 112 100 51 57 139 120 77 25 178 2
B	23 68 43 167 148 175 4
C	191 135 39 66
D	123 99 24 14 37
E	75 92 183 117 103 55
F	91 101 36 20 1 127 132 173 164 180 154
G	185 7 93 151 138 118
H	81 143 114 152 165 131
I	18 88 125 6 45 170 133 35 22 155
J	190 89 98 61 9
K	27 122 157 17 176 47 54
L	44 146 48 52 160 113
M	34 140 187 109 15
N	134 172 13 161 129 149
O	87 97 31 182 71 76 10 67 70
P	64 95 147 169 184 108 150 19 78
Q	49 58 107 29 181 42 156 188
R	145 174 130 84 124 69 106 60
S	82 137 119 16 105 46 163
T	26 63 85 5 73 38 116 3 90 33
U	94 53 121 11 111 168
V	142 136 194 159 40 86
W	12 144 186 193 32
X	41 72 189 141 80 126 115 8
Y	56 171 179 166 162 21 50 104 28 96
Z	158 192 65 83 79 153 30 74 110 59 177 102

GRID

7 G	8 X	9 J	■	10 O	11 U	1 F	2 A	3 T	■	12 W	13 N	14 D	■	15 M
16 S	17 K	18 I	■	19 P	20 F	21 Y	22 I	23 B	24 D	
25 A	26 T	27 K	28 Y	■	29 Q	30 Z	31 O	32 W	33 T	34 M	35 I
36 F	37 D	38 T	39 C	40 V	41 X	42 Q	43 B	44 L	
45 I	46 Y	47 K	48 L	49 Q	50 Y	51 A	52 L	53 U	54 K	
55 E	56 Y	57 A	58 Q	59 Z	60 R	61 J	62 A	63 T	
64 P	65 Z	66 C	67 O	68 B	69 R	70 O	71 O	72 X	
73 T	74 Z	75 E	76 O	77 A	78 P	79 Z	80 X	81 H	
82 S	83 Z	84 R	85 T	86 V	87 O	88 I	89 J	90 T	91 F	
92 E	93 G	94 U	95 P	96 Y	97 O	98 J	99 D	100 A	101 F	
102 Z	103 E	104 Y	105 S	106 R	107 Q	108 P	109 M	110 Z	111 U	112 A
113 L	114 H	115 X	116 T	117 E	118 G	119 S	120 A	121 U	
122 K	123 D	124 R	125 I	126 X	127 F	128 A	129 N	130 R	131 H	
132 F	133 I	■	134 N	135 C	136 V	137 S	138 G	139 A	140 M	
141 X	142 V	143 W	144 W	145 R	146 L	147 P	148 B	149 N	150 P	151 G
152 H	153 Z	154 F	155 I	156 Q	157 K	158 Z	159 V	160 L	161 N	
162 Y	163 S	164 F	165 H	166 Y	167 B	168 U	169 P	
170 I	171 Y	172 N	173 F	174 R	175 B	176 K	177 Z	178 A	179 Y	
180 F	181 Q	182 O	183 E	184 P	185 G	186 W	187 M	188 Q	
189 X	190 J	191 C	192 Z	193 W	194 V	

20

CLUES

		WORDS
A	Detested	104 162 126 46 183 172 10
B	Opposite	63 56 200 186 211 100 78 144 38 45
C	Natural, unaffected	115 14 20 96 202 121 213 181 117 109 55 204 88
D	Withdrew	83 4 54 107 150 161 116 135 170
E	Pool game; clod, sad sack	148 174 111 19 195 51 112 22 85
F	Article of menswear	209 62 42 145 140 205 95
G	Goatlike mountain antelope of Europe	206 37 139 102 47 158 167
H	Standards of dealing	74 91 31 17 123 154
I	Indirect, dubious, insincere	3 28 41 128 134 90 169 160 2 65
J	Sanction, approval	188 9 214 114 137 87 50 57 119 29 155
K	Shafted, gypped, swindled	16 101 32 124 97 217
L	Intermediary (hyph.)	33 58 113 8 24 94 178 147 64
M	Tawdry, disreputable	127 131 5 138 27 93 71
N	Utterance showing affection	152 110 157 36 67 143 39 192 199 182
O	"Putting it mildly"	142 61 164 1 194 89 190 153 133 76 26
P	"There is a —— passage to the intellectual world" (hyph.; Sterne, "Tristram Shandy")	191 21 163 177 212 30 11 53 130
Q	Idle, wool-gathering fellow (hyph.)	66 52 201 108 34 173 6 82 98 151 77
R	Avaricious, grasping	216 84 203 156 23 120 136 175 68 35 198
S	What one should do on getting the long end of a furcula (3 wds.)	125 176 207 184 106 196 7 44 49
T	The one little possession of Nathan's poor man (2 wds., II Sam. 12:3)	105 70 166 189 86 171 193
U	Newspapers; sails; lines for trimming sails	165 118 92 215 81 18
V	Was in contact with	40 179 149 180 15 187 103 210
W	Quarter inhabited by a racial group	60 141 80 99 132 122
X	Raise the spirits of; cheer; make happy	129 79 75 25 73 208 59 13 48 43
Y	Fire that rakes a line or position from end to end	159 146 185 72 69 168 12 197

21

CLUES

A. French tabloid on a road for painter . .
B. Going for ungainly giant holding lure .
C. Join a venture designed for making one young . . . .
D. Express glee with plug hat and heart-less i.o.u. (3 wds.) . . . .
E. Lures into trouble with parents going out . . . .
F. Composer of so many U arrangements
G. Modus operandi not on. Ring us! That's tiresome. . . . .
H. First possibility might be on heathen don (4 wds.) . . . .
I. Grief that might stop a horse . . . . . .
J. North Dakota—bad state about serves
K. Count a loonybird . . . .
L. A demo shoe rebuilt for a lake . . . . .
M. Add honey, throw off rose shrub (2 wds.) . . . .
N. The latest fad, edgewise, has dimmed .
O. Shape troop up for "Where are you now, Elvis Presley?" e.g. . . . .
P. Hang on ugliest perversion of a repri-mand (hyph.) . . . .
Q. Caliph in Flatbush—as sane as ever one was! . . . .
R. Hoist a cue; play an anatomist . . . . .
S. Tories' scared to bits in Revolution . .
T. Extremities of spirit and heart of youth are superior . . . .
U. Bribe or, if 99, this should make you drowsy . . . .
V. Second possibility as her hot tone changes (3 wds.) . . . .
W. Bobby: No day's off for a title (2 wds.) . . . .

WORDS

A	115	162	155	179	99	29	61	52	14		
B	199	181	40	139	112	5	1	13	166	23	
C	80	118	30	143	152	85	17	134	19	177	158	198
D	156	194	90	136	142	164	174	55	84		
E	151	169	141	119	183	98	173				
F	148	41	68	48	8	188	37				
G	67	54	59	38	123	197	203	114	22	91	
H	172	190	43	24	106	31	77	109	2	49	63	18
I	60	89	137								
J	16	65	103	3	127	191	95				
K	72	26	175	133	12	140					
L	126	153	82	180	6	108	113	87	71		
M	32	70	124	170	165	110	79	9	184	73	4	56	46
N	131	76	129	28	196						
O	120	171	186	94	163	86	104	97	150	51	
P	160	192	178	47	27	92	81	125	11	34	132	195	185
Q	20	168	62	57	10	200					
R	101	122	75	36	189	157	182	93	111		
S	176	128	201	78	161	66	50	100			
T	69	138	35	159	146	58	96	107			
U	144	202	117	187	39	45	42	130	154		
V	83	135	33	88	145	64	149	44	74	7	
W	193	21	147	116	102	53	167	121	15	105	25

Grid (diagram)

1 B	2 H	3 J	4 M	5 B	6 L	7 V				
8 F	9 M	10 Q	11 P	12 K	13 B	14 A	15 W	16 J		
17 C	18 H	19 C	20 Q	21 W	22 G	23 B	24 H	25 W	26 K	
27 P	28 N	29 A	30 C	31 H	32 M	33 V	34 V	35 P	36 R	
37 F	38 G	39 U	40 B	41 F	42 U	43 H	44 V	45 V		
46 M	47 P	48 F	49 H	50 S	51 O	52 A	53 W	54 G	55 D	
56 M	57 Q	58 T	59 G	60 I	61 A	62 G	63 H	64 V		
65 J	66 S	67 G	68 F	69 T	70 M	71 L	72 K	73 M	74 V	
75 R	76 N	77 H	78 S	79 M	80 C	81 C	82 L	83 V		
84 D	85 D	86 C	87 L	88 V	89 I	90 D	91 G	92 R	93 R	
94 O	95 J	96 J	97 O	98 E	99 E	100 S	101 R	102 W	103 J	
104 O	105 W	106 H	107 T	108 L	109 H	110 M	111 R	112 L		
113 L	114 G	115 A	116 W	117 T	118 U	119 E	120 O	121 W		
122 R	123 G	124 M	125 P	126 L	127 J	128 S	129 N	130 O	131 N	
132 P	133 K	134 C	135 V	136 D	137 L	138 T	139 B			
140 K	141 E	142 D	143 C	144 U	145 V	146 T	147 M	148 F	149 V	
150 O	151 E	152 C	153 L	154 U	155 E	156 D	157 R	158 C	159 T	
160 P	161 S	162 A	163 O	164 D	165 M	166 B	167 W	168 O	169 E	170 M
171 O	172 H	173 E	174 C	175 P	176 W	177 C	178 P	179 A	180 L	
181 B	182 R	183 E	184 M	185 P	186 O	187 U	188 F	189 R		
190 H	191 J	192 P	193 W	194 D	195 P	196 N	197 G	198 C		
199 B	200 Q	201 S	202 U	203 G						

22

	CLUES	WORDS
A	Chicken; Italian seaport on the Ligurian Sea	66 3 44 28 174 148 111
B	Most bulky or muscular	108 135 86 164 116 23 7 190
C	Elongated freshwater fish, family Petromizontidae	159 89 168 74 175 106 57
D	Benign, easygoing, pleasant	58 157 130 97 136 153 38
E	Corrupting, ruining	90 18 149 128 87 43 49 189 131
F	Environment conducive to rapid growth	191 182 125 40 119 27
G	Person in a cast if he's lucky	142 134 180 32 8
H	1934 song by Hudson and DeLange	39 177 185 79 53 156 169 45
I	Lacking zest	16 163 24 124 176 197 144
J	Beneficial covering for plants	73 151 172 93 61
K	Scheduled, synchronized	146 166 4 80 35 14
L	Cheerfully stimulating	52 17 11 68 187 122 88 25 150 33 183 98
M	John Updike's Harry Angstrom	5 152 117 170 77 96
N	Unsettled	9 114 173 65 95 71 41 82 195 171 193 127
O	Disposition	133 51 83 147 200 155 105 99
P	Plant with small, aromatic seeds used for seasoning	123 102 31 192 115 205
Q	Peak in the Pennine Alps	161 196 165 107 91 206 48 78 132 85
R	Wearing down	138 47 6 37 181 1 55 129 59
S	Makes less severe	63 72 67 36 202 143 30
T	1st cen. A.D. Roman rhetorician	120 139 110 19 56 104 160 84 12 21
U	Set free from trouble	186 76 201 121 101 60 94 69
V	"In a dream you are never ___" says Anne Sexton ("Old")	194 158 70 2 112 141
W	Featuring nonstop occurrence (hyph.)	92 113 100 46 188 154 199 13 137
X	Roman general (40–93), conqueror of Britain	179 64 54 42 81 20 118 75
Y	Serving to identify	198 26 145 204 62 15 22 140 29 103 109
Z	Unconventional, odd	167 184 10 162 50 203 178 126 34

■	■	■	■	1 R	2 V	3 A	■	4 K	5 M	6 R	7 B
■	8 G	9 N	10 Z	11 L	12 T	13 W	14 K	■	15 Y	16 I	17 L
18 E	19 T	■	20 X	21 T	22 Y	23 B	■	24 I	25 L	26 Y	27 F
■	28 A	29 Y	30 S	■	31 P	32 G	33 L	34 Z	35 K	■	36 S
37 R	38 D	39 H	40 F	41 N	42 X	43 E	44 A	■	45 H	46 W	47 R
48 Q	■	49 E	50 Z	51 O	52 L	53 H	54 X	55 R	56 T	57 C	■
58 D	59 R	60 U	■	61 J	62 Y	63 S	■	64 X	65 N	66 A	67 S
68 L	69 U	70 V	■	71 N	72 S	73 J	74 C	75 X	76 U	77 M	78 Q
79 H	80 K	■	81 X	82 N	83 O	■	84 T	85 Q	■	86 B	87 E
88 L	■	89 C	■	90 E	91 Q	92 W	93 J	94 U	95 N	96 M	97 D
98 L	99 O	■	100 W	101 U	102 P	103 Y	104 T	105 O	106 C	■	107 Q
108 B	109 Y	■	110 T	111 A	112 V	113 W	114 N	115 P	116 B	117 M	118 X
119 F	■	120 T	121 U	122 L	123 P	124 I	125 F	126 Z	127 N	128 E	■
129 R	130 D	■	131 E	132 Q	133 O	134 G	135 B	■	136 D	137 W	138 R
139 T	140 Y	141 V	■	142 G	143 S	144 I	■	145 Y	146 K	147 O	148 A
149 E	150 L	151 J	152 M	153 D	■	154 W	155 O	156 H	157 D	158 V	159 C
160 T	161 Q	162 Z	163 I	164 B	■	165 Q	166 K	167 Z	■	168 C	169 H
170 M	171 N	172 J	■	173 N	174 A	175 C	176 I	177 H	178 Z	179 X	180 G
181 R	182 F	183 L	■	184 Z	185 H	186 U	187 L	188 W	189 E	190 B	■
191 F	192 P	193 N	194 V	■	195 N	196 Q	197 I	198 Y	■	199 W	200 O
■	201 U	202 S	203 Z	204 Y	205 P	206 Q	■	■	■	■	■

23

WORDS

24

CLUES

A. Undecided; perturbed (4 wds.)
B. Drug of the ancients, bringing forgetfulness of sorrow
C. American Indian tribe, once of Colorado, now in Oklahoma and Wyoming
D. Conduct causing petty annoyance
E. Commotion
F. "I make it a rule never to look into a ___" (Sheridan, "The Critic")
G. Poisonous shrub of the dogbane family
H. Nonsticking stuff
I. Hero of Margaret Mitchell's 1936 novel (full name)
J. Written declaration on oath
K. "A trip to the moon on ___" (2 wds.; Cole Porter, "Just One of Those Things")
L. Uninformed; without sin
M. Split, division
N. "The little dogs and all, / Tray, Blanch, and ___" (hyph. "King Lear")
O. Quaver (2 wds.)
P. Viceroy under the former Mogul Empire in India
Q. Tidy, trim
R. Soil
S. With uncritical grounds for belief (2 wds.)
T. Just come
U. Setbacks; failures
V. Sturdy woolen fabric (2 wds.)
W. Celebrations; dines
X. Articulate, expressive

WORDS

Clue	Cell numbers
A	108 29 146 53 13 90 183 84 125 92
B	72 25 96 49 81 121 141 42
C	101 140 50 117 160 27 74 111
D	73 35 59 64 100 151 166 7
E	88 24 75 77 69 113
F	124 58 145 18 138 107 102 181 159
G	91 106 94 15 36 187 61 67
H	105 193 78 129 52 175
I	26 41 32 16 133 161 170 66 155 68 191
J	87 31 156 123 188 63 165 104 179
K	109 185 144 162 28 19 60 10 93 120 47 89 70
L	149 85 62 174 158 192 21 44
M	184 34 116 171 57 157 190 76
N	30 1 11 168 134 180 33 20 48 82
O	9 173 37 55 40 45 137 71 4 98
P	150 142 114 65 131
Q	23 135 14 143 118 83 46 97 95
R	115 56 38 147 2
S	112 186 130 3 6 172 110
T	8 99 139 167 122
U	164 177 153 127 17 51
V	22 43 54 176 148 79 119 189 128 5
W	178 154 39 103 126 182
X	80 86 163 169 132 136 12 152

Grid (cell number with clue letter)

9 O	10 K	11 N	12 X	13 A	14 Q	15 G	16 I	17 U	18 F	19 K
20 N	21 L	22 V	23 Q	24 E	25 B	26 I	27 C	28 K	29 A	
30 N	31 J	32 I	33 N	34 M	35 D	36 G	37 O	38 R	39 W	
40 O	41 I	42 B	43 V	44 L	45 O	46 Q	47 K	48 N	49 B	
50 C	51 U	52 H	53 A	54 V	55 O	56 R	57 M	58 F		
59 D	60 K	61 G	62 L	63 J	64 D	65 P	66 I	67 G		
68 I	69 E	70 K	71 O	72 B	73 D	74 C	75 E	76 M	77 E	
78 H	79 V	80 X	81 B	82 N	83 Q	84 A	85 L	86 X	87 J	
88 E	89 K	90 A	91 G	92 A	93 K	94 G	95 Q	96 B		
97 Q	98 O	99 T	100 D	101 C	102 F	103 W	104 J	105 H	106 G	
107 F	108 A	109 K	110 S	111 C	112 S	113 E	114 P	115 R	116 M	
117 C	118 Q	119 V	120 K	121 B	122 T	123 J	124 F	125 A	126 W	
127 U	128 V	129 H	130 S	131 P	132 X	133 I	134 N	135 Q	136 X	
137 O	138 F	139 T	140 C	141 B	142 P	143 Q	144 K	145 F	146 A	
147 R	148 V	149 L	150 P	151 D	152 X	153 U	154 W	155 I	156 J	
157 M	158 L	159 F	160 C	161 I	162 K	163 X	164 U	165 J	166 D	
167 T	168 N	169 X	170 I	171 M	172 S	173 O	174 L	175 H	176 V	
177 U	178 W	179 J	180 N	181 F	182 W	183 A	184 M	185 K	186 S	
187 G	188 J	189 V	190 M	191 I	192 L	193 H				

Grid (cell number — clue letter)

Row	Cells
1	1-P 2-R 3-C 4-E 5-G 6-L 7-V 8-Q 9-H
2	10-P 11-V 12-M 13-R 14-F 15-K 16-E 17-J 18-F
3	19-T 20-B 21-Q 22-P 23-O 24-E 25-T 26-K 27-E 28-J 29-H
4	30-F 31-J 32-P 33-B 34-T 35-W 36-B 37-G 38-K 39-H
5	40-T 41-R 42-M 43-P 44-T 45-S 46-M 47-R 48-V
6	49-W 50-B 51-M 52-F 53-N 54-O 55-S 56-P 57-A
7	58-N 59-V 60-F 61-S 62-L 63-N 64-K 65-L 66-I 67-T
8	68-M 69-R 70-N 71-U 72-P 73-O 74-R 75-B 76-A
9	77-M 78-P 79-G 80-M 81-Q 82-V 83-V 84-R 85-B 86-A
10	87-A 88-V 89-S 90-I 91-C 92-V 93-G 94-O 95-C
11	96-M 97-U 98-H 99-G 100-S 101-K 102-D 103-B 104-E 105-A
12	106-P 107-G 108-G 109-V 110-U 111-A 112-A 113-K 114-W
13	115-V 116-A 117-U 118-C 119-H 120-A 121-E 122-D 123-R 124-H
14	125-J 126-P 127-N 128-H 129-L 130-N 131-B 132-Q 133-D
15	134-Q 135-W 136-A 137-P 138-S 139-L 140-H 141-F 142-N
16	143-M 144-C 145-F 146-S 147-L 148-P 149-D 150-F 151-U
17	152-Q 153-L 154-C 155-K 156-G 157-U 158-A 159-F 160-P 161-R 162-O
18	163-A 164-V 165-H 166-B 167-M 168-I 169-J 170-U 171-C
19	172-S 173-T 174-Q 175-P 176-D 177-P 178-E 179-W 180-C

CLUES   **WORDS**

A "There's small choice in ___" (2 wds., "Taming of the Shrew") 136 112 86 76 57 111 163 158 87 120 116 105

B Journeying 36 131 33 85 103 20 75 166 50

C Honeymooner, perhaps 91 154 118 95 171 3 180 144

D Trace: word game 176 149 133 122 102

E "In ___ palm and southern pine" (2 wds., Tennyson, "The Daisy") 178 16 104 27 24 4 121

F Gr. goddess of love and beauty 60 18 14 145 159 141 150 30 52

G City in N Illinois; TV role for James Garner 156 79 93 99 5 108 107 37

H Wild with excitement 9 98 140 39 29 165 119 124 128

I Dark blue 66 139 168 90

J Upper regions, heavens 169 125 31 28 17

K Withdrawn; abed 26 15 101 155 113 64 38

L Informed, drilled, trained 6 65 147 129 153 62

M On the spot, behind the 8-ball (3 wds.) 96 143 51 12 46 68 77 42 167 80

N "Yet will I bring one plague more upon ___" (Exodus 11:1) 58 53 142 70 127 130 63

O Brief fight or argument (hyph.) 162 94 23 73 54

P Contemptuous, haughty, stuck-up (4 wds.) 106 175 43 22 32 56 78 137 148 1 126 10 160 72 177

Q English actress Cathleen ___ (1888–1982, "So Long at the Fair," "Separate Tables") 8 21 81 134 174 152 132

R 1958 film starring Cary Grant 74 2 13 41 69 123 47 84 161

S "There's no such thing as bad publicity except your own ___" (Dominic Behan, "My Brother Brendan") 146 138 100 172 45 89 55 61

T Golden shiners, e.g. 34 25 19 44 173 40 67

U One who drives draft animals 157 97 71 117 151 110 170

V Without competition 7 109 83 88 48 164 92 115 82 59 11

W Form of trapshooting 179 35 114 135 49

26

WORDS / Grid

Col	1	2	3	4	5	6	7	8	9	10	11
	1 D	2 Y	3 Q	4 E	5 L	6 M	7 N	8 B	9 W	10 R	11 W
	12 Y	13 Q	14 T	15 B	■	16 G	17 L	18 A	19 Y	20 O	21 E
	22 X	23 C	24 A	25 J	26 P	27 F	28 U	29 E	30 I	31 T	■
	32 S	33 O	34 H	35 R	36 H	37 D	38 Y	39 F	40 V	41 Z	■
	42 E	43 B	44 Q	45 C	46 R	47 P	48 W	49 S	50 J	51 P	52 B
	53 S	54 F	55 A	56 M	57 R	58 H	59 Y	60 N	61 W	62 U	63 G
	64 C	65 F	66 E	67 T	68 N	69 B	70 P	71 V	72 M	73 J	74 B
	75 I	76 E	77 W	78 V	79 P	80 A	81 Y	82 G	83 O	84 N	85 F
	86 K	87 C	88 P	89 B	90 A	91 Z	92 E	93 B	94 O	95 S	■
	96 R	97 W	98 K	99 S	100 H	101 E	102 M	103 Q	104 O	105 D	106 X
	107 V	108 F	109 A	110 I	111 K	112 L	113 V	114 G	115 B	116 N	■
	117 D	118 U	119 Y	120 P	121 W	122 K	123 T	124 O	125 E	126 L	■
	127 T	128 W	129 S	130 M	131 V	132 N	133 U	134 I	135 H	136 W	■
	137 F	138 O	139 A	140 Z	141 L	142 Q	143 M	144 F	145 G	146 K	■
	147 H	148 E	149 V	150 B	151 J	152 V	153 X	154 G	155 L	156 M	■
	157 U	158 J	159 W	160 Y	161 B	162 U	163 N	164 K	165 H	■	■
	166 S	167 Q	168 B	169 A	170 F	171 M	172 U	173 T	174 U	175 Y	■
	176 N	177 A	178 G	179 K	180 K	181 E	182 Z	183 H	184 C	185 Y	■
	186 G	187 D	188 N	189 B	190 W	191 Z	192 H	193 Z	194 T	195 L	■
	196 S	197 B	198 R	199 A	200 K	201 Q	202 H	203 I	204 F	205 Z	■

CLUES

A Raised platform on which a body lies in state

B Science of planning and constructing buildings

C Split apart

D "Cool ___" (1918 Carl Sandburg poem)

E The throwing off of scales or flakes

F Absurd, nonsensical

G Rise or float in air

H 425 B.C. Aristophanes play

I Ornamental recess in a wall

J Hoarse, harsh

K Experienced

L Checks; detentions

M Type of tip

N Sea urchins and sand dollars, e.g.

O Largest of the Ryukyus

P "Every woman adores a ___, / The boot in the face, the brute" (Sylvia Plath, "Daddy")

Q Seethes

R Came forth

S Pit in which water is collected

T The act of drawing or pulling

U Conducted by letters

V Rues

W Injured

X Snake-worship

Y Parliament of the Republic of Ireland

Z Release, remove

WORDS

A 55 80 18 169 177 109 24 199 139 90

B 150 168 89 69 115 74 161 15 52 8 197 93 189 43

C 64 45 87 23 184

D 117 187 105 37 1

E 148 101 29 76 92 42 66 4 125 181 21

F 108 137 85 65 170 54 144 27 39 204

G 178 16 186 82 63 154 114 145

H 183 34 147 100 58 202 135 36 192 165

I 110 30 134 75 203

J 50 151 73 25 158

K 200 164 111 86 122 180 179 98 146

L 112 17 155 5 141 126 195

M 102 6 72 56 130 143 156 171

N 132 68 7 176 84 163 188 60 116

O 138 94 20 33 83 124 104

P 120 70 51 26 88 47 79

Q 13 167 44 142 201 103 3

R 198 46 96 57 35 10

S 53 32 166 95 49 99 129

T 127 14 67 123 190 31

U 194 133 62 162 172 118 157 28

V 152 131 78 174 40 173 71 107 113 149

W 121 61 11 48 9 136 128 159 77 97

X 22 196 106 153

Y 38 2 81 59 19 119 160 175 12 185

Z 41 193 140 182 191 205 91

27

CLUES

	Clue	Letters
A	Type of shark	22 93 148 53 7 27 45 145 115 58
B	Foolishly fond of one's wife	80 63 100 160 40 166 162 146
C	Predaceous insect of devout aspect	139 106 116 21 103 99
D	Apparition	66 6 110 150 72 154 94 55
E	Adjective for, e.g. Mt. Everest	39 73 177 143 165 159 54 26 57
F	Share taken illicitly (hyph.)	50 64 155 180 30 102 59
G	Distinguished	105 65 18 131 91 47 71
H	River of Scotland, flowing into the Tweed	181 49 3 61 89 33
I	"Friendship needs a certain parallelism of life, a —— of thought" ("Education of Henry Adams")	170 15 153 90 167 41 86 95 8
J	Mountain, SW Szechwan, sacred to Buddhists	52 129 176 112
K	Cover so as to make watertight (2 wds.)	92 149 38 142 10 124 108 60 48 179
L	Guitar-like Russian instrument	161 83 67 46 29 157 140 175 147
M	Officials charged with maintaining order	11 97 119 104 51 135 35 32
N	Secretary	171 173 164 74 120 156 113 88 138 128
O	1904 Cecil Mack–Albert Von Tilzer song	141 62 12 4 70 121 114
P	Heavy rope for moving or towing	126 96 158 36 25 136
Q	Print; cancel (2 wds.)	69 14 9 56 144 23 152 19 134
R	Arrange by clever maneuvering	76 24 118 137 132 168 163 81 2 151 37
S	Most able, qualified, competent	101 123 5 44 68 43 31
T	Ogling, staring stupidly	75 174 1 111 84 172 42
U	Hit high in the air	85 79 16 122 169 117
V	Study of the nature of being	178 77 82 130 17 34 125 78
W	"The pulp so bitter, how shall taste the ——" (Thompson, "The Hound of Heaven")	13 127 87 98
X	SW part of Arabia, cap. San'a	133 20 109 28 107

WORDS (grid)

1	2	3	4	5	6	7	8	9	10
1 T	2 R	3 H	4 O	5 S	6 D	7 A	8 I	9 Q	10 K
11 M	12 O	13 W	14 Q	15 I	16 U	17 V	18 G	19 Q	20 X
■	21 C	22 A	23 Q	24 R	25 P	26 E	27 A	28 X	29 L
30 F	31 S	32 M	33 H	34 V	35 M	36 P	37 R	38 K	39 E
40 B	41 I	42 T	43 S	44 S	45 A	46 L	47 G	48 K	49 H
■	50 F	51 M	52 J	53 A	54 E	55 D	56 Q	57 E	58 A
59 F	60 K	61 H	62 O	63 B	64 F	65 G	66 D	67 L	68 S
■	69 Q	70 O	71 G	72 D	73 E	74 N	75 T	76 R	77 V
78 V	79 U	80 B	81 R	82 V	83 L	84 T	85 U	86 I	87 W
88 N	89 H	90 I	91 G	92 K	93 A	94 D	95 I	96 P	97 M
98 W	99 C	100 B	101 S	102 F	103 C	104 M	105 G	106 C	107 X
108 K	109 X	110 D	111 T	112 J	113 N	114 O	115 A	116 C	117 U
118 R	119 M	120 N	121 O	122 U	123 S	124 K	125 V	126 P	127 W
■	128 N	129 J	130 V	131 G	132 R	133 X	134 Q	135 M	136 P
137 R	138 C	139 C	140 L	141 O	142 K	143 E	144 A	145 A	146 B
■	■	147 L	148 A	149 K	150 D	151 R	152 Q	153 I	154 D
■	155 F	156 N	157 L	158 P	159 E	160 B	161 L	162 B	163 R
■	164 N	165 E	166 B	167 I	168 R	169 U	170 I	171 N	172 T
■	173 N	174 T	175 L	176 J	177 E	178 V	179 K	180 F	181 H

CLUES

A Condition characterized by brief attacks of deep sleep — 18 175 32 84 173 120 193 60 143 111

B Act of bestowing or assigning — 28 187 176 2 114 110 76 83 41 68 156

C Most strict or secure — 61 100 116 94 139 127 44 10

D Scottish pudding — 4 163 161 172 183 105

E Family of plants including yucca and century plant — 141 145 11 22 16

F Wink — 122 59 39 203 21 157 191

G Showing little or no change — 99 6 85 108 51 57

H Belonging to a thing by its very nature — 90 190 79 50 82 174 113 43 150

I Republic at the east end of the Mediterranean — 12 74 166 92 38 65 164

J Clarity — 63 47 97 170 14 86 27 36 102

K Involving charity — 7 148 119 89 133 69 195 81 115 125 179 167

L Brings to a pure state — 197 40 72 159 171 132 71

M Vilifying — 121 19 42 147 30 13 155 137 168

N Belonging to a time not long past — 103 180 3 189 201 153

O Harvest mites — 192 118 144 126 202 185 152 109

P Extinct prairie chicken of the eastern U.S. (2 wds.) — 158 98 49 9 140 131 200 78

Q Involve as a necessary circumstance — 62 184 45 67 95 8 196 24 151

R Pigs' feet, e.g. — 138 58 25 177 91 35 73 162

S "A pleasant thing it is for the ___ the sun." (3 wds. Eccl. 11:7) — 181 53 64 149 34 15 26 23 188 128 199 165

T Squidlike cephalopod — 29 112 117 101 52 136 66 5 56 20

U Faculty of speech — 142 134 160 123 31 77

V Leaves, straw, rushes, etc., used for covers — 182 204 1 130 93 178 55 17

W Eng. poet (1880–1958, "The Highwayman"; full name) — 154 80 129 46 96 54 146 169 198 104 186

X Offshoots — 107 37 135 88 194

Y Small, orange-colored citrus fruit — 70 124 48 75 106 33 87

WORDS (grid)

1 V	2 B	3 N	4 D	5 T	6 G	7 K	8 Q	9 P		
10 C	11 E	12 I	13 M	14 J	15 S	16 E	17 V	18 A	19 M	
20 T	21 F	22 E	23 S	24 Q	25 R	26 S	27 J			
28 B	29 T	30 M	31 U	32 A	33 Y	34 S	35 R	36 J	37 X	38 I
39 F	40 L	41 B	42 M	43 H	44 C	45 Q	46 W	47 J		
48 Y	49 P	50 H	51 G	52 T	53 S	54 W	55 V	56 T	57 G	58 R
59 F	60 A	61 C	62 Q	63 J	64 S	65 I	66 T	67 Q	68 B	
69 K	70 Y	71 L	72 L	73 R	74 I	75 Y	76 B	77 U	78 P	79 H
80 W	81 K	82 H	83 B	84 A	85 G	86 J	87 Y	88 X		
89 K	90 H	91 R	92 I	93 V	94 C	95 Q	96 W	97 J	98 P	
99 G	100 C	101 T	102 J	103 N	104 W	105 D	106 Y	107 X	108 G	
109 O	110 B	111 A	112 T	113 H	114 B	115 K	116 C	117 T		
118 O	119 K	120 A	121 M	122 F	123 U	124 Y	125 K	126 O	127 C	
128 S	129 W	130 V	131 P	132 L	133 K	134 U	135 X	136 T	137 M	
138 R	139 C	140 P	141 E	142 U	143 A	144 O	145 E	146 W	147 M	
148 K	149 S	150 H	151 Q	152 O	153 N	154 W	155 M	156 B	157 F	
158 P	159 L	160 U	161 D	162 R	163 D	164 I	165 S	166 I	167 K	
168 M	169 W	170 J	171 L	172 D	173 A	174 H	175 A	176 B		
177 R	178 V	179 K	180 N	181 S	182 V	183 D	184 Q	185 O	186 W	
187 B	188 S	189 N	190 H	191 F	192 O	193 A	194 X	195 K	196 Q	
197 L	198 W	199 S	200 P	201 N	202 O	203 F	204 V			

29

Diagram

Grid cells in reading order (white squares), shown as **number·clue-letter**; black squares are not numbered.

1 I	2 X	3 C	4 M	5 V	6 W	7 B	8 J	9 A	10 E	
11 T	12 I	13 Q	14 N	15 F	16 H	17 M	18 D	19 D		
20 V	21 N	22 I	23 K	24 P	25 V	26 Y	27 A	28 W	29 L	
30 J	31 I	32 L	33 W	34 O	35 O	36 B	37 S	38 V	39 N	40 U
41 H	42 O	43 D	44 J	45 K	46 A	47 M	48 Z	49 E	50 H	
51 W	52 D	53 Z	54 C	55 K	56 B	57 A	58 Q	59 L		
60 R	61 U	62 I	63 N	64 P	65 E	66 W	67 J	68 F		
69 S	70 E	71 M	72 E	73 X	74 U	75 Z	76 X	77 O	78 R	
79 K	80 A	81 B	82 P	83 H	84 M	85 A	86 B	87 N	88 E	
89 B	90 Z	91 Z	92 J	93 S	94 X	95 S	96 F	97 L		
98 U	99 V	100 B	101 G	102 Z	103 K	104 Q	105 P	106 D	107 R	108 T
109 S	110 U	111 O	112 A	113 P	114 G	115 S	116 O	117 P	118 Z	
119 T	120 F	121 X	122 D	123 R	124 F	125 V	126 M			
127 J	128 F	129 Q	130 G	131 Z	132 N	133 C	134 L	135 G	136 G	
137 K	138 R	139 J	140 E	141 D	142 B	143 R	144 P	145 M	146 U	147 I
148 H	149 T	150 X	151 A	152 Y	153 C	154 A	155 M	156 F	157 O	
158 X	159 W	160 Y	161 U	162 H	163 E	164 O	165 G			
166 V	167 S	168 T	169 X	170 Y	171 P	172 E	173 C	174 M	175 Z	176 L
177 F	178 U	179 U	180 B	181 N	182 B	183 A	184 S	185 X	186 O	
187 Q	188 Y	189 R	190 E	191 C	192 T	193 J	194 V	195 H	196 B	197 O
198 Y	199 A	200 B	201 J	202 Q	203 O	204 I	205 E			

CLUES / WORDS

	Clue	Words
A	Laudable	46 183 9 151 112 57 154 199 27 85 80
B	Quick to learn; fearful	182 100 7 196 89 180 200 142 36 81 56 86
C	Jacob's favorite wife, mother of Joseph and Benjamin (Gen. 29–35)	191 3 173 153 133 54
D	"Teach the young idea how ___" (2 wds.; Thomson, "The Season: Spring")	122 106 43 19 141 18 52
E	Deep thoughts; unfavorable comments	10 172 163 140 88 190 205 49 72 70 65
F	Unfortunate divinations (2 wds.)	156 96 177 120 15 68 128 124
G	County in S England	130 135 101 165 114 136
H	Irish lad	83 195 148 16 50 162 41
I	Heart, core	147 1 12 204 62 31 22
J	Paddle-wheeler, e.g.	44 139 8 193 67 201 92 127 30
K	"The breathless ___ (WORD N)" (2 wds.; Hammerstein, "All the Things You Are")	137 45 103 23 55 79
L	Drifting, as on water	59 97 176 32 29 134
M	Coyly playful	4 174 84 17 47 126 145 71 155
N	See WORD K	14 21 181 132 39 87 63
O	Wary	186 116 197 34 77 157 42 111 164 203
P	Having royal privileges	171 117 144 64 113 105 82 24
Q	Behaves theatrically	202 58 129 187 13 104
R	Skeptically, suspiciously	123 78 60 138 107 189 143
S	Reward; retribution	93 95 115 167 37 184 69 109
T	Property, possessions	192 149 168 108 119 11
U	Impressive seriousness	74 40 161 98 110 146 61 179 178
V	Old-time weapon of war; domineering, aggressive person (hyph.)	166 20 38 194 25 5 125 99
W	Building used as a religious retreat in Hinduism	159 6 28 51 66 33
X	Beluga, perhaps	150 2 185 76 169 73 121 94 158
Y	Situated away from the point of origin or attachment	26 188 170 152 198 160
Z	Long, trumpet-shaped drinking glass with a bulb at the closed end (hyph.)	131 175 48 90 53 91 75 118 102

30

CLUES

A. Stuck down here; coming here
B. Evil
C. Render empty, as, e.g. a log (2 wds.)
D. Comes into possession of
E. Break
F. Flourishing
G. Sharp, with it, alert (3 wds.)
H. American port on the Thames (2 wds.)
I. Earthquakes
J. Plant, genus Crataegus, of the rose family
K. Outlines sharply, delineates
L. Reach a goal
M. Unit of acceleration, one centimeter per second per second
N. Fill the mind of with prejudice by insinuations
O. Ratio of probability
P. Making, contriving
Q. Require, urge
R. Whim
S. Big panjandrum
T. Conservative element (2 wds.)
U. Member of a Bantu-speaking people of Malawi
V. Delight, bliss
W. Saccharine secretion of a plant
X. Touch, immediate proximity
Y. Capable, economical

WORDS

Clue	Positions
A	110 166 116 10 30 63 140 57 101 138
B	60 103 170 38 115 149
C	23 8 153 127 40 97 44 20 139
D	112 169 56 51 150 161 3 132
E	92 144 7 1 106 45 34
F	125 109 142 66 89 31 98 117
G	73 151 114 27 120 21 61 167 49
H	39 5 121 95 160 86 82 93 43
I	36 64 119 105 19 143 9 124
J	146 28 6 158 37 16 70
K	154 99 129 33 83 176
L	122 136 54 77 47 15
M	71 147 128
N	152 118 81 22 133 65
O	90 134 76 162
P	159 96 62 14 24 163 67 85 42 145
Q	126 102 78 46 123 113
R	148 174 32 165 55 131
S	68 48 50 168 74
T	130 111 84 155 91 171 12 29
U	13 2 135 41 80
V	164 141 175 59 88 25 107
W	4 137 79 52 11 35
X	58 18 104 72 156 172 17
Y	100 87 94 173 53 69 75 157 108

Grid

1 E	2 U	3 D	4 W	5 H	6 J	7 E	8 C	9 I	
10 A	11 W	12 T	13 U	14 P	15 L	16 J	17 X	18 X	19 I
20 C	21 G	22 N	23 C	24 P	25 V	27 G	28 J	29 T	
30 A	31 F	32 R	33 K	34 E	35 W	36 I	37 J	38 B	39 H
40 C	41 U	42 P	43 H	44 C	45 E	46 Q	47 L	48 S	49 G
50 S	51 D	52 W	53 Y	54 L	55 R	56 D	57 A	58 X	59 V
60 B	61 G	62 P	63 A	64 I	65 N	66 F	67 P	68 S	69 Y
70 J	71 M	72 X	73 G	74 S	75 Y	76 O	77 L	78 Q	
79 W	80 U	81 N	82 H	83 K	84 T	85 P	86 H	87 Y	88 V
89 F	90 O	91 T	92 E	93 H	94 Y	95 H	96 P	97 C	98 F
99 K	100 Y	101 A	102 Q	103 B	104 X	105 I	106 E	107 V	
108 Y	109 F	110 A	111 T	112 D	113 Q	114 G	115 B	116 A	117 F
118 N	119 I	120 G	121 H	122 L	123 Q	124 I	125 F	126 Q	127 C
128 M	129 K	130 T	131 R	132 D	133 N	134 O	135 U	136 L	137 W	138 A
139 C	140 A	141 V	142 F	143 I	144 E	145 P	146 J	147 M	
148 R	149 B	150 D	151 G	152 N	153 C	154 K	155 T	156 X	157 Y	158 J
159 P	160 H	161 D	162 O	163 P	164 V	165 R	166 A	167 G	
168 S	169 D	170 B	171 T	172 X	173 Y	174 R	175 V	176 K	

31

CLUES

A. Making habitual petty criticisms (hyph.) — 101 167 111 176 94 48 35 191 201 143 153 86

B. Works to one's advantage or disadvantage — 85 206 19 204 55 71 149 174

C. Remarkable, noteworthy — 25 112 134 82 181 49 16 65 38 53 31 208 6

D. Wild with excitement, enthusiasm, etc. — 170 84 182 117 99 57 155 45 193

E. Texas pioneer who didn't brand his calves — 80 178 142 165 66 91 116 187

F. Inappropriate — 175 188 79 67 106 54 123 150 140 100

G. Beak, beezer, snoot — 78 180 199 68 195 32

H. Alarm bell — 42 95 14 60 126 36

I. "The Lord _____ Job out of the whirlwind" (Job 38:1) — 103 72 59 203 152 96 12 196

J. Highwaymen, e.g. — 114 202 161 20 40 56 146

K. Infers — 92 119 30 2 144 58 27

L. Recurrent phrase in Pepys' diary (3 wds. after "and") — 198 113 44 189 10 130 109

M. E.R. Burrough's outstanding creation — 177 8 105 33 192 157

N. Adversaries — 18 137 151 76 115 11 186

O. Gusted — 154 7 183 122 29 61 171 46

P. Greek version of the Romans' Mars — 148 22 93 75

Q. Plant, genus Hesperis, of the mustard family — 168 158 90 4 52 135

R. Pathetic, affective — 163 172 159 107 185 128 88 131

S. Disordered — 63 89 133 74 141 145 129

T. Place for incubating eggs — 147 139 209 51 164 110 3 21

U. Mass. Senator since 1962 (2 wds.) — 47 118 190 200 102 83 69 87 124 205 5 9 138

V. Theme, subject — 160 62 166 43 127

W. Through extensive experience (4 wds.) — 108 179 1 64 73 24 136 121 194 50 15 39

X. As a matter of fact — 207 184 41 26 77 120 17 70 197

Y. Determines the value of — 23 34 59 98 104 125 132 156 162 173 210

Z. Candy of nuts in a sweet paste — 13 28 81 37 169 97

WORDS / Grid

1	W2	K3	T4	Q5	U6	7	O8	M9	U10
L11	N12	I13	14	H15	W16	C17	N18	B19	J20
T21	P22	23	W24	C25	X26	K27	Z28	O29	K30
C31	G32	M33	34	A35	H36	Z37	C38	W39	J40
X41	H42	V43	L44	D45	O46	U47	A48	C49	W50
T51	Q52	C53	F54	B55	J56	D57	K58	59	H60
O61	V62	S63	W64	C65	E66	F67	G68	U69	X70
B71	I72	W73	S74	P75	N76	X77	G78	F79	E80
Z81	C82	U83	D84	B85	A86	U87	R88	S89	Q90
E91	K92	P93	A94	H95	I96	Z97	98	D99	F100
A101	U102	I103	104	M105	F106	R107	W108	L109	T110
A111	C112	L113	J114	N115	E116	D117	U118	K119	X120
W121	O122	F123	U124	125	H126	V127	R128	S129	L130
R131	132	S133	C134	Q135	W136	N137	U138	T139	F140
S141	E142	A143	K144	S145	J146	T147	P148	B149	F150
N151	I152	A153	O154	D155	156	M157	Q158	R159	V160
J161	162	R163	T164	E165	V166	A167	Q168	Z169	D170
O171	R172	173	B174	F175	A176	M177	E178	W179	G180
C181	D182	O183	X184	R185	N186	E187	F188	L189	U190
A191	M192	D193	W194	G195	I196	X197	L198	G199	U200
A201	J202	I203	B204	U205	B206	X207	C208	T209	210

32

Grid (each white cell shown as *number·clue-letter*; cell 97 is a black square)

```
Row 1:  1·S  2·R  3·B  4·N  5·R  6·T  7·O
Row 2:  8·E  9·K  10·D  11·P  12·L  13·B  14·T  15·K  16·A  17·J
Row 3:  18·R  19·E  20·A  21·V  22·W  23·U  24·F  25·D  26·U  27·Q  28·L
Row 4:  29·N  30·Y  31·D  32·U  33·W  34·O  35·N  36·L  37·C  38·D
Row 5:  39·F  40·P  41·G  42·H  43·D  44·X  45·H  46·G  47·L
Row 6:  48·M  49·K  50·T  51·J  52·Y  53·G  54·C  55·L  56·G  57·K
Row 7:  58·E  59·Y  60·V  61·P  62·A  63·M  64·G  65·Q  66·D  67·E
Row 8:  68·K  69·G  70·M  71·P  72·N  73·O  74·U  75·O  76·G  77·F
Row 9:  78·R  79·U  80·H  81·F  82·X  83·B  84·J  85·F  86·Q
Row 10: 87·W  88·M  89·V  90·Q  91·N  92·M  93·P  94·T  95·J  96·B
Row 11: 97·■  98·I  99·D  100·Q  101·C  102·X  103·Y  104·N  105·K  106·F  107·L
Row 12: 108·G  109·E  110·U  111·D  112·Q  113·P  114·N  115·A  116·S
Row 13: 117·O  118·U  119·L  120·N  121·V  122·U  123·I  124·S  125·F  126·P
Row 14: 127·K  128·C  129·F  130·I  131·E  132·L  133·V  134·N  135·P  136·B
Row 15: 137·H  138·C  139·B  140·N  141·F  142·X  143·H  144·W  145·O
Row 16: 146·J  147·G  148·T  149·G  150·Q  151·P  152·U  153·V  154·H  155·Q
Row 17: 156·X  157·M  158·W  159·I  160·Q  161·B  162·D  163·V  164·O  165·J  166·E
Row 18: 167·A  168·H  169·C  170·V  171·O  172·A  173·L  174·Y  175·N  176·W  177·T
Row 19: 178·S  179·R  180·K  181·V  182·E  183·A  184·U  185·K  186·R  187·Q
Row 20: 188·T  189·P  190·O  191·W  192·P  193·D  194·I  195·G  196·R  197·S
Row 21: 198·B  199·L  200·Q  201·X  202·S  203·R  204·M  205·U  206·N  207·T
Row 22: 208·Y  209·J  210·A  211·E  212·B  213·S  214·X
```

CLUES / WORDS

A Walked aimlessly, tramped 115 183 167 20 210 16 172 62

B Supported, rooted for (2 wds.) 139 198 13 136 212 3 83 96 161

C Offended, irritated 128 169 138 54 101 37

D Small N American rabbit, genus sylvilagus 162 193 10 25 31 43 38 66 99 111

E One who is morally or sexually unrestrained 19 211 109 8 166 182 58 67 131

F Baseless, unjustified 141 106 125 39 81 85 24 77 129

G Home, fireside 56 64 108 195 46 76 69 149 53 147 41

H Mexican salamander, genus Ambystoma 42 45 80 168 137 143 154

I "April Morning" and "David," for instance 123 194 159 130 98

J State of SE Mexico, cap. Villahermosa 165 146 17 84 209 95 51

K "I may justly say with the ___ fellow of Rome, 'I came, saw, and overcame'" (hyph., "Henry IV, Part 2") 180 185 127 15 9 105 49 57 68

L Undertaking, venture 199 36 55 47 173 132 12 28 119 107

M Tearful 157 92 88 70 63 48 204

N "I to the world am like ___" (4 wds., "Comedy of Errors") 35 104 72 140 120 134 114 91 4 175 206 29

O Last name of Greek brothers, early 19th-cent. revolutionary leaders 145 171 164 7 34 117 190 75 73

P Haughtily arrogant 61 135 113 126 40 151 189 93 71 192 11

Q Young, coiled fern-fronds, eaten as a vegetable 90 112 100 200 155 187 150 27 160 86 65

R Dentition 186 18 203 179 2 196 5 78

S Most distinguished 116 213 124 202 178 197 1

T Manifested, made clear 14 177 50 188 207 6 94 148

U Female symbol of life (2 wds.) 23 122 79 74 152 32 184 118 26 110 205

V Sound of NE North Carolina 153 133 60 163 170 181 121 89 21

W Amended, altered 144 158 22 176 87 33 191

X New Jersey city on the Delaware 214 102 44 142 201 156 82

Y Have a restless longing 30 174 52 208 103 59

33

Grid

The acrostic grid (each white cell shows its sequence number and the letter of the clue-word it belongs to):

Row	Cells (number + clue-letter)
1	1 K · 2 R · 3 E · 4 M · 5 F · 6 E · 7 T · 8 F · ■
2	10 E · 11 B · 12 O · 13 Y · 14 P · 15 R · 16 T · 17 I · 18 N · 19 Z · 20 Z₂
3	21 M · 22 L · 23 G · 24 V · 25 R · 26 G · 27 D · 28 U · 29 F · 30 E
4	31 A · 32 K · 33 F · 34 Z · 35 X · 36 B · 37 Z₁ · 38 F · 39 M · 40 Y · 41 Z₂
5	42 Z₁ · 43 E · 44 T · 45 R · 46 S · 47 Z · 48 M · 49 N · 50 Y · 51 B · 52 D
6	53 B · 54 K · 55 L · 56 T · 57 Z₁ · 58 Z · 59 E · 60 D · 61 L
7	62 Q · 63 C · 64 A · 65 Z₁ · 66 B · 67 O · 68 C · 69 D · 70 Z₂ · 71 B
8	72 A · 73 Z · 74 I · 75 P · 76 G · 77 K · 78 Z₁ · 79 O · 80 T · 81 D · 82 L
9	83 F · 84 Q · 85 B · 86 K · 87 Z₁ · 88 U · 89 T · 90 B · 91 I · 92 P · 93 A
10	94 K · 95 Z₂ · 96 V · 97 G · 98 Z₂ · 99 O · 100 H · 101 E · 102 A · 103 U
11	104 M · 105 D · 106 R · 107 J · 108 E · 109 M · 110 Z · 111 I · 112 S · 113 P · 114 O
12	115 A · 116 C · 117 E · 118 J · 119 O · 120 E · 121 D · 122 J · 123 B · 124 Y · 125 Z₁
13	126 M · 127 F · 128 N · 129 U · 130 Z₂ · 131 J · 132 O · 133 Z₂ · 134 Z · 135 J · 136 F
14	137 H · 138 S · 139 P · 140 D · 141 T · 142 X · 143 O · 144 W · 145 L · 146 U · 147 W
15	148 V · 149 F · 150 J · 151 J · 152 F · 153 Z · 154 H · 155 N · 156 C · 157 O · 158 X
16	159 O · 160 E · 161 F · 162 V · 163 T · 164 R · 165 A · 166 S · 167 Y · 168 B
17	169 C · 170 R · 171 O · 172 D · 173 S · 174 Q · 175 Q · 176 I · 177 Z · 178 M · 179 L
18	180 C · 181 J · 182 G · 183 H · 184 T · 185 P · 186 O · 187 C · 188 H · 189 D · 190 Z₂
19	191 F · 192 K · 193 X · 194 E · 195 A · 196 P · 197 W · 198 R · 199 Y · 200 B · 201 X · 202 S
20	203 I · 204 L · 205 D · 206 Z₁ · 207 Z · 208 S · 209 Z · 210 B · 211 V
21	212 T · 213 D · 214 F · 215 V · 216 Y · 217 T · 218 L · 219 K · 220 K · 221 B · 222 D
22	223 Z · 224 Q · 225 E · 226 N · 227 O · 228 V · 229 F · 230 H · 231 G · 232 L · 233 Q
23	234 G · 235 F · 236 H · 237 E · 238 S · 239 L · 240 D · 241 W · 242 N

CLUES

A. Get rid of . . . .

B. "Where they most breed and haunt, I have observed / The ___," says Banquo (3 wds., "Macbeth")

C. Linus Pauling or Melvin Calvin, e.g.

D. Being the most perfect, pure embodiment of something . . . . . .

E. Father of King Arthur (full name) . . .

F. Conveyer of arsenic in "Arsenic and Old Lace" (2 wds.) . . . . . .

G. Member of a Bantu people of Zanzibar . . . . . .

H. Group of islands in the British W Indies

I. Star of the second magnitude in Ursa Major

J. Overflowing; escaping . . . . . .

K. 1959 one-act play by Edward Albee (2 wds. after "The") . . . .

L. "The ___ man and his pain" (Yeats, "A Dialogue of Self and Soul")

M. State of being a beginner . . . .

N. Slender, lithe; urbane . . . .

O. Very much, extremely (4 wds.) . . . .

P. Peppermint camphor . . . .

Q. One who makes a display of book-learning; hairsplitter

R. Disagreeable, bilious, crabbed . .

S. Gives grounds for laying claim . . . .

T. Fruit of a West Indian tree, Grias cauliflora (2 wds.) . . . .

U. Anc. Egyptian goddess, mother of Ra

V. Habitual object of abuse or humiliation

W. Dreadful, terrible . . . . .

X. As a follower or admirer (2 wds.) . . . .

Y. ___ State Mountains, of W West Germany

Z. Instance of advancing beyond established limits

Z₁. Mocking, teasing . . . .

Z₂. "I drink to the general joy of table, / And to our dear friend Banquo," says Macbeth (2 wds.)

WORDS

A	31 64 102 93 115 72 195 165
B	36 200 90 53 66 11 210 123 221 85 71 51 168
C	180 63 68 169 156 116 187
D	81 172 105 240 27 121 52 222 189 60 205 213 140 69
E	108 101 160 30 10 225 3 120 237 6 59 194 43 117
F	235 29 38 83 191 127 149 136 152 161 8 33 214 5
G	23 97 231 234 26 182 76
H	137 183 188 236 154 100 230
I	176 17 91 203 111 74
J	131 181 229 220 135 150 122 118 151 107
K	54 219 192 94 1 32 77 86
L	82 22 204 179 232 239 218 145 55 61
M	109 4 126 178 48 21 39 104
N	242 155 49 128 226 18
O	227 114 119 99 157 67 143 79 171 132 159 12 186
P	196 75 92 14 139 113 185
Q	175 174 233 224 84 62
R	25 15 45 164 106 170 198 2
S	46 202 208 112 166 238 138 173
T	217 44 16 163 56 141 7 89 80 212 184
U	88 129 146 28 103
V	148 228 96 215 211 24 162
W	147 197 144 241
X	142 193 35 201 158
Y	13 167 216 50 124 199 40
Z	134 47 223 177 153 58 110 209 19 207 34 73
Z₁	42 206 65 78 57 87 37 125
Z₂	98 95 20 190 133 130 70 41

34

CLUES

A. Its capital is Rabat

B. Disagreeable; repugnant (hyph.)

C. At once; uncontrolled (3 wds.)

D. Bulbous plant of the amaryllis family, *Narcissus pseudonarcissus*

E. Seaport, S Ukraine, on the Black Sea

F. Large rooms or buildings devoted to painting, photography, shooting, etc.

G. Firmness of purpose

H. Poet-musician, son of Calliope

I. Move unsteadily from side to side

J. Insert

K. Wimps, boobs, jerks

L. Distort

M. "These ___ call for the building of plans" (2 wds., F.D. Roosevelt, radio address 1932)

N. In braids

O. Tender of horses

P. Requirements

Q. "This passion, and ___ a dear friend, would go near to make a man look sad" (3 wds., "A Midsummer-Night's Dream")

R. Wandering, not fixed

S. Closes tightly

T. Parasitic plant growing on another plant or an animal

U. Abdominal

V. Not authorized

W. Pele's game

X. Trespass, interference

Y. Person of great authority

Z. Be naturally situated

WORDS

Clue	Numbers
A	36 93 197 88 46 1 37
B	133 174 33 89 83 119 87 116 13 121
C	184 105 132 127 50 178 32 30 70
D	16 91 188 38 48 141 55 113
E	67 78 191 142 135
F	195 166 73 65 186 109 57 18 84
G	182 62 156 10 81 145 148 125 21 107
H	143 26 158 99 108 181 43
I	134 175 163 75 66 15
J	9 94 202 40 6 86 167 47 117
K	20 170 23 199 103
L	154 139 61 111 11 76
M	64 49 96 39 183 196 92 22 193 126 72 28
N	180 51 60 112 79 27 168
O	17 58 123 106 97 77
P	140 150 59 130 189 185 45 136 100 122 19
Q	44 129 85 71 179 68 157 124 159 63
R	147 176 131 152 54 74 137
S	101 110 31 14 149 155 203
T	160 187 201 172 12 128
U	190 53 4 120 25 138 82 177 165
V	104 80 171 41 35 2 164
W	52 144 90 162 98 42 115
X	169 194 95 153 200 161 114 5 69
Y	198 8 29 3 151 34 146 102
Z	7 24 118 56 192 173

GRID (cell number — clue letter)

Row	Cells
1	1·A 2·V 3·Y 4·U 5·X 6·J 7·Z
2	8·Y 9·J 10·G 11·L 12·T 13·B 14·S 15·I 16·D 17·O 18·F
3	19·P 20·K 21·G 22·M 23·K 24·Z 25·U 26·H 27·N 28·M
4	29·Y 30·C 31·S 32·C 33·B 34·Y 35·V 36·A 37·A
5	38·D 39·M 40·J 41·V 42·W 43·H 44·Q 45·P 46·A 47·J
6	48·D 49·M 50·C 51·N 52·W 53·U 54·R 55·D 56·Z 57·F
7	58·O 59·P 60·N 61·L 62·G 63·Q 64·M 65·F 66·I 67·E
8	68·Q 69·X 70·C 71·Q 72·M 73·F 74·R 75·I 76·L 77·O 78·E
9	79·N 80·V 81·G 82·U 83·B 84·F 85·Q 86·J 87·B 88·A
10	89·B 90·W 91·D 92·M 93·A 94·J 95·X 96·M 97·O
11	98·W 99·H 100·P 101·S 102·Y 103·K 104·V 105·C 106·O 107·G
12	108·H 109·F 110·S 111·L 112·N 113·D 114·X 115·W 116·B 117·J 118·Z
13	119·B 120·U 121·B 122·P 123·O 124·Q 125·G 126·M 127·C
14	128·T 129·Q 130·P 131·R 132·C 133·B 134·I 135·E 136·P
15	137·R 138·U 139·L 140·P 141·D 142·E 143·H 144·W 145·G
16	146·Y 147·R 148·G 149·S 150·P 151·Y 152·R 153·X 154·L 155·S
17	156·G 157·Q 158·H 159·Q 160·T 161·X 162·W 163·I 164·V 165·U
18	166·F 167·J 168·N 169·X 170·K 171·V 172·T 173·Z 174·B 175·I 176·R
19	177·U 178·C 179·Q 180·N 181·H 182·G 183·M 184·C 185·P 186·F
20	187·T 188·D 189·P 190·U 191·E 192·Z 193·M 194·X 195·F
21	196·M 197·A 198·Y 199·K 200·X 201·T 202·J 203·S

35

CLUES

WORDS

A Lofty falcon's nest, e.g. . . . .
152 125 136 37 114

B Of course . . . .
34 78 150 158 169 17 99 70 32

C Co-authors of "Mutiny on the Bounty" (3 wds.) . . . .
117 20 103 148 134 11 60 57 71 66 102 122 52 41 132

D "Bring on the ___ horses!" said Michael Curtiz, directing "The Charge of the Light Brigade" . . . .
92 48 26 139 79

E Lash, change, substitute . . . .
138 68 44 13 106 155

F Disrepute, opprobrium . . . .
130 153 183 141 143 42

G Fit of trembling . . . .
10 177 121 85 35 129

H "How now! A rat? Dead for a ___, dead!" cries Hamlet . . . .
18 128 7 105 38

I Egg-shaped . . . .
157 36 131 97 59

J Egyptian goddess of hunting and war
63 108 171 137 100

K Angry, enraged . . . .
25 181 15 87 167 2 64

L Of the ancient Greeks . . . .
95 67 175 22 56 110 19 127

M Long-ago places for storing napkins, towels, pitchers, etc. . . . .
73 77 98 88 5 173 43

N Of Mennonites now living chiefly in Pennsylvania, Ohio, Indiana, and Canada . . . .
39 112 182 164 84

O Catarrh . . . .
151 1 31 62 166

P Hitches . . . .
154 140 83 124 53 29

Q Good times . . . .
51 116 75 179 3

R Am. author ("Portnoy's Complaint," "Good-bye, Columbus") . . . .
27 96 178 107

S Entrance, transport . . . .
176 12 126 93 69 74 165 156 123

T Prototypical fiend (2 wds.) . . . .
135 91 46 8 23 33 82 170 65 149 120

U Erudition . . . .
172 147 180 4 55 163 76 159 118

V Goddess of youth and spring, daughter of Zeus and Hera, wife of Hercules . . .
160 28 113 21

W Remote settlements, esp. in Australia
61 49 6 40 174 72 94

X "Is ___ in Sodom?" ("Brothers Karamazov," Bk.3, Ch.3) . . . .
142 50 104 16 168 90 47 146 111 161 145

Y Gyp, chisel, dupe, screw . . . .
86 80 133 14 115 9

Z Horatio Nelson's main squeeze (2 wds.)
81 144 109 54 162 101 58 24 30 89 119 45

36

CLUES		WORDS
A	Concentrate, causing process shift about mental opening	142 163 167 121 63 137 9 131
B	Gravity permits comedy, but of a grave nature (2 wds.)	84 99 5 160 97 21 58 61 75 46 42 52
C	Escaped East to West with hot stuff on a railroad (2 wds.)	89 127 133 118 51 152
D	Lou took change to prospect	59 93 154 19 88 53 38
E	Insecure as result of terrible bout with flu after disastrous start	146 166 184 162 135 26 140 150
F	Like the Devil, I'm quiet before his breakup	147 156 30 116 176 122
G	Wicked Furies on a tear	179 120 159 22 164 16 81 144 165
H	Honor begun in Greece, O shifting reverence!	136 112 54 173 92 3
I	I know a new way to a Pacific island	123 90 82 117 40 171 14
J	Female wanly holding a Hindu mantra	55 183 172 91 13 15 94
K	Any white formation being a hindrance (3 wds.)	72 78 85 34 12 95 161 141
L	Oh, gee! to start getting mixed up for a poet?!	139 134 69 43 110 104
M	Join gang broken between Edie's opening and closing	157 148 68 7 80 20
N	Removes a weak stay in trouble (2 wds.)	64 4 103 11 185 56 33 77 50
O	Novel aspect of sleepy town's return	60 57 27 125 49
P	A couple of thousands in hock for simple sleeping arrangement	96 105 111 177 170 98 174
Q	Being cowardly regarding strange trance	138 180 109 23 39 149 48 18
R	Now I've gone out, as anyone can plainly see (2 wds.)	143 100 182 155 28 6
S	Muscle an unusual symbolic character (2 wds.)	108 67 126 41 62 106 130 36
T	Cared in an odd way, managed about a five (3 wds.)	74 102 2 114 66 79 37 107 124
U	Fictional Teddy reverting to old English bird	169 158 86 76 44 32
V	Crestfallen nymph holding a Steinbeck character	128 153 73 119 115
W	Briny ailment roiling without surcease	151 113 71 168 181 101 1 83 132 10 129 24
X	Crazy fool, about fifty, while beginning to succeed	45 35 31 145 25 87
Y	Canine living in a moist zone	175 8 178 70 29 47 17 65

■	■	■	1 W	2 T	3 H	■	4 N	5 B	6 R	7 M	8 Y
9 A	■	10 W	11 N	12 K	13 J	■	14 I	■	15 J	16 G	17 Y
18 Q	19 D	20 M	■	21 B	22 G	23 Q	24 W	■	25 X	26 E	■
27 O	28 R	29 Y	30 F	31 X	32 U	■	33 N	34 K	35 X	■	36 S
37 T	38 D	39 Q	■	40 I	■	41 S	42 B	43 L	■	44 U	45 X
■	46 B	47 Y	48 Q	49 O	50 N	■	51 C	52 B	53 D	54 H	■
55 J	56 N	57 O	58 B	■	59 D	60 O	61 B	62 S	63 A	■	64 N
65 Y	66 T	67 S	■	68 M	69 L	70 Y	71 W	72 K	73 V	74 T	■
75 B	76 U	■	77 N	78 K	79 T	■	80 M	81 G	82 I	83 W	84 B
■	85 K	86 U	■	87 X	88 D	89 C	90 I	■	91 J	■	92 H
93 D	94 J	■	95 K	96 P	97 B	■	98 P	99 B	100 R	■	101 W
102 T	103 N	104 L	■	105 P	106 S	■	107 T	108 S	109 Q	110 L	■
111 P	112 H	113 W	114 T	115 V	■	116 F	117 I	■	118 C	119 V	120 G
■	121 A	122 F	123 I	124 T	125 O	■	126 S	127 C	128 V	129 W	■
130 S	131 A	■	132 W	133 C	134 L	135 E	136 H	137 A	138 Q	■	139 L
140 E	141 K	■	142 A	143 R	144 G	145 X	146 E	■	147 F	148 M	■
149 Q	■	150 E	151 W	152 C	153 V	154 D	155 R	156 F	157 M	■	158 U
159 G	■	160 B	161 K	162 E	163 A	164 G	■	165 G	166 E	167 A	168 W
169 U	170 P	171 I	■	172 J	173 H	174 P	175 Y	176 F	■	177 P	178 Y
■	179 G	180 Q	181 W	182 R	183 J	184 E	185 N	■	■	■	■

37

CLUES / WORDS

Clue	Definition	Word (cell numbers)
A	Wife of Ahab	9 29 72 118 84 88 151
B	Utter, absolute; offensive	39 137 97 12
C	Backed, supported	158 119 30 48 122 77 177 110
D	Simpleton	70 132 66 42 170 141
E	Plant, source of linen	166 138 79 157
F	Eng. architect (1573–1652, full name)	91 59 103 136 112 87 108 23 76 80
G	Otalgia	56 58 153 22 104 37 3
H	E.B. White's Stuart ___	150 165 89 34 63 54
I	Commented at great length	14 176 57 106 6 161 1 62 24
J	Fr. colonial governor in N America (1657–1730), founder of Detroit	46 43 143 147 5 68 160 111
K	One concerned with improving humans by improving the environment	8 142 167 82 50 148 28 174 33
L	Leaned, careened; in the book	175 134 49 36 114 60
M	Down	13 156 164 81 117 120 149 17 95
N	Evasive	133 126 45 61 98 55
O	In layers	25 145 168 130 154 21
P	Immediate apprehension	140 135 93 32 96 64 67 16 41
Q	Elbow	171 40 51 86 94
R	Esau; anc. country, bordering anc. Palestine	127 169 35 52
S	Stewed, potted, fried, loaded	178 71 125 105 107 144 162
T	Landing strip; habitual path	115 109 7 116 19 152
U	Efflux	99 131 172 92 47 31 18
V	Unnecessarily tedious and wordy	4 20 173 155 74 27
W	Ventured, risked	102 100 73 65 11 128 121 69
X	As anyone can see	83 113 85 159 38 75 101 90 53
Y	Kidded, ribbed	129 2 26 146 15 123 163
Z	Irish poet (1865–1939, "Down by the Salley Gardens")	44 10 124 139 78

Grid (cells: number·word)

Row	Cells
1	1·I 2·Y 3·G 4·V 5·J 6·I
2	7·T 8·K 9·A 10·Z 11·W 12·B 13·M 14·I 15·Y 16·P
3	17·M 18·U 19·T 20·V 21·O 22·G 23·F 24·I 25·O 26·Y
4	27·V 28·K 29·A 30·C 31·U 32·P 33·K 34·H 35·R
5	36·L 37·G 38·X 39·B 40·Q 41·P 42·D 43·J 44·Z 45·N
6	46·J 47·U 48·C 49·L 50·K 51·Q 52·R 53·X 54·H
7	55·N 56·G 57·I 58·G 59·F 60·L 61·N 62·I 63·H 64·P
8	65·W 66·D 67·P 68·J 69·W 70·D 71·S 72·A 73·V
9	74·V 75·X 76·F 77·C 78·Z 79·E 80·F 81·M 82·K 83·X
10	84·A 85·X 86·Q 87·F 88·A 89·H 90·X 91·F 92·U
11	93·P 94·Q 95·M 96·P 97·B 98·N 99·U 100·W 101·X
12	102·W 103·F 104·G 105·S 106·I 107·S 108·F 109·T 110·C 111·J
13	112·F 113·X 114·L 115·T 116·T 117·M 118·A 119·C 120·M 121·W
14	122·C 123·Y 124·Z 125·S 126·N 127·R 128·W 129·Y 130·O 131·U
15	132·D 133·N 134·L 135·P 136·F 137·B 138·E 139·Z 140·P 141·D 142·K
16	143·J 144·S 145·O 146·Y 147·J 148·K 149·M 150·H 151·A 152·T
17	153·G 154·O 155·V 156·M 157·E 158·C 159·X 160·J 161·I 162·S
18	163·Y 164·M 165·H 166·E 167·K 168·O 169·R 170·D 171·Q 172·U
19	173·V 174·K 175·L 176·I 177·C 178·S

Grid

1 F	2 Z	3 M	4 T	5 K	6 B	7 K	8 G			
9 P	10 A	11 N	12 D	13 X	14 J	15 Y	16 I	17 Q	18 M	19 E
20 V	21 T	22 N	23 C	24 Y	25 D	26 M	27 Z	28 B	29 O	30 S
31 L	32 V	33 M	34 R	35 B	36 W	37 V	38 F	39 R	40 E	
41 A	42 D	43 B	44 C	45 M	46 T	47 U	48 D	49 X	50 S	
51 A	52 P	53 O	54 R	55 W	56 S	57 Q	58 L	59 Z	60 P	
61 F	62 K	63 C	64 G	65 R	66 I	67 O	68 H	69 P	70 E	
71 M	72 Q	73 G	74 I	75 A	76 X	77 F	78 N	79 G	80 N	
81 F	82 I	83 N	84 H	85 C	86 U	87 R	88 K	89 D	90 P	
91 N	92 R	93 L	94 T	95 Y	96 P	97 M	98 Q	99 D	100 Z	
101 E	102 Y	103 X	104 A	105 H	106 W	107 F	108 P	109 B	110 C	111 J
112 B	113 D	114 W	115 U	116 I	117 H	118 U	119 J	120 B	121 M	
122 P	123 B	124 I	125 C	126 N	127 M	128 E	129 X	130 J	131 F	
132 I	133 P	134 D	135 W	136 R	137 F	138 J	139 A	140 T	141 M	
142 Y	143 O	144 S	145 Z	146 W	147 Y	148 W	149 K	150 K		
151 J	152 C	153 A	154 Z	155 S	156 W	157 G	158 P	159 I	160 K	
161 W	162 N	163 W	164 Y	165 Z	166 H	167 E	168 D	169 Q	170 S	171 V
172 B	173 C	174 D	175 V	176 Z	177 N	178 M	179 F	180 N		
181 V	182 L	183 W	184 T	185 J	186 N	187 V	188 W			

CLUES / WORDS

A — Anc. Greek and Roman storage jar 104 153 51 10 41 139 75

B — Type of fresh term 123 28 109 112 6 35 172 120 43

C — Game of bowls 110 44 63 152 125 85 173 23

D — Easy 25 12 42 113 134 99 168 89 48 174

E — Two-point play on the gridiron 40 101 128 167 19 70

F — Native, natural 77 137 107 61 1 81 38 179 131

G — Drumming "Baby" (1898–1959) 73 157 64 8 79

H — Pop dance music 117 68 166 105 84

I — Quirks; rarae aves, freaks 16 124 82 66 132 159 116 74

J — Improvises a passage experimentally 130 14 119 138 185 151 111

K — Laden, burdened 150 62 88 160 7 5 149

L — Posterior 182 93 58 31

M — Am. singer and actress (1896–1977, "Member of the Wedding"; full name) 178 121 33 18 26 141 71 3 97 127 45

N — Post; job; meeting; date 80 91 83 186 11 78 162 177 126 180 22

O — Covered with tiny particles of ice 29 53 67 143

P — "Till he unseam'd him from the nave ___ / And fix'd his head upon our battlements" (3 wds., "Macbeth") 108 133 69 158 60 9 96 122 52 90

Q — Eng. political leader, trade unionist (1897–1960) 17 57 169 98 72

R — Disconcerted, discomposed, confused 92 136 39 87 54 34 65

S — Young chicory plant; witloof 170 144 155 50 56 30

T — Filled with sudden horror 140 184 4 21 46 94

U — Type of furnace used for baking or drying 115 47 118 86

V — Highly successful and aggressive 175 37 181 171 20 187 32

W — Returning from travels, e.g. (4 wds.) 106 148 156 163 161 146 55 135 36 114 188 183

X — University in eastern Mass. 76 129 13 103 49

Y — Captivate, spellbind 164 102 95 24 15 147 142

Z — Deplored, bewailed, grieved 100 176 165 154 2 27 145 59

WORDS / Grid

1 D	2 T	3 E	4 S	5 C	■	6 A	7 P	8 D	9 B
10 Z₁	11 J	12 L	13 W	14 J	15 T	16 E	17 Y	18 Y	19 B	20 D
21 Z	22 Q	23 G	24 E	25 L	26 E	27 F	28 J	29 R
30 Z	31 Z₁	32 F	33 L	34 U	35 S	36 Y	37 A	38 P	39 X
40 R	41 X	42 R	43 O	44 Z	45 L	46 M	47 L	48 R
49 L	50 V	51 T	52 X	53 Y	54 N	55 R	56 J	57 G	58 H
59 F	60 P	61 Y	62 S	63 Q	64 C	65 H	66 J	67 Z
68 E	69 B	70 E	71 L	72 M	73 C	74 J	75 D	76 R	77 G
78 O	79 U	80 N	81 Q	82 I	83 M	84 B	85 R	86 L	87 Y
88 E	89 M	90 P	91 B	92 S	93 A	94 L	95 Q	96 A	97 K
98 F	99 E	100 I	101 O	102 Z₁	103 W	104 I	105 L	106 C	107 E
108 W	109 M	110 T	111 F	112 Y	113 P	114 Z	115 B	116 T	117 V
118 S	119 F	120 G	121 E	122 P	123 R	124 V	125 T	126 Y	127 X
128 C	129 K	130 V	131 V	132 K	133 L	134 U	135 I	136 F
137 I	138 B	139 O	140 N	141 U	142 K	143 C	144 U	145 W	146 A	147 H
148 W	149 H	150 X	151 T	152 U	153 U	154 N	155 E	156 C	157 A
158 Z₁	159 X	160 S	161 I	162 L	163 Q	164 Y	165 B
166 C	167 D	168 E	169 Y	170 Z	171 E	172 V	173 G	174 Z₁	175 J

CLUES

A "Good night, sweet ___, good night, good night," says Ophelia 96 6 37 93 157 146

B Family name in Wilder's "The Skin of Our Teeth" 9 91 19 165 84 115 138 69

C Answered 166 143 73 128 106 5 64

D Occasion of merrymaking 75 20 156 167 8 1

E 1936 Pulitzer Prize–winning Kaufman & Hart comedy (4 wds. followed by WORD F) 70 121 88 16 168 3 24 107 155 68 171 99 26

F See WORD E (2 wds.) 119 32 111 27 136 59 98

G Cold, callous, savage, brutish 23 141 120 173 57 77 152

H Heaps, piles 65 149 147 58

I Disheartenment, consternation, fear . . 137 104 100 135 82 161

J Blemish, blot, fright 74 175 28 14 66 56 11

K Japanese general executed for war crimes (1885–1948) 142 97 132 129

L Critical though false evidence in "Othello" 25 12 94 105 45 162 86 33 49 133 71 47

M Show or feign strong feelings 89 83 46 72 109

N City of Philistia, home of Goliath . . . 80 140 54 154

O Mature, mellow 139 43 78 101

P Wrap, surround 90 113 60 38 7 122

Q "He's mad that trusts in the tameness of ___," says The Fool (2 wds., "King Lear") 95 22 63 81 163

R "Oh, for ___ of a vanished hand" (2 wds.; Tennyson. "Break. Break. Break.") 40 76 55 48 123 85 29 42

S Prairie wolf 4 62 118 35 92 160

T Diffusion of fluids through membranes 15 151 51 116 125 2 110

U Grandeur, imposing character 134 18 144 131 79 153 34

V Dodge, get around by trickery 124 130 172 117 50

W Smears 148 103 145 108 13

X Purpose, design 52 159 127 150 39 41

Y New York hotel, home of a famous "Round Table" 112 169 61 164 126 87 36 17 53

Z Nonentity 44 67 170 30 21 114

Z₁ Hurt, sting 102 31 158 10 174

40

CLUES / WORDS

	Clue	Letters
A	Clans within a tribe	145 176 158 139 169 63 3 44 62
B	Begone! (obs.)	159 45 6 133 151 95
C	Vague, indistinct	118 60 96 188 182 19 193
D	Clear, transparent; calm	72 115 12 125 121 168
E	Suitable	172 17 178 170 141 83 175 124
F	Does; binds; obligates	23 10 194 171 153 110 26
G	One of a Dumas trio	56 108 43 129 32
H	Practice chicanery	82 187 86 165 22 8 14 132
I	Disappointment	130 40 85 54 66 15 71
J	Specialized vocabulary	87 80 137 192 180
K	Semiaquatic salamanders	191 112 7 68 2
L	Laugh self-consciously	50 58 21 155 73 34
M	Successes	39 48 61 84
N	Lightens, mitigates, soothes	79 94 69 186 90
O	Ship's small boat; two-masted sailboat	13 81 27 146
P	Hone	51 128 76 98 65 114 183
Q	Aid	195 49 74 107 113 77 31 136 57
R	Fictional Faulkner county	147 35 88 122 46 55 189 127 179 106 160 78 163
S	Cry out sharply	161 64 196 47
T	Getting well (3 wds.)	37 53 42 109 59 144 28 154 123
U	Bathsheba's husband (II Sam. 11)	70 41 150 126 111
V	Negligent	18 99 36 181 142 75
W	River from W Czechoslovakia through Germany to the North Sea	93 30 190 177
X	Divided	162 105 24 33 184
Y	Thoughts; unfavorable observations	92 149 185 29 103 20 100 143 131 5 120
Z	"___, ye that dwell in dust'' (3 wds.. Isaiah 26:19)	1 138 25 4 174 97 164 102 116 135 16 152
Z₁	1964 film starring Anthony Quinn (3 wds.)	134 101 67 148 52 38 156 119 91 9 89 166 173
Z₂	Sycophant (hyph.)	

Grid

Row	Cells (number·letter)
1	1 Z · 2 K · 3 A · 4 Z · 5 Y · 6 B · 7 K · 8 H
2	9 Z₁ · 10 F · 11 Z₂ · 12 D · 13 O · 14 H · 15 I · 16 Z · 17 E
3	18 V · 19 C · 20 Y · 21 L · 22 H · 23 F · 24 X · 25 Z · 26 F · 27 O
4	28 T · 29 Y · 30 W · 31 Q · 32 G · 33 X · 34 L · 35 R · 36 V
5	37 T · 38 Z₁ · 39 M · 40 I · 41 U · 42 T · 43 G · 44 A · 45 B · 46 R · 47 S
6	48 M · 49 Q · 50 L · 51 P · 52 Z₁ · 53 T · 54 I · 55 R · 56 G · 57 Q
7	58 L · 59 T · 60 C · 61 M · 62 A · 63 A · 64 S · 65 P · 66 I · 67 Z₁ · 68 K
8	69 N · 70 U · 71 I · 72 D · 73 L · 74 Q · 75 V · 76 P · 77 Q
9	78 R · 79 N · 80 J · 81 O · 82 H · 83 E · 84 M · 85 I · 86 H · 87 J · 88 R
10	89 Z₁ · 90 N · 91 Z₁ · 92 Y · 93 W · 94 N · 95 B · 96 C · 97 Z · 98 P
11	99 V · 100 Y · 101 Z₁ · 102 Z · 103 Y · 104 Z₂ · 105 X · 106 R · 107 Q
12	108 G · 109 T · 110 F · 111 U · 112 K · 113 Q · 114 P · 115 D · 116 Z · 117 Z₂
13	118 C · 119 Z₁ · 120 Y · 121 D · 122 R · 123 T · 124 E · 125 D · 126 U · 127 R
14	128 P · 129 G · 130 I · 131 Y · 132 H · 133 B · 134 Z₁ · 135 Z · 136 Q · 137 J · 138 Z
15	139 A · 140 Z₂ · 141 E · 142 V · 143 Y · 144 T · 145 A · 146 O · 147 R · 148 Z₁
16	149 Y · 150 U · 151 B · 152 Z · 153 F · 154 T · 155 L · 156 Z · 157 Z₂ · 158 A
17	159 B · 160 R · 161 S · 162 X · 163 R · 164 Z · 165 H · 166 Z₁ · 167 Z₂ · 168 D
18	169 A · 170 E · 171 F · 172 E · 173 Z₁ · 174 Z · 175 E · 176 A · 177 W
19	178 E · 179 R · 180 J · 181 V · 182 C · 183 P · 184 X · 185 Y · 186 N · 187 H
20	188 C · 189 R · 190 W · 191 K · 192 J · 193 C · 194 F · 195 Q · 196 S

41

WORDS

A Injured slightly · · · · · · · · · 119 27 14 85 170 62 53

B Major city of the Ruhr Valley · · · · 83 149 7 129 46

C Crests, raised narrow strips · · · · 169 45 4 179 84 147

D Commercial seaport, E Co. Cork, Eire 73 43 48 87 118 139 10

E Appearance · · · · · · · · · · · 155 42 134 72 126

F Flat, subdued · · · · · · · · · · 39 26 153 68 137

G Mortified, humiliated · · · · · · · 132 24 167 36 101 165 19

H Partial return of payment · · · · · 104 6 112 166 174 163

I Accepted, current, bruited about · · 44 8 168 158 80

J Shelter at J.F.K. or O'Hare, e.g. · · · 29 56 99 145 94 52

K Confront boldly · · · · · · · · · 100 28 93 12 71 150

L Fairy queen of folklore · · · · · · 140 51 65

M Scourge; beat, trounce · · · · · · 124 133 30 143

N 1872 novel by Samuel Butler · · · · 144 63 77 92 106 109 31

O Calm, unruffled · · · · · · · · · 76 70 81 152 96 113

P High and low, from stem to stern · · 105 2 164 34 121 47 69 103 148 89

Q Means · · · · · · · · · · · · · 54 97 107 35 78 1 58 60 90 17 41

R Imminent (3 wds.) · · · · · · · · 88 122 74 25 176 173 95 142

S "And there is nothing hid from —— thereof" (Psalms 19:6. 2 wds.) · · 67 108 102 55 40 79 127

T Am. novelist ("The Blood Oranges") · 151 159 157 13 114 82

U Accomplish quickly (2 wds.) · · · · 57 91 160 59 75 154 33

V Accumulated, amassed · · · · · · 175 131 38 110 156 123

W Baked pottery · · · · · · · · · · 111 115 135 9 162 22 37 16 125 130 98

X Snare · · · · · · · · · · · · · 138 120 3 136 171

Y Unskillful · · · · · · · · · · · · 177 23 64 15 117

Z Adult · · · · · · · · · · · · · · 32 116 5 20 178 66 49

Z₁ Hole for an anchor cable · · · · · 61 146 172 180 141

Z₂ "A cucumber should be well sliced, and dressed with pepper and vinegar, and then —— out," said Dr. Johnson (Boswell, "A Tour to the Hebrides") · 161 128 18 11 50 86

Puzzle grid (cell number / clue letter):

1	Q 2	P 3	X	4	C 5	Z 6	H 7	B 8	I 9	W
10 D	Z₂ 11	K 12	K 13	T	14 A	15	Y 16	W 17	Q 18	Z₂ 19 · G
20 Z	R 21	W 22	W 23	Y	24	G 25	R 26	F 27	A 28	K 29 · J
30 M	N 31	Z 32	33	U 34	P 35	36	G	37	W 38 · V	
39 F	S 40	41 Q	Q 42	E 43	D 44	I 45	C 46	B 47	P	48 · D
49 Z	Z₂ 50	L 51	J 52	53 A	54	Q 55	S 56	J 57	U	58 · Q
59 U	Q 60	Z₁ 61	A 62	N 63	Y 64	65	L 66	Z 67 · S		
68 F	P 69	O 70	71 K	K 72	E 73	74	R 75	U	76 · O	
77 N	S 78	S 80	I 81	O	82	T 83	B 84	C 85	A 86 · Z₂	
87 D	R 88	P 89	90	Q 91	U 92	N	93 K	94	J 95 · R	
96	Q 97	W 98	99	J 100	K 101	G 102	S	103	P 104 · H	
105 P	N 106	N 107	S 108	N 109	V 110	W 111	112	H 113 · O		
114 T	W 115	Z 116	Z 117	D 118	A 119	X 120	P 121	P 122	R 123 · V	
124 M	W 125	E 126	S 127	Z₂ 128	B 129	B 130	W 131	132 · G		
133 M	E 134	W 135	X 136	F 137	X 138	D 139	L 140	Z₁ 141	R 142	
143 M	N 144	J 145	Z₁ 146	C 147	P 148	B 149	150 · K			
151 T	152 T	O 153	F							
154 U	E 155	V 156	T 157	158	V	E 156	T	U 160	159 T	161 Z₂ · W 162
163 H	P 164	G 165	H 166	G 167	I 168	G	C 169	A 170	X 171	
172 Z₁	R 173	R 174	H	V 175	H 175	R 176	Y 177	Z 178	Z 179	Z₁ 180

42

Puzzle grid (numbered cells with clue-letter; reconstructed in reading order):

1 R	2 E	3 C	4 S	5 K	6 G
8 R	9 Q	10 C	11 I	12 W	13 C	14 B	15 J
16 O	17 W	18 Q	19 M	20 V	21 B	22 X	23 P	24 X
25 R	26 C	27 V	28 O	29 R	30 R	31 Y	32 Q	33 H
34 T	35 T	36 Y	37 I	38 G	39 B	40 X	41 P	42 H	43 M
44 R	45 O	46 X	47 Y	48 T	49 Z	50 S	51 W	52 P	53 T
54 S	55 Y	56 O	57 L	58 M	59 D	60 K	61 I	62 K
63 L	64 F	65 W	66 E	67 K	68 U	69 P	70 Y	71 R	72 P
73 Q	74 W	75 V	76 Q	77 T	78 E	79 I	80 H	81 B	82 U
83 V	84 Y	85 Z	86 C	87 P	88 H	89 R	90 O	91 P	92 V
93 S	94 K	95 D	96 G	97 Q	98 P	99 C	100 V	101 N	102 X	103 A
104 N	105 U	106 B	107 S	108 N	109 W	110 A	111 J	112 I
113 O	114 Y	115 D	116 J	117 N	118 H	119 M	120 Z	121 S	122 Y	123 L
124 H	125 L	126 Y	127 S	128 Z	129 U	130 Y	131 I	132 Q
133 Y	134 R	135 B	136 U	137 A	138 H	139 D	140 X	141 L	142 E
143 T	144 B	145 M	146 P	147 A	148 K	149 Z	150 R	151 K
152 J	153 W	154 T	155 M	156 M	157 Q	158 B	159 J	160 F	161 R	162 L
163 Z	164 T	165 N	166 A	167 P	168 S	169 E	170 D	171 D
172 G	173 F	174 V	175 J	176 C	177 E	178 U	179 R	180 U	181 C	182 A
183 O	184 H	185 R	186 B	187 J	188 A	189 N	190 B	191 F	192 T
193 R	194 Z	195 I	196 T	197 E	198 Z	199 E

CLUES

WORDS

A Critiques 188 110 137 147 182 166 103

B Of two minds 190 186 144 158 106 14 39 135 21 81

C Movable pieces of personal property 176 181 99 26 3 86 13 10

D Professional surname assumed by actor Leslie Stainer 59 115 139 95 171 170

E Wreathe 78 169 66 199 177 2 142

F Epithet for Leo Ernest Durocher 197 64 173 160 191

G Matter for consideration 96 38 6 172

H Fervor, keenness 184 42 80 124 33 118 88 138

I Dinghy or dory, perhaps 79 61 37 195 11 112 131

J Type of wrench 152 159 175 111 15 187 116

K Resentment, indignation 151 94 62 67 148 60 5

L City near Boston, Mass.; city in central Kansas; city E of Des Moines . . . 162 123 63 141 125 57

M Usually itinerant menders of pots, pans, etc. 58 43 119 155 145 19 156

N Limp; frustrate; cramp 104 165 117 108 189 101

O Bent, vaulted 45 28 113 56 183 90 16

P Industrial work period from midafternoon to midnight (2 wds.) . . . 91 98 69 167 146 87 72 23 41 52

Q Short-lived, transitory 73 18 132 97 76 7 32 9 157

R ''The very casques / That did ___ at Agincourt'' (3 wds... ''Henry V'') . . . 25 44 30 193 161 179 89 71 150 134 29 8 1 185

S Supporter; follower 168 127 4 107 93 54 50 121

T Chide, upbraid 143 34 77 48 192 53 196 154 164

U Having a fling or a bender (3 wds.) . . . 129 178 136 180 82 105 68

V Employ 92 100 20 174 27 83 75

W Settling in 65 109 17 74 153 12 51

X Is tediously protracted (2 wds.) . . . 46 102 140 22 24 40 35

Y Noxious 47 70 130 122 84 126 36 114 31 55 133

Z Monotonous in rhythm and pitch . . . 194 49 85 120 149 198 128 163

43

CLUES

A U.S. senator (1903–63) identified with hearings on organized crime
B Closing statement
C Italian port on the Adriatic
D Rom. Cath. sacrament for the dying (2 wds.)
E Common term for a lady's sleepwear
F Contiguous
G Member of the Eng. Parliamentarians during 17th-cent. Civil Wars
H Maiden name of sister comedians Audrey and Jane
I Wrapped closely in cloth or other material
J Weedy, strong-smelling Old-World herbs having flat-topped corymbs of yellow flowers
K Situation in which one is hopelessly doomed; dilapidated hovel
L First-rate (3 wds.)
M Beauts; pips; zingers
N Great jazz clarinetist–bandleader (1909–86)
O Disconcert, embarrass
P Tract of open, uncultivated land
Q Not up to scratch
R Set to right
S "It was my duty to have loved ___" (2 wds.; Tennyson, "Idylls of the King")
T Like most birds, regarding reproduction
U Type of wheel often involved with tennis nets
V Rotten coward (2 wds.)
W Cereal ingredient of a haggis
X Previous, past
Y Trick, prank; plaything, toy
Z Eggshell or ivory, e.g. (hyph.)
Z_1 Causing anxiety

WORDS

Clue	Numbers
A	49 111 108 165 163 58 85 25
B	102 120 164 18 6 80 92 210 15
C	136 36 68 28 12 201
D	142 131 109 33 3 19 105 189 84 27 79 7 48 65
E	154 53 183 172 52 38 42
F	193 178 166 143 186 20 205 124
G	184 26 200 133 41 170 177 179 147
H	211 117 81 191 107 46 155
I	82 168 146 100 47 203 180
J	202 69 151 152 61 40 198
K	57 132 9 86 141 71 121
L	153 188 99 195 24 162 209 77 144
M	70 115 157 207 88 59 98
N	140 29 156 161 35 173 62
O	128 116 197 93 66
P	138 56 212 91 110
Q	75 60 112 11 32 204 148 122 17
R	8 44 118 185 34 13 208 1 130 54 215 175
S	37 5 135 2 181 90 145 192 31 103
T	160 39 10 51 113 76 119 67 182
U	127 123 214 4 101 187 194
V	45 139 129 114 83 196 174 126 95
W	171 74 137 104 167 22 190
X	72 125 216 97 159 14 89 50
Y	63 158 94 21
Z	206 73 23 169 87 64 213 149
Z_1	134 43 16 199 30 176 150 55 78 106 96

Diagram

```
 1  R2  S3  D  ■  4  U5  S6  B
 7  D8  R9  K10 T11 Q12 C  ■  13 R14 X15 ■ 16 Z1
17  Q18 B19 D20 F21 Y  ■  22 W  ■  23 Z24 L25 A26 G
27  D28 C29 N30 Z1,31 S ■ 32 Q33 D34 R35 N36 C37 S
38  E39 T40 J  ■  41 G42 E43 Z1,44 R45 V46 H47 I
48  D  ■  49 A50 X51 T52 E53 E54 R55 Z1,56 P57 K
58  A59 M60 Q61 J62 Y63 ■ 64 Z65 D66 O67 T
68  C69 J70 M71 K72 X73 Z74 W75 Q76 T77 L
78  Z1,79 D ■ 80 B81 H82 I83 V84 D85 A 86 K
87  Z88 M89 X90 S ■ 91 P92 B93 ■ 94 Y95 V96 Z1
97  X98 M99 L100 I101 U102 B103 S ■ 104 W105 D106 Z1
107 H108 A109 D110 P111 A112 Q113 T114 M115 M
116 O117 H118 R119 T120 B121 K122 U123 F124 X125 S
126 V127 U128 O129 V130 R131 D132 K133 G134 Z1,135 S
136 C137 W138 P139 V ■ 140 N141 K142 D143 F144 L
145 S146 I147 G148 Q149 Z150 J151 J152 J153 L154 E
155 H156 N157 M158 Y159 X160 T161 N162 L
163 A164 B165 A ■ 166 F167 W168 R169 Z170 G171 W
172 E173 N174 V175 R176 Z1,177 G178 F179 G
180 I181 S182 T183 E184 G185 F186 U187 L188 D189 W190
191 H192 S193 F194 U195 L ■ 196 V197 O198 J199 Z1,200 G
201 C202 J203 Q204 G205 F206 Z207 M208 R209 L210 B
211 H212 P213 Z214 U215 R216 X
```

44

CLUES

A Song about young Johnny Jones, who "had a cute little boat" (3 wds.) · · ·
B Determine · · · · · · · · · · · ·
C Coarse goldenrod · · · · · · · ·
D Nuisances, troublesome things · ·
E Let · · · · · · · · · · · · · · · ·
F Was like · · · · · · · · · · · · ·
G Pro football player and politician for Buffalo, N.Y. · · · · · · · ·
H Filled turnover or mold of Latin American cookery · · · · · · · ·
I Word for a light, dry, white wine · ·
J Rehearsal, e.g. · · · · · · · · · ·
K Lodes, streaks, natural channels · ·
L Led · · · · · · · · · · · · · · · ·
M Azrael, who separates the soul from the body (3 wds.) · · · · · · · ·
N Truman, Barkley, Nixon, Humphrey et al. held this title · · · · · · ·
O Uninformed, unaware · · · · · · ·
P Loony bin · · · · · · · · · · · · ·
Q Circumference · · · · · · · · · · ·
R Witty, jocular, whimsical · · · · ·
S BBC show that was very big on PBS over here (2 wds.) · · · · · · · ·
T Lack of being; death; nonexistence ·
U Summer resort in SW Nova Scotia · ·
V Special stresses · · · · · · · · · ·
W "___ are stirring—birds are on the wing" (2 wds.; Coleridge, "Work Without Hope") · · · · · · · · ·

WORDS

A 48 95 166 73 85 125 63 110 101
B 11 94 185 150 173 52 126 2 70
C 178 14 186 129 105 139 24 58 18 8
D 10 138 181 98 115
E 128 5 106 136 149 22 69
F 27 76 158 148 21 39 177 92 171
G 42 80 59 86
H 72 96 161 40 88 29 107 169
I 123 84 75 111 78 157 3
J 176 124 34 28 19 87 16 9 54 164
K 118 141 163 155 43
L 17 187 44 152 1 30
M 35 7 33 182 151 160 45 15 99 25 174 113
N 71 153 143 36
O 144 89 32 103 38 82 66 56
P 120 172 134 57 131 51 159 37
Q 81 20 154 168 140
R 55 184 41 156 62 65 132 122 53
S 133 162 74 146 23 31 142 61 117 50 67 145 127 90 6 114 100 109
T 83 60 112 91 180 77 165 170 119 130 104
U 26 64 183 137 97 108 121 102
V 68 179 93 147 116 135 47 13
W 46 49 175 79 4 167 12

Grid (cell number / clue letter)

Row (start)	Cells
1	1 L · 2 B · 3 I · 4 W · 5 E · 6 S · 7 M · 8 C · 9 J
10	10 D · 11 B · 12 W · 13 V · 14 C · 15 M · 16 J · 17 L · 18 C · 19 J
20	20 Q · 21 F · 22 E · 23 S · 24 C · 25 M · 26 U · 27 F · 28 J · 29 H
30	30 L · 31 S · 32 O · 33 M · 34 J · 35 M · 36 N · 37 P · 38 O · 39 F · 40 H
41	41 R · 42 G · 43 K · 44 L · 45 M · 46 W · 47 V · 48 A · 49 W · 50 S
51	51 P · 52 B · 53 R · 54 J · 55 R · 56 O · 57 P · 58 C · 59 G
60	60 T · 61 S · 62 R · 63 A · 64 U · 65 R · 66 O · 67 S · 68 V · 69 E
70	70 B · 71 N · 72 H · 73 A · 74 S · 75 I · 76 F · 77 T · 78 I
79	79 W · 80 G · 81 Q · 82 O · 83 T · 84 I · 85 A · 86 G · 87 J · 88 H
89	89 O · 90 S · 91 T · 92 F · 93 V · 94 B · 95 A · 96 H · 97 U · 98 D
99	99 M · 100 S · 101 A · 102 U · 103 O · 104 T · 105 C · 106 E · 107 H
108	108 U · 109 S · 110 A · 111 I · 112 T · 113 M · 114 S · 115 D · 116 V
117	117 S · 118 K · 119 T · 120 P · 121 U · 122 R · 123 I · 124 J · 125 A · 126 B · 127 S
128	128 E · 129 C · 130 T · 131 P · 132 R · 133 S · 134 P · 135 V · 136 E
137	137 U · 138 D · 139 C · 140 Q · 141 K · 142 S · 143 N · 144 O · 145 S · 146 S
147	147 V · 148 F · 149 E · 150 B · 151 M · 152 L · 153 N · 154 Q · 155 K · 156 R · 157 I
158	158 F · 159 P · 160 M · 161 H · 162 S · 163 K · 164 J · 165 T · 166 A · 167 W
168	168 Q · 169 H · 170 T · 171 F · 172 P · 173 B · 174 M · 175 W · 176 J · 177 F
178	178 C · 179 V · 180 T · 181 D · 182 M · 183 U · 184 R · 185 B · 186 C · 187 L

45

The grid (each white square shows its number and the clue-letter it belongs to):

1	W2	S3	P4	N	5	B6	H7	G8	U9	Y
10 S	11	M12	E13	S14	B15	H16	17	A18	K19	R
20	X21	P22	E23	Y24		V25	P26	N27	28	K / G
29 E	30 U	31	X32	P33	V34	35	R36	A37	D38	A
39 N	40 X	41	42	U43	R44	Q45	X46	O47	W48	W49 / H
50 D	51 W	52 W	B53	V54	K55	56	A	O57	X58	C59 / A
60 I	61 R	62	Y63	W	64	I65	Y66	X67	X68	L
69 Q	70 T	71	L72	Q73	A74	I75	E76	S77	H78	N79 / Y
80 X	81	X82	83	F84	I85	E86	M87	P88	K	
89 T	90 A	B92	D93	P94	95	H96	J97	B98	N99	I
100 U	101 W	102 E	103 N	104 C	105 X	106 X	107 B	108 P	109 E	
110 I	111 V	112 V	113 A	114 T	115 F	116 G	117 L	118 C	119 C	M
120 F	121 E	122 P	123 S	124 Y	125 C	126 X	127 E	128 U	129 F	
130 Q	131 H	132 V	133 R	134 O	135 I	136 V	137 E	138 S	139 Q	
140 R	141 Y	142 C	143 X	144 K	145 O	146 G	147 O	148 C	Q	
149 B	150 C	151 W	152 L	153 M	154 X	155 R	156 L	157 F	158 A	
159 E	160 P	161 T	162 G	163 H	164 D	165 S	166 D	167 K		
168 T	169 H	170 E	171 E	172 S	173 O	174 O	175 S	176 M	177 Q	
178 N	179 T	180 Q	181 T	182 O	183 N	184 A	185 V			

CLUES

A. Excited, transported (2 wds.) .....
B. Decamp (2 wds.) .....
C. Coat worn by an usher, in, e.g., a formal wedding .....
D. Starve .....
E. "There's ___ / In the frying pan" (4 wds.: De la Mare, "Peacock Pie, Alas, Alack") .....
F. Am. educator and library administrator (1851–1931) .....
G. Soak with water .....
H. Visual range .....
I. Overabundance .....
J. "The Georgia Peach," briefly .....
K. Lover's novel of 1842 (2 wds.) .....
L. Draw forth .....
M. Surging of waves .....
N. Gift, grant .....
O. Firmness, strictness .....
P. Insert, insinuate .....
Q. N. Am. Indian of Algonquian speech stock .....
R. Extents, durations .....
S. Depose, vanquish .....
T. "___ but no girl wants to laugh all the time" (3 wds.: Loos, "Gentlemen Prefer Blondes") .....
U. Overly emotional or sentimental .....
V. Very .....
W. Enumerate; deem, estimate .....
X. A mediating; a pleading on someone's behalf .....
Y. Cipher, goose egg .....

WORDS

A. 112 184 73 90 59 36 55 158 17 38 105
B. 149 52 14 97 107 91 5
C. 142 118 148 150 104 125 58
D. 34 50 166 92 164 37
E. 75 137 29 170 102 22 65 85 127 121 12 116 109 159
F. 114 129 157 120 83
G. 146 7 115 162 27
H. 15 169 131 95 77 49 6 163
I. 60 135 99 74 84 64 110
J. 96 16
K. 28 18 54 144 94 167 82 41 88
L. 156 71 117 68 152
M. 119 153 176 86 11
N. 178 4 46 78 183 98 103 26 39
O. 173 47 174 145 134 147 56 182
P. 25 21 93 32 108 160 3 122 87
Q. 72 139 44 177 180 130 69
R. 133 140 155 61 43 35 19
S. 171 2 138 175 76 10 13 165 123
T. 89 172 181 113 179 70 161 168
U. 30 8 42 128 100
V. 111 24 136 53 33 132 185
W. 51 1 101 151 63 48
X. 154 45 126 143 57 106 40 80 31 20 81 67
Y. 141 23 62 124 66 79 9

46 CLUES

WORDS

A "Stirring / Dull ___ with spring rain" (Eliot, "The Waste Land: I, The Burial of the Dead") 120 21 141 158 38

B Mental, intelligent 129 166 143 188 110 199 72 17 56 178 153 92

C Uncomfortably close 111 101 193 24 207 64 97

D Recklessly determined; moving very fast 172 181 189 159 164 75 89 62

E Daughter of Oedipus and Jocasta, play by Sophocles 145 96 73 162 103 88 33 185

F Supporting timbers; flocks of turkeys . 104 34 80 151 221 11 59

G Sunrise (3 wds.) 139 128 7 50 148 183 126 98 176

H Beat it 116 84 167 32 225

I Boyfriends and girlfriends; keeps calm; holds firm 201 214 107 224 123 192 4 39

J Unwritten laws, customs 121 182 213 5 190 55 23 165 43 127

K Speed 187 91 99 170 118 215 117 28

L Talus 37 69 220 45 160 163 196 19 131

M Bend, angle; change of pitch 208 106 168 16 67 198 203 174 83 125

N Wanderer, one who shifts from place to place 51 15 132 119 63 204 115 212

O Elevating 144 77 49 149 81 61 138 205

P "My Cutey's Due at ___ Today": 1926 song by Robin, Van Tilzer, and Bibo (hyph.) 76 66 47 209 1 70 90 177

Q "He that lives upon hope will die ___" (Franklin, "Poor Richard's Almanack") 140 54 13 173 219 22 191

R Knavish conduct 161 95 195 14 211 169 29 154 40

S Popeye's sweetie (2 wds.) 46 27 156 180 100 6 87 60

T Large gamefish of the pike family . . . 9 194 94 136 68 218 186 52 8 35 122

U Roman emperor, 98–117 . . . . 222 147 124 114 25 2

V Port in E Hupeh, on the Yangtze . . . 152 134 30 44 206 82

W X-ray photo of the brain 217 86 135 179 78 71 10 93 112 31 142 42 53 57

X Remove by chopping (2 wds.) 74 85 3 48 200 108 175

Y Deserving of respect 184 150 157 12 216 137 41 130 58

Z Sweet and lovely, saintly 18 113 171 202 155 105 146

Z_1 Apparel, dress 197 79 133 102 26

Z_2 Inferior in quality . . . . [illegible]

				1 P	2 U	3 X	4 I		5 J	6 S	7 G
8 T		9 T	10 W	11 F	12 Y	13 Q	14 R	15 N	16 M		17 B
18 Z	19 L	20 Z_2	21 A	22 Q		23 J		24 C	25 U	26 Z_1	
27 S	28 K	29 R	30 V	31 W		32 H	33 E		34 F		35 T
36 Z_2	37 L	38 A	39 I	40 R		41 Y	42 W	43 J	44 V		45 L
46 S	47 P	48 X	49 O	50 G	51 N		52 T	53 W		54 Q	55 J
	56 B	57 W	58 Y		59 F	60 S	61 O	62 D		63 N	64 C
65 Z_2	66 P	67 M	68 T	69 L		70 P	71 W	72 B		73 E	74 X
75 D		76 P	77 O	78 W		79 Z_1	80 F		81 O	82 V	83 M
	84 H	85 X	86 W	87 S	88 E	89 D		90 P	91 K	92 B	93 W
94 T		95 R	96 E	97 C		98 G		99 K	100 S	101 C	102 Z_1
103 E	104 F	105 Z	106 M	107 I		108 X	109 Z_2	110 B	111 C	112 W	113 Z
	114 U	115 N	116 H	117 K		118 K	119 N	120 A	121 J	122 T	123 I
	124 U	125 M	126 G		127 J	128 G	129 B	130 Y	131 L	132 N	
133 Z_1	134 V	135 W	136 T		137 Y	138 O	139 G		140 Q	141 A	142 W
143 B	144 O		145 E	146 Z	147 U	148 G	149 O	150 Y		151 F	152 V
153 B	154 R		155 Z	156 S	157 Y	158 A	159 D	160 L		161 R	162 E
163 L	164 D	165 J	166 B		167 H	168 M		169 R	170 K	171 Z	172 D
173 Q		174 M	175 X		176 G	177 P	178 B		179 W	180 S	181 D
182 J		183 G	184 Y	185 E	186 T		187 K	188 B	189 D	190 J	191 Q
192 I	193 C	194 T	195 R		196 L	197 Z_1		198 M	199 B	200 X	201 I
202 Z		203 M	204 N		205 O	206 V	207 C		208 M	209 P	210 Z_2
	211 R	212 N		213 J		214 I	215 K	216 Y	217 W		218 T
219 Q	220 L	221 F		222 U	223 Z_2	224 I	225 H				

47

CLUES

A Firm, stout — 21 99 110 50 169 38 31 104 78 108 150

B Uproar — 127 153 142 45 86 166

C "Gone before / To that ___ and silent shore" (Lamb, "Hester") — 111 79 171 124 152 41 96

D Stupid — 164 66 172 119 105 52 75

E Muffled sound — 58 186 9 70 27 141

F Capable of being drawn out; pertaining to strain — 176 179 134 65 73 167 23

G Participating (2 wds.) — 100 39 47 181 22 137 103 80 87 173

H Recluse — 2 115 84 33 62 163

I Bothers — 184 63 48 160 29 72

J Distorts, swindles, tightens — 144 159 187 122 1 117

K Intensity — 49 180 146 128 26 43 113 11

L Woven fabrics of light texture — 178 175 76 112 151 102 139

M "Nourish / (Not too far from the ___ / The life of significant soil" (2 wds.; Eliot, "Dry Salvages") — 55 131 126 185 35 91 158

N Fr. philosopher (1712–78; "Du Contrat Social") — 8 97 13 77 162 34 170 68

O Public performer — 32 92 106 25 154 138 140

P Centaur who tried to seduce the wife of Hercules — 16 188 116 61 57 95

Q Punctilios — 165 15 37 182 6 42 20 46

R "Thou hast nor ___," says Vicentio to Claudio (3 wds., "Measure for Measure") — 107 40 4 90 161 156 148 118 174 83 60

S Become rigid or inflexible — 53 18 133 10 149 168

T Products, results, effects — 88 183 71 30 155 19

U Circular file — 121 3 143 89 64 44 5 98 123 17 54

V Indecent — 135 67 51 24 81 114 147

W John Updike's Harry Angstrom — 130 85 12 157 36 69

X Undoing; legal termination — 120 132 177 109 125 28 145 136 94 56 82

Y Speakeasy in Scotland, Ireland, England — 14 101 129 59 93 7 74

WORDS (grid)

```
  1:J   2:H   3:U   4:R   5:U   6:Q   7:Y   8:N   9:E
 10:S  11:K  12:W  13:N  14:Y  15:Q  16:P  17:U  18:S  19:T
 20:Q  21:A  22:G  23:F  24:V  25:O  26:K  27:E  28:X  29:I  30:T
 31:A  32:O  33:H  34:N  35:M  36:W  37:Q  38:A  39:G  40:R
 41:C  42:Q  43:K  44:U  45:B  46:Q  47:G  48:I  49:K  50:A
 51:V  52:D  53:S  54:U  55:M  56:X  57:P  58:E  59:Y
 60:R  61:P  62:H  63:I  64:U  65:F  66:D  67:V  68:N  69:W
 70:E  71:T  72:I  73:F  74:Y  75:D  76:L  77:N  78:A  79:C
 80:G  81:V  82:X  83:R  84:H  85:W  86:B  87:G  88:T  89:U
 90:R  91:M  92:O  93:Y  94:X  95:P  96:C  97:N  98:U
 99:A 100:G 101:Y 102:L 103:G 104:A 105:D 106:O 107:R 108:A
109:X 110:A 111:C 112:L 113:K 114:V 115:H 116:P 117:J 118:R
119:D 120:X 121:U 122:J 123:U 124:C 125:X 126:M 127:B
128:K 129:Y 130:W 131:M 132:X 133:S 134:G 135:V 136:X
137:G 138:O 139:L 140:O 141:E 142:B 143:U 144:J 145:X 146:K
147:V 148:R 149:S 150:A 151:L 152:C 153:B 154:O 155:T 156:R
157:W 158:M 159:J 160:I 161:R 162:N 163:I 164:D 165:Q 166:B 167:G
168:S 169:A 170:N 171:C 172:D 173:H 174:R 175:L 176:G 177:X
178:L 179:G 180:K 181:H 182:Q 183:T 184:I 185:M 186:E 187:J 188:P
```

48

CLUES

A. 1920s jazz style revived in England in the '50s, featuring washboards, WORD Ks, etc.

B. "The very casques that did — at Agincourt," ("King Henry V")

C. Elegance of taste, feeling, etc.

D. Attached without full status

E. Name for stereotypical Am. small town

F. All but

G. Pardon or forgive (a sin, etc.)

H. 1930s Gershwin song from "Girl Crazy" (2 wds.)

I. Building for religious devotion

J. Port, SW Spain, on the Guadalquivir River

K. Instrument popular with WORD A bands

L. Two-masted, fore-and-aft-rigged sailing vessel

M. Small, harmless tropical lizard

N. Marked increase

O. Detest

P. Joplin specialty

Q. Get rid of

R. Douse, plunge into liquid

S. 1934 Cole Porter song from "Anything Goes" (4 wds.)

T. Dome, conk

U. Be present at

V. Hell (2 wds.)

W. Blunder

X. Am. writer 1899–1985, "Stuart Little," "Charlotte's Web," etc.; full pen name)

Y. Pendant, perhaps, holding snaps, perhaps

WORDS

Clue																	
A	144	165	44	185	86	170	136										
B	177	184	112	92	35	174	149	78	82	126	33	155	164	89			
C	85	17	124	134	101	76	146	179	67	1							
D	100	34	133	40	173	12	148										
E	20	5	77	183	104	13											
F	118	157	115	145	62	24											
G	72	56	21	127	31												
H	91	39	9	113	169	6	3	141	59	43	80	178	19	71			
I	30	166	94	137	18	111											
J	53	161	16	172	8	68	84										
K	171	116	110	158	51												
L	69	167	90	4													
M	52	22	140	160	143												
N	88	70	108	168	139	23	175										
O	58	130	48	122	119												
P	135	61	105	156	109	28	15										
Q	14	103	97	25	55												
R	106	27	182	131	75	98	121										
S	7	163	57	38	154	181	66	95	102	79	142	42	129	107	29	120	64 47
T	132	114	87	50	10	147											
U	180	128	54	32	151	36											
V	37	73	96	2	49	99	125	26	176	117	162						
W	152	81	11	123													
X	93	74	60	83	150	63	46										
Y	138	159	41	45	65	153											

Grid (cell number + clue letter)

Row											
1	1 C	2 V	3 H	4 L	5 E	6 H	7 S	8 J			
2	9 H	10 T	11 W	12 D	13 E	14 Q	15 P	16 J	17 C	18 C	19 H
3	20 E	21 G	22 M	23 N	24 F	25 Q	26 V	27 R	28 P	29 S	30 I
4	31 G	32 U	33 B	34 D	35 B	36 U	37 V	38 S	39 H	40 D	
5	41 Y	42 S	43 H	44 A	45 Y	46 X	47 S	48 O	49 V		
6	50 T	51 K	52 M	53 J	54 U	55 Q	56 G	57 S	58 O	59 H	
7	60 X	61 P	62 F	63 X	64 S	65 Y	66 S	67 C	68 J		
8	69 L	70 N	71 H	72 G	73 V	74 X	75 R	76 C	77 E	78 B	
9	79 S	80 H	81 W	82 B	83 X	84 J	85 C	86 A	87 T	88 N	
10	89 B	90 L	91 H	92 B	93 X	94 I	95 S	96 V	97 Q	98 R	
11	99 V	100 D	101 C	102 S	103 Q	104 E	105 P	106 R	107 S		
12	108 N	109 P	110 K	111 I	112 B	113 H	114 T	115 F	116 K		
13	117 V	118 F	119 O	120 S	121 R	122 O	123 W	124 C	125 V	126 A	
14	127 G	128 U	129 S	130 O	131 R	132 T	133 D	134 C	135 P	136 A	
15	137 I	138 Y	139 N	140 M	141 H	142 S	143 M	144 A	145 F	146 C	
16	147 T	148 D	149 B	150 X	151 U	152 W	153 Y	154 S	155 B	156 P	
17	157 F	158 K	159 Y	160 M	161 J	162 V	163 S	164 B	165 A	166 I	
18	167 L	168 N	169 H	170 A	171 K	172 J	173 D	174 B	175 N	176 V	
19	177 B	178 H	179 C	180 U	181 S	182 R	183 E	184 B	185 A		

49

CLUES	WORDS
A One who makes arrows	137 88 168 63 71 18 109 98
B Former Dodger Peewee	128 33 84 62 177
C Luring by the cops into the commission of a crime	115 3 179 132 45 74 28 102 90 118
D Eminence; difference	91 81 146 66 116 8 26 181 147 9 104
E Jerking, taking away by force	85 58 110 70 49 171 79 92
F Something very clear (2 wds.)	72 193 1 43 37 94 21 157
G Projecting part	38 151 163 46
H One who enjoys short-lived success (4 wds.)	96 87 144 139 41 15 178 148 64 78 29 89 10
I Illiberal, uncharitable	164 93 191 4 31 99 120 42 56 76
J Nonindulgent	121 184 35 17 166 20 55 156 138 202
K Character played in films by Errol Flynn, Don Taylor et al. (2 wds.)	142 103 82 2 117 51 155 47 16
L Mutual understanding	65 101 36 192 195
M ___ Lenya: Austrian singer-actress	83 100 5 23 39
N Middle name of an American King	153 124 135 32 19 165
O Inflammable gas used as refrigerant and anesthetic (2 wds.)	60 40 182 122 145 161 130 152 27 185 111 95 52
P "He that ___ for my sake shall find it" (3 wds., Matt. 10:39)	154 141 59 12 150 167 188 24 22 106 197 126 131
Q Confuse, disturb	48 54 80 190 114 143 173 133
R Cathleen ___: Eng. actress (1888–1982, "Nicholas Nickleby," "Separate Tables")	112 57 158 172 61 201 189
S Putting out	159 200 134 53 67 34 187
T Beautiful sight	176 186 196 107 162 25
U Am. songwriter and performer (1815–1904, "Dixie")	105 73 140 175 129 50
V Areas, parts of the space or body	75 6 44 199 119 169 113
W Dapper Dan, ladykiller	149 194 174 69 108
X Caustic, producing a hard crust	183 170 198 77 14 30 180 125 7 11
Y Imminent (hyph.)	13 127 97 160 68 136 123 86

■	■	■	■	■	1 F	2 K	3 C	4 I	5 M	6 V	7 X
8 D	■	9 D	10 H	11 X	12 P	■	13 Y	14 X	15 H	16 K	■
17 J	18 A	19 N	■	20 J	21 F	22 P	23 M	■	24 P	25 T	26 D
27 O	28 C	29 H	30 X	31 I	32 N	33 B	34 S	35 J	36 L	37 F	38 G
39 M	■	40 O	41 H	42 I	43 F	44 V	■	45 C	46 G	47 K	48 Q
49 E	■	50 U	51 K	52 O	■	53 S	54 Q	55 J	56 I	57 R	58 E
59 P	60 O	■	61 R	62 B	■	63 A	64 H	65 L	66 D	■	67 S
68 Y	■	69 W	70 E	■	71 A	72 F	73 U	74 C	75 V	76 I	77 X
78 H	79 E	80 Q	81 D	82 K	83 M	84 B	■	85 E	86 Y	87 H	88 A
■	89 H	90 C	91 D	■	92 E	93 I	94 F	95 O	■	96 H	97 Y
98 A	■	99 I	100 M	101 L	102 C	103 K	104 D	105 U	■	106 P	107 T
108 W	109 A	■	110 E	111 O	112 R	113 V	114 Q	115 C	116 D	117 K	■
118 C	119 V	■	120 I	121 J	122 O	■	123 Y	124 N	125 X	■	126 P
127 Y	128 B	■	129 U	130 O	131 P	■	132 C	133 Q	134 S	135 N	■
136 Y	137 A	■	138 J	139 H	■	140 U	141 P	142 K	143 Q	144 H	145 O
146 D	■	147 D	148 H	■	149 W	150 P	151 G	152 O	153 N	■	154 P
155 K	156 J	157 F	158 R	■	159 S	160 Y	161 O	162 T	163 G	164 I	165 N
166 J	167 P	168 A	169 V	170 X	171 E	172 R	173 Q	174 W	■	175 U	176 T
177 B	178 H	■	179 C	180 X	■	181 D	182 O	183 X	■	184 J	185 O
186 T	187 S	188 P	189 R	190 Q	191 I	192 L	■	193 F	194 W	195 L	196 T
197 P	198 X	199 V	200 S	201 R	202 J	■	■	■	■	■	■

50

CLUES	WORDS
A The crack of dawn	118 103 193 64 145 3 71 85
B Revolt, uprising	93 44 23 137 119 174 130 84 170 175 133 189
C Elia	99 195 6 129
D Dolt	207 144 38 49 136 191
E Something gained; mastery of a language	50 36 81 105 197 112 1 24 123 143 187
F Nickname of former Cardinal Rogers Hornsby	196 34 51 68 46
G Cleft stick attached to a spinning wheel	140 147 106 113 159 108 80
H Transparent block for transfusing light	39 181 208 200 126
I Induced, presumable	88 41 28 210 124 141 35 14 186 61 176
J Attic, garret	199 37 27 182
K Laugh, snicker	57 164 117 121 96 190
L Cleft	203 63 165 152
M Rash, indiscreet	184 4 48 114 120 70 59 87 162
N Area of stables built around a small street	128 86 10 62
O Quality, character, property	173 192 19 78 83 138 97 13 154
P Altogether	76 153 79 9 25 95 188 132 67 135
Q Prime Minister of England, 1979–90	157 163 74 146 17 11 29 2
R Exemption from any natural or usual liability	100 94 111 58 151 18 204 206
S Dexterous, quick	69 47 205 60 198 5
T They come in many shapes and sizes, such as bread, butter, fish, pen, and scout	166 160 42 185 125 98
U "'Twas from Kathleen's eyes he flew, / ___ blue!" (4 wds.; Moore, "Irish Melodies; By that Lake")	55 158 127 91 115 209 148 26 122 75 32 89 15 110 177 20
V Am. astronomer, telescope-maker (1732–96), 1st director of U.S. Mint	30 139 201 179 8 167 21 52 82 45 16
W Vessel formed of two hulls held side by side by a frame above them	155 202 92 180 33 12 131 22 116
X Eng. mathematician, physicist (1842–1919), Nobel Prize for physics, 1904	53 40 142 73 102 156 90 107
Y Coloring cosmetic applied above the cilia	77 171 168 178 31 65 161 43 134
Z Abhorrent	194 169 172 72 104 56 7 183 149
Z_1 Small, shrimplike crustaceans, food	101 109 150 54 66

			1 E		2 Q	3 A	4 M	5 S	6 C	7 Z	8 V
9 P		10 N	11 Q	12 W	13 O		14 I	15 U	16 V		17 Q
18 R	19 O	20 U		21 V	22 W	23 B		24 E	25 P		26 U
27 J	28 I	29 Q	30 V		31 Y	32 U	33 W	34 F	35 I		36 E
37 J	38 D	39 H	40 X	41 I	42 T	43 Y	44 B	45 V	46 F	47 S	48 M
	49 D	50 E	51 F	52 V	53 X	—	54 Z_1	55 U	56 Z	57 K	58 R
59 M		60 S	61 I	62 N	63 L	64 A	65 Y	66 Z_1	67 P		68 F
69 S	70 M		71 A		72 Z	73 X	74 Q	75 U	76 P	77 Y	78 O
	79 P	80 G		81 E	82 V	83 O	84 B	85 A	86 N	87 M	88 I
89 U	90 X		91 U	92 W	93 B	94 R	95 P	96 K	97 O	98 T	
99 C	100 R	101 Z_1	102 X		103 A		104 Z	105 E	106 G	107 X	
108 G	109 Z_1	110 U	111 R		112 E	113 G	114 M	115 U	116 W	117 K	
118 A	119 B	120 M	121 K	122 U		123 E		124 I	125 T	126 H	127 U
128 N	129 C	130 B	131 W		132 P	133 B	134 Y		135 P	136 D	137 B
	138 O	139 V	140 G	141 I		142 X	143 E	144 D	145 A		146 Q
147 G	148 U	149 Z		150 Z_1	151 R		152 L	153 P	154 O		155 W
156 X	157 Q	158 U		159 G	160 T	161 Y		162 M	163 Q	164 K	165 L
166 T		167 V	168 Y	169 Z	170 B		171 Y	172 Z	173 O	174 B	
175 B	176 I	177 U		178 Y	179 V	180 W	181 H	182 J		183 Z	184 M
185 T	186 I	187 E	188 P		189 B	190 K	191 D	192 O		193 A	194 Z
195 C	196 F		197 E	198 S	199 J		200 H	201 V	202 W	203 L	204 R
	205 S	206 R		207 D	208 H	209 U	210 I				

51

CLUES / WORDS

A Untidy 4 135 148 50 178 91 168

B "God help us, for we knew the worst ___" (2 wds.; Kipling, "Gentlemen Rankers") 86 66 2 99 189 187 164 32

C "Ye have heard that it hath been said, An ___" (4 wds., Matt. 5:38) 181 98 14 177 28 102 105 121 17 3 9

D View of an extensive area in all directions 19 127 31 72 125 163 194 5

E To midpoint 104 80 147 155 198 182 62

F That to which anything is fastened . . 173 10 128 55 186 75 116 209 100

G Deprives of physical sensation 160 216 115 64 76

H Shuts in; confines 145 48 83 132 183 175 39

I Sooner or later 114 95 129 23 15 44 134 196 146 214

J Slaughter 43 124 69 54 16 74 93 130

K Annulment 188 96 73 22 140 53 90 211 24 202

L Given free rein 156 143 41 56 20 213 113 27 153 60

M Emaciated, excessively thin 171 207 97 35 67 46 122

N Feeding on solid food, as do most animals 11 123 158 92 212 70 199 161

O Brief stops in the course of a journey . 201 101 185 208 174 94 133 51

P Sideways, in a roundabout way 40 59 7 117 205 109 71 106 139 197

Q Accomplished, achieved 167 137 82 25 78 200 157 149 112

R Britons who were nomadic, said T.H. White in "Farewell Victoria" 84 184 29 154 111 165 142 107 118 38

S Humble, degrade 12 108 179 47 34

T Relinquishment of a right or interest . 190 58 166 13 151 65

U Fondly tender 138 192 126 42 150 103 159 131 191 110 204 63

V Type of oblique-angled parallelogram 45 141 169 8 88 120 21 152

W Tolerable, fair (3 wds.) 79 176 136 68 203 1 193 37

X Hep, hip, squared away, with it (3 wds.) 195 85 52 162 206 77 6 215 144

Y Fosters 210 18 89 36 30 57 172 61 87

Z (Of a heavenly body) convex at both edges 26 81 33 180 49 170 119

					1 W	2 B	3 C	4 A		5 D	6 X
7 P		8 V	9 C	10 F		11 N	12 S	13 T	14 C		15 I
16 J	17 C		18 Y	19 D	20 L	21 V	22 K	23 I		24 K	25 Q
	26 Z	27 L	28 C	29 R	30 Y	31 D	32 B		33 Z	34 S	35 M
36 Y	37 W	38 R		39 H	40 P	41 L	42 U	43 J	44 I	45 V	46 M
47 S		48 H	49 Z	50 A	51 O	52 X	53 K	54 J	55 F	56 L	57 Y
	58 T	59 P	60 L		61 Y	62 E	63 U	64 G	65 T	66 B	67 M
68 W		69 J	70 N		71 P	72 D	73 K	74 J	75 F		76 G
77 X	78 Q	79 W		80 E	81 Z	82 Q	83 H	84 R	85 X	86 B	87 Y
	88 V	89 Y	90 K		91 A	92 N	93 J		94 O	95 I	96 K
97 M	98 C		99 B	100 F	101 O	102 C		103 U	104 E	105 C	106 P
	107 R		108 S	109 P	110 U	111 R	112 Q		113 L	114 I	115 G
116 F	117 P	118 R	119 Z		120 V	121 C		122 M	123 N	124 J	125 D
	126 U	127 D	128 F	129 I		130 J	131 U	132 H	133 O		134 I
135 A	136 W	137 Q	138 U	139 P		140 K	141 V	142 R	143 L		144 X
145 H	146 I	147 E		148 A	149 Q	150 U	151 T	152 V	153 L		154 R
	155 E	156 L	157 Q	158 N		159 U	160 G	161 N	162 X		163 D
164 B	165 R		166 T	167 Q		168 A	169 V	170 Z		171 M	172 Y
173 F	174 O	175 H		176 W	177 C	178 A		179 S		180 Z	181 C
182 E	183 H	184 R		185 O	186 F	187 B	188 K		189 B	190 T	191 U
	192 U	193 W	194 D	195 X	196 I	197 P		198 E	199 N	200 Q	201 O
	202 K	203 W	204 U		205 P	206 X	207 M	208 O	209 F	210 Y	211 K
212 N	213 L		214 I	215 X	216 G						

52

CLUES

A Most bizarre . . . . — 135 9 188 204 102 54 130 223

B Dogmatically, with insistence . . . — 31 15 51 169 53 156 126 213 226 220 117

C Fr. priest, confessor to Louis XIV (2 wds.) . . . . — 119 12 81 225 124 192 42 228

D Traveling as a theatrical company . — 24 211 136 174 162 4 189 146

E Apparel featured in a Berlin song from "As Thousands Cheer" (1933; 2 wds.) . . . . — 41 161 165 199 175 75 101 2 193 60 88

F Type of robin, sunfish, or dowitcher . — 147 73 120 30 168 127 16 11 202

G Board game; exclusive control . . . — 91 64 154 37 107 22 196 106

H Abruptly detain (someone) in conversation . . . . — 71 216 14 149 19 93 25 115 57 176

I Chicago airport . . . . — 221 177 208 68 139

J Russian pianist, composer, conductor (1873–1943) . . . . — 8 148 43 104 116 74 181 111 128 215 38 23

K "Brought up in this city at —— Gamaliel" (3 wds., Acts 22:3) . . . . — 47 205 212 87 96 61 78 67 27

L Boozy and creamy sponge-cake dessert from Italy (2 wds.) . . . . — 227 83 210 172 70 48 13 194 56 185 134 105

M Cajole, coax . . . . — 29 34 6 18 112 72 206

N Am. "King" idolized for years after his death (full name) . . . . — 183 144 198 133 179 7 44 28 158 218 21 58

O Modern . . . . — 143 171 103 224 90 40 5 92 219

P Beginning to appear; nascent . . . — 180 137 63 94 46 178 160 167 230

Q Spoil; mar; corrupt . . . . — 110 45 98 153 195 32 85

R Marketplaces; city in Kansas . . . — 121 65 39 76 17 150 200

S Cozily warm . . . . — 173 157 1 36 129 145

T One who clothes . . . . — 109 142 3 59 197 69 187 80 164

U Dominated by persistent thoughts or drives . . . . — 86 190 186 35 84 222 203 209

V Humble, bashful, modest (hyph.) . — 229 159 62 66 26 95 201 82 33 214 20 99

W "Borrowing dulls the edge of ——," says Polonius . . . . — 207 77 217 79 55 50 138 184 152

X Post, station, situation . . . . — 100 141 151 52 170 113

Y Chanticleers . . . . — 108 49 166 10 132 191 122 97

Z Support for circus acrobats . . . — 182 131 155 89 114 140 118 123 163

WORDS

53

The Grid

1 Z	2 T	3 H	4 J	5 X	6 G	7 L	8 D			
9 B	10 M	11 D	12 C	13 U	14 I	15 R	16 Z	17 G	18 H	
19 G	20 K	21 Z	22 L	23 K	24 W	25 F	26 N	27 O	28 Z	
29 A	30 N	31 K	32 B	33 S	34 W	35 G	36 G	37 D	38 R	39 A
40 P	41 T	42 Q	43 C	44 W	45 R	46 Y	47 D	48 Y		
49 P	50 V	51 R	52 M	53 L	54 T	55 K	56 J	57 U	58 W	59 I
60 B	61 V	62 I	63 H	64 A	65 E	66 Q	67 Y	68 I	69 V	
70 U	71 M	72 S	73 S	74 Q	75 X	76 E	77 F	78 R	79 Z	
80 Q	81 K	82 O	83 S	84 J	85 D	86 T	87 N	88 U	89 Q	
90 K	91 M	92 Y	93 Z	94 W	95 S	96 T	97 N	98 P	99 L	
100 G	101 K	102 G	103 P	104 F	105 D	106 X	107 Z	108 U	109 B	
110 D	111 H	112 L	113 C	114 Y	115 P	116 T	117 F	118 Z	119 O	120 Q
121 E	122 K	123 A	124 T	125 W	126 K	127 H	128 Q	129 P	130 N	
131 X	132 D	133 B	134 H	135 F	136 X	137 X	138 N	139 X	140 A	
141 Y	142 N	143 U	144 G	145 O	146 E	147 V	148 B	149 T	150 D	
151 A	152 W	153 E	154 C	155 K	156 Y	157 T	158 K	159 O		
160 R	161 K	162 Q	163 P	164 E	165 Y	166 X	167 G	168 U	169 J	
170 Y	171 N	172 E	173 J	174 Y	175 C	176 D	177 X	178 P	179 F	
180 N	181 Y	182 A	183 U	184 V	185 T	186 D				

CLUES

A Harness-racing horse

B Way or means of approach

C Watch

D Paine's defense of the French Revolution (3 wds. after "The")

E Charmingly simple or rustic

F Simmered; fretted; potted; gassed

G Major portion of the Bible

H Bray (hyph.)

I Discharge

J Large, long-tailed parrot

K "Your chimneys I sweep and _____" (4 wds.: Blake, "The Chimney Sweeper")

L Permeates; filters

M Stables built around a small street

N Found; prove

O Expert

P Bonbon, candy

Q Excessively suave or smug

R Hoi polloi, masses

S Defendant in Gilbert's "Trial by Jury"

T Manipulative therapy

U Distraught, overwrought

V Quay

W Presented, tendered

X Impetus

Y Powerful, controversial herbicide (2 wds.)

Z Playing favorites for familial reasons

WORDS

A 151 123 29 182 39 140 64

B 148 60 32 133 109 9

C 12 154 175 113 43

D 105 176 85 37 110 150 11 47 186 132 8

E 172 121 153 146 76 65 164

F 25 117 104 179 135 77

G 17 144 35 100 19 6 167 102 36

H 18 127 3 111 63 134

I 62 14 59 68

J 173 84 56 169 4

K 101 155 81 161 158 90 31 20 126 55 122 23

L 53 7 112 22 99

M 10 52 91 71

N 26 130 171 142 97 30 87 138 180

O 145 27 82 159 119

P 136 40 178 163 103 49 98 115 129

Q 120 66 128 162 42 74 80 89

R 160 38 78 45 51 15

S 72 83 73 33 95

T 41 96 116 124 185 54 86 157 2 149

U 183 143 13 88 70 108 57 168

V 147 69 50 184 61

W 24 58 125 34 152 94 44

X 139 5 131 106 177 137 75 166

Y 174 67 48 170 165 92 114 181 141 156 46

Z 16 79 28 21 1 118 107 93

54

	CLUES	WORDS
A	Impudent whippersnapper	165 198 78 131 162 5 74 168 191 143
B	Children's game involving capture and release of team players	114 90 133 105 164 57 135 60 146 68 178
C	Petroleum product used for making candles, sealing jelly glasses, etc.	207 104 10 169 161 40 42 130
D	Generally (3 wds.)	21 151 171 41 4 113 32 110 208 63
E	Am. novelist (1876–1916; "Martin Eden," "White Fang")	108 150 99 67 137 83
F	It. anatomist (1524?–1574)	1 49 23 69 156 100 190 95 166
G	Natives of Riga, e.g.	89 180 16 181 142
H	Defensive substance produced by an organism in response to, e.g., the action of a parasitic toxin	176 148 50 2 25 76 157 56
I	Subjacent, inferior	77 206 44 51 112 17
J	Flowed out copiously; issued suddenly	119 195 19 97 140 87
K	Unsound, sick	102 75 94 145 152 62 204 73 172
L	Fundamentally, truly (2 wds.)	202 55 187 27 80 205 197
M	Left; alit; escaped punishment (2 wds.)	134 39 138 182 125 28
N	Blockage, occlusion by a blood vessel	158 194 48 124 81 52 153 46
O	Increasing (3 wds.)	15 22 127 184 106 35 45 111 88
P	Study of argumentation and formal debate	85 109 141 18 121 193 71 96 13
Q	Site; status	20 101 43 132 199 185 188 136
R	Percussionists' strokes that hit the skin and the metal or wood simultaneously	30 117 163 54 139 7 126 53
S	Possible, conceivable	9 12 59 177 128 200 209
T	Change, alteration	173 11 36 116 186 79
U	Very much (4 wds.)	115 14 84 6 47 93 160 159 123 189 70 120 92
V	Flaws	107 147 37 174 64 31 3
W	Hungarian-born U.S. nuclear physicist (1908– ; full name)	58 34 183 82 170 122 91 66 26 154 33 167
X	Wife of Amenhotep IV	179 98 61 201 192 72 129 175 86
Y	Fr. painter, engraver, enameller (1836–1902)	65 24 149 203 29 38
Z	Broadcast, scattered	196 144 103 155 8 118

					1 F	2 H	3 V	4 D	5 A	6 U	7 R
8 Z	9 S	10 C		11 T	12 S	13 P		14 U	15 O	16 G	
17 I	18 P	19 J	20 Q	21 D	22 O	23 F	24 Y	25 H	26 W	27 L	
28 M	29 Y	30 R		31 V	32 D	33 W		34 W	35 O	36 T	37 V
38 Y		39 M	40 C		41 D	42 C	43 Q		44 I	45 O	46 N
47 U		48 N	49 F	50 H		51 I	52 N	53 R		54 R	55 L
56 H	57 B	58 W		59 S	60 B	61 X	62 K	63 D	64 V	65 Y	66 W
67 E		68 B	69 F		70 U	71 P	72 X	73 K		74 A	
75 K	76 H	77 I	78 A	79 T	80 L	81 N	82 W	83 E	84 U		85 P
86 X	87 J	88 O	89 G	90 B	91 W	92 U		93 U	94 K	95 F	96 P
97 J		98 X	99 E	100 F	101 Q	102 K	103 Z	104 C	105 B	106 O	107 V
	108 E	109 P	110 D	111 O	112 I		113 D	114 B	115 U	116 T	117 R
118 Z	119 J		120 U	121 P	122 W		123 U	124 N	125 M	126 R	
127 O	128 S	129 X	130 C	131 A	132 Q	133 B	134 M		135 B	136 Q	
137 E	138 M	139 R	140 J	141 P	142 G		143 A	144 Z	145 K	146 B	147 V
148 H	149 Y	150 E	151 D		152 K	153 N		154 W	155 Z	156 F	157 H
158 N	159 U		160 U	161 C		162 A		163 R	164 B	165 A	166 F
167 W		168 A	169 C	170 W	171 D	172 K		173 T	174 V	175 X	
176 H		177 S	178 B	179 X	180 G		181 G	182 M		183 W	184 O
185 Q	186 T	187 L		188 Q	189 U	190 F	191 A	192 X	193 P		194 N
195 J	196 Z	197 L		198 A	199 Q		200 S	201 X	202 L	203 Y	204 K
	205 L	206 I	207 C	208 D	209 S						

55

Grid

		F3	G4	H	5	S6	T7	R8	I9	F10	K
11	O12	E13	D14	L	15	U	17	P18	N19	Q20	J
21	W	22	F23	U24	O	25	K26	S27	H28	G29	I30 · P
31 · C	32	R33	H34	G	35	O36	Q37	U	38 · N		
39	P40	M41	L42	W	43	G44	G45	J46	B47 · M		
48 · W	49	P50	D51	S52	A	53	V54	I55	C56	T57	B58 · H
59 · H	60	I61	U	62	C63	C64	A65	S	66 · G		
67 · F	68	D69	S70	71	B72	N73	E74	Q75	A	76 · P77	S
78 · O	79	O80	U	81	D82	C83	R84	S85	E86	J87	T
	88 · A89	O90	C91	M92	U	93	H94	U95	I	96 · Q	
97 · B	98 · U99	S100	D101	V102	P103	W	104	I105	E106	Q	
107 · P	108 · K109	B110	S	111	F112	U113	H	114	U115	C116	S
117 · V	118 · L	119	F120	U121	M122	D123	S	124	S125	B	
126 · U127	A128	C	129	E130	T131	K132	C133	I134	R135	V136	N
137 · H138	L139	O140	G	141	I142	S143	J	144	E145	U146	I
147 · D148	A149	B150	R151	W152	T	153	N154	V155	H156	H157	U
158 · I159	M160	G161	L	162	C163	B164	U165	M166	L167	L168	E
169 · S170	H171	V172	O173	N174	A175	J176	J177	U178	K		
179 · P180	I181	D182	G	183	U184	B185	Q186	I187	O		

CLUES / WORDS

A. Put lots of holes in 127 148 52 88 175 75 64

B. Topple 57 149 109 163 71 184 46 125 97

C. "There were his young ___ all at play" (Byron, "Childe Harold") . . . 162 90 82 15 115 55 31 63 132 128

D. Intensified 13 122 68 50 181 100 147 81

E. Solid round file 144 168 129 12 73 85 105

F. Contorts 111 2 9 67 22 119

G. Island republic in the Indian Ocean . . . 28 165 182 3 140 66 34 44 43 160

H. Long Island, N.Y. town a bit west of Montauk . . . 93 27 59 156 33 58 4 113 137 170

I. 1915 song by Gus Chandler, Bert White, and Henry Cohen (2 wds.) . . . 8 54 158 180 95 1 141 60 146 104 186 29 70 133

J. Water nymph 86 45 20 176 143

K. Surname of Maurice and Dame Edith, of stage and screen . . . 178 108 131 10 25

L. Folly 138 14 118 41 167 161

M. Filthy rich; stinko, blotto . . . 91 40 159 166 121 47

N. Elk 72 18 174 153 136 38

O. Intractable; perverse 173 79 187 78 89 139 11 35 24

P. Cocks 30 49 107 179 102 17 76

Q. Pesters, plagues 19 36 74 185 106 96

R. Title for a Hindu teacher . . . 7 32 83 134 150

S. Henry James novel (4 wds. after "The") . . . 99 26 51 142 69 5 123 124 65 169 116 110 77 84

T. Shabby, disheveled 130 6 152 56 155 87

U. 1822 opus in B minor by Franz Schubert (2 wds. after "The") . . . 126 177 114 157 94 98 183 112 145 61 92 80 62 120 23 164 37 16

V. "In the course of one revolving moon / Was ___ fiddler, statesman, and buffoon" (Dryden, "Absalom and Achitophel") . . . 53 101 117 154 135 171 172

W. Rounded protuberances 42 151 21 48 103

Puzzle grid (number–letter cells; ■ = black square)

1	2	3	4	5	6	7	8	9	10	11	
■1	T2	X3	C4	E5	Y6	A7	Z8	R9	P10	N11	U
12	P13	Z₁14	■	15	I16	V17	V18	B19	■	20	B
21	Z₁22	M23	A24	■	25	X26	27	Q28	T29	X30	N
31	W32	Q33	34	D35	F36	N37	J38	S39	■	B
40	W41	■	J43	K44	C45	V46	Y47	Z48	H49	N
50	Z51	E52	53	A54	S55	L56	Q57	V58	■	59	J
60	G61	R62	■	63	N64	P65	L66	J67	■	68	I	69	K
70	C71	S72	■	73	H74	W75	V76	U	77	V78	Z₁79	W
80	D81	■	82	G83	E84	K85	V86	W87	J88	Z89	M
90	■	91	G92	■	93	T94	Z95	S96	H97	G98	Q
99	B100	Z₁101	S102	Q103	T104	A105	J106	R107	■	108	T109	C
110	J	111	W112	L113	■	114	R115	G116	A117	D118	T119	J
120	D121	Q	122	X123	O124	X125	F126	J127	S	128	Z₁
129	O130	L131	Z132	K	133	T134	N135	Y136	Z137	W138	H139	H
140	X141	C142	H143	I144	J145	N146	B147	Y148	F	149	Z
150	B151	I152	N153	P154	Z₁155	156	E	157	M158	W159	V
160	Y	161	F162	Y163	J164	C165	W166	X	167	L168	D169	M
170	U171	P	172	W173	A174	U175	O176	H177	I178	I179	Q
180	B	181	Z182	B183	M184	Y	185	P186	A187	I188	E
189	W190	Z₁191	Z192	L193	F194	195	H196	E197	I198	Z₁
199	J200	F201	L202	O203	Q204	P205	G206	R207	R
208	B209	A210	I211	Z₁212	D213	O214	F215	P216	Y217	E218	E
219	T	220	G221	J222	C223	H224	U225	K226	M227	E228	Q
229	C230	J231	O232	M233	X234	E235	236	E237	R238	P	239	Q
240	V241	U	242	J243	H244	L245	F246	L247	Y248	Q

CLUES

A. Children's blowgun . . . .
B. Number One, nationally (3 wds.) . .
C. Make better than, go one up (2 wds.) . . .
D. Am. actor (1911–76) first to portray Willy Loman in "Death of a Salesman" (full name)
E. "Satan finds some mischief still / For ___ to do" (2 wds.; Watts, "Divine songs for Children")
F. Quibble over trifles; practice chicanery . . . .
G. Speakeasy, in Ireland . . . .
H. Dubbed, perhaps, as film (hyph.) . . . .
I. Amazed, startled, shocked . . . . . .
J. Subject of well-known practice sentence (4 wds.) . . . .
K. Defeats by a narrow margin (2 wds.) . . .
L. Gawk with curiosity . . . .
M. Exhausting, tiresome . . . .
N. One of the objects of a Spiro Agnew barb (2 wds.) . . . .
O. Excite, stir to action . . . .
P. Bestowing profusely . . . .
Q. WORD J's prepositional object (3 wds.) . . . .
R. Expedite, press . . . .
S. Dogface, as opposed to, e.g., swabby (2 wds.) . . . .
T. Little sack for a swabby (2 wds.) . . . .
U. Deified mortal . . . .
V. Contumely, denunciation . . . .
W. Small intestines of swine, prepared as food . . . .
X. Rebellious young Englishman of late '50s and early '60s (2 wds.) . . . . . .
Y. Crossroads . . . .
Z. Supplying . . . .
Z₁. Fr. astrologer (1503–66) . . . .

WORDS

A. 53 23 116 14 104 209 173 6 186 174
B. 182 180 146 90 150 208 99 39 244 20 18
C. 223 70 164 141 151 3 229 109 44
D. 117 34 168 213 233 201 120 80
E. 196 24 236 4 51 83 218 156 188
F. 161 194 148 245 125 35 200 215
G. 82 60 220 91 115 206 97
H. 177 96 224 139 67 73 48 243 142 195
I. 143 187 228 210 15 178 33 68 197 152
J. 59 119 81 221 110 105 42 144 199 66 163 242 126 87 37 230
K. 226 211 107 52 132 43 69 84
L. 19 130 55 167 65 193 246 112 235 202
M. 157 89 183 232 22 227 169
N. 49 145 36 63 113 30 153 10 134 122
O. 176 129 214 123 203 231
P. 185 154 64 9 238 12 205 171 216
Q. 32 27 102 56 239 179 121 204 247 98
R. 114 61 8 207 237 106
S. 71 38 101 95 127 54 92
T. 133 28 103 118 108 93 1 219
U. 76 175 225 170 11 137 241
V. 85 240 45 159 77 25 57 17 75
W. 58 158 31 172 40 74 138 165 189 79 111 86
X. 62 166 2 29 234 140 26 124
Y. 46 72 248 162 5 147 16 135 184 217 41 160
Z. 192 94 136 149 7 181 50 88 47 131
Z₁. 165 100 212 198 21 78 128 13 191 222 190

CLUES

A Strict; unadorned — 113 11 171 188 201 67

B Directly imperiled by weapons' trajectory (5 wds.) — 170 61 110 159 43 80 136 184 89 198 100 95 141 66 23

C Stimulus — 178 55 129 157 199 85

D Excel, surpass — 34 174 169 64 151 15 115 82

E Requirement — 16 45 58 10 126 84 146 107 3

F Bright, cheerful, hunky-dory — 56 72 119 68

G 1933 Eugene O'Neill comedy (2 wds.) — 143 6 155 168 74 37 131 175 32 117 109 40

H "Kindling her undazzled eyes at the full ___ beam" (Milton, "Areopagitica") — 33 108 28 8 83 187

I Book of the Old Testament; Minor Prophet — 179 9 105 163 195 7 20

J Vicious, malicious — 13 104 38 41 161 54

K Not hobbled, hindered, restrained — 73 18 19 88 65 148 132 120 98 93 140

L Run-down, shabby — 116 149 133 75 50

M Washington Irving's fictional schoolmaster (full name) — 106 197 111 145 190 94 76 90 130 60 27 164

N 1939 film starring Greta Garbo — 137 166 144 81 25 96 59 57 91

O Languor, lassitude — 162 150 193 123 99

P Kept at a distance (2 wds.) — 124 47 101 4 114 39 2 152

Q Luster —

R Norse explorer, fl. 880 — 69 42 186 30 191 102 176

S Engaged in lasting hostility, as did the Capulets and the Montagues — 165 127 5 203 87 183

T Rutabagas, esp. in England — 177 71 172 49 125 142

U Light, open carriage — 173 156 26 17 24 200

V Act of calling upon a spirit, deity, etc., for aid — 112 139 35 185 158 48 160 1 153 51

W Summarize, condense — 79 103 121 182 134 92 70 147 138 189 36

X Vogue or movement that breaks with tradition (2 wds.) — 12 63 22 53 122 78 21

Y "The trail has its own stem ___" (Service, "The Cremation of Sam McGee") — 46 14 194 52

Z Unrestrained excess, profusion — 202 128 29 154 97 86 118 180 135 44 62 77

WORDS

(Acrostic puzzle grid)

58

Grid

1 J	2 J	3 V	4 O	5 B	6 T					
7 G	8 H	9 F	10 X	11 S	12 K	13 V	14 J	15 U	16 R	
17 P	18 S	19 O	20 V	21 M	22 H	23 N	24 B	25 U	26 X	
27 F	28 Y	29 N	30 X	31 M	32 G	33 R	34 Y	35 M		
36 N	37 A	38 K	39 G	40 L	41 P	42 F	43 J	44 Y	45 W	
46 B	47 N	48 V	49 R	50 H	51 L	52 L	53 M	54 B	55 Y	56 J
57 B	58 W	59 M	60 L	61 P	62 J	63 I	64 R	65 G	66 D	67 X
68 E	69 V	70 A	71 G	72 I	73 O	74 F	75 M	76 S	77 L	
78 I	79 R	80 U	81 T	82 F	83 Q	84 Y	85 O	86 W	87 S	
88 E	89 P	90 F	91 C	92 L	93 Y	94 J	95 W	96 P		
97 F	98 O	99 A	100 G	101 V	102 I	103 M	104 S	105 Q	106 D	107 C
108 E	109 E	110 F	111 T	112 S	113 V	114 A	115 C	116 I	117 R	118 U
119 E	120 U	121 F	122 K	123 Q	124 W	125 N	126 F	127 S		
128 D	129 E	130 C	131 R	132 S	133 O	134 K	135 F	136 X	137 Y	
138 U	139 W	140 G	141 H	142 O	143 I	144 U	145 B	146 X		
147 P	148 L	149 I	150 K	151 J	152 R	153 N	154 U	155 K	156 J	
157 L	158 V	159 R	160 X	161 Q	162 O	163 D	164 I	165 S	166 J	
167 N	168 K	169 M	170 P	171 I	172 O	173 E	174 V	175 G		
176 H	177 F	178 W	179 T	180 K	181 F	182 I	183 U	184 C	185 A	
186 F	187 Q	188 T	189 X	190 N	191 V	192 C	193 Q	194 W		
195 C	196 F	197 U	198 D	199 A	200 A	201 S	202 H	203 B	204 Y	
205 O	206 V	207 Q	208 N	209 G	210 R	211 K	212 C	213 S	214 A	
215 H	216 D	217 Y	218 F	219 Q	220 L	221 B	222 N	223 U	224 D	
225 T	226 S	227 F	228 C	229 A	230 P					

CLUES

A. Dietetic nursery-rhyme character (full name) . . . . — 70 114 99 185 199 37 229 200 214

B. Interred . . . . — 221 54 24 5 46 203 145 57

C. Did a double-take, perhaps . . . . . . — 184 107 115 212 130 195 192 228 91

D. Sincere . . . . — 163 128 224 106 66 216 198

E. Paving material . . . . . . — 109 173 129 119 108 88 68

F. Romeo's words that might make us think of a hard-hit baseball or a vandal-tossed stone (3 wds.) . . — 135 110 126 121 42 218 74 186 2 90 181 27 97 82 177 9 196 227

G. Grabbed hold (2 wds.) . . . . . — 39 32 65 100 140 7 175 71 209

H. Equipped, furnished . . . . . . — 215 22 8 141 176 50 202

I. Poet who claimed to have "wandered lonely as a cloud" . . . . — 78 171 149 63 102 182 143 72 164 116

J. Unsettled, argued over (2 wds.) . . — 62 151 43 1 56 94 14 166 156

K. Endures, waits until the end of (2 wds.) . . . . . — 155 211 168 122 134 12 150 38 180

L. Covering made of jipijapa leaves (2 wds.) . . . . . — 220 60 51 40 157 52 77 92 148

M. One of Swift's imaginary countries . . — 59 21 169 31 75 35 53 103

N. "The words of the wise ———" (3 wds. Eccl. 12:11) . . . . — 208 153 125 47 29 23 36 190 222 167

O. Type of marina (2 wds.) . . . . . — 85 98 162 4 172 142 205 73 133 19

P. Laundry quandaries (2 wds.) . . . . — 170 89 17 230 61 96 41 147

Q. Russian dancer–choreographer (1890–1950) . . . . . . — 161 105 193 219 187 123 207 83

R. Greeted warmly (hyph.) . . . . — 152 159 64 210 16 79 33 131 117 49

S. Discord . . . . . . — 127 104 132 76 213 165 226 112 201 18 87 11

T. Dull . . . . — 225 188 179 111 6 81

U. Metal-polishing powder . . . . — 144 25 223 80 154 138 118 15 183 120 197

V. Cigar-store owner . . . . . . — 113 101 158 69 206 191 13 174 48 20 3

W. Serving as a hindrance (3 wds.) . . — 58 178 95 124 86 139 194 45

X. Kipling poem . . . . — 136 160 26 67 146 189 30 10

Y. Fortified . . . . — 84 93 44 28 217 55 204 137 34

59

Diagram

1 D	2 J	3 N	4 H	5 M	6 P	7 B	8 F	9 Q
10 K	11 T	12 B	13 Q	14 C	15 A	16 U	17 S	18 F
19 P	20 N	21 J	22 Q	23 E	24 W	25 B	26 Y	27 C	28 F
29 A	30 D	31 R	32 L	33 E	34 D	35 F	36 T	37 E
38 V	39 C	40 B	41 G	42 P	43 Q	44 E	45 X	46 N	47 Y
48 F	49 E	50 M	51 F	52 D	53 L	54 R	55 M	56 D
57 W	58 T	59 I	60 O	61 Q	62 M	63 U	64 L	65 H
66 H	67 V	68 E	69 I	70 N	71 T	72 F	73 C	74 P	75 T	76 Q	77 M
78 D	79 S	80 K	81 B	82 I	83 H	84 F	85 C	86 P	87 Y
88 E	89 N	90 X	91 A	92 M	93 R	94 U	95 A	96 V	97 G	98 U
99 S	100 X	101 K	102 E	103 I	104 Y	105 S	106 R	107 P	108 W	109 K
110 M	111 K	112 F	113 V	114 G	115 K	116 V	117 I	118 P
119 M	120 Y	121 Q	122 F	123 I	124 L	125 V	126 N	127 S	128 C	129 P
130 O	131 T	132 B	133 F	134 N	135 P	136 S	137 Q	138 H
139 T	140 O	141 Q	142 A	143 R	144 O	145 U	146 G	147 H
148 W	149 K	150 M	151 D	152 F	153 L	154 J	155 W	156 A	157 Y
158 U	159 T	160 X	161 J	162 T	163 O	164 G	165 E	166 A	167 N	168 X
169 R	170 V	171 W	172 L	173 H	174 T	175 F	176 Y	177 C	178 D
179 K	180 I	181 H	182 V	183 G	184 H	185 U	186 Q	187 A
188 L	189 G	190 L	191 O	192 N	193 E	194 G	195 B	196 A	197 O
198 N	199 P	200 Y	201 W	202 O	203 X	204 J	205 I	206 B

CLUES

A Speech of denunciation

B 1818 narrative poem by Keats

C Walks laboriously, wearily

D Anticipated, looked forward to

E "___ shapes of foul disease" (3 wds.; Tennyson, "In Memoriam")

F Regard apprehensively (3 wds.)

G Plant, genus Sagittaria

H O.K., tolerable, fair-to-middling (3 wds.)

I Foolproof

J Notions, conceptions

K British army chaps

L Real stuff, genuine article (2 wds.)

M Desertion from one's principles, faith, etc.

N High-wire performer (2 wds.)

O Highest level in rank or importance (2 wds.)

P "___ workers came out too early to catch any sinners" (2 wds.; Runyon, "The Idyll of Miss Sarah Brown")

Q Intercepting (2 wds.)

R Wipe out, expunge

S Provender, food for livestock; search about, seek

T Lack of ability, strength, etc.

U Soft, limp, not firm

V "It is the business of a comic poet to paint ___ and follies of human kind" (2 wds.; Congreve, "The Double Dealer")

W "The Emperor of ___" (hyph.; Wallace Stevens poem, 1923)

X Make manifest, prove

Y Depressed, discouraged

WORDS

A 166 29 196 15 142 156 95 187 91

B 195 132 40 206 81 25 7 12

C 128 177 14 73 27 39 85

D 56 178 1 52 78 151 30 34

E 37 88 102 44 165 23 193 68 33 49

F 51 84 72 35 8 152 28 112 133 18 48 122 175

G 97 164 146 101 189 194 41 183 114

H 83 138 181 184 147 173 4 65

I 180 82 205 59 103 123 69 117

J 2 21 204 161 154

K 111 115 80 149 179 109 10

L 188 64 190 124 32 53 172 153

M 150 55 50 110 92 119 5 77

N 167 20 134 46 198 70 126 3 192 89

O 144 202 163 130 197 140 60 66 191

P 86 118 129 74 199 42 6 135 19 107

Q 61 137 9 22 43 76 141 121 13 186

R 106 143 54 169 31 93

S 17 79 105 127 136 99

T 131 139 159 75 162 36 58 11 71 174

U 145 16 158 98 63 185 94

V 170 38 96 116 125 67 113 182

W 62 108 171 201 24 155 57 148

X 90 203 168 45 100 160

Y 200 176 87 47 104 26 157 120

60

CLUES

A. 1925 Sinclair Lewis novel — 92 84 140 147 1 52 113 5 102 19

B. Not reliable; untrustworthy (hyph.) — 131 41 17 199 117 4 153 106 85 107

C. 4-wheeled, 2-seated carriage with a convertible top — 181 67 167 77 162 114

D. Argentine poet (1805–51; "El Matadero") — 178 128 81 36 14 44 201 30 160 123

E. Virgin, untried — 35 156 176 112 65 21

F. Permeate, saturate; charge; fire — 83 171 43 108 136

G. Foul, repulsive, indecent — 122 54 188 148 101

H. Lawn, turf — 185 109 99 174 195 157 126 120 66 137

I. Inspired, touched — 193 51 75 60 168

J. Frequently — 58 79 135 62 37 6 121 145 127 158

K. 1918 poem by Aleksandr Blok (after "The f") — 61 179 97 26 93 71

L. One of those "Creatures that by a rule in nature teach / The act of order to a peopled kingdom" (hyph. "Henry V") — 103 78 68 76 49 59 166 9

M. 1894 Theodor Fontane novel (2 wds.) — 152 87 170 196 90 132 183 74 7 50

N. Last book of the New Testament — 164 56 98 3 72 159 34 20 194 143

O. Former name of city in E Hubei province, China — 2 46 184 31 138 155

P. Sedative, narcotic, soporific — 29 48 104 118 88 191

Q. Finessing — 129 33 18 23 73 189 57 165 124 202

R. Cul-de-sac, blind alley (2 wds.) — 27 15 94 125 198 173 69

S. Duke's domain — 95 25 197 45 89

T. Stable, lasting — 111 134 115 40 91 144 63 22

U. Celebrated — 163 192 10 39 139 203

V. Exalt, invest with great authority — 11 105 154 53 70 133 150 82

W. Supposed to be so — 16 8 47 186 80 86 42

X. Count; judgment — 55 200 151 182 141 130 172 110 119

Y. Mary Chase's Harvey's human pal (full name) — 149 175 38 24 32 12 187 116 169 142 161

Z. Game in which players can get a used-card trade-in deal (2 wds.) — 64 100 180 28 146 96 177 13 190

WORDS (grid)

1 A	2 O	3 N	4 B	5 A	6 J	7 M				
8 W	9 L	10 U	11 V	12 Y	13 Z	14 D	15 R	16 W	17 B	18 Q
19 A	20 N	21 E	22 T	23 Q	24 Y	25 S	26 K	27 R	28 Z	
29 P	30 D	31 O	32 Y	33 Q	34 N	35 E	36 D	37 J		
38 Y	39 U	40 T	41 B	42 W	43 F	44 D	45 S	46 O	47 W	
48 P	49 L	50 M	51 I	52 A	53 V	54 G	55 X	56 N		
57 Q	58 J	59 L	60 I	61 K	62 J	63 T	64 Z	65 E	66 H	
67 C	68 L	69 R	70 V	71 K	72 N	73 Q	74 M	75 I	76 L	
77 C	78 L	79 J	80 W	81 D	82 V	83 F	84 A	85 B		
86 W	87 M	88 P	89 S	90 M	91 T	92 A	93 K	94 R	95 S	96 Z
97 K	98 N	99 H	100 Z	101 Z	102 A	103 L	104 P	105 P	106 B	
107 B	108 F	109 H	110 X	111 X	112 E	113 A	114 C	115 T	116 Y	117 B
118 P	119 X	120 H	121 J	122 G	123 D	124 Q	125 R	126 H		
127 J	128 D	129 Q	130 X	131 B	132 M	133 V	134 T	135 J	136 F	137 H
138 O	139 U	140 A	141 X	142 Y	143 N	144 T	145 J	146 Z		
147 A	148 G	149 Y	150 V	151 X	152 M	153 B	154 V	155 O	156 E	
157 H	158 J	159 N	160 D	161 Y	162 C	163 U	164 N	165 Q		
166 L	167 C	168 I	169 Y	170 M	171 F	172 X	173 R	174 R		
175 Y	176 E	177 Z	178 D	179 K	180 Z	181 C	182 X	183 M	184 O	185 H
186 W	187 Y	188 G	189 Q	190 Z	191 P	192 U	193 I	194 N	195 H	
196 M	197 S	198 R	199 B	200 X	201 D	202 Q	203 U			

61

Grid

9 C	10 P	11 Y	12 D	13 Q	14 X	15 S	16 K	17 I	18 F	19 O
20 E	21 I	22 S	23 E	24 D	25 O	26 E	27 N	28 A	29 U	
30 J	31 S	32 L	33 X	34 F	35 V	36 W	37 X	38 Q	39 C	
40 E	41 A	42 X	43 R	44 Z	45 A	46 T	47 H	48 D	49 S	50 Q
51 L	52 W	53 R	54 V	55 R	56 I	57 Y	58 M	59 F	60 T	
61 C	62 R	63 B	64 Q	65 F	66 M	67 Y	68 W	69 J		
70 Y	71 V	72 I	73 U	74 T	75 W	76 Q	77 X	78 Z	79 N	
80 N	81 J	82 B	83 S	84 U	85 D	86 K	87 G	88 W	89 C	90 Y
91 M	92 Y	93 X	94 C	95 P	96 B	97 F	98 N	99 E	100 W	
101 U	102 D	103 H	104 O	105 E	106 N	107 Z	108 X	109 U	110 D	
111 Z	112 I	113 L	114 X	115 E	116 Y	117 B	118 O	119 A	120 W	
121 K	122 U	123 W	124 H	125 O	126 I	127 O	128 P	129 J	130 V	
131 B	132 Y	133 J	134 Q	135 I	136 R	137 C	138 X	139 J	140 W	
141 U	142 T	143 Y	144 A	145 P	146 K	147 M	148 B	149 L	150 R	
151 T	152 H	153 K	154 Y	155 A	156 M	157 G	158 D	159 O	160 P	161 X
162 A	163 H	164 F	165 W	166 D	167 F	168 P	169 I	170 R	171 E	
172 Y	173 O	174 Q	175 N	176 A	177 C	178 S	179 L	180 M	181 U	
182 H	183 G	184 Z	185 V	186 F	187 T	188 W	189 J	190 A	191 G	192 X
193 Y	194 L	195 F	196 O	197 U	198 V	199 J	200 L	201 Q	202 W	
203 C	204 H	205 C	206 W	207 F	208 H	209 E				

CLUES

A Commanding respect because of age

B Make coarse

C Ill-favored (3 wds.)

D "Those blessed feet / Which fourteen hundred ___ were nail'd" (2 wds., "Henry IV, Part I")

E Brazen, immodest

F Discusses exhaustively (2 wds.)

G Titular hyena of a short story by Saki (H.H. Munro)

H "Lives of great men all ___ / We can make our lives sublime" (2 wds.; Longfellow, "Psalm of Life" st. 7)

I Consider as belonging; sanction; believe

J Plundering, foraging (Brit. slang)

K Gr. island off the SW coast of Turkey

L Its cap. is Reykjavik

M Extended shortage

N Worn out, exhausted of vigor

O N.Y. town on the N shore of Long Island (2 wds.)

P Big fuss; much ado about nothing

Q Apparition, specter

R Rot, drivel

S Younger son of Joseph (Gen. 41:52)

T "All looks yellow to the ___" (2 wds.; Pope, "Essay on Criticism, Pt. II")

U Not related; not numbered or counted

V Imagining, fancying

W Place into office

X Type of nonsurgical treatment of disease

Y Discomposure

Z 1924 Pulitzer Prize–winning novel by Edna Ferber (2 wds.)

WORDS

A 190 28 119 41 176 155 144 45 162

B 117 63 96 82 2 131 148

C 137 89 9 177 61 205 203 94 39

D 12 24 85 158 110 102 166 48

E 20 99 171 115 40 105 209 26 23

F 65 34 167 186 18 164 59 97 8 207 195

G 191 87 183 157

H 103 152 204 124 163 208 182 47

I 56 126 21 112 72 169 17 135

J 133 69 129 81 30 189 139 199

K 121 7 146 86 153 16

L 194 179 51 32 113 200 149

M 4 58 180 147 156 66 91

N 80 175 79 106 27 98

O 125 196 159 19 173 127 104 118 25

P 145 10 128 68 168 52 95 160

Q 13 50 201 38 76 134 174 64

R 62 170 55 136 53 150 43

S 31 49 83 15 22 5 178

T 187 74 151 46 181 60

U 141 73 84 122 197 109 29 101

V 185 130 54 71 198 1 35

W

X 6 161 14 114 138 33 108 93 192 37 42 77

Y 3 143 92 70 132 57 116 193 90 11 67 154 172

Z 107 78 184 44 111

62

CLUES

A. Molière comedy

B. Fr. abbess (1101–64) who was secretly married

C. "He hath left you all his walks, / His private arbours and new-planted ——," says Antony ("Julius Caesar")

D. Resort city, SE France, on the Mediterranean

E. "Advice-to-the-Lovelorn" ladies, e.g. (2 wds.)

F. Causing resentment; insulting

G. Most disgusting

H. Offends by disrespect

I. Give up, relinquish, annul

J. "An —— is nothing but his imagination" (2 wds.; Shaw, "John Bull's Other Island")

K. Using old material in a somewhat new form

L. Think of and develop (an idea) slowly in the mind

M. Congenital, hereditary

N. Phospholipid used commercially in candy, cosmetics, inks, etc.

O. Paving material composed largely of coarsely crushed stone

P. Home, fireside

Q. 1911 Denni & Lewis song (2 wds. after "The")

R. Contest; counterpart

S. State in detail

T. Of the eye

U. Compels, forces, obliges

V. Period of economic decline

W. Exalt; invest with sovereign authority

X. Formless; indeterminate

Y. Behead

Z. New Testament book, written by Paul

Z1. Symbolizes; acts in place of; speaks

WORDS

Clue	Letters / positions
A	112 99 183 159 201 142 20 43
B	2 203 168 14 154 165 21
C	164 86 189 25 148 206 212 74
D	117 39 9 24 75 108
E	176 107 197 78 122 31 133 157 5 18
F	211 29 218 11 132 38 30 52 116
G	196 214 180 219 77 155 89 103
H	28 64 84 215 97 191 53 113
I	42 92 146 32 209 178
J	23 128 179 202 69 207 181 149 102 220 188 41 44 135
K	65 3 147 101 170 58 36 98 16
L	182 126 7 143 158 140 110
M	223 15 115 195 95 6
N	47 221 68 94 161 104 192 37
O	60 174 125 13 81 70 88 93 79 87
P	71 34 138 111 187 62
Q	85 109 198 72 153 12 40 19 175 226
R	224 59 186 106 136
S	120 26 48 173 96 124 45
T	54 4 177 229 144 123 100 35 172 193
U	80 66 10 137 134 228 160 57 169 83 56 50
V	91 8 199 184 130 171 118 141 55
W	131 76 90 190 33 151 67 227
X	185 163 114 156 225 204 217 17 213
Y	22 129 167 51 121 194 166 200 1 208
Z	105 127 210 63 150 27 49 73 222
Z1	139 216 46 82 205 119 145 152 61 162

Grid

1	Y2	B3	K 4	T5	E6	M7	L					
8	V9	D10	U11	12	Q13	O14	B15	M16	K 17	X		
18	E19	Q20	A 21	B22	Y23	J24	D25	C26	S			
27	Z28	H29	F 30	F31	32	33	W34	P35	T			
36	K37	N38	F39	D40	41	J 42	I43	A44	J45	S		
46	Z1,47	N48	S49	Z50	U51	Y52	F53	54	T55	V		
56	U57	U58	K59	R60	O 61	Z1,62	P63	64	H			
65	K66	U67	W68	N69	J 70	O71	P72	Q73	Z74	C75	D	
76	W77	G78	E 79	O80	U 81	O82	Z1,83	U				
84	H85	Q86	C87	O 88	O89	G 90	W91	V92	I93	O		
94	N95	M96	S97	H98	K99	A100	T 101	K102	J 103	G		
104	N105	Z 106	R107	E108	D109	Q110	L111	P112	A 113	H		
114	X115	M116	F 117	D118	V119	Z1,120	S 121	Y122	E123	T		
124	S 125	O126	L127	Z128	J129	Y130	V131	W132	F133	E134	U	
135	J136	R137	U 138	P139	Z1,140	L 141	V142	A				
143	L144	T145	Z1, 146	I147	K148	C149	J150	Z151	W152	Z1,153	Q	
154	B155	G156	X157	E 158	L159	A 160	U161	N162	Z1			
163	X164	C165	B166	Y 167	Y168	B169	U170	K171	V172	T173	S	
174	O175	Q 176	E177	T178	I 179	J180	G 181	J				
182	L183	A184	V185	X186	R 187	P188	J189	C190	W191	H192	N	
193	T194	Y195	M196	G 197	E198	Q199	V200	Y201	A202	J203	B	
204	X205	Z1,206	C 207	J208	Y209	Z210	I211	F212	C213	X		
214	G215	H216	Z1, 217	X218	F 219	G220	J221	N				
222	Z223	M224	R225	X226	Q227	W228	U229	T				

63

CLUES

A Adorned, ornamented — 192 181 170 14 168 106 1 147 49 189 59

B In accord with logic — 33 119 2 26 7 98 99 188 140 163

C Immeasurable extent — 4 127 62 107 86 110 94 159

D Norman _____ : Am. dramatist, novelist (born 1910), great writer for radio — 67 128 146 100 125 75

E Heed — 34 20 37 74 157 9 22 176 112

F Men's underwear (2 wds.) — 115 167 48 6 122 40 134 24 179 84 92 111

G Process, course — 56 65 78 165 178 195 113 43

H Contrived, perhaps (2 wds.) — 141 45 …

I Turned weird; started fooling around (2 wds.) — 27 199 149 172 166 83 63

J Distributed, set apart — 23 101 160 61 46 200 152 197

K Eponym — 18 196 130 142 158 71 148 136

L Tropical Am. shrub, Morinda royoc — 15 186 102 164 117 153 133 73

M Hone — 93 193 161 72 109 58 54

N Fawning, sycophantic — 155 184 70 56 191 28 132 91 16

O Peak in the Pennine Alps — 131 69 190 55 120 116 60 41 171 19

P Prosperous, rich — 187 85 154 79 90 50 3 126 64 138

Q Loony bin (2 wds.) — 151 129 8 47 182 202 104 25

R 1924 hit play by George Kelly (hyph. after "The") — 175 121 88 10 180 42 105 156

S "Methinks I have a great desire to a _____ of hay," says Bottom ("A Midsummer-Night's Dream") — 123 29 145 177 137 81 108

T Inside scoop — 35 162 95 203 77 144 5

U Crude, raw, sketchy — 53 201 76 173 21 135 12 38 11 87

V "His fate and fame shall be / An _____ unto eternity" (4 wds.; Shelley, "Adonais") — 30 183 150 96 103 66 169 32 17 51 44 57 139

W Awkward situation (chiefly Brit., 2 wds.) — 194 52 97 198 174 80 89 185 13 143 39 124

WORDS (grid)

Cell (number–clue letter)
1 A · 2 B · 3 P · 4 C · 5 T · 6 F
7 B · 8 Q · 9 E · 10 R · 11 U · 12 U · 13 W · 14 A · 15 L · 16 N
17 V · 18 K · 19 O · 20 E · 21 U · 22 E · 23 J · 24 F · 25 Q
26 B · 27 I · 28 N · 29 S · 30 V · 31 ? · 32 V · 33 B · 34 E
35 T · 36 ? · 37 E · 38 U · 39 W · 40 F · 41 O · 42 R · 43 G · 44 V
45 H · 46 J · 47 Q · 48 F · 49 A · 50 P · 51 V · 52 W · 53 U · 54 M · 55 O
56 G · 57 V · 58 M · 59 A · 60 O · 61 J · 62 C · 63 I · 64 P · 65 G
66 V · 67 D · 68 ? · 69 O · 70 N · 71 K · 72 M · 73 L · 74 E · 75 D
76 U · 77 T · 78 G · 79 P · 80 W · 81 S · 82 ? · 83 I · 84 F · 85 P
86 C · 87 ? · 88 R · 89 W · 90 P · 91 N · 92 F · 93 M · 94 C · 95 T
96 V · 97 W · 98 B · 99 B · 100 D · 101 J · 102 L · 103 V · 104 Q
105 R · 106 A · 107 C · 108 S · 109 M · 110 C · 111 F · 112 E · 113 G
114 ? · 115 F · 116 O · 117 L · 118 ? · 119 B · 120 O · 121 R · 122 F
123 S · 124 W · 125 D · 126 P · 127 C · 128 D · 129 Q · 130 K · 131 O · 132 N
133 L · 134 F · 135 U · 136 K · 137 S · 138 P · 139 V · 140 B · 141 H
142 K · 143 W · 144 T · 145 S · 146 D · 147 A · 148 K · 149 I · 150 V · 151 Q
152 J · 153 L · 154 P · 155 N · 156 R · 157 E · 158 K · 159 C · 160 J
161 M · 162 T · 163 B · 164 L · 165 G · 166 I · 167 F · 168 A · 169 V
170 A · 171 O · 172 I · 173 U · 174 W · 175 R · 176 E · 177 S · 178 G
179 F · 180 R · 181 A · 182 Q · 183 V · 184 N · 185 W · 186 L · 187 P
188 B · 189 A · 190 O · 191 N · 192 A · 193 M · 194 W · 195 G · 196 K · 197 J
198 W · 199 I · 200 J · 201 U · 202 Q · 203 T

Acrostic Puzzle

(Grid: each cell shows its cell number and the clue-letter to which it belongs. The puzzle is unsolved, so only cell numbers and clue letters are present.)

Cell	Clue	Cell	Clue	Cell	Clue	Cell	Clue	Cell	Clue
1	O	2	U	3	P	4	L	5	W
6	R	7	L	8	M	9	Y	10	V
11	B	12	X	13	S	14	K	15	B
16	Q	17	U	18	J	19	I	20	X
21	B	22	R	23	Y	24	B	25	S
26	A	27	R	28	P	29	Q	30	D
31	C	32	I	33	M	34	Q	35	N
36	K	37	J	38	E	39	W	40	P
41	V	42	Y	43	B	44	Y	45	V
46	W	47	H	48	X	49	R	50	G
51	S	52	N	53	M	54	U	55	B
56	P	57	G	58	Y	59	A	60	O
61	D	62	M	63	V	64	G	65	O
66	D	67	J	68	V	69	E	70	K
71	Q	72	U	73	O	74	Q	75	S
76	V	77	C	78	O	79	J	80	T
81	K	82	E	83	N	84	B	85	Y
86	O	87	V	88	K	89	O	90	V
91	Q	92	R	93	K	94	L	95	U
96	M	97	X	98	V	99	D	100	H
101	U	102	S	103	M	104	A	105	K
106	P	107	G	108	D	109	V	110	M
111	T	112	W	113	K	114	H	115	Y
116	H	117	G	118	X	119	F	120	F
121	V	122	H	123	B	124	F	125	I
126	W	127	M	128	F	129	B	130	V
131	D	132	K	133	C	134	I	135	N
136	G	137	X	138	Y	139	W	140	N
141	X	142	V	143	O	144	M	145	Y
146	T	147	W	148	K	149	K	150	H
151	W	152	J	153	F	154	N	155	Y
156	H	157	L	158	V	159	P	160	M
161	R	162	X	163	P	164	V	165	M
166	K	167	Y	168	P	169	N	170	J
171	H	172	C	173	B	174	X	175	W
176	A	177	S	178	V				

CLUES / WORDS

A Hurt; feel great sympathy, pity, etc. · · ·
176 26 104 59

B Norman Thomas and Upton Sinclair, e.g. · · · ·
55 84 11 173 15 129 21 43 123 24

C Backs of thighs · · · · · ·
77 31 133 172

D Period of unemployment or inactivity
99 66 30 108 131 61

E "We shall rest, and, faith, we shall need it—lie down for an ___ or two" (Kipling, "When Earth's Last Picture Is Painted")
82 69 38

F Lout, yokel; character from "Gulliver's Travels" · ·
153 120 124 128 119

G Scrooge's late partner · · · · · ·
64 117 107 57 50 136

H Unbalanced; partial; unfair (hyph.) · ·
150 156 47 171 116 100 114 122

I Critical; exacting; pleasant · · · · · ·
32 134 19 125

J Vestiges · · · · · · · ·
18 37 152 67 170 79

K Oval or round building with tiers of seats for public contests · · · · ·
36 81 166 113 93 149 88 105 132 70 14 148

L Flush, redden · · · · · ·
157 94 4 7

M Low-lying vegetation · · · · ·
53 110 33 8 62 160 165 144 96 103 127

N Nancy Lopez and Patty Sheehan, e.g. · ·
140 52 135 169 35 83 154

O Bring to mind, have the earmarks of · ·
73 65 60 89 86 1 143 78

P Transgressor · · · · · · ·
168 3 163 56 159 40 28 106

Q Besides, as well · · · · · ·
16 74 29 71 91 34

R Early enough (2 wds.) · · · · · ·
27 22 49 161 92 6

S Regular · · · · · · · · ·
75 25 51 13 102 177

T Son of Zilpah (Gen. 30:11); move about · · · · · · ·
146 80 111

U U.S. aviator, born 1923, first person to fly supersonically · · ·
95 2 17 101 72 54

V Impossible; unthinkable (4 wds.) · ·
63 109 87 142 90 41 68 10 45 98 130 178 76 158 164 121

W Experienced, suffered · · · · · ·
46 175 151 39 5 126 147 139 112

X "He rode that tide / To Ararat: all men are ___" (2 wds.; R.P. Wilbur, "Still, Citizen Sparrow") · ·
118 174 12 20 48 137 97 141 162

Y Large, venomous snake of tropical African forests (2 wds.)
23 138 9 85 42 145 58 155 115 44 167

65

CLUES

A. 1941 W.C. Fields film (2 wds. after "The")
B. Certain; absolutely trustworthy
C. Tethered
D. Preferable direction in which to spit
E. Lea
F. Structure at the center of L'Étoile (3 wds.)
G. Improper; inauspicious
H. German-born Am. composer ("Camelot," "My Fair Lady")
I. Seaport, cap. of the Northern Territory, Australia
J. Refreshing summer drink (2 wds.)
K. Town in Rhode Island; nearly extinct Indian tribe of Rhode Island
L. Part of a radio or TV receiver
M. English Prime Minister, 1970–74
N. "By the old Moulmein Pagoda, lookin' ___ to the sea" (Kipling, "Mandalay")
O. Animal in Job (40:15–24)
P. Series of paintings and engravings by Hogarth (2 wds. after "The")
Q. "O Mary, ___ be!" (3 wds.; Burns, "Mary Morison")
R. Place of low-paid drudgery
S. "O God! that men should put an enemy in their mouths to ___ their brains" (2 wds.; "Othello")
T. Mount in the Black Hills, with Borglum carvings
U. Irish-Sea-bound place whose cap. is Douglas (3 wds.)
V. Execrable, impious, not to be spoken of
W. Showy ornament

WORDS

A. 117 36 32 88 162 165 22 72
B. 127 71 18 96 142 118 149 55 14 54
C. 146 110 31 53 66 56 75
D. 87 59 23 97 181 109 93
E. 45 98 111 135 175 10
F. 63 12 94 106 6 173 41 184 116 30 34 108 89
G. 52 92 107 103 46 185 125 99
H. 95 140 113 153 28
I. 160 156 29 102 122 134
J. 161 37 13 143 115 67 172
K. 61 47 176 64 24 186 49 128 9 44 166 152
L. 57 141 7 163 69
M. 83 80 73 42 100
N. 11 133 174 144 120 91 5 68
O. 124 35 137 84 180 77 170 121
P. 182 51 16 138 129 3 76 40 27 19 101 82 48
Q. 70 177 132 148 33 62 15 25 90 159 167
R. 136 139 187 168 8 123 43 158 50
S. 155 112 17 126 105 78 58 20 2
T. 183 131 169 171 1 178 79 145
U. 151 65 147 38 130 39 150 4 74
V. 114 60 179 154 21 81 119 104 85
W. 157 164 86 26

Diagram (number · clue-letter)

Row	Cells
1	T1 S2 P3 U4 N5 F6 L7 R8
2	K9 E10 E11 F12 J13 B14 Q15 P16 S17
3	B18 P19 S20 V21 A22 D23 K24 Q25 W26 P27
4	H28 I29 F30 C31 A32 Q33 F34 O35 A36 J37 U38
5	U39 P40 F41 M42 R43 K44 E45 G46 K47
6	P48 K49 R50 P51 G52 C53 B54 B55 C56
7	L57 S58 D59 V60 K61 Q62 F63 K64 U65 C66
8	J67 N68 L69 Q70 B71 A72 M73 U74 C75
9	P76 O77 S78 T79 M80 V81 P82 M83 O84 V85
10	W86 D87 A88 F89 Q90 N91 G92 D93 F94 H95
11	B96 D97 E98 G99 M100 P101 I102 G103 V104 S105
12	F106 G107 F108 D109 C110 E111 S112 H113 V114 J115
13	F116 A117 B118 V119 N120 O121 I122 R123 O124
14	G125 S126 B127 K128 P129 U130 T131 Q132 N133 I134
15	E135 R136 O137 P138 R139 H140 L141 B142 J143
16	N144 T145 C146 U147 Q148 B149 U150 U151 K152
17	H153 V154 S155 I156 W157 R158 Q159 I160 J161
18	A162 L163 W164 A165 K166 Q167 R168 T169 O170
19	T171 J172 F173 N174 E175 K176 Q177 T178 V179
20	O180 D181 P182 T183 F184 G185 K186 R187

66

Grid

(Numbered answer cells; each cell shows its clue-letter and cell number.)

```
K1  G2  Y3  I4  J5  W6  L7  H8
N9  X10 G11 O12 D13 F14 U15 W16 Z17 T18 Z19
R20 K21 C22 I23 N24 L25 K26 F27 G28 V29
C30 B31 J32 I33 K34 W35 B36 J37 V38 Z39
X40 A41 O42 R43 U44 X45 B46 I47 X48 V49
L50 G51 C52 R53 J54 Z55 L56 G57 F58 B59
Z60 A61 M62 W63 P64 X65 V66 U67 R68 T69
B70 Y71 K72 D73 N74 H75 K76 F77 Y78 C79 L80
S81 B82 A83 L84 E85 W86 T87 Q88 J89 O90
K91 L92 W93 K94 S95 H96 R97 M98 P99
U100 D101 C102 J103 M104 O105 G106 N107 U108 T109
C110 F111 H112 B113 M114 J115 K116 C117 E118
J119 M120 P121 U122 F123 N124 C125 O126 E127 Y128
C129 M130 F131 L132 Z133 O134 G135 F136 I137 V138
P139 K140 J141 Q142 X143 A144 Y145 W146 O147 H148
N149 K150 X151 D152 K153 O154 F155 H156 S157 E158 B159
C160 V161 M162 X163 P164 W165 Z166 D167 S168 K169
B170 A171 T172 Y173 O174 M175 E176 K177 X178 Q179 W180
A181 X182 Q183 S184 X185 M186 U187
```

CLUES

A Spotted 61 181 144 83 41 171

B King of Israel 159 113 59 82 36 170 31 46 70

C Artificial gem of paste 129 102 79 52 160 110 30 22 117 125

D Marshal 13 167 152 73 101

E Queer, suspect 85 158 127 118 176

F Avid, eager, insatiable 131 155 27 58 123 136 77 14 111

G Norse explorer, fl. 880 . . . .   51 2 106 135 28 11 57

H Type of slum 156 112 8 75 148 96

I Granular mineral used for grinding and polishing 33 137 4 47 23

J Center of public attention, notoriety . .   89 119 54 115 5 103 32 141 37

K Prophet who prepared the way for Jesus (3 wds.) 21 169 76 150 140 177 153 94 91 26 34 116 72 1

L Fine workmanship or quality 25 56 80 132 84 7 92 50

M Female officer in a religious house . . .   62 175 162 130 186 114 98 120 104

N Primitive adding machine 107 9 149 124 74 24

O Requisite 42 12 154 134 126 105 174 147 90

P Away, in reserve 64 121 139 99 164

Q Member of an ascetic, mystical Muslim sect 142 179 183 88

R Dark-bodied term, often so tame as to seem stupid 20 68 43 53 97

S Incautious, heedless 95 157 184 168 114 81

T Muslim jurist expert in religious law . .   87 109 69 18 172

U Unexpectedly large quantity 100 122 15 187 67 108 44

V Avoid, shun 38 29 66 161 49 138

W 1942 Ginger Rogers film (2 wds.) 16 146 165 6 93 35 86 180 63

X Forbidden, prohibited (3 wds.) 178 10 40 185 45 48 182 143 65 151 163

Y Young lad; large claw 173 71 145 128 3 78

Z Demanded, required, compelled 19 39 17 60 166 55 133

Grid

1	R2	O3	I4	M5	L6	N7	F8	■ 9	O10 · P
11 L	12	U13	B14	L15	D16	P17	18	F19	Q20 · P
21	A22	G23	N ·24	O25	M26	G27	X28	E29	F ■
30 X31	P32	N ·33	K34	C35	I36	U37	H ·38	F39	U
40 G	41	S42	H43	G44	F45	X46	Q47	P48	L49 · U
50 G51	C ·52	U53	J54	N ·55	M56	N57	T ·58	B	
59 L60	T ·61	W62	P63	C64	K ·65	S66	E67	H68	U
69 B70	X71	Q ·72	E73	V74	N75	C ·76	P77	T78	O
79 E80	S81	J ·82	X83	F ·84	N85	Q86	X ·87	J	
88 A89	U90	M91	I ·92	K93	D ·94	Q95	N96	T	
97 M98	U99	T ·100	T101	V102	O103	G ·104	I105	W106 · P	
107 S108	M109	X ·110	H111	C112	V ·113	V114	Q115	S	
116 H117	V118	W119	K ·120	A121	Q122	E123	R124	G	
125 R126	V127	T128	S ·129	W130	X131	W ·132	T133	R134	X
135 A ·136	G137	Q138	B139	A140	S ·141	M142	H143	K	
144 O145	E146	C147	S148	I ·149	X150	J ·151	I152	G153	C
154 V ·155	P156	G157	A158	B ·159	D160	R161	K162	I	
163 T164	I165	W166	A ·167	X168	N169	N ·170	E ·171	N	
172 J173	A174	S175	K ·176	U177	B178	D ·179	G180	W181 · I	

CLUES

A Bunker's term for his son-in-law ("All in the Family") — 173 139 135 21 88 166 120 157

B Chief wife of Mohammed — 69 158 138 177 13 58

C Destructive — 34 153 146 111 51 63 75

D Recognize — 178 15 93 159

E Demanding great effort — 170 145 28 66 122 79 72

F City, south central New Hampshire, on the Merrimack River — 83 38 29 7 44 18

G Uncover, as in respect (3 wds.) — 40 156 124 179 152 103 26 136 22 43 50

H "Mother of arts and eloquence" and "The olive grove of Academe," said Milton ("Paradise Regained") — 110 142 116 42 37 67

I Clem's surname in Hardy's "The Return of the Native" — 151 35 164 104 181 3 148 91 162

J At all; carelessly, neglectfully — 168 150 81 53 172 87

K Coming close to — 175 119 161 64 143 92 33

L Disinterest — 5 59 11 48 14

M Cheat — 90 97 25 141 55 4 8 108

N Adjective for the "Yellow Polka-dot Bikini" in a 1960 song (hyph.) — 6 54 32 169 84 171 23 74 95 56

O Once more — 78 24 144 102 9 2

P Removed by friction (2 wds.) — 31 10 76 155 16 20 62 47 106

Q Hornbeam or hop hornbeam, e.g. — 46 121 114 19 137 94 85 71

R Not at all — 133 125 160 123 1

S Doctor, physician to Queen Anne, to whom Pope wrote an epistle in 1735 — 174 128 41 115 80 65 147 107 140

T Flavoring, source of a cooking oil, sometimes called benne, or benny (2 wds.) — 17 77 100 132 163 127 99 96 57 60

U "Gentle child of gentle Mother, / born our Brother" (3 wds.; 1906 hymn by Percy Dearmer) — 89 39 98 12 52 176 68 49 36

V Commonplace — 101 126 73 154 129 112 117 113

W Peeping Tom — 118 180 61 105 131 165

X Enlightenment, clarification — 109 27 86 167 149 134 30 45 82 130 70

68

CLUES

A. Supplement, with considerable effort (2 wds.)
B. Guarding, protecting
C. Neighs (chiefly East Coast U.S.)
D. Commendation, sanction
E. Over and over
F. Division, as of an organization
G. "Stars in the purple dust above ___" (2 wds.; Aiken, "Senlin Morning Song")
H. Popular style for breakfast potatoes
I. Adaptation, modification
J. Raised embankments
K. Dismisses merrily (2 wds.)
L. Type of sheath
M. Airplane maneuver named for a WWI German fighter pilot (2 wds.)
N. Elongated fish with a jawless, sucking mouth
O. Throwing out
P. "Cape St. Vincent to the ___ died away" (Browning, "Home Thoughts, from the Sea")
Q. "It seems she hangs upon ___ of night / Like a rich jewel in an Ethiop's ear," says Romeo (2 wds.)
R. Of inferior importance, size, etc.
S. Remission, deferral
T. Pitifully inept, shy person
U. Intentional snub, e.g. (hyph.)
V. Aggressive Yuppies, e.g. (hyph.)
W. Arrive at, accomplish
X. Hoods, goons, Mafiosi, etc.
Y. Tuba-like instrument with a higher pitch

WORDS

A	140	84	48	203	96	125						
B	199	126	202	2	158	27	209	62	173			
C	1	171	122	83	94	212	163	49				
D	59	97	175	207	79	161	170	69	19	200	7	
E	22	130	194	42	71	151	18	103	88	186		
F	104	12	45	134	95	40	160	193	76	15		
G	116	70	61	9	118	155	201	128	78	133	25	
H	144	114	24	90	91	6	206	53	168	137		
I	92	14	131	180	214	89	64	26	102	107		
J	81	8	55	50	198	127						
K	121	191	63	169	51	10	156	205	113			
L	39	184	46	65	28	101	192	157				
M	31	35	153	136	196	73	124	47	13	98	159	67 204
N	182	132	20	120	57	74	100					
O	208	43	138	115	4	111	188	154				
P	135	52	176	109	108	85	189	3	11			
Q	139	58	86	123	41	179	105	185				
R	141	37	190	112	152	213						
S	106	36	162	29	75	146	117	56				
T	93	5	30	17	172	164	129					
U	32	16	165	149								
V	183	143	87	211	80	178	187	119	23	38	150	
W	44	99	110	167	147	60	54					
X	210	195	33	77	68	72	142	166	148			
Y	66	34	21	174	145	181	177	82	197			

Diagram (cell number / letter)

1 C	2 B	3 P	4 O	5 T	6 H	7 D				
8 J	9 G	10 K	11 P	12 F	13 M	14 I	15 F	16 U		
17 T	18 E	19 D	20 N	21 Y	22 E	23 V	24 H	25 G	26 I	27 B
28 L	29 S	30 T	31 M	32 U	33 X	34 Y	35 M	36 S		
37 R	38 V	39 L	40 F	41 Q	42 E	43 O	44 W	45 F	46 L	
47 M	48 A	49 C	50 J	51 K	52 P	53 H	54 W	55 J	56 S	57 N
58 Q	59 D	60 W	61 G	62 B	63 K	64 I	65 L	66 Y	67 M	
68 X	69 D	70 G	71 E	72 X	73 M	74 N	75 S	76 F		
77 X	78 G	79 D	80 V	81 J	82 Y	83 C	84 A	85 P	86 Q	
87 V	88 E	89 I	90 H	91 H	92 I	93 T	94 C	95 F	96 A	97 D
98 M	99 W	100 N	101 L	102 I	103 E	104 F	105 Q	106 S	107 I	
108 P	109 P	110 W	111 O	112 R	113 K	114 H	115 O	116 G		
117 S	118 G	119 V	120 N	121 K	122 C	123 Q	124 M	125 A	126 B	127 J
128 G	129 T	130 E	131 I	132 N	133 G	134 F	135 P	136 M	137 H	138 O
139 Q	140 A	141 R	142 X	143 V	144 H	145 Y	146 S	147 W	148 X	
149 U	150 V	151 E	152 R	153 M	154 O	155 G	156 K	157 K	158 B	
159 M	160 F	161 D	162 S	163 C	164 T	165 U	166 X	167 W	168 H	169 K
170 D	171 C	172 T	173 B	174 Y	175 D	176 P	177 Y	178 V		
179 Q	180 I	181 Y	182 N	183 V	184 L	185 Q	186 E	187 V	188 O	
189 P	190 R	191 K	192 L	193 F	194 E	195 X	196 M	197 Y	198 J	
199 B	200 D	201 G	202 B	203 A	204 M	205 K	206 H	207 D		
208 O	209 B	210 X	211 V	212 C	213 R	214 I				

69

Grid

■	1 M	2 S	3 C	4 B	5 E	6 B	7 G	8 K	9 T
10 H	11 J	12 C	13 Q	■	14 M	15 Y	16 R	17 O	18 R
19 Q	20 M	21 J	22 B	23 W	24 V	25 E	26 M	27 F	■
28 D	29 U	30 D	31 S	■	32 A	33 M	34 V	35 R	36 Y
37 N	38 R	39 Y	40 N	41 W	42 P	43 L	44 A	45 O	46 P
47 V	48 L	49 O	50 I	51 V	■	52 D	53 M	54 R	55 C
56 S	57 I	58 L	59 H	60 J	61 U	62 I	63 V	64 N	65 L
66 J	67 E	68 B	69 O	70 W	71 P	72 X	73 L	74 O	■
75 J	76 G	77 X	78 W	79 X	80 D	81 B	82 A	83 O	84 P
85 O	86 D	87 Q	88 A	89 M	90 Y	91 X	92 H	93 O	■
94 U	95 Y	96 N	97 F	98 P	99 W	100 U	101 E	102 X	103 A
104 R	105 F	106 K	107 M	■	108 F	109 C	110 X	111 B	112 Y
113 T	114 W	115 S	116 G	117 A	118 H	119 L	120 S	121 P	122 J
123 B	124 R	125 R	126 Q	127 N	128 T	129 A	■	130 T	131 K
132 Y	133 P	134 C	135 H	136 A	137 O	138 J	139 P	140 V	141 G
142 N	143 M	144 F	145 D	146 I	147 D	148 L	149 T	150 F	■
151 G	152 E	153 O	154 V	155 N	156 S	157 A	158 B	159 D	160 X
161 Y	162 P	163 H	164 N	165 F	166 M	167 E	168 H	169 K	■
170 I	171 A	172 P	173 X	174 B	175 U	176 C	177 D	178 S	■

CLUES / WORDS

A Self-important official — 136 129 44 88 117 82 32 103 171 157

B Scarlet pimpernel — 6 174 158 22 4 81 68 111 123

C Theatrical performance in preparation for an official opening — 55 134 12 109 3 176

D Type of canine — 86 52 177 159 80 145 147 30

E It. composer (1792–1868, "Barber of Seville") — 152 101 5 25 167 67 27

F With unyielding inflexibility — 28 97 105 150 144 165 108

G Anc. linear unit: elbow to tip of the middle finger — 7 76 141 151 116

H Background, past; annals, record — 92 10 168 118 163 59 135

I Merit, usefulness, importance — 50 170 146 57 62

J Conceited braggart, e.g. — 21 122 75 11 66 138 60

K Fr. painter, lithographer, and decorator (1877–1953) associated with Fauvism — 131 8 106 169

L Advocating belligerence — 119 58 73 65 43 48 148

M He often wonders for "60 Minutes" (full name) — 14 20 166 143 33 89 26 53 107 1

N "And with the blast of thy ___ the waters were gathered" (Ex. 15:8) — 64 37 127 155 164 40 142 96

O Foolishly amorous glances (hyph. & wds.) — 45 137 85 83 69 49 93 74 17 153

P Being planned (3 wds.) — 46 121 84 71 133 162 98 172 42 139

Q In 1995, he started pitching for the Dodgers — 87 126 13 19

R Nut, dingbat: narcotic pill — 18 54 124 38 16 35 125 104

S Sardonic outcomes — 120 178 2 115 156 31 56

T Fortitude; impertinence — 130 128 9 113 149

U Lovers' meeting — 61 94 100 175 29

V Bathsheba's Uriah, e.g. — 51 140 154 24 63 47 34

W Pour forth, disseminate — 114 99 70 23 41 78

X Sketch in outline (2 wds.) — 77 173 102 79 160 72 110 91

Y Common, usual — 95 132 161 39 90 36 112 15

70

The grid

Cells shown as *number + clue-letter* (black squares omitted):

```
  1B   2A   3N   4M   5T   6A   7X   8Z
  9R  10Q  11Q  12S  13B  14F  15W  16Y  17U  18D
 19E  20W  21T  22Z  23S  24V  25P  26K  27X  28R  29Q  30Y
 31G  32R  33F  34Q  35A  36X  37I  38V  39X
 40F  41A  42T  43E  44L  45F  46M  47X  48Y  49H  50G
 51K  52Q  53E  54J  55A  56Z  57A  58C  59R  60B  61T
 62D  63N  64R  65F  66K  67C  68U  69Z  70A  71I  72W
 73X  74B  75P  76W  77F  78E  79M  80L  81Z  82V  83J
 84K  85R  86B  87V  88R  89T  90J  91M  92P  93W  94L
 95F  96S  97P  98X  99D 100G 101O 102T 103T
104C 105I 106Z 107V 108R 109A 110L 111Q 112M 113H
114A 115Z 116S 117X 118A 119Q 120P 121J 122W 123D
124U 125H 126X 127O 128D 129Y 130K 131V 132N 133U
134Q 135O 136T 137N 138I 139V 140Y 141A 142T 143U
144W 145X 146U 147P 148J 149I 150K 151V 152Z 153S
154T 155V 156K 157D 158H 159L 160F 161S 162R 163X 164Z
165G 166B 167E 168R 169R 170D 171L 172D 173B 174Y
175G 176Z 177C 178F 179U 180R 181A 182K 183F 184P
185C 186Z 187I 188N 189E 190M 191Z 192D 193B 194F 195O
196C 197O 198D 199N 200K 201Z 202C 203M
```

CLUES

A Great vigor, force, etc. (3 wds.)

B Causing to penetrate; steeping, soaking, etc.

C Abundant stream of anything

D Formally conventional

E Aromatic herb of the mint family

F Locale, ambience

G Be darkening or threaten

H Lacking vitality; flaccid

I Murky, roiled

J Pursue; harass

K Flagrant, gross

L Small flag used for identification

M Bring back to former condition

N "And the ___ tree shall flourish, and the grasshopper shall be a burden" (Eccl. 12:5)

O WORDS G, J, M, P, and Q, e.g.

P Surround with foliage

Q Add stakes to (a pot)

R Castration

S Measurable; subject to limitations

T Approval, favor

U Patron saint of shoemakers

V Bunk, hooey

W 1936 Shirley Temple film

X System of doctrines concerning death, the Judgment, etc.

Y River flowing from Derbyshire to the Irish Sea; river in SW Nova Scotia

Z Excessive reverence for churchly tradition

WORDS

A 41 109 57 6 114 70 141 2 181 55 35 118

B 13 74 86 60 193 1 173 166

C 177 104 58 185 196 67 202

D 62 18 11 172 157 128 170 99 123 198 192

E 78 167 19 43 53 189

F 33 160 183 194 95 40 45 65 178 14 77

G 100 165 31 50 175

H 125 113 158 49

I 71 105 149 37 187 138

J 90 83 148 54 121

K 182 84 51 130 200 26 156 66 150

L 171 159 44 80 94 110

M 112 91 203 46 79 190 4

N 132 3 188 63 137 199

O 195 101 135 197 127

P 120 75 25 147 97 184 92

Q 52 111 10 134 29 119 34

R 59 88 162 32 28 108 168 9 180 64 85

S 12 161 116 153 23 96

T 136 142 5 21 61 89 102 154 103 42

U 146 17 68 179 133 143 124

V 24 139 131 82 151 107 169 87 155 38

W 15 72 93 20 144 76 122

X 47 145 39 98 7 36 73 27 163 117 126

Y 129 174 48 16 140 30

Z 191 22 69 164 201 152 115 81 56 176 8 106 186

71

CLUES

A Puffy, full .... `199` `169` `113` `53` `126` `160` `82` `71`

B Bold, recklessly brave .... `152` `89` `110` `81` `77` `28` `40` `198` `116`

C Integrity, principle .... `87` `121` `164` `153` `194` `57` `205` `192` `52`

D "Fair laughs the morn, and soft the ___" (2 wds.; Gray, "The Bard") ... `188` `9` `64` `80` `180` `58` `86` `156` `141` `122` `148`

E Adverse, contrary .... `6` `187` `168` `63` `22` `95` `145` `48` `39` `137` `84`

F Of the kidneys .... `195` `101` `161` `51` `72` `54` `119` `127` `179`

G Annul, repeal .... `59` `155` `18` `35` `173` `30` `97` `37`

H German city .... `102` `123` `178` `16` `183` `207`

I Generous, bountiful .... `66` `197` `189` `174` `120` `138` `118` `20` `47` `34`

J Nasty, offensive, esp. in smell or taste ... `55` `147` `33` `202` `172` `115`

K Death .... `44` `150` `79` `208` `1` `11` `133`

L Navel; central point .... `166` `106` `68` `62` `108` `177` `125` `159`

M Iterative .... `170` `19` `175` `146` `154` `50` `130` `12` `90`

N It. poet (1544–95, "Rinaldo," "Aminta") ... `92` `3` `111` `49` `181`

O Decline, deteriorate .... `60` `13` `134` `61` `25` `100`

P Cocktail of whiskey, bitters, sugar, etc. (2 wds.) ... `176` `2` `149` `31` `158` `107` `91` `140` `69` `109` `193` `46`

Q "___ haven't any hair: / Old men's heads are just as bare" (Hoffenstein, "Songs of Faith in the Year After Next, VIII") ... `94` `206` `124` `23` `163` `143`

R Town near Kampala, on Lake Victoria ... `75` `190` `139` `65` `151` `184` `17`

S "When the ___ bares his steel. / Tarantara" (Gilbert, "Pirates of Penzance") ... `103` `186` `157` `38` `93` `76`

T Hurrying; evading arrest (3 wds.) ..... `88` `4` `27` `74` `165` `105` `32` `132`

U Nullify, withdraw .... `185` `70` `85` `24` `10` `142` `41`

V Crude representations, esp. for ridicule ... `136` `67` `36` `201` `83` `26` `171` `203`

W Appetite, thirst .... `99` `43` `196` `135` `114` `117` `131` `5`

X King of Norway, 995–1000 (2 wds.) .... `112` `200` `7` `167` `45`

Y Omnipresence .... `96` `98` `42` `204` `191` `162` `14` `73`

Z Irritates, nettles; rasps .... `8` `182` `15` `128` `78` `29`

Z₁ Fertile areas in a desert .... `104` `144` `56` `21` `129`

WORDS

Diagram

1·W	2·S	3·Z	4·Y	5·E	6·D	7·K		
8·C	9·B	10·A	11·N	12·S	13·B	14·E	15·U	16·P
17·N	18·M	19·L	20·B	21·H	22·E	23·C	24·B	25·Y
26·Z_1	27·P	28·X	29·I	30·V	31·M	32·I	33·A	34·U
35·Z_1	36·C	37·K	38·O	39·A	40·G	41·Z_1	42·B	43·P
44·T	45·K	46·O	47·N	48·R	49·Y	50·H	51·V	52·Q
53·B	54·H	55·L	56·G	57·Y	58·T	59·Z	60·T	61·P
62·V	63·E	64·I	65·H	66·W	67·U	68·S	69·F	70·N
71·X	72·L	73·Q	74·Y	75·S	76·W	77·J	78·T	79·S
80·N	81·V	82·P	83·Q	84·U	85·F	86·Z_1	87·I	88·N
89·Y	90·W	91·M	92·T	93·F	94·G	95·O	96·P	97·B
98·W	99·W	100·Z	101·D	102·Y	103·R	104·U	105·O	106·L
107·M	108·D	109·K	110·P	111·R	112·R	113·S	114·S	115·Z
116·M	117·U	118·T	119·B	120·L	121·F	122·W	123·R	124·E
125·F	126·T	127·A	128·W	129·C	130·O	131·U	132·S	133·I
134·T	135·W	136·D	137·P	138·Z	139·Y	140·M	141·B	142·X
143·Z	144·S	145·Z	146·Y	147·Z	148·A	149·P	150·B	151·J
152·C	153·E	154·F	155·K	156·G	157·E	158·B	159·J	160·Q
161·H	162·U	163·W	164·Z	165·E	166·H	167·Z	168·L	169·G
170·V	171·S	172·J	173·T	174·R	175·U	176·X	177·M	178·F
179·V	180·U	181·I	182·M	183·G	184·X	185·Q	186·M	187·Z_1
188·U	189·I	190·T	191·G	192·X	193·O	194·D	195·C	

CLUES

WORDS

A Irritated, vexed 127 33 148 39 10

B Eng. poet (1844–81, "Ode") 13 24 141 114 20 150 97 9 42 158 53 119

C Appropriate; compatible 195 129 23 152 8 36

D Belief, faith 101 6 194 136 108

E Fire directed along a line of troops, a trench, battery, etc. 157 14 5 124 63 165 22 153

F Snowy 85 178 125 69 93 121 154

G Settle, smooth over (2 wds.) 94 40 169 191 156 183 56

H "All the perfumes of ____ will not sweeten this little hand," says Lady Macbeth. 65 21 161 166 54 50

I Eliot character described as "erect," "among the nightingales," etc. 133 32 87 64 189 29 181

J Mound in which fairies live (Irish folklore) 172 159 77 151

K 1868–69 Dostoevski novel (after "The") 37 45 7 109 155

L Alloy of copper and zinc, "mosaic gold" 120 72 55 19 106 168

M Staircase rail support (2 wds.) 186 116 177 18 107 91 182 140 31

N Gyps; refuses to tip; corpses 17 80 47 88 70 11

O Not quite 105 95 46 193 38 130

P Vile, execrable 27 96 137 43 82 149 110 16 61

Q First appearance 73 52 83 185 160

R Anatomical structure associated with young Presley 111 103 123 99 174 48

S Bring back; raise from the dead 68 171 79 132 113 75 2 12 144

T Russ. theatrical and film director (1898–1948; "Alexander Nevsky") 92 78 190 58 44 173 134 126 60 118

U King Richard II's uncle (3 wds.) 131 188 180 162 117 15 104 84 67 175 34

V Disheveled 81 30 51 112 170 62 179

W Disadvantages, hindrances 1 122 98 90 128 135 163 76 66

X Member of a Malay people of northern Luzon 192 176 142 184 71 28

Y Acrobatic feat, a favorite among youngsters 25 74 4 49 139 102 146 89 57

Z Cosmetic applied subciliously (2 wds.) 100 164 138 147 145 3 59 167 143

Z_1 Crush, stamp out, foil 41 187 26 115 86 35

73

CLUES

A. Remove hurriedly (2 wds.) — 24 158 45 166 6 95 181 165

B. "We are all in the gutter, but some of us are looking ___" (Wilde, "Lady Windemere's Fan"; 3 wds.) — 42 176 2 148 113 57 142 154 102 204

C. Wanted — 12 83 108 172 199 107

D. Enticement — 125 101 191 111 97 185 37 193 202 46

E. Type of whip formerly used in Russia for flogging — 84 49 20 132 27

F. Removal — 77 112 203 196 121 96 178 104 93 54 63

G. Portrayed, described — 186 182 82 190 29 122

H. Ceremonial forms of prayer; enumerations — 44 60 179 200 33 1 115 163

I. Hicks, rubes — 117 65 198 192 43 153

J. Drift, purport, gist — 114 10 66 34 69

K. Old Icelandic literary work — 52 134 170 127

L. A specialty of Edward Lear (1812–88), e.g. — 169 89 155 137 146 119 17 67

M. America's Cup contender — 159 105 126 76 61

N. Conspicuousness, note — 56 110 48 21 205 173 152 40

O. Chiefly nocturnal mammal, family *Dasypodidae* — 36 32 145 139 13 19 187 195 109

P. Authoritative demand — 136 144 14 168 5 3 180 58 80 174 72

Q. Treated unfairly — 86 51 68 184 138 7 120

R. "Nine ___": 3 pagan, 3 Christian, and 3 Jewish heroes of medieval romances — 59 70 79 50 9 161 135 103

S. Sloping — 151 133 162 4 90 106 39 73

T. Ignited, gave rise to (2 wds.) — 74 22 71 147 177 129 156 31 41 53

U. Enthusiastically (3 wds.) — 28 85 87 38 81 78 150 94 91 64 98 194

V. Doric temple of Athena on the Acropolis at Athens — 157 197 128 18 25 92 99 131 124

W. No kidding, as a solemn promise (3 wds.) — 164 201 75 88 16 188 189 149 130 143

X. Bestowed. esp. by formal act — 47 55 118 140 183 26 100

Y. Fantastic; incredible; unreal (4 wds.) — 167 15 35 123 23 8 62 171 160 175 11 30 116 141

Grid

Row 1: 1H 2B 3P 4S 5P 6A 7Q

Row 2: 8Y 9R 10J 11Y 12C 13O 14P 15Y 16W 17L

Row 3: 18V 19O 20E 21N 22T 23Y 24A 25V 26X 27E

Row 4: 28U 29G 30Y 31T 32O 33H 34J 35Y 36O

Row 5: 37D 38U 39S 40N 41T 42B 43I 44H 45A 46D

Row 6: 47X 48N 49E 50R 51Q 52K 53T 54F 55X

Row 7: 56N 57B 58P 59R 60H 61M 62Y 63F 64U

Row 8: 65I 66J 67L 68Q 69J 70R 71T 72P 73S 74T

Row 9: 75W 76M 77F 78U 79R 80P 81U 82G 83C

Row 10: 84E 85U 86Q 87U 88W 89L 90S 91U 92V

Row 11: 93F 94U 95A 96F 97D 98U 99V 100X 101D 102B

Row 12: 103R 104F 105M 106S 107C 108C 109O 110N 111D 112F 113B

Row 13: 114J 115H 116Y 117I 118X 119L 120Q 121F 122G

Row 14: 123Y 124V 125D 126M 127K 128V 129T 130W 131V

Row 15: 132E 133S 134K 135R 136P 137L 138Q 139O 140X 141Y 142B

Row 16: 143W 144P 145O 146L 147T 148B 149W 150U 151S 152N 153I

Row 17: 154B 155L 156T 157V 158A 159M 160Y 161R 162S 163H

Row 18: 164W 165A 166A 167Y 168P 169L 170K 171Y

Row 19: 172C 173N 174P 175Y 176B 177T 178F 179H 180P 181A

Row 20: 182G 183X 184Q 185D 186G 187O 188W 189W 190G

Row 21: 191D 192I 193D 194U 195O 196F 197V 198I 199C

Row 22: 200H 201W 202D 203F 204B 205N

Puzzle Grid

1 N	2 N	3 V	4 L	5 T						
6 E	7 D	8 B	9 W	10 K	11 R	12 J	13 R	14 H	15 K	
16 F	17 M	18 Q	19 E	20 R	21 A	22 U	23 C	24 N	25 O	
26 D	27 B	28 C	29 P	30 N	31 E	32 W	33 N	34 L		
35 F	36 D	37 M	38 V	39 A	40 S	41 N	42 T	43 A	44 I	
45 B	46 P	47 S	48 D	49 N	50 H	51 I	52 U	53 K	54 L	
55 M	56 O	57 L	58 H	59 B	60 K	61 J	62 F	63 S	64 C	
65 U	66 G	67 M	68 K	69 O	70 E	71 N	72 C	73 B	74 Q	
75 U	76 W	77 V	78 O	79 K	80 R	81 S	82 F	83 G	84 E	85 B
86 A	87 V	88 T	89 W	90 A	91 T	92 S	93 B	94 M	95 E	
96 D	97 H	98 N	99 U	100 T	101 K	102 C	103 U	104 Q	105 H	106 P
107 G	108 O	109 W	110 G	111 B	112 Q	113 F	114 O	115 W	116 J	
117 R	118 Q	119 L	120 H	121 B	122 G	123 J	124 B	125 R		
126 W	127 H	128 D	129 L	130 M	131 V	132 P	133 C	134 T	135 I	
136 T	137 K	138 T	139 U	140 O	141 N	142 H	143 O	144 C	145 V	
146 E	147 P	148 T	149 N	150 U	151 F	152 D	153 E	154 C	155 I	156 Q
157 S	158 N	159 P	160 U	161 V	162 M	163 W	164 R	165 U		
166 D	167 L	168 H	169 K	170 T	171 A	172 G	173 H	174 O		
175 V	176 D	177 O	178 P	179 B						

CLUES

A Immature; untried; puerile · · · · · · · · ·

B 1934 Cole Porter hit from "Anything Goes" (3 wds.)

C Nocturnal carnivores valued for their fur · · · · · · ·

D Largeness · · · · · · · ·

E One skilled in the use of tools; card-sharp

F Immense, stupendous, vast · · · · ·

G Substitute (inferior goods) in cheating someone (2 wds.) · · · · · ·

H Pugnacious · · · · · ·

I Queen of Carthage who killed herself when Aeneas abandoned her

J Am. labor leader, Socialist candidate for president, 1900–1920

K Am. poet, editor, and critic; supporter of Fascism (1885–1972, "Instigations"; full name)

L Some nursemaids · · · · ·

M Responded to a stimulus · · · · ·

N Spectacular, magnificent (hyph.) · · · ·

O Allurement · · · · · ·

P "Neither do men put ___ into old bottles" (2 wds. Matt. 9:17)

Q Choice · · · · · · ·

R Causes · · · · · · · ·

S Stuff, cram full · · · · · · · ·

T Quarters, home · · · · · ·

U Newness · · · · · · · ·

V Most unpleasant · · · · · · ·

W Cherish as sacred · · · · · ·

WORDS

A	39	43	86	21	171	90						
B	27	73	45	111	124	8	93	59	179	121	85	
C	72	133	154	23	144	28	64	102				
D	176	26	7	96	166	36	152	128	48			
E	84	95	146	19	6	153	31	70				
F	82	151	35	113	62	16						
G	110	83	172	107	122	66						
H	127	50	120	142	168	105	14	97	58	173		
I	135	155	44	51								
J	12	116	123	61								
K	53	10	60	15	68	79	101	137	169			
L	57	54	167	119	34	129	4					
M	94	37	17	55	130	67	162					
N	24	2	141	1	149	33	71	158	49	41	30	98
O	78	108	143	177	114	174	25	69	56	140		
P	46	132	159	29	106	178	147					
Q	118	74	18	104	112	156						
R	125	11	13	164	20	80	117					
S	81	92	63	47	157	40						
T	42	148	5	138	88	136	170	91	100	134		
U	99	150	52	75	103	160	165	22	65	139		
V	38	3	175	77	145	87	161	131				
W	163	126	109	115	76	9	32	89				

75

CLUES

WORDS

A Pacify, calm, gladden 28 174 60 114 81 3 115

B Hamlet near Ayr, Scotland: Robert Burns' birthplace 4 134 119 186 126 35 90

C Mongrel; simpleton 97 145 42 168

D Marine sculpin, genus Hemilepidotus (2 wds.) 107 178 78 15 116 46 59 111 139

E Fish-eating, diving bird 200 193 96 80

F "Minnehaha, ___ Water" (Longfellow, "The Song of Hiawatha") 57 199 194 167 66 43 51 87

G Singer played by Doris Day in "Love Me or Leave Me" (last name) 38 84 63 196 112 173

H Biblical book of 150 songs, hymns, and prayers 192 50 14 133 20 198 185

I "The ___ shall flourish, and the grasshopper shall be a burden" (2 wds. Eccl. 12:5) 10 156 180 110 137 197 54 151 127 104

J ___ pea; peanut 56 141 179 91 44 85

K Sack 163 32 102 64

L Lay to rest 34 147 53 124 37

M Inflexible, unyielding 25 5 120 68 48 129 30

N 1924 hit play by George Kelly (hyph. after "The") 16 122 6 157 135 177 76

O Mission 47 191 61 94 201 22 106

P Yellow 7 23 166 19 29 153 118

Q Strange, rare, curious 172 36 92 195 62 130 12

R Fortunate, promising 148 187 108 131 165 101 75 190 175 79

S Fine, hard-twisted cotton thread 164 41 154 11 88

T Comeliness 189 181 40 9 169 171 140 82 67 138 17

U Miss Vye in Hardy's "The Return of the Native" 117 162 121 149 136 95 8 83

V Tributes for fun 70 58 2 45 93 160

W Demanded, was particular about (2 wds.) 146 125 69 55 99 21 182

X Statement of total opposition (4 wds.) 132 24 77 73 103 143 89 170 158 183 109 52 49 100

Y Hungarian political leader (1896–1958); premier, 1953–55, 1956 .... 18 155 26 13

Z Pet, favorite, darling (4 wds.) 39 1 161 74 128 65 71 113 33 152 144 27 159 184

Z₁ Lacking in imagination or sophistication 98 86 188 176 31 123 72 150 142 105

76

CLUES

A Puzzles, eludes

B Dress, vesture

C "I will ___ them from the power of the grave" (Hosea 13:14)

D Check, stop, veto

E Tasteless, crude

F Ablution: laundry

G N Am. fish resembling a small shad

H Core of a type of WORD R

I Realms, states

J Small monkey of S America, genus Callicebus

K Blacksmiths' concerns

L Allowing no equivocation (hyph.)

M A spirit of fertility (classical myth)

N Divination

O Fiddles, fools, plays idly

P Region N of Khartoum, from the Nile to the Red Sea

Q Rankle, sour

R Type of playing field

S Type of pipe

T Lead, conduct, escort

U Huge, grotesque, horrible

V Lofty nest

W Eng. satirist (1567–1601; "The Unfortunate Traveller")

X Easily won: renegade

Y Overhead systems for transport of people or cargo

Z Confirms, validates

Z₁ Puzzle, mystery

WORDS

Clue	Cell numbers
A	7 43 156 137 89 77 34 154 144
B	155 124 21 53 79 92 149
C	96 125 35 8 10 67
D	48 75 11 29 160 33
E	19 41 132 54 110
F	40 37 25 66 126 3 117
G	139 107 70 161 15 74 158
H	134 56 91 64 6 153 165
I	90 106 9 62 44 113 4
J	98 150 28 119
K	102 162 26 168 176 111
L	123 83 46 166 18 116 95 174
M	114 86 72 81 13
N	47 163 121 45 127 20
O	172 118 170 17 100 39 69
P	135 71 60 78 2
Q	84 130 152 99 63 140 12 14
R	57 94 143 52 58 120 88
S	50 23 73 175 151 157
T	68 105 133 148 93
U	1 22 38 65 32 122 171 112 142
V	31 49 24 97 103
W	87 109 85 138 136
X	27 145 76 173 108 167 42
Y	131 141 61 164 104 30 177 101
Z	16 5 147 82 51 59 159 169 128
Z₁	115 146 55 36 80 129

Grid (reading order, cell number + clue letter)

Row	Cells
1	1-U · 2-P · 3-F · 4-I · 5-Z · 6-H · 7-A
2	8-C · 9-I · 10-C · 11-D · 12-Q · 13-M · 14-Q · 15-G
3	16-Z · 17-O · 18-L · 19-E · 20-N · 21-B · 22-U · 23-S · 24-V · 25-F
4	26-K · 27-X · 28-J · 29-D · 30-Y · 31-V · 32-U · 33-D · 34-A
5	35-C · 36-Z₁ · 37-F · 38-U · 39-O · 40-F · 41-E · 42-X · 43-A
6	44-I · 45-N · 46-L · 47-N · 48-D · 49-V · 50-S · 51-Z · 52-R
7	53-B · 54-E · 55-Z₁ · 56-H · 57-R · 58-R · 59-Z · 60-P · 61-Y
8	62-I · 63-Q · 64-H · 65-U · 66-F · 67-C · 68-T · 69-O · 70-G · 71-P · 72-M
9	73-S · 74-G · 75-D · 76-X · 77-A · 78-P · 79-B · 80-Z₁ · 81-M · 82-Z
10	83-L · 84-Q · 85-W · 86-M · 87-W · 88-R · 89-A · 90-I · 91-H · 92-B
11	93-T · 94-R · 95-L · 96-C · 97-V · 98-J · 99-Q · 100-O · 101-Y · 102-K · 103-V
12	104-Y · 105-T · 106-I · 107-G · 108-X · 109-W · 110-E · 111-K · 112-U
13	113-I · 114-M · 115-Z₁ · 116-L · 117-F · 118-O · 119-J · 120-R · 121-N · 122-U · 123-L
14	124-B · 125-C · 126-F · 127-N · 128-Z · 129-Z₁ · 130-Q · 131-Y · 132-E · 133-T
15	134-H · 135-P · 136-W · 137-A · 138-W · 139-G · 140-Q · 141-Y · 142-U
16	143-R · 144-A · 145-X · 146-Z₁ · 147-Z · 148-T · 149-B · 150-J · 151-S · 152-Q · 153-H
17	154-A · 155-B · 156-A · 157-S · 158-G · 159-Z · 160-D · 161-G
18	162-K · 163-N · 164-Y · 165-H · 166-L · 167-X · 168-K · 169-Z · 170-O · 171-U
19	172-O · 173-X · 174-L · 175-S · 176-K · 177-Y

Grid

Reading the numbered/lettered cells (cell number followed by clue-letter):

1 O	2 A	3 M	4 C	5 R	6 V	7 Q	8 P	
9 U	10 C	11 W	12 S	13 P	14 G	15 L	16 P	17 M
18 N	19 T	20 I	21 V	22 F	23 D	24 C	25 K	26 B	27 T
28 N	29 J	30 X	31 U	32 G	33 N	34 O	35 K	36 Q	37 L	38 E
39 F	40 A	41 T	42 B	43 D	44 G	45 J	46 W	47 V	48 G
49 F	50 G	51 O	52 K	53 E	54 U	55 V	56 P	57 F	58 C	59 R
60 T	61 X	62 L	63 F	64 V	65 S	66 I	67 H	68 N
69 D	70 K	71 A	72 P	73 C	74 S	75 T	76 R	77 J	78 Q	79 I
80 X	81 D	82 N	83 W	84 M	85 R	86 S	87 I	88 D
89 B	90 G	91 N	92 G	93 B	94 L	95 J	96 V	97 X
98 O	99 R	100 U	101 G	102 Q	103 O	104 H	105 Q	106 V	107 J
108 R	109 F	110 X	111 V	112 O	113 P	114 B	115 Q	116 J	117 M	118 E
119 N	120 W	121 F	122 A	123 L	124 I	125 J	126 D	127 U	128 J
129 I	130 G	131 N	132 J	133 R	134 M	135 A	136 L	137 A
138 J	139 U	140 H	141 X	142 L	143 C	144 K	145 P	146 E	147 R
148 Q	149 S	150 B	151 D	152 T	153 I	154 C	155 K	156 O	157 H
158 V	159 J	160 O	161 G	162 O	163 I	164 S	165 M	166 L	167 D
168 L	169 O	170 B	171 E	172 C	173 G	174 W	175 A	176 Q

CLUES

A Tender
B Whomp
C Chess champion from France in the '20s, '30s, and '40s
D Am. labor leader, pres. Am. Federation of Musicians, 1940–58
E (Music): slow, in a broad, dignified style
F Show enthusiastic approval
G "___, wherefore should I fast?" (4 wds., II Sam. 12:23)
H Abram "pitched his ___ toward Sodom" (Gen. 13:12)
I Divine, sublime
J Authority; right; sanction
K Petty officer; valiant, useful
L Companions on the same vessel
M Song of praise or devotion
N Juvenile
O Type of moorage (2 wds.)
P "The sweet" of Queen Gertrude's "Sweets to the sweet"
Q Revealed, displayed
R Affected with disgust
S Absolute dominion
T Hotshot, buckaroo
U Beat
V Result, outcome
W Piquant
X Idle talk

WORDS

A 122 40 71 2 137 175 135
B 114 93 170 42 26 89 150
C 143 73 154 24 10 58 172 4
D 69 88 126 167 81 43 23 151
E 38 146 118 171 53
F 63 109 39 57 22 121 49
G 48 32 130 161 44 173 14 101 92 50 90
H 104 140 67 157
I 20 79 66 163 124 87 153 129
J 107 132 125 95 29 116 159 45 128 77 138
K 144 70 35 155 25 52
L 123 62 136 94 142 37 166 168 15
M 117 165 3 84 134 17
N 68 131 28 33 91 82 18 119
O 160 162 169 98 112 51 1 156 34 103
P 16 72 145 13 8 113 56
Q 115 36 105 102 7 176 148 78
R 5 99 147 76 108 59 85 133
S 164 65 149 74 12 86
T 19 41 75 152 27 60
U 54 139 100 9 127 31
V 47 96 64 106 111 55 6 21 158
W 174 11 46 83 120
X 141 110 97 61 30 80

78

CLUES

A Am. illustrator-cartoonist (1840–1902), creator of elephant and donkey political symbols

B 1864 poem by Tennyson (2 wds.)

C Approving, supporting

D Tools for cowboys, Will Rogers, etc.

E 1938 Marjorie Kinnan Rawlings novel (after "The")

F Plant of the genus Chenopodium

G Obtain by force, threat, etc.

H Full of louse eggs

I Attracted by (2 wds.)

J Synthetic, artificial

K Proportional relations

L Occult

M Infectious febrile disease of warm climates (2 wds.)

N Food substance, product of cassava

O African people also called Khoikhoi

P Past one's prime (3 wds.)

Q Had an angry look, looked displeased

R Fill with delight or wonder; way in

S Wild carrot (3 wds.)

T Monoceros

U Precision, exactness

V Lustful, lewd

W Sense, feel, divine

X White Russians

Y Source of Juliet's "light" for Romeo (2 wds.)

WORDS

Clue	Cell numbers
A	121 191 177 91
B	112 185 75 83 157 96 14 142 120 198
C	18 49 65 149 164 156 138 172 126
D	148 78 137 20 189 192
E	42 152 51 64 24 132 167 17
F	151 2 143 111 129 190 106 30 39
G	181 194 62 11 175 155
H	67 92 13 9 8
I	165 146 15 159 136 186 110
J	48 180 131 40 34 128
K	88 68 102 154 103 125
L	4 54 99 134 161 45 60 187
M	70 135 52 197 158 21 179 203 86 53 3
N	108 5 145 124 84 61 199
O	119 37 178 77 87 115 59 27 200 97
P	93 26 105 31 50 36 73 123 66 7 23
Q	139 107 57 118 104 71 47
R	176 76 169 202 196 58 32 184
S	182 101 141 170 150 25 16 1 174 35 95 127 56 193
T	33 85 81 79 114 144 162
U	90 44 113 201 38 168 74 188
V	6 28 100 22 153 130 133 163 195 160
W	166 94 173 183 46 122
X	80 89 43 69 171 12 98 117
Y	72 147 41 116 55 19 109 140 82 29 63 10

Grid (cell number / word-letter)

1 S	2 F	3 M	4 L	5 N	6 V	7 P			
8 H	9 H	10 Y	11 G	12 X	13 H	14 B	15 I	16 S	17 E
18 C	19 Y	20 D	21 M	22 V	23 P	24 E	25 S	26 P	27 O
28 V	29 Y	30 F	31 P	32 R	33 T	34 J	35 S	36 P	
37 O	38 U	39 F	40 J	41 Y	42 E	43 X	44 U	45 L	46 W
47 Q	48 J	49 C	50 P	51 E	52 M	53 M	54 L	55 Y	56 S
57 Q	58 R	59 O	60 L	61 N	62 G	63 Y	64 E	65 C	66 P (+67 H)
68 K	69 X	70 M	71 Q	72 Y	73 P	74 U	75 B	76 R	77 O
78 D	79 T	80 X	81 T	82 Y	83 B	84 N	85 T	86 M	87 O
88 K	89 X	90 U	91 A	92 H	93 P	94 W	95 S	96 B	97 O (+98 X)
99 L	100 V	101 S	102 K	103 K	104 Q	105 P	106 F	107 Q	
108 N	109 Y	110 I	111 F	112 B	113 U	114 T	115 O	116 Y	117 X
118 Q	119 O	120 B	121 A	122 W	123 P	124 N	125 K	126 C	
127 S	128 J	129 F	130 V	131 J	132 E	133 V	134 L	135 M	136 I
137 D	138 C	139 Q	140 Y	141 S	142 B	143 F	144 T	145 N	146 I
147 Y	148 D	149 C	150 S	151 F	152 E	153 V	154 K	155 G	156 C
157 B	158 M	159 I	160 V	161 L	162 T	163 V	164 C	165 I	166 W (+167 E)
168 U	169 R	170 S	171 X	172 C	173 W	174 S	175 G	176 R	177 A (+178 O)
179 M	180 J	181 G	182 S	183 W	184 R	185 B	186 I	187 L	188 U
189 D	190 F	191 A	192 D	193 S	194 G	195 V	196 R	197 M	
198 B	199 N	200 O	201 U	202 R	203 M				

79

CLUES		WORDS
A	City in central Mass.; city in central England	6 130 159 36 63 169 178 126 1 72 92
B	European fish, family Zoarcidae	61 31 135 188 137 5 157
C	Remove by cutting (2 wds.)	138 82 179 16 30 4
D	Have a gloomy, threatening look	107 115 102 108 153
E	Flagrant, appalling	55 192 78 32 14 163 60 37 131 112
F	Bittersweet or tomato, e.g.	77 109 118 59 113 190 87 127 27 183
G	Thief, swindler, rascal (Yiddish)	160 104 34 9 50
H	Utters bitter denunciation	68 156 73 20 149
I	Gershwin hit of 1930	33 165 22 65 48 185 194 175 85 17 3 170 181 125
J	Junkie	43 80 172 91 19 46
K	Reproach; insignificant klutz	89 47 28 101
L	Causes as a consequence	171 74 41 39 133 105 142
M	Wrapped round with bandages	49 70 158 66 184 83 57 38
N	Under the influence, mellow, a bit juiced	191 144 167 56 86
O	Hoofer in a Broadway chorus	93 40 62 121 129
P	Eggshell or pearl, e.g. (hyph.)	95 139 18 187 2 88 162 79
Q	Obtained from milk	134 164 151 124 177 96
R	Knock down; steamroll	13 145 152 8 110 76 25
S	Film actor (1924–63, "Elephant Boy")	120 189 147 21
T	Scripture (2 wds.)	71 12 154 122 132 193 23 35
U	"The Spell ___": reprint title of Service's "Songs of a Sourdough" (3 wds.)	10 29 53 42 166 155 119 116 186 174
V	Sometimes the makings of hula skirts (2 wds.)	143 140 168 67 148 182 106 24
W	Engaging, gripping	161 44 81 180 26 98 128 45 176 15
X	Calls on, goes to	75 99 69 123 90 117
Y	Large oboe (2 wds.)	64 11 136 146 114 141 54 111 51 94 100
Z	Striped bass, e.g.	52 173 7 97 84 150 58 103

	1 A	2 P	3 I	■	4 C	5 B	6 A	7 Z	8 R	9 G	10 U
11 Y		12 T	13 R	■	14 E	■	15 W	16 C	17 I	18 P	
19 J	20 H	21 S	22 I	■	23 T	24 V	■	25 R	26 W	■	27 F
28 K	29 U	30 C	31 B	32 E	33 I	34 G	35 T	■	36 A	37 E	38 M
39 L	40 O	■	41 L	42 U	43 J	44 W	■	45 W	46 J	■	47 K
48 I	49 M	■	50 G	51 Y	52 Z	■	53 U	54 Y	55 E	56 N	57 M
■	58 Z	59 F	60 E	61 B	62 O	63 A	64 Y	65 I	66 M	67 V	68 H
69 X	■	70 M	71 T	72 A	■	73 H	74 L	75 X	76 R	77 F	78 E
79 P	80 J	■	81 W	82 C	83 M	84 Z	■	85 I	86 N	■	87 F
88 P	89 K	90 X	91 J	92 A	93 O	■	94 Y	95 P	96 Q	97 Z	98 W
■	99 X	100 Y	101 K	102 D	■	103 Z	104 G	105 L	106 V	107 D	■
108 D	109 F	110 R	111 Y	■	112 E	113 F	114 Y	115 D	116 U	117 X	■
118 F	119 U	120 S	121 O	122 T	■	123 X	124 Q	■	125 I	126 A	■
127 F	128 W	■	129 O	130 A	131 E	■	132 T	133 L	134 Q	135 B	■
136 Y	137 B	138 C	139 P	■	140 V	141 Y	■	142 L	143 V	144 N	145 R
146 Y	■	147 S	148 V	149 H	150 Z	151 Q	152 R	153 D	154 T	155 U	■
156 H	■	157 B	158 M	159 A	160 G	161 W	162 P	■	163 E	164 Q	165 I
166 U	■	167 N	168 V	169 A	170 I	171 L	172 J	■	173 Z	174 U	■
175 I	176 W	■	177 Q	178 A	179 C	180 W	181 I	182 V	183 F	184 M	■
185 I	186 U	187 P	■	188 B	189 S	190 F	191 N	192 E	193 T	194 I	■

80

CLUES

		Word letters
A	Site of 1864 battle near Atlanta (2 wds.)	189 69 46 183 84 55 74 64 98 79 118 135 165 62 20 41
B	Female name from the Hebrew for "rebirth"	148 180 107 153
C	Invalidating	14 178 100 87 151 91 22 157
D	Of the mind	17 106 163 169 12 150
E	Uncanny	44 93 145 105 27
F	"Friendship is constant in all other things / Save in ___ and affair of love," (2 wds. "Much Ado About Nothing")	56 124 109 138 89 39 4 43 129
G	Am. bird of prey distinguished by its cry (2 wds.)	29 49 88 119 38 73 155
H	Claim presumptuously	45 78 192 173 132 149 11 35
I	Bridal outfit	172 36 158 170 81 85 59 6 113
J	Pick	58 83 50 21 112 125
K	Most arrogant	2 182 54 7 177 94 164 142 115 82
L	Enmity (2 wds.)	101 154 110 147 8 90 24
M	It's free if on this; freely if off (2 wds.)	137 108 86 52 193 92 190
N	Faulkner's county	156 175 26 102 60 111 179 1 76 128 171 95 67
O	Have an impact	57 31 143 65 184 104
P	Desires, longs	123 25 114 160 140 63
Q	Was borne on	51 13 174 168
R	Not to be endured	134 61 167 121 47 15 3 72 10 141 34 96
S	Memento, souvenir	19 187 68 32 9
T	Lifts	146 48 127 181 99 122 133 130 23
U	Rakes	188 144 152 161 37
V	Fatty	166 185 139 103 116 33 42 16 194
W	"Boast not thyself of ___" (Prov. 27:1)	159 191 66 120 53 126 70 186
X	Aloof	97 77 75
Y	Silent	5 71 28 131
Z	French delicacy having a muscular ventral foot	30 80 18 40 162 136 117 176

WORDS

Grid (each square shows its clue letter and number):

N1	K2	R3	F4	Y5	I6	K7	L8	S9	R10	H11		
D12	Q13	C14	R15	V16	D17	Z18	S19	A20	J21	C22		
T23	L24	P25	N26	E27	Y28	G29	Z30	O31				
S32	V33	V34	H35	I36	U37	G38	F39	Z40	A41			
V42	F43	E44	H45	A46	R47	T48	G49	J50	Q51			
M52	W53	K54	A55	F56	O57	J58	I59	N60	R61			
A62	P63	A64	O65	W66	N67	S68	A69	W70				
Y71	R72	G73	A74	X75	N76	X77	H78	A79	Z80			
I81	K82	J83	A84	I85	M86	C87	G88	F89				
L90	C91	M92	E93	K94	N95	R96	X97	A98				
T99	C100	L101	N102	V103	O104	E105	D106	B107	M108	F109		
L110	N111	J112	I113	P114	K115	V116	Z117	A118	G119			
W120	R121	T122	P123	F124	J125	W126	T127	N128				
F129	T130	Y131	H132	T133	R134	A135	Z136	M137	F138			
V139	P140	R141	K142	O143	U144	E145	T146	L147				
B148	H149	D150	C151	U152	B153	L154	G155	N156	C157			
I158	W159	P160	U161	Z162	D163	K164	A165	V166				
R167	Q168	D169	I170	N171	I172	H173	Q174	N175				
Z176	K177	C178	N179	B180	T181	K182	A183	O184	V185			
W186	S187	U188	A189	M190	W191	H192	M193	V194				

81

CLUES

A. Contrite parent worried about tangled net

B. Added coach brained a legendary schoolmaster (2 wds.)

C. Chest holding a note for Linus Pauling, perhaps

D. Suspicion: Quasimodo's back in Notre Dame?

E. Pop, having his beginning with the industrial giant's 2-letter signature, follows a brief statement of principle

F. Falls back, runs briefly, pleases wildly

G. Di, starting to indulge in wild living, has pasties scattered about

H. City swinging only to the South

I. Ancient once messed up before his beginning

J. Note cute little flunky's sway

K. Importance of hemp shredded as is

L. Having a spat in a skull, you might say

M. Decorates me turning heads

N. Disgusting street: one for polish

O. The Old Man could make a stink here

P. Evil's price could be insincerity (2 wds.)

Q. Innovation holding back a river

R. G.I. jerks

S. Always theatrical awards screwed up! Sobeit, without end!

T. Carp, perhaps, about love—softly, softly

U. Complaining about a win, holding one heart? Gin! strangely

V. O, Night! New! New, and active! (3 wds.)

W. Being in charge unhinges. Thrown out! (3 wds.)

X. "Hands up!" I relay to princes

Y. Going through, if in pain

WORDS

Clue	Letters
A	51 2 194 68 112 150 169 46 113
B	103 53 110 133 48 80 160 168 183 95 93 181
C	129 114 47 81 39 177 78
D	99 89 59 3 118
E	123 62 45 16 151 50 164 82 41 75
F	139 10 63 143 120 34 161 167
G	145 188 155 122 159 180 115 96 76
H	73 149 12 189 173
I	28 8 60 134 35
J	44 70 146 175 5 42 86 65
K	157 142 38 178 57 13 121 43
L	56 131 109 36 25 94
M	130 71 171 182 21 117 111 101
N	61 125 100 55 24 29 163 30 19 87 172
O	72 136 187 58 195 6 64 84
P	135 7 176 191 85 88 106 97 69 22
Q	147 23 140 91
R	49 179 186 54 79
S	18 156 165 105 138
T	126 83 37 104 92 137 174
U	67 14 152 40 193 90 17
V	4 153 33 27 107 1 185 124 98
W	132 52 148 170 119 144 154 11 192 66 162 31 141 26
X	20 32 9 166 102 128 77 184
Y	158 74 127 116 15 108 190

GRID

(Each cell: square number + clue letter)

1 V	2 A	3 D	4 V	5 J	6 O	7 P	8 I	9 X	10 F	
11 W	12 H	13 K	14 U	15 Y	16 E	17 U	18 S	19 N	20 X	
21 M	22 P	23 Q	24 N	25 L	26 W	27 V	28 I	29 N		
30 N	31 W	32 X	33 V	34 F	35 I	36 L	37 T	38 K	39 C	40 U
41 E	42 J	43 K	44 J	45 E	46 A	47 C	48 B	49 R		
50 E	51 A	52 W	53 B	54 R	55 N	56 L	57 K	58 O	59 D	
60 I	61 N	62 E	63 F	64 O	65 J	66 W	67 U	68 A		
69 P	70 J	71 M	72 O	73 H	74 Y	75 E	76 G	77 X	78 C	
79 R	80 B	81 C	82 E	83 T	84 O	85 P	86 J	87 N	88 P	
89 D	90 U	91 Q	92 T	93 B	94 L	95 B	96 G	97 P	98 V	
99 D	100 N	101 M	102 X	103 B	104 T	105 S	106 P	107 V	108 Y	
109 L	110 B	111 M	112 A	113 A	114 C	115 G	116 Y	117 M		
118 D	119 W	120 F	121 K	122 G	123 E	124 V	125 N	126 T		
127 Y	128 X	129 C	130 M	131 L	132 W	133 B	134 I	135 P		
136 O	137 T	138 S	139 F	140 Q	141 W	142 K	143 F	144 W	145 G	
146 J	147 Q	148 W	149 H	150 A	151 E	152 U	153 V	154 W	155 G	
156 S	157 K	158 Y	159 G	160 B	161 F	162 W	163 N	164 E	165 S	166 X
167 F	168 B	169 A	170 W	171 M	172 N	173 H	174 T	175 J		
176 P	177 C	178 K	179 R	180 G	181 B	182 M	183 B	184 X	185 V	
186 R	187 O	188 G	189 H	190 Y	191 P	192 W	193 U	194 A	195 O	

82

CLUES

A Sketch in outline (2 wds.) . . . .
B Weave, braid . . . .
C Broadcasting system, e.g. . . . .
D Hindu religious leader (1869–1948) . . .
E Colorado city near Denver . . . .
F Capital of Jordan . . . .
G Firmness . . . .
H Hated . . . .
I Snowy . . . .
J Grommet . . . .
K Restoration . . . .
L "The lusty horn / Is not ___ to laugh to scorn" (2 wds., "As You Like It")
M Shriveled . . . .
N Clerical (3 wds.) . . . .
O Exchange, mart . . . .
P Woman said to have been Adam's first wife
Q Silent . . . .
R Pet phrase of a sect or party . . . .
S "The ___ is a ship's upon the sea" (4 wds.; Kipling, "The Long Trail")
T Decorate brightly . . . .
U Extended in undulations . . . .
V Exaggerated; shameless . . . .
W Markets for goods . . . .
X Insalubrious . . . .
Y "Factory windows are always broken. / ___ throwing bricks" (2 wds.; Lindsay, "Factory Windows") . . . .

WORDS

Clue	Cells
A	107 91 28 146 176 49 56 103
B	109 173 172 99 25 122 86 73 67 121
C	84 162 110 45 115 100 6
D	38 132 82 68 31 26
E	108 136 14 183 163 36 5 134
F	171 126 135 92 133
G	198 13 63 1 58 18 153 184
H	94 139 148 85 83 2 11 199
I	128 123 50 77 79 33 55
J	190 131 141 96 44 8
K	166 22 98 186 151 197 145
L	130 41 164 194 57 175
M	185 143 195 147 150 71 180
N	119 87 75 64 46 90 12 104 20 114
O	52 174 59 48 181 32
P	193 152 3 62 74 170
Q	35 106 161 43
R	17 39 97 189 53 127 72 165 65 182
S	118 78 154 24 177 113 168 169 140 191 54 69 4 116 15
T	101 124 138 188 81 196 156 179
U	89 27 187 47 117 129
V	149 120 10 160 102 51 29 40
W	9 88 111 144 95 158 7
X	37 61 70 167 16 76 93 21 19 157 34
Y	159 105 80 125 192 42 155 60 23 178 112 142 66 137 30

Grid (cell number · clue letter)

Row	Cells
1	1-G 2-H 3-P 4-S 5-E 6-C 7-W 8-J
2	9-W 10-V 11-H 12-N 13-G 14-E 15-S 16-X 17-R
3	18-G 19-X 20-N 21-X 22-K 23-Y 24-S 25-B 26-D
4	27-U 28-A 29-V 30-Y 31-D 32-O 33-I 34-X 35-Q 36-E
5	37-X 38-D 39-R 40-V 41-L 42-Y 43-Q 44-J 45-C
6	46-N 47-U 48-O 49-A 50-I 51-V 52-O 53-R 54-S
7	55-I 56-A 57-L 58-G 59-O 60-Y 61-X 62-P 63-G 64-N 65-R
8	66-Y 67-B 68-D 69-S 70-X 71-M 72-R 73-B 74-P
9	75-N 76-X 77-I 78-S 79-I 80-Y 81-T 82-D 83-H 84-C
10	85-H 86-B 87-N 88-W 89-U 90-N 91-A 92-F 93-X
11	94-H 95-W 96-J 97-R 98-K 99-B 100-C 101-T 102-V 103-A 104-N
12	105-Y 106-Q 107-A 108-E 109-B 110-C 111-W 112-Y 113-S
13	114-N 115-C 116-S 117-U 118-S 119-N 120-V 121-B 122-B 123-I
14	124-T 125-Y 126-F 127-R 128-I 129-U 130-L 131-J 132-D 133-F
15	134-E 135-F 136-E 137-Y 138-T 139-H 140-S 141-J 142-Y
16	143-M 144-W 145-K 146-A 147-M 148-H 149-V 150-M 151-K 152-P
17	153-G 154-S 155-Y 156-T 157-X 158-W 159-Y 160-V 161-Q 162-C
18	163-E 164-L 165-R 166-K 167-X 168-S 169-S 170-P 171-F 172-B
19	173-B 174-O 175-L 176-A 177-S 178-Y 179-T 180-M 181-O 182-R
20	183-E 184-G 185-M 186-K 187-U 188-T 189-R 190-J 191-S
21	192-Y 193-P 194-L 195-M 196-T 197-K 198-G 199-H

83

Grid

Each white square below is given as cell-number · clue-letter, in reading order by row.

Row	Cells
1	1·I 2·W 3·Z₁ 4·Z 5·L 6·H 7·G
8	8·H 9·E 10·Z₁ 11·B 12·J 13·M 14·V 15·F 16·X 17·Y 18·J
19	19·S 20·D 21·E 22·U 23·I 24·Q 25·Z 26·K 27·H 28·Z₁
29	29·B 30·R 31·M 32·K 33·U 34·O 35·R 36·D 37·Q
38	38·X 39·T 40·U 41·J 42·N 43·H 44·F 45·R 46·D
47	47·K 48·M 49·R 50·H 51·E 52·T 53·X 54·J 55·I 56·A
57	57·B 58·H 59·I 60·C 61·P 62·G 63·Z₁ 64·L 65·M 66·J 67·J
68	68·P 69·T 70·Q 71·E 72·X 73·R 74·H 75·W 76·R 77·P
78	78·J 79·N 80·E 81·O 82·I 83·Q 84·L 85·F 86·W
87	87·I 88·P 89·V 90·C 91·L 92·O 93·C 94·B 95·N 96·R 97·K
98	98·L 99·J 100·S 101·U 102·T 103·A 104·N 105·Z₁ 106·C
107	107·P 108·Y 109·V 110·L 111·P 112·S 113·V 114·D 115·G 116·Z₁
117	117·S 118·B 119·I 120·L 121·S 122·Z 123·U 124·F 125·L
126	126·O 127·A 128·C 129·H 130·G 131·V 132·T 133·B 134·R
135	135·A 136·X 137·B 138·F 139·D 140·E 141·V 142·X 143·K 144·R
145	145·Y 146·Q 147·P 148·S 149·V 150·N 151·W 152·K 153·X 154·E
155	155·V 156·O 157·W 158·V 159·U 160·S 161·D 162·F 163·Q 164·M
165	165·M 166·G 167·U 168·T 169·I 170·X 171·D 172·W 173·Z₁
174	174·Y 175·Z 176·P 177·W 178·G 179·O 180·B 181·A 182·P
183	183·T 184·V 185·Q 186·U 187·M 188·J 189·W 190·E 191·P 192·Z
193	193·M 194·H 195·A 196·J 197·Y 198·G 199·G 200·H 201·C 202·F
203	203·Z₁ 204·Q 205·P 206·Y 207·B 208·X 209·L 210·E 211·G 212·J
213	213·Y 214·V 215·P 216·X 217·T 218·L

CLUES

A Be worthwhile; show profit (2 wds.)

B Ophthalmia

C Vexatious, full of difficulties

D One on the run

E Of great assistance (hyph.)

F Access, portal

G Hydrated magnesium sulphate (2 wds.)

H Censure harshly, revile

I Caused distaste or aversion

J Fair; apathetic

K Application, exertion, try

L Small N American bird, Aegolius acadicus with a repeated, mechanical-sounding note (hyph. and wd.)

M 1882 Wagnerian opera

N Embroidered vestment of the Jewish high priest

O Stingy person; inexpensive, inferior product (hyph.)

P Members of a U.S. political party of the 1850s (hyph.)

Q Trouble, a jam (2 wds.)

R Self-evident

S Brahman sage

T Newcomer

U Type of rail (2 wds.)

V Female sharpshooter; theater pass (2 wds.)

W With impressively skeletal prominence

X Person or thing that assumes leadership

Y French tennis player who beat Tilden in the 1927 U.S. Open

Z Serpentine ridge of gravelly and sandy drift

Z₁ Jeering at

WORDS

A: 135 195 103 127 56 181

B: 94 180 11 57 133 29 137 207 118

C: 201 106 60 93 128 90

D: 20 46 139 114 171 161 36

E: 80 210 190 140 154 71 9 51 21

F: 85 124 202 162 44 15 138

G: 130 178 198 199 7 166 62 115 211

H: 194 50 58 200 27 8 74 6 129 43

I: 59 55 1 23 87 169 82 119

J: 188 196 99 18 66 67 41 12 54 78 212

K: 26 47 143 152 97 32

L: 91 84 125 120 5 98 218 64 110 209

M: 187 31 193 164 48 65 165 13

N: 79 95 42 104 150

O: 126 81 156 179 92 34

P: 147 77 182 88 215 68 176 205 107 111 61 191

Q: 83 146 204 37 163 70 185 24

R: 96 49 76 134 35 45 30 73 144

S: 112 148 160 121 19 100 117

T: 217 132 183 168 102 52 39 69

U: 167 101 40 159 33 22 186 123

V: 158 131 149 141 214 109 89 184 155 113 14

W: 172 86 157 151 177 189 2 75

X: 53 142 170 136 16 72 153 38 216 208

Y: 213 17 174 145 108 197 206

Z: 192 122 4 175 25

Z₁: 116 3 28 203 105 173 63 10

84

CLUES

A. Don't worry, it doesn't matter (2 wds.)
B. Working, functioning
C. Eng. philosopher, mathematician, author (1872–1970), 1950 Nobel Prize winner for Literature
D. Continue, proceed; attack as a military target (2 wds.)
E. Bitter gum resin formerly used as a carminative and antispasmodic
F. "There is —— with edge tools" (2 wds.; Fletcher and Massinger, "The Little French Lawyer")
G. Thick, stout, stocky
H. African starling that rides on large animals to feed on their ticks
I. Undecided, unsettled (4 wds.)
J. Beast of burden
K. "To post / With such dexterity to ——" (2 wds.; "Hamlet")
L. Jitters
M. Stamps out, puts an end to
N. "If a man say, I love God, and ——, he is a liar" (3 wds.; I John 4:20)
O. Unprecedented; outrageous (hyph.)
P. Robert W. Service's "Dangerous Dan"
Q. Source of a great oak, perhaps
R. What Nixon said there could be at the White House (2 wds.; TV speech on Watergate, Apr. 30, 1973)
S. Fail to mention
T. Exceptional valor, ability, etc.
U. Endure or resist hardship or adversity (3 wds.)
V. Nude, stripped (3 wds.)
W. Long series of wanderings, adventures, etc.
X. Wicked
Y. Loose, lightweight overgarments

WORDS

A. 105 70 99 108 58 2 151 119 138
B. 106 88 169 126 102 159 69 26 4 44 137
C. 25 193 154 117 178 21 140
D. 120 59 107 104 174 80
E. 142 95 125 171 181 164 23 72 84 115
F. 73 14 48 141 189 166 206 176 28
G. 5 111 167 196 12 113
H. 146 165 124 56 186 45 32 109
I. 49 33 191 182 10 97 148 155 89 82
J. 63 208 7 180 30 83 93
K. 118 144 201 8 179 149 79 64 37 62 47 24 112 77 54 145
L. 188 184 168 68 39 85
M. 209 35 86 75 60 41 133 183
N. 78 1 91 61 101 132 55 34 19 200 177 170 110 31 42 116
O. 92 13 150 67 195 136 81 11 22
P. 147 90 153 143 114 175
Q. 3 205 6 38 122
R. 203 135 71 16 96 131 46 15 98 40 76
S. 157 18 139 160
T. 57 66 207 134 162 194 185
U. 127 202 158 74 161 52 43 192 27 51
V. 17 152 36 29 94 156 199 87 65
W. 187 197 123 9 50 100 173
X. 53 20 130 121 204 163
Y. 198 172 129 190 103 128

Grid (cell number and clue letter)

1 N	2 A	3 Q	4 B	5 G	6 Q
7 J	8 K	9 W	10 I	11 O	12 G	13 O	14 F	15 R
16 R	17 V	18 S	19 N	20 X	21 C	22 O	23 E	24 K	25 C	26 B
27 U	28 F	29 V	30 J	31 N	32 H	33 I	34 N	35 M	36 V
37 K	38 Q	39 L	40 R	41 M	42 N	43 U	44 B	45 H	46 R
47 K	48 F	49 I	50 W	51 U	52 U	53 X	54 K	55 N
56 H	57 T	58 A	59 D	60 M	61 N	62 K	63 J	64 K	65 V
66 T	67 O	68 L	69 B	70 A	71 R	72 E	73 F	74 U	75 M
76 R	77 K	78 N	79 K	80 D	81 O	82 I	83 J	84 E	85 L
86 M	87 V	88 B	89 I	90 P	91 N	92 O	93 J	94 V	95 E
96 R	97 I	98 R	99 A	100 W	101 N	102 B	103 Y	104 D	105 A
106 B	107 D	108 A	109 H	110 N	111 G	112 K	113 G	114 P
115 E	116 N	117 C	118 K	119 A	120 D	121 X	122 Q	123 W
124 H	125 E	126 B	127 U	128 Y	129 Y	130 X	131 R	132 N	133 M
134 T	135 R	136 O	137 B	138 A	139 S	140 C	141 F	142 E
143 P	144 K	145 K	146 H	147 P	148 I	149 K	150 O	151 A	152 V
153 P	154 C	155 I	156 V	157 S	158 U	159 B	160 S	161 U	162 T
163 X	164 E	165 H	166 F	167 G	168 L	169 B	170 N	171 E
172 Y	173 W	174 D	175 P	176 F	177 N	178 C	179 K	180 J	181 E
182 I	183 M	184 L	185 T	186 H	187 W	188 L	189 F	190 Y	191 I	192 U
193 C	194 T	195 O	196 G	197 W	198 Y	199 V	200 N	201 K	202 U
203 R	204 X	205 Q	206 F	207 T	208 J	209 M

85

CLUES

A Temperamental — 103 39 109 58 43

B What foil on fir usually represents — 45 3 75 40 122 81 54

C King of 1933 film — 125 157 19 98

D Occurrences, happenings — 177 82 198 94 191 33

E Fervent, ardent — 41 99 185 171 111

F Courtier whom Hamlet refers to as "this water-fly" — 141 128 71 90 30

G Browning poem beginning "It once might have been, once only" (3 wds.) — 119 105 1 146 9

H Acquaintance; familiarity; information — 24 10 113 108 181 60 27 88 15 127 80

I Burdensome — 152 97 173 166 42 104 37 162 57

J Blue, depressed (4 wds.) — 17 168 186 44 102 174 50

K Royal office or state — 52 20 158 143 190 18 77 115 134 126 28 164 175 155

L Does away with — 32 14 95 136 161 163 196

M Seat of government in the White House (2 wds.) — 193 135 26 170 150 61 110 8 69 139

N Acting as a corporate director (3 wds.) — 22 118 187 78 12 121 2 195 154 67

O Small, rounded hills — 4 65 87 73 145 7

P "___ of fragrance, lily-silver'd vales" (Pope, "The Dunciad") — 96 47 183 142 16

Q Bewitch — 153 63 25 180 79 167 114

R 1925 Gus Kahn–Walter Donaldson hit (2 wds. followed by WORD Z₁) — 85 116 74 92 51 120

S For the eyes — 112 151 133 184 35 38

T Dickensian character whose villainy is exposed by Wilkins Micawber (full name) — 6 117 70 169 138 56 31 62 178

U N Calif. city on the Sacramento River — 107 53 197 23 93 36 189

V Queer; wandering; eccentric — 49 149 13 165 34 64 46

W Harry Leon Wilson's Eng. butler, played by Chas. Laughton in a 1935 film — 84 179 194 144 130 72 76

X Enrage; pleasant perfume — 160 137 124 59 100 91 68

Y Shining, polished — 66 182 132 147 101 89

Z "She knocks 'em dead when she's dressed in red, but she looks like ___" (2 wds. from a 1936 song by Billy Rose & Fred Fisher) — 148 176 159 83 29 48 199 106 129 11

Z₁ See WORD R (3 wds.) — 192 156 123 55 188 5 172 86 140 21 131

WORDS (Grid)

1 G	2 F	3 N	4 B	5 O	6 Z₁	7 T	8 O	9 M	
10	11 G	12 Z	13	14 U	15 K	16 G	17 P	18 I	19 C
20	21 Z₁	22 N	23 U	24 G	25 Q	26 M	27 G		28 J	29 Z
30 E	31 T	32 K	33 K	34 D	35 V	36 S	37 U	38 S	39 A	40 B
41 L	42 H	43 H	44 A	45 I	46 B	47 Z	48 Z	49 Z	50 I
51 R	52 J	53 U	54 U	55 Z₁	56 Z₁	57 T	58 A	59 A	60 G
61 M	62 T	63 Q	64 Q	65 V	66 Y	67 O	68 Y	69 N	70 U
72 W	73 O	74 O	75 B	76 W	77 J	78 J	79 N	80 H
81 R	82 B	83 Z	84 W	85 Z₁	86 R	87 Z₁	88 G	89 G	90 E	91 E
92	93 R	94 U	95 D	96 K	97 P	98 H	99 C	100 X
101 Y	102 I	103 A	104 H	105 F	106 Z	107 Z	108 U	109 A	110 M
111 M	112 L	113 H	114 R	115 K	116 S	117 R	118 N	119 F	120 R
121 N	122 B	123 Z₁	124 X	125 C	126 J	127 J	128 E	129 Z	130 W
131 Z₁	132 Y	133 S	134 K	135 M	136 L	137 X	138 K	139 N
140 Z₁	141 E	142 P	143 K	144 W	145 O	146 F	147 Z	148 Z
150 M	151 S	152 H	153 J	154 N	155 J	156 Z₁	157 C	158 J	159 Z	160 X
161 K	162 H	163 K	164 K	165 H	166 H	167 Q	168 Q	169 U	170 M
171 L	172 Z₁	173 I	174 H	175	176 J	177 D	178 T	179 W
180 G	181 G	182 Y	183 S	184 S	185 L	186 I	187 N	188 Z₁	189 U
190 J	191 D	192 Z₁	193 M	194 W	195 O	196 K	197 V	198 D	199 Z

86

CLUES / **WORDS**

A High-flown; ornate, as in speech or writing 90 26 16 73 46 95 130 10 124 212

B Cornflower (hyph.) 209 38 14 153 166 51 127 84 98 65 192 72 146 132 163

C Be on guard (2 wds.) 113 78 137 56 174 150 162 122

D Campaign trail in politics 63 97 136 119 40 102 159 179

E Not useful; lacking sense 68 25 189 199 57 37 186 126 11 108 176

F 4 wds. following "to" in "The Marines' Hymn" 147 8 198 185 181 17 89 2 168 96 191 28 47 178 104 49 67 129

G Adopted, embraced 143 218 91 41 208 27 118 171

H Deaths 31 101 39 154 158 107 200 175 66 61

I Deny; cast aside 140 115 134 34 81 18

J Inspired by an improbable surmise (4 wds.) 59 24 13 155 141 109 116 187 36 44 76 203

K Inmost, essential part; strength, vitality 87 9 60 92 112 62

L Struck lightly, drew off (liquid) 58 172 207 197 21 6

M Crowded together closely; gathered round for a conference 100 151 164 177 114 182 52

N Try 71 3 144 29 145 123 196 50

O Principal longitudinal area of a church 170 23 70 204

P Taro (hyph.) 105 193 69 194 120 74 131 82 216 5 169 205

Q Packed tightly, jammed, crowded . . . 20 156 54 117 93 35

R "___ is come out of the west" (2 wds.; Scott, "Marmion") 201 88 55 111 152 157 45 106 77 211 128 142 215 33

S Chiefly aquatic insectivore, potamogale velox (2 wds.) 184 99 75 53 139 19 148 30 83 1

T Overwhelming defeat 149 161 135 217

U Touch the forehead to the ground while kneeling 110 64 48 133 32 7

V Thunder-and-lightning episode (2 wds.) 190 210 4 173 202 12 85 22 80 165 103 180 214 195 183

W Think hard (3 wds.) 160 138 94 15 188 42 206 125 213 79 121 43 167 86

1 S	2 F	■	3 N	4 V	5 P	6 L	■	7 U	8 F	9 K	10 A
■	11 E	12 V	13 J	14 B	15 W	16 A	17 F	18 I	19 S	■	20 Q
21 L	■	22 V	23 O	24 J	■	25 E	26 A	27 G	28 F	29 N	30 S
■	31 H	32 U	33 R	■	34 I	35 Q	36 J	37 E	38 B	39 H	40 D
41 G	42 W	■	43 W	44 J	■	45 R	46 A	47 F	■	48 U	49 F
50 N	51 B	52 M	■	53 S	54 Q	55 R	56 C	57 E	58 L	59 J	60 K
61 H	■	62 K	63 D	64 U	■	65 B	66 H	67 F	68 E	69 P	70 O
71 N	■	72 B	73 A	74 P	75 S	■	76 J	77 R	78 C	79 W	80 V
81 I	82 P	83 S	84 B	■	85 V	86 W	■	87 K	88 R	89 F	90 A
■	91 G	92 K	93 Q	94 W	95 A	96 F	97 D	98 B	■	99 S	100 M
101 H	102 D	■	103 V	104 F	105 P	106 R	107 H	108 E	109 J	■	110 U
111 R	112 K	113 C	114 M	115 I	116 J	117 Q	118 G	■	119 D	120 P	121 W
122 C	■	123 N	124 A	125 W	126 E	127 B	128 R	■	129 F	130 A	■
131 P	132 B	133 U	■	134 I	135 T	136 D	137 C	■	138 W	139 S	140 I
141 J	142 R	143 G	144 N	■	145 N	146 B	■	147 F	148 S	149 T	150 C
151 M	152 R	153 B	■	154 H	■	155 J	156 Q	157 R	158 H	—	159 D
160 W	161 T	162 C	163 B	164 M	■	165 V	166 B	167 W	168 F	■	169 P
170 O	171 G	■	172 L	■	173 V	174 C	175 H	176 E	177 M	■	178 F
179 D	■	180 V	181 F	182 M	■	183 V	184 S	185 F	186 E	■	187 J
188 W	189 E	190 V	191 F	192 B	193 P	■	194 P	195 V	196 N	197 L	198 F
199 E	200 H	201 R	■	202 V	203 J	204 O	■	205 P	206 W	207 L	208 G
209 B	210 V	211 R	212 A	■	213 W	214 V	215 R	216 P	217 T	218 G	■

CLUES

A Fell off in vigor, energy, etc. . . . .

B "'Tis an ——— thing to play with souls" (Browning, "A Light Woman"). . . . .

C 1954 Ross & Adler song from "The Pajama Game" (2 wds.) . . . . . .

D Kind of double (hyph.) . . . .

E Weeping . . . .

F Self-imposed penance or punishment (2 wds.) . . . .

G Philosophy associated with Ortega, Unamuno, Sartre, Heidegger, etc. . . .

H Safest wagers, outstanding golfers, top marksmen, etc. (2 wds.) . . . . . .

I Organized illegal activities . . . .

J Charge, slur, aspersion . . . .

K Harm, mischief . . . .

L Type of overshoe; type of puttee . . . . .

M Symbol of life or fertility (2 wds.) . . . . .

N Title of respect derived from the Hindi for "brave person" . . . .

O Groundless, idle, false . . . .

P Seriousness; priority; closeness . . . . . .

Q Sanctioned, valid, not spurious . . . .

R Disagree; be at variance . . . .

S Causing vomiting . . . .

T Infrequency; unusual excellence . . . . . .

U Tightwad, miser . . . .

V Get hot; play that thing! (2 wds.) . . . . .

W "But let a lord once own the happy lines. / How ——— brightens!" (2 wds.: Pope, "Essay on Criticism") . . . . . .

X At once (3 wds.) . . . .

Y Fame, high repute . . . .

Z "An 'Oh!' or 'Ah!' of joy or misery. / Or a 'Ha! ha!' or 'Bah!' a ———" (3 wds.: Byron, "Don Juan") . . . .

WORDS

A 81 102 184 32 18 125 45

B 38 175 25 194 115 160 80

C 159 41 2 195 117 12 137 44 169

D 61 92 72 39 82 168 156 189 29

E 114 188 193 71 65

F 89 163 133 77 210 43 40 50 140

G 128 151 94 108 9 183 17 119 139 204 178 67 35 200

H 149 209 147 83 106 37 10 69 56

I 164 36 201 187 53 148 129

J 46 23 126 177 208 57 95 166 199 113

K 179 180 162 107 135 85

L 76 90 202 181 96 146

M 206 105 124 132 170 74 150 11 141 161 198

N 120 78 62 33 97 110 205

O 98 167 70 24 28 8 111 121 91

P 103 136 142 112 54 42 157 30 75

Q 14 26 66 59 109 155 191 93 100 4

R 63 173 68 153 49 86

S 88 73 130 186 118 154

T 127 64 34 101 52 143

U 22 165 145 47 122 182 7 5 207

V 185 1 51 131 203 123 16 20

W 174 48 192 104 31 116

X 21 144 197 172 84 19 58 55 6

Y 158 13 134 15 3 99

Z 196 171 138 79 176 60 190 27 152 87

88

Grid (cell number followed by clue letter, in reading order)

Row	Cells
1	1‑N 2‑R 3‑D 4‑S 5‑U 6‑I 7‑V 8‑E
2	9‑J 10‑X 11‑Q 12‑K 13‑J 14‑Q 15‑D 16‑S 17‑H 18‑G 19‑O
3	20‑Z 21‑X 22‑A 23‑G 24‑A 25‑W 26‑B 27‑X 28‑V 29‑F
4	30‑D 31‑V 32‑N 33‑S 34‑B 35‑Y 36‑C 37‑X 38‑H 39‑Z
5	40‑U 41‑T 42‑J 43‑A 44‑H 45‑W 46‑S 47‑V 48‑J 49‑U
6	50‑B 51‑K 52‑R 53‑C 54‑J 55‑Y 56‑O 57‑L 58‑S 59‑T
7	60‑X 61‑G 62‑H 63‑V 64‑Y 65‑D 66‑N 67‑M 68‑K 69‑T
8	70‑O 71‑Z 72‑X 73‑U 74‑E 75‑N 76‑K 77‑P 78‑J
9	79‑D 80‑U 81‑Z 82‑U 83‑G 84‑V 85‑U 86‑A 87‑A
10	88‑B 89‑A 90‑Y 91‑X 92‑Z 93‑O 94‑Y 95‑W
11	96‑P 97‑M 98‑I 99‑X 100‑M 101‑H 102‑C 103‑Z 104‑S 105‑F
12	106‑N 107‑K 108‑N 109‑X 110‑K 111‑I 112‑H 113‑M 114‑G 115‑Z
13	116‑G 117‑J 118‑S 119‑N 120‑B 121‑Z 122‑I 123‑V 124‑H 125‑R
14	126‑U 127‑C 128‑Q 129‑N 130‑R 131‑D 132‑A 133‑B 134‑G
15	135‑R 136‑W 137‑F 138‑Z 139‑W 140‑G 141‑P 142‑N 143‑Y 144‑L
16	145‑C 146‑B 147‑L 148‑U 149‑N 150‑B 151‑N 152‑B 153‑R
17	154‑W 155‑H 156‑U 157‑R 158‑L 159‑B 160‑E 161‑F 162‑A 163‑V
18	164‑Z 165‑D 166‑T 167‑G 168‑P 169‑X 170‑B 171‑N 172‑T
19	173‑V 174‑D 175‑R 176‑O 177‑M 178‑Q 179‑N 180‑J 181‑N 182‑P
20	183‑J 184‑I 185‑A 186‑M 187‑E 188‑M 189‑Y 190‑L 191‑P 192‑A
21	193‑N 194‑Z 195‑K 196‑W 197‑J 198‑H 199‑X 200‑R 201‑U

CLUES / WORDS

A "What'll I do with just a ____ to tell my troubles to?" (Irving Berlin, "What'll I Do?")
24 132 192 86 43 89 162 185 22 87

B Am. poet (1850–95, "Wynken, Blynken, and Nod"; full name)
120 34 159 150 50 133 170 152 88 26 146

C River along part of England's NE border
53 127 36 145 102

D Strongly expressive
79 174 30 131 165 15 65 3

E Clan, stock, people
74 8 160 187

F Tristan Tzara's school of art, founded to mock traditional values
29 161 137 105

G Former
167 18 23 140 61 134 116 83 114

H Hallowed by lofty associations
44 124 101 112 38 62 155 198 17

I Prepare; unhesitant
184 122 98 111 6

J Attractive; of interest
78 117 9 54 197 13 48 180 42 183

K Province federated with Ethiopia, cap. Asmara
107 110 195 76 12 51 68

L Hit (a golf ball) badly
190 144 147 158 57

M "Have sat in ____ while the tempest hurled" (Housman, "Last Poems, ix")
67 100 186 177 188 113 97

N Character played by William Boyd (full name)
149 32 106 171 142 1 193 108 119 75 66 181 129 151 179

O Oust
19 93 70 56 176

P Outcast
191 96 168 141 182 77

Q Titaness; large South American bird
178 128 11 14

R Mediate
157 2 200 175 125 130 153 52 135

S Blatant pretense or deception
104 16 58 46 118 33 4

T Special aptitude
166 59 41 172 69

U "You would pluck out the heart ____," says Hamlet to Guildenstern (3 wds.)
73 80 40 201 5 126 85 82 156 49 148

V Former term for the Republic of Ireland (2 wds.)
7 31 163 173 63 47 84 123 28

W Had a shot at the bait
139 25 196 95 136 45 154

X Erumpent scenic feature of Wyoming
169 99 60 37 109 199 91 10 72 21 27

Y Upshot
94 55 143 35 90 64 189

Z Fr. astrologer (1503–66)
71 39 194 164 115 81 20 92 121 138 103

89

CLUES

A Polka-like round dance

B Me (2 wds.)

C Station, terminal

D Myself (2 wds.)

E Zoarces viviparus; burbot

F Long, trumpet-shaped drinking glass (hyph.)

G Expedite, speed

H Dolt, scatterbrain

I Automatons

J Despoil, plunder

K Nation centering in the Tigris-Euphrates basin

L Short gaiter covering the instep, worn in the late 19th and early 20th cen.

M Embellished (2 wds.)

N "Of all the trees that grow so fair, / Old ___ adorn" (2 wds.; Kipling, "Puck of Pook's Hill")

O Lock; clasp

P 1847 narrative poem by Longfellow

Q Petroleum distillate used as a solvent, fuel, etc.

R Breaking, cracking, destroying

S Authorize; give power to

T Vacancies; first performances

U Quarrel; estrangement (hyph.)

V Show disdain toward (2 wds.)

W Place; settle

X Title character of "The Merchant of Venice"

Y Of the mind

Z Indian prime minister, 1966—77

WORDS

Clue	Letters (cell numbers)
A	101 116 58 119 86 128 162 30 13 93 149
B	43 2 69 130 151 171 136 38 161 177
C	22 24 190 40 63
D	115 169 97 23 157 145 19 29 94
E	170 109 70 52 199 100 31
F	91 121 140 74 107 147 102 21 117
G	172 72 8 143 114 200
H	131 78 110 9 11 138 113
I	65 99 37 133 50 201
J	106 25 195 135 5 180
K	89 134 34 125
L	32 108 59 39 153 80 16 67 175 62 156
M	68 76 66 118 163 137 104 126 105
N	179 167 160 71 87 35 75 92 146
O	83 173 186 132 158 48 85 1 36
P	152 84 12 4 168 184 33 47 73 127
Q	41 123 98 14 197 18 27
R	17 164 112 60 155 54 185 191 176 26
S	3 192 46 122 188 53
T	154 95 141 150 189 79 45 51
U	187 44 6 42 61 159 183 82 20 57
V	49 181 198 148 120 142 165
W	88 129 55 196 178 15
X	77 174 90 194 103 64 166
Y	124 96 144 10 7 111
Z	139 182 193 81 56 28

Diagram (cell number with its clue letter)

1 O	2 B	3 S	4 P	5 J	6 U					
7 Y	8 G	9 H	10 Y	11 H	12 P	13 A	14 Q	15 W	16 L	
17 R	18 Q	19 D	20 U	21 F	22 C	23 D	24 C	25 J	26 R	
27 Q	28 Z	29 D	30 A	31 E	32 L	33 P	34 K	35 N	36 O	
37 I	38 B	39 L	40 C	41 Q	42 U	43 B	44 U	45 T	46 S	
47 P	48 O	49 V	50 I	51 T	52 E	53 S	54 R	55 W	56 Z	
57 U	58 A	59 L	60 R	61 U	62 L	63 C	64 X	65 I	66 M	
67 L	68 M	69 B	70 E	71 N	72 G	73 P	74 F	75 N		
76 M	77 X	78 H	79 T	80 L	81 Z	82 U	83 O	84 P	85 O	
86 A	87 N	88 W	89 K	90 X	91 F	92 N	93 A	94 D	95 T	
96 Y	97 D	98 Q	99 I	100 E	101 A	102 F	103 X	104 M	105 M	
106 J	107 F	108 L	109 E	110 H	111 Y	112 R	113 H	114 G	115 D	116 A
117 F	118 M	119 A	120 V	121 F	122 S	123 Q	124 Y	125 K		
126 M	127 P	128 A	129 W	130 B	131 H	132 O	133 I	134 K	135 J	
136 B	137 M	138 H	139 Z	140 F	141 T	142 V	143 G	144 Y	145 D	
146 N	147 F	148 V	149 A	150 T	151 B	152 P	153 L	154 T		
155 R	156 L	157 D	158 O	159 U	160 N	161 B	162 A	163 M	164 R	
165 V	166 X	167 N	168 P	169 D	170 E	171 B	172 G	173 O	174 X	
175 L	176 R	177 B	178 W	179 N	180 J	181 V	182 Z	183 U	184 P	
185 R	186 O	187 U	188 S	189 T	190 C	191 R	192 S	193 Z	194 X	
195 J	196 W	197 Q	198 V	199 E	200 G	201 I				

90

Grid

Cell (number · clue letter)
1 I · 2 R · 3 M · 4 N · 5 B · 6 A · 7 W
8 I · 9 E · 10 M · 11 H · 12 C · 13 B · 14 Y · 15 G · 16 E · 17 U
18 T · 19 U · 20 P · 21 A · 22 Y · 23 K · 24 W · 25 M · 26 I
27 E · 28 Z · 29 T · 30 O · 31 L · 32 B · 33 F · 34 A · 35 H
36 Q · 37 I · 38 C · 39 W · 40 U · 41 L · 42 E · 43 S · 44 W · 45 Q · 46 U
47 O · 48 E · 49 B · 50 H · 51 S · 52 I · 53 E · 54 O · 55 B · 56 N
57 C · 58 D · 59 M · 60 R · 61 U · 62 P · 63 L · 64 P · 65 J
66 C · 67 A · 68 R · 69 S · 70 B · 71 W · 72 A · 73 B · 74 C · 75 Z
76 V · 77 P · 78 C · 79 E · 80 A · 81 L · 82 H · 83 C · 84 Q
85 D · 86 X · 87 W · 88 W · 89 N · 90 E · 91 Q · 92 G · 93 B
94 J · 95 C · 96 D · 97 Z · 98 X · 99 V · 100 H · 101 G · 102 W
103 J · 104 Y · 105 A · 106 N · 107 B · 108 L · 109 I · 110 F · 111 A · 112 X · 113 Y
114 B · 115 D · 116 E · 117 Q · 118 A · 119 L · 120 I · 121 N · 122 X · 123 G
124 J · 125 U · 126 L · 127 B · 128 S · 129 N · 130 X · 131 M · 132 D · 133 F
134 E · 135 Z · 136 U · 137 P · 138 L · 139 K · 140 R · 141 D · 142 C · 143 B
144 Q · 145 X · 146 Z · 147 G · 148 T · 149 L · 150 K · 151 B · 152 F · 153 Z
154 A · 155 L · 156 I · 157 N · 158 Q · 159 I · 160 D · 161 H · 162 E · 163 R
164 M · 165 X · 166 J · 167 W · 168 U · 169 M · 170 G · 171 O · 172 X · 173 K
174 F · 175 M · 176 F · 177 Z · 178 Y · 179 R · 180 X · 181 M · 182 K
183 X · 184 C · 185 Z · 186 M · 187 W · 188 X · 189 T · 190 K · 191 O
192 S · 193 K · 194 U · 195 T · 196 J · 197 X · 198 H · 199 W · 200 V · 201 E
202 V · 203 I · 204 O · 205 U · 206 Y · 207 R

CLUES

A Terribly evil deeds 6 72 111 67 105 118 21 34 80 154

B Unruly, resisting 114 127 5 151 70 32 143 13 93 73 107 49

C Injurious, evil, ill-disposed 83 57 38 12 142 66 184 95 74 78

D Turk 141 96 85 132 160 115 58

E State in N India (2 wds.) 53 162 27 42 16 116 201 90 134 9 48 79

F Dissolute, jaunty 133 110 33 152 174 176

G Audacious, bold 123 101 92 15 170 147

H Ease, alleviate 11 82 198 50 100 161 35

I "Honored among wagons I was prince of the ——" (2 wds.; Thomas, "Fern Hill") 203 109 52 8 159 1 37 120 156 26

J Light vehicle on runners 103 65 166 196 94 124

K Attempt to persuade by using flattery 139 23 193 173 150 182 190

L Medieval script, a standard for fine penmanship; subtlety, craftiness (2 wds.) 55 81 31 138 41 155 149 126 63 119 108

M Eng. essayist, novelist, and poet (1874–1936; "Ballad of the White Horse") 186 131 3 59 10 169 164 175 25 181

N Vociferated 4 121 106 129 56 89 157

O Eldest son of Jacob and Leah (Gen. 29, 30) 54 47 204 30 191 171

P Mournful poem, song for the dead 62 137 20 64 77

Q Secured, confirmed 158 45 144 36 117 84 91

R Timber wolf, western U.S. 179 207 2 68 60 163 140

S Sporting venue for strikes, etc. 128 43 192 51 69

T Warm-water marine fish, family Centropomidae 18 29 189 148 195

U Covering closely or thickly 19 46 194 125 168 136 61 17 40 205

V Son of Abraham and Hagar; outcast 202 200 76 99

W Pirates 199 7 187 102 24 39 71 44 87 88 167

X Between the devil and the deep blue sea (4 wds.) 122 197 112 130 165 145 86 188 180 183 172 98

Y Racing-shell crews 104 22 113 206 14 178

Z Reject; veto 75 177 97 185 146 153 28 135

WORDS

91

CLUES

A Solves, as a problem (2 wds.) 48 45 93 192 120 14 136 35

B Tireless, persevering 98 170 213 138 125 195 89 186 109 26 142 209 71

C "Din! Din! Din! / You ___ o' brick-dust, Gunga Din!" (2 wds.; Kipling) . . 113 86 177 201 119 66 31 154 215 81 92

D "Din! Din! Din! / You ___ Gunga Din!" (hyph.; Kipling) 64 12 74 182 165 34 10 24 134 108 184 25 123 151 126 90 80 216

E Take, as food, into the body 41 135 28 91 18 222

F Fix firmly 30 11 191 103 20 179

G Sass, talk back (2 wds.) 79 99 221 87 127 130 19 204

H Snappy retorts 75 50 100 67 84 46 143

I Free of spot or stain, irreproachable 5 107 129 39 181 174 139 69 167 128

J Deprives of physical sensation 196 29 133 44 105

K Put away, packed 188 175 16 164 208 185

L Trembles 223 7 96 152 63 219 131

M Am. Unitarian clergyman (1794–1865) 153 62 52 83 162 189 132

N Decomposing, putrid 163 54 168 149 1 47

O Unites, fuses 85 43 115 72 159

P Tottering, unsteady; firm, steadfast 53 203 199 15 140

Q Deepest, superlatively profound 116 2 122 94 111 56 157 78 23

R Golfers' equipment 60 169 218 198

S "Carousel" hit (4 wds.) 166 55 61 76 101 161 178 148 193 37 21

T Type of cured salmon, or lox 27 114 17 9

U Old French dance in moderately quick quadruple meter 70 183 42 206 117 51 32

V What George Washington Cable taught Mark Twain to "abhor and detest" (3 wds.; letter to William Dean Howells) 40 220 147 6 176 13 33 171 187 88 197 211 57

W Across, in excess of 124 146 110 22

X Short chest of drawers on short legs 4 82 8 155 121 112

Y Manner of speaking or reading in public 144 194 173 95 68 207 106 156 212

Z "Bigotry may be roughly defined as the ___ who have no opinions" (3 wds.; Chesterton, "Heretics") 200 58 3 77 150 141 102 205 160 36

Z₁ Some indoor antennas (2 wds.) 49 73 214 172 104 137 202 190 145 210

Z₂ Japanese port 38 65 217 118 97 59 158 180

WORDS

Cell	Cell	Cell	Cell	Cell	Cell	Cell	Cell	Cell	Cell	Cell
1 N	2 Q	3 Z	4 X	5 I	6 V	7 L	8 X	9 T	10 D	11 F
12 D	13 V	14 A	15 P	16 K	17 T	18 E	19 G	20 F	21 F	22 W
23 Q	24 D	25 D	26 B	27 B	28 E	29 J	30 F	31 C	32 U	33 V
34 D	35 A	36 Z	37 S	38 Z₂	39 I	40 V	41 E	42 U	43 O	44 J
45 A	46 H	47 N	48 A	49 Z₁	50 H	51 U	52 M	53 P	54 N	55 S
56 Q	57 V	58 Z	59 Z₂	60 R	61 S	62 M	63 L	64 D	65 Z₂	66 C
67 H	68 Y	69 I	70 U	71 B	72 O	73 Z₁	74 D	75 H	76 S	77 Z
78 Q	79 G	80 D	81 C	82 X	83 M	84 H	85 O	86 C	87 G	88 V
89 B	90 D	91 E	92 C	93 A	94 Q	95 Y	96 L	97 Z₂	98 B	99 G
100 H	101 S	102 Z	103 F	104 Z₁	105 J	106 Y	107 I	108 D	109 B	110 W
111 Q	112 X	113 C	114 T	115 O	116 Q	117 U	118 Z₂	119 C	120 A	121 X
122 Q	123 D	124 W	125 B	126 D	127 G	128 I	129 I	130 G	131 L	132 M
133 J	134 D	135 E	136 A	137 Z₁	138 B	139 I	140 P	141 Z	142 B	143 H
144 Y	145 Z₁	146 W	147 V	148 S	149 N	150 Z	151 D	152 L	153 M	154 C
155 X	156 Y	157 Q	158 Z₂	159 O	160 Z	161 S	162 M	163 N	164 K	165 D
166 S	167 I	168 N	169 R	170 B	171 V	172 Z₁	173 Y	174 I	175 K	176 V
177 C	178 S	179 F	180 Z₂	181 I	182 D	183 U	184 D	185 K	186 B	187 V
188 K	189 M	190 Z₁	191 F	192 A	193 S	194 Y	195 B	196 J	197 V	198 R
199 P	200 Z	201 C	202 Z₁	203 P	204 G	205 Z	206 U	207 Y	208 K	209 B
210 Z₁	211 V	212 Y	213 B	214 Z₁	215 C	216 D	217 Z₂	218 R	219 L	220 V
221 G	222 E	223 L								

CLUES

A. Great Am. jazz pianist (1885–1941), originally named Ferdinand Joseph La Menthe (3 wds.)
B. Existing power structure
C. Sprang back; recovered, as from illness
D. Stems used for wickerwork
E. Type of pudding baked under roasting meat
F. "Plucked his gown, to ___ good man's smile" (Goldsmith, "The Deserted Village"; 2 wds.)
G. Writing in praise of a deceased person
H. Greek island, legendary home of Ulysses
I. Impossible; out of the question (2 wds.)
J. Inane
K. Eulogist
L. Big guy of Steinbeck's "Of Mice and Men"
M. "A woman is a ___ gods" ("Antony and Cleopatra"; 3 wds.)
N. Slightly marred, as goods exposed and handled
O. Thing
P. One who deceives under an assumed character
Q. Naiad, e.g.
R. Dubious, shady, disreputable
S. Elementary math
T. Spruce, trim
U. Street urchin
V. Plant of the ginseng family, cultivated for its edible shoots
W. Reaches, realizes
X. Ger. poet-playwright-philosopher (1749–1832)
Y. Gingrich's orb, perhaps (3 wds.)

WORDS

Clue	Numbers
A	44 43 58 93 185 125 134 106 146 82 87 21 100 4 96
B	98 11 37 124 167 17 55 36 151 133 60 155 6
C	61 165 46 156 26 79 99 83 86
D	76 176 107 59 117 116
E	95 115 65 154 178 7 35 19 160
F	42 48 84 27 112 174 180 97
G	152 15 63 158 163 111 109
H	67 182 159 131 56 92
I	85 14 88 72 34
J	5 10 1 71 194 122 175
K	136 195 128 41 190 78 57 172 141
L	130 51 40 2 191 184
M	32 147 104 77 140 171 113 177 162 28
N	73 142 189 13 179 31 132 170
O	24 192 119 168 12 75
P	127 9 20 69 114 47 80 145
Q	103 161 62 70 183
R	94 22 129 188 53 149
S	166 90 102 30 66 135 143 150 81 52
T	137 18 74 126 181
U	193 105 50 118 91 186 29 68 121 123 173
V	16 25 139
W	33 23 38 144 8 164 89 64
X	169 101 49 108 120 39
Y	187 153 3 45 148 54 110 157 138

Diagram (cell number : clue letter)

1 J	2 L	3 Y	4 A	5 J	6 B	7 B	8 W	9 P		
10 J	11 B	12 O	13 N	14 I	15 G	16 V	17 B	18 T	19 E	
20 P	21 A	22 R	23 W	24 O	25 V	26 C	27 F	28 M	29 U	30 S
31 N	32 M	33 W	34 I	35 E	36 B	37 B	38 W	39 X		
40 L	41 K	42 F	43 A	44 A	45 Y	46 C	47 P	48 F	49 X	
50 U	51 L	52 S	53 R	54 Y	55 B	56 H	57 K	58 A	59 D	
60 B	61 C	62 Q	63 G	64 W	65 E	66 S	67 H	68 U	69 P	
70 Q	71 J	72 I	73 N	74 T	75 O	76 D	77 M	78 K	79 C	80 P
81 S	82 A	83 C	84 F	85 I	86 C	87 A	88 I			
89 W	90 S	91 U	92 H	93 A	94 R	95 E	96 A	97 F	98 B	
99 C	100 A	101 X	102 S	103 Q	104 M	105 U	106 A	107 D		
108 X	109 G	110 Y	111 G	112 F	113 M	114 P	115 E	116 D	117 D	
118 U	119 O	120 X	121 U	122 J	123 U	124 B	125 A	126 T	127 P	
128 K	129 R	130 L	131 H	132 N	133 B	134 A	135 S	136 K	137 T	138 Y
139 V	140 M	141 K	142 N	143 S	144 W	145 P	146 A	147 M		
148 Y	149 R	150 S	151 B	152 G	153 Y	154 E	155 B	156 C	157 Y	
158 G	159 H	160 E	161 Q	162 M	163 G	164 W	165 C	166 S		
167 B	168 O	169 X	170 N	171 M	172 K	173 U	174 F	175 J		
176 D	177 M	178 E	179 N	180 F	181 T	182 H	183 Q	184 L	185 A	
186 U	187 Y	188 R	189 N	190 K	191 L	192 O	193 U	194 J	195 K	

93

CLUES

A Moral purity

B Sign

C Cruel

D "Busy ___, unruly sun" (2 wds.; Donne, "The Sun Rising")

E Small round beetle

F Holler (2 wds.)

G What there was in Mudville at game's end (2 wds.)

H Kept at a distance (2 wds.)

I Set of moral principles

J Am. novelist (1879–1951, "Private Life of Helen of Troy")

K Wander away (2 wds.)

L Dinghy or skiff, perhaps

M Adopt, support

N With all water removed (of a chemical compound)

O Popular Canadian writer (1921–; "A Whale for the Killing," "My Father's Son")

P "___ my Master went, / Clean, forspent, forspent" (3 wds.; Lanier, "Ballad of Trees and the Master")

Q Desert in Saudi Arabia

R Castrated cat

S Large wading bird, family Threskiornithidae

T Bottom

U Crosswise

V Gay, jolly

W Great circle

X Fame

Y Slowly, in increments (3 wds.)

Z Became fond of (2 wds.)

Z₁ Exculpates

WORDS

A: 8 48 72 160 78 132 54 112

B: 53 101 46 140 134 19 174 119 167

C: 157 129 12 114 181 63 138 97

D: 191 120 137 3 9 150 169

E: 83 13 71 124 33 185 130

F: 7 115 15 187 180 35 123

G: 136 61 29 45 107

H: 118 102 152 178 172 90 103 82

I: 165 113 74 143 44 16

J: 173 186 31 11 109 144 75

K: 153 56 65 108 142 2 17 126

L: 25 80 52 37 184 135 93

M: 170 23 162 34 147 176 55

N: 92 133 156 154 42 36 168 190 69

O: 62 158 91 77 111

P: 104 5 64 38 155 131 117 166 100 18 51 43

Q: 50 4 110 141 182

R: 145 79 99

S: 22 151 171 60

T: 39 40 28 84 76

U: 98 148 164 159 49 95 89

V: 66 14 88 177 139 105 161 127

W: 94 189 86 128 73 81 116

X: 192 121 41 70 27 1

Y: 175 149 24 179 146 183 96 58 6 21

Z: 47 87 32 20 26 122 67 59 163 125

Z₁: 57 10 85 30 188 106 68

Grid

1	2	3	4	5	6	7	8	9	10
1 V	2 R	3 J	4 B	5 W	6 Q	7 G	8 Y	9 S	10 F
11 R	12 Z₁	13 C	14 G	15 Q	16 Y	17 Z₁	18 O	19 H	20 R
21 Z	22 Y	23 K	24 N	25 S	26 B	27 D	28 M	29 F	30 Z
31 J	32 Z₁	33 U	34 O	35 I	36 F	37 X	38 G	39 D	40 F
41 K	42 W	43 T	44 I	45 P	46 Z₁	47 F	48 J	49 H	50 M
51 G	52 Z	53 Y	54 R	55 B	56 H	57 Z	58 L	59 N	60 E
61 T	62 M	63 Q	64 L	65 E	66 J	67 H	68 O	69 W	70 G
71 K	72 I	73 N	74 O	75 P	76 M	77 C	78 O	79 F	80 W
81 K	82 Z	83 Y	84 B	85 C	86 W	87 Z₁	88 N	89 E	90 T
91 H	92 C	93 N	94 A	95 U	96 Q	97 O	98 R	99 T	100 Y
101 P	102 K	103 H	104 A	105 Z₁	106 C	107 F	108 K	109 Q	110 A
111 U	112 F	113 I	114 R	115 H	116 O	117 Z₁	118 M	119 X	120 P
121 B	122 Y	123 W	124 I	125 H	126 N	127 M	128 V	129 H	130 C
131 R	132 D	133 F	134 A	135 V	136 L	137 Z₁	138 J	139 N	140 W
141 C	142 U	143 Z₁	144 S	145 Q	146 M	147 W	148 F	149 R	150 Z₁
151 T	152 E	153 A	154 I	155 M	156 X	157 R	158 J	159 C	160 T
161 A	162 S	163 H	164 Z₁	165 X	166 W	167 V	168 P	169 U	170 I
171 J	172 B	173 F	174 R	175 P	176 Z	177 I	178 O	179 Q	180 G
181 F	182 M	183 T	184 O	185 P	186 L	187 S	188 B	189 X	190 Q
191 L	192 K	193 E	194 M	195 A	196 F	197 N	198 W	199 G	200 U
201 B	202 I	203 M	204 Y	205 V	206 J	207 L	208 Y	209 P	210 Y
211 B	212 I	213 N	214 X	215 U	216 N	217 J	218 E	219 V	220 Q
221 U									

CLUES

A "He has gone to the demnition ___" (Dickens, "Nicholas Nickleby") · 110 195 161 94 104 153 134

B Not real, illusory · 172 201 4 188 26 121 211 84 55

C Unfortunate · 77 130 85 13 106 159 141 92

D Conducted · 132 27 39

E Crowded noisily · 218 152 193 65 60 89

F Terrific, great, super, fantastic (4 wds.) · 148 79 196 143 112 10 40 133 47 181 107 36 173 29

G Cap. of Armenia · 180 38 199 14 70 51 7

H Genus of often very tall trees of the myrtle family · 115 56 49 91 67 103 129 163 19 125

I Building for locomotive repair; sometimes K.O. punch · 35 202 170 212 72 154 113 124 177 44

J Trim, orderly · 171 138 48 3 206 31 217 158 66

K Am. actress Wanda ("Prince of Foxes," "The Highwayman") · 81 71 108 102 23 41 192

L Finger-shaped creampuff · 136 58 64 207 186 191

M "Ne'er a villain dwelling in all Denmark, / But he's an ___," says Hamlet (2 wds.) · 182 194 118 146 127 76 50 28 62 203 155

N Conn. town, birthplace of Ethan Allen, Henry Ward Beecher, and Harriet Beecher Stowe · 88 126 73 216 197 24 139 93 59 213

O Conspiring (2 wds.) · 68 116 184 78 74 34 18 97 178

P Part of a fastener, sometimes used ornamentally · 175 120 168 45 185 101 75 209

Q Old man, sage · 109 220 190 145 179 6 96 63 15

R Walking · 11 54 131 149 174 98 20 157 114 2

S Am. novelist (1870–1902, "McTeague") · 187 117 25 144 162 9

T Dumps, discards · 160 99 183 61 151 90 43

U "Between the motion / And the act / Falls ___" (2 wds.; Eliot, "The Hollow Men") · 142 164 111 200 95 221 215 169 33

V Anc. Gr. god of roads, commerce, and theft · 135 219 167 1 205 128

W Common loon · 198 42 147 69 5 80 123 86 140 166

X Apes, simulates · 119 37 189 214 156 165

Y Instilled, taught persistently and earnestly · 204 208 122 22 100 210 16 8 83 53

Z Eng. philosopher and mathematician (1642–1727) · 57 176 30 82 21 52

Z₁ Indecisive, unsettled · ...

WORDS

95

Puzzle Grid

Each cell is shown below as **number + clue-letter**.

1 E	2 D	3 L	4 B	5 C	6 A	7 Z	8 W	9 Q	10 M	
11 B	12 Q	13 C	14 A	15 Z	16 U	17 S	18 P	19 M	20 K	21 E
22 I	23 M	24 W	25 Q	26 E	27 D	28 G	29 O	30 C		
31 R	32 A	33 E	34 T	35 O	36 M	37 L	38 E	39 F	40 I	
41 D	42 H	43 M	44 R	45 Y	46 U	47 X	48 Q	49 G		
50 W	51 J	52 A	53 L	54 O	55 Y	56 J	57 B	58 U	59 A	
60 L	61 P	62 U	63 C	64 N	65 G	66 A	67 Z	68 G		
69 V	70 J	71 Q	72 R	73 I	74 K	75 H	76 H	77 O		
78 F	79 E	80 I	81 M	82 B	83 W	84 D	85 J	86 U	87 T	88 I
89 Z	90 G	91 O	92 K	93 W	94 V	95 A	96 M	97 P	98 T	
99 D	100 J	101 C	102 Y	103 V	104 T	105 G	106 P	107 I	108 A	
109 S	110 Y	111 X	112 P	113 T	114 G	115 D	116 H	117 H	118 F	
119 N	120 B	121 I	122 F	123 F	124 H	125 D	126 R	127 K	128 L	
129 R	130 F	131 B	132 E	133 L	134 K	135 T	136 W	137 X	138 V	
139 R	140 T	141 C	142 U	143 G	144 S	145 Z	146 X	147 Q	148 G	149 L
150 V	151 M	152 J	153 N	154 O	155 F	156 S	157 J	158 H	159 Z	
160 D	161 R	162 K	163 H	164 O	165 N	166 S	167 R	168 X	169 X	
170 N	171 M	172 O	173 R	174 T	175 H	176 A	177 P	178 F		
179 K	180 H	181 F	182 D	183 A	184 T	185 O	186 F	187 S		

CLUES

A Impromptu jazz performance (2 wds.)
B Flowing freely; changeable
C Point of time
D Discuss (2 wds.)
E Zealot, hothead
F Using a type of line (3 wds.)
G Good, honest
H Process of lessening
I Draw, lure
J Force, compel
K Promote life or zeal in
L Fundamental; thoroughgoing; extreme
M About to happen
N Intimidated
O Pledge; self-confidence
P Dolt
Q Conclusion of an activity
R Permission, approval; stipend
S Sycophant (hyph.)
T Taking an official tour for the fun of it (3 wds.)
U Angles
V Cluster, group, lot
W Native
X Comedy series that starred Valerie Harper
Y Bark of the paper mulberry
Z Break in the continuity of something

WORDS

Clue	Numbers
A	183 52 6 14 32 95 176 66 59 108
B	11 82 4 120 131 57
C	63 169 13 141 5 30 101
D	115 84 2 41 160 125 27 99 182
E	132 79 38 1 26 21 33
F	181 78 186 122 130 123 178 118 155 39
G	28 90 114 65 68 49 143 105 148
H	117 175 180 76 163 124 75 42 116 158
I	88 80 121 73 107 40 22
J	152 51 100 56 85 70
K	179 157 74 20 162 134 127 92
L	60 3 37 149 128 133 53
M	81 171 19 23 36 10 96 43 151
N	64 165 119 153 170
O	35 91 185 29 54 154 77 164 172
P	97 18 106 61 112 177
Q	71 12 9 25 147 48
R	173 161 126 72 129 44 31 139 167
S	109 187 17 166 156 144
T	104 113 140 98 184 174 34 135 87
U	58 142 16 62 46 86
V	103 138 150 94 69
W	93 83 24 8 50 136
X	47 111 146 137 168
Y	110 102 45 55
Z	145 15 7 89 159 67

96

CLUES

A. Natural habitat, sphere of activity

B. "Ship me somewhere east of —— is like the worst" (4 wds.; Kipling, "Mandalay")

C. Appearing at regular intervals

D. "A whoreson Achitophel! A rascally ——," (hyph. & wd.; "Henry IV, Part 2")

E. On both sides of, in a dominant position within

F. State or period of being a beginner

G. Manner; position; posture

H. "If this be magic, let it be an art / —— as eating," says King Leontes ("The Winter's Tale")

I. Doubtful issue, something debatable (2 wds.)

J. Anne Nichols's 1922 play that had 2,237 performances in New York (3 wds.)

K. Anonymity, obscurity; worthless

L. With cunning, ingenuity, cleverness, etc.

M. Contribute, participate (2 wds.)

N. "What! is Brutus sick, / And will he steal out ——" (4 wds., "Julius Caesar")

O. Be partial to; prefer

P. Type of dash, usually part of a conditioning program to develop endurance (2 wds.)

Q. 1818 sonnet by Shelley, ironic commentary on a "King of Kings"

R. Licentious, dissolute man

S. On or toward the lee side

T. Hip, in the groove, with it

U. "They told me I was every thing; 'tis a lie, I am not ——" (hyph.; "King Lear")

V. Facing, in the direction of

W. Forgiveness

X. Having a discolored, bluish appearance; enraged, furiously angry

Y. Public discussion or disclosure

Z. Lout, yokel; in "Gulliver's Travels," one of a race of brutes subject to the Houyhnhnms

WORDS

Clue	Numbers
A	79 183 10 58 116 129 19
B	122 53 153 156 193 166 143 173 132 92 161 111 3 105 223 47
C	171 150 191 89 137 46 38 71
D	23 17 30 113 81 218 62 147 43 196 7 127 186 57 211 215
E	194 200 207 65 70 120 83
F	110 204 184 169 27 134 175 114 121
G	118 24 213 185 141 222 11 146
H	154 72 165 216 44 149
I	202 190 198 220 54 208 128 103 160
J	162 139 59 167 41 217 119 192 56 85 159 182 32 91
K	51 174 12 115 203 67 212
L	178 108 123 140 63 158 73 37
M	176 25 66 221 86 101
N	48 197 117 157 219 29 177 33 74 180 21 20 1 64 42 8 84
O	90 26 80 93 179
P	124 61 136 77 31 148 94 50 133 6
Q	100 36 75 131 151 163 106 210 55 87
R	4 40 135 95 214 206 88 34
S	104 5 144 14 39 99 168 18
T	16 49 97 205 187 13 45 209
U	22 130 15 76 172 152 201 112 142
V	82 125 138 102 199 52
W	145 170 9 188 109 60
X	96 164 181 28 78
Y	155 195 126 107 69 98
Z	2 35 224 68 189

Diagram

1 N	2 Z	3 B	4 R	5 S	6 P	7 D	8 N	9 W		
10 A	11 G	12 K	13 T	14 S	15 U	16 T	17 D	18 S		
19 A	20 N	21 N	22 U	23 D	24 G	25 M	26 O	27 F		
28 X	29 N	30 D	31 P	32 J	33 N	34 R	35 Z	36 Q		
37 L	38 C	39 S	40 R	41 J	42 N	43 D	44 H	45 T		
46 C	47 B	48 N	49 T	50 P	51 K	52 V	53 B	54 I		
55 Q	56 J	57 D	58 A	59 J	60 W	61 P	62 D	63 L		
64 N	65 E	66 M	67 K	68 Z	69 Y	70 E	71 C	72 H	73 L	74 N
75 Q	76 U	77 P	78 X	79 A	80 O	81 D	82 V	83 E	84 N	
85 J	86 M	87 Q	88 R	89 C	90 O	91 J	92 B	93 O		
94 P	95 R	96 X	97 T	98 Y	99 S	100 Q	101 M	102 V	103 I	
104 S	105 B	106 Q	107 Y	108 L	109 W	110 F	111 B			
112 U	113 D	114 F	115 K	116 A	117 N	118 G	119 J	120 E	121 F	
122 B	123 L	124 P	125 V	126 Y	127 D	128 I	129 A	130 U	131 Q	
132 B	133 P	134 F	135 R	136 P	137 C	138 V	139 J	140 L		
141 G	142 U	143 B	144 S	145 W	146 G	147 D	148 P	149 H	150 C	
151 Q	152 U	153 B	154 H	155 Y	156 B	157 N	158 L	159 J		
160 I	161 B	162 J	163 Q	164 X	165 H	166 B	167 J	168 S		
169 F	170 W	171 C	172 U	173 B	174 K	175 F	176 M	177 N	178 L	
179 O	180 N	181 X	182 J	183 A	184 F	185 G	186 D	187 T	188 W	
189 Z	190 I	191 C	192 J	193 B	194 E	195 Y	196 D	197 N		
198 I	199 V	200 E	201 U	202 I	203 K	204 F	205 T	206 R	207 E	
208 I	209 T	210 Q	211 D	212 K	213 G	214 R	215 D	216 H		
217 J	218 D	219 N	220 I	221 M	222 G	223 B	224 Z			

97

CLUES / WORDS

A Mysterious character in the Watergate affair (2 wds.) — 37 136 86 106 118 27 93 98 94 73

B Vivacity — 190 48 56 135 16 74 130 122 164

C Relieve by giving expression to something — 125 83 19 150

D Imprudent, unwise — 111 41 54 168 71 143 154 12 186 35 26

E Token, device, badge — 133 31 159 69 18 36

F Slender, flexible rod — 49 40 183 88 178 46

G Scratch, tear; make fumbling motions — 189 112 39 89

H One of Isaac and Rebekah's twin sons (Gen. 25:21–25) — 87 116 52 55

I Former chief whaling port of Mass. (2 wds.) — 64 145 123 66 78 193 43 179 169 96

J Checks — 146 158 61 139

K "Dingbat" of "All in the Family" — 177 144 63 185 8

L Infernal; lower — 141 175 77 155 9 127

M Equivocal — 75 152 176 188 65 161 5 50 21

N Chess castles — 34 42 32 82 84

O Affectedly erudite borrowing from Greek, e.g. (2 wds.) — 68 171 104 147 163 38 95 4 119 30 180

P Short sock — 22 174 14 97 105 138

Q Final, totally conclusive — 137 25 191

R Rejected; left behind (2 wds.) — 117 129 99 2 17 29 23 132

S Town in NE Illinois (2 wds.) — 67 107 100 6 160 134 115 182 128

T Horizontal band across the middle of an escutcheon — 28 92 101 60

U Flipped — 91 151 142 79 58 172

V Fireside; home — 121 181 90 11 15 166

W Symbol constructed for the exposition of 1889 in Paris (2 wds.) — 47 20 44 33 165 114 162 173 85 148 24

X Lack of appetite, inability to eat — 120 13 167 53 109 187 59 170

Y Rivals a person cannot best — 157 126 110 70 3 62 131

Z "Just hint a fault, and hesitate ___" (Pope, "Epistle to Dr. Arbuthnot") — 10 156 76 80 72 113 192

Z₁ Perplexing, mysterious — 124 184 103 51 1 153 7 81 57

Z₂ Kitchen refuse given to pigs, hogwash — 149 45 140 108 102

GRID

Each square is shown as **number·clue-letter**.

Row	Cells
1	1·Z1 2·R 3·Y 4·O 5·M 6·S 7·Z1 8·K
2	9·L 10·Z 11·V 12·D 13·X 14·P 15·V 16·B 17·R 18·E
3	19·C 20·W 21·M 22·P 23·R 24·W 25·Q 26·D 27·A
4	28·T 29·R 30·O 31·E 32·N 33·W 34·N 35·D 36·E
5	37·A 38·O 39·G 40·F 41·D 42·N 43·I 44·W 45·Z2
6	46·F 47·W 48·B 49·F 50·M 51·Z1 52·H 53·X 54·D 55·H
7	56·B 57·Z1 58·U 59·X 60·T 61·J 62·Y 63·K 64·I 65·M
8	66·I 67·S 68·O 69·E 70·X 71·D 72·Z 73·A 74·B
9	75·M 76·Z 77·L 78·I 79·U 80·Z 81·Z1 82·N 83·C 84·N
10	85·W 86·A 87·H 88·F 89·G 90·V 91·U 92·T 93·A 94·A
11	95·O 96·I 97·P 98·A 99·R 100·S 101·T 102·Z2 103·Z1 104·O
12	105·P 106·A 107·S 108·Z2 109·X 110·Y 111·D 112·G 113·Z 114·W
13	115·S 116·H 117·R 118·A 119·O 120·X 121·V 122·B 123·I 124·Z1
14	125·C 126·Y 127·L 128·S 129·R 130·B 131·Y 132·R 133·E 134·S
15	135·B 136·A 137·Q 138·P 139·J 140·Z2 141·L 142·U 143·D 144·K 145·I
16	146·J 147·O 148·W 149·Z2 150·C 151·U 152·M 153·Z1 154·D 155·L
17	156·Z 157·Y 158·J 159·E 160·S 161·M 162·W 163·O 164·B
18	165·I 166·V 167·X 168·D 169·I 170·X 171·O 172·U 173·W
19	174·P 175·L 176·M 177·K 178·F 179·I 180·O 181·V 182·S 183·F
20	184·Z1 185·K 186·D 187·X 188·M 189·G 190·B 191·Q 192·Z 193·I

98

CLUES / WORDS

	Clue	Cell numbers
A	Lack of personal identification	35 33 52 97 19 99 202 217 45
B	Young man in Shaw's "Candida"	147 57 101 26 197 176 137 13 50 6
C	All right, fair enough, yep (hyph.)	24 166 200 95 30 191 82 113 120
D	Under the guardianship of another (2 wds.)	178 60 110 195 14 138 136
E	Posers	198 79 9 76 177 125 218
F	Choleric; lustful	56 148 172 143 75 212 170 155 7 123
G	One who is short-tempered	151 23 196 41 150 165 74
H	Feign; mask; hide	146 83 16 184 86 175 43 153 130
I	Squire, guardian of Fielding's Tom Jones	134 85 72 122 208 31 164 67 160
J	Cap. of Meurthe-et-Moselle, France	4 144 2 216 10
K	Wastes away	149 186 207 145 190 84 5 117
L	Pies, cakes, sherbets, etc.	98 115 80 46 89 124 47 156
M	Building traditionally considered the northernmost point of Britain (hyph.)	214 96 27 36 61 183 58 11 158 88 116
N	Abashes, disconcerts	167 157 118 171 107 15 185 92 81 63 73
O	Conveying a hint, esp. of something improper	187 8 180 69 194 168 59 128 112 42
P	Rigidity	206 126 140 39 12 189 68 105 20
Q	Eng. pianist-composer, and Rocket Man (full name)	102 25 192 119 114 181 3 78 62
R	Began (2 wds.)	142 215 91 48 133 154
S	Appropriate, proper	93 174 65 111 66 40 28 209 139
T	Mad, violently intense	71 210 213 162 103
U	Wild, the greatest, incredibly cool	55 127 17 173 44 203 94
V	Slender, carnivorous, weasel-like mammal of Egypt	182 21 193 179 204 108 161 38 159
W	Am. cartoonist, illustrator (1840–1902)	205 131 135 51
X	Overly romantic or idealistic (hyph.)	132 106 188 18 141 53 32 37 100 201
Y	Basics	199 163 121 104 90 77 169 152 29 54
Z	Lake of Mexico, famed for floating gardens	87 49 109 22 70 34 1 211 129 64

Grid (cell number–clue letter, by row)

Row											
1	1 Z	2 J	3 Q	4 J	5 K	6 B	7 F	8 O	9 E	10 J	
2	11 M	12 P	13 B	14 D	15 N	16 H	17 U	18 X	19 A		
3	20 P	21 V	22 Z	23 G	24 C	25 Q	26 B	27 M	28 S	29 Y	30 C
4	31 I	32 X	33 A	34 Z	35 A	36 M	37 X	38 V	39 P		
5	40 S	41 G	42 O	43 H	44 U	45 A	46 L	47 L	48 R	49 Z	
6	50 B	51 W	52 A	53 X	54 Y	55 U	56 F	57 B	58 M	59 O	
7	60 D	61 M	62 Q	63 N	64 Z	65 S	66 S	67 I	68 P		
8	69 O	70 Z	71 T	72 I	73 N	74 G	75 F	76 E	77 Y		
9	78 Q	79 E	80 L	81 N	82 C	83 H	84 K	85 I	86 H	87 Z	
10	88 M	89 L	90 Y	91 R	92 N	93 S	94 U	95 C	96 M	97 A	98 L
11	99 A	100 X	101 B	102 Q	103 T	104 Y	105 P	106 X	107 N	108 V	
12	109 Z	110 D	111 S	112 O	113 C	114 Q	115 L	116 M	117 K	118 N	119 Q
13	120 C	121 Y	122 I	123 F	124 L	125 E	126 P	127 U	128 O	129 Z	
14	130 H	131 W	132 X	133 R	134 I	135 W	136 D	137 B	138 D		
15	139 S	140 P	141 X	142 R	143 F	144 J	145 K	146 H	147 B		
16	148 F	149 K	150 G	151 G	152 Y	153 H	154 R	155 F	156 L		
17	157 N	158 M	159 V	160 I	161 V	162 T	163 Y	164 I	165 G	166 C	167 N
18	168 O	169 Y	170 F	171 N	172 F	173 U	174 S	175 H	176 B	177 E	
19	178 D	179 V	180 O	181 Q	182 V	183 M	184 H	185 N	186 K	187 O	
20	188 X	189 P	190 K	191 C	192 Q	193 V	194 O	195 D	196 G	197 C	
21	198 E	199 Y	200 C	201 X	202 A	203 U	204 V	205 W	206 P	207 K	208 I
22	209 S	210 T	211 Z	212 F	213 T	214 M	215 R	216 J	217 A	218 E	

99

CLUES

A. Conventional piles in the wild — 73 101 26 147 62 129 159 170 120 167

B. Poet's Ground Zero and up (2 wds.) — 172 82 135 94 86 78 98 117 132

C. To hug could be quite difficult — 19 7 44 151 158

D. Package returned; talk of care in detail! — 162 169 68 63 67 80 141 128 92

E. Queen Gertrude stayed with the most primitive — 168 125 96 160 88 100

F. Pip sought in process of leaving (2 wds.) — 60 34 51 1 149 15 85 75 144 156 29

G. Devils laid off without due consideration (hyph.) — 150 64 56 81 173 123 108 153 165 107

H. In reverse, very softly you start biting — 131 46 5 58 20

I. Dance backwards from minuet to vague two-step — 36 113 171 84 118 103 180

J. Collection of poetry from the dearly remembered days of old — 134 115 40 28

K. Passes on after scrap with ruffians — 3 18 112 179 12 65 16

L. Island of Moonlight and Roses — 155 17 31 91 2 52

M. We French come to mind — 126 42 175 48

N. Soil spread about 500 graven images — 116 23 41 142 109

O. Mixed-up creatures mixed longer in short manuscript — 25 111 39 157 104 124 69 76

P. Peaks of a thousand escapades — 146 14 163 119 177

Q. Missing from motel, ostensibly — 57 24 139 50

R. Toper returning in Irish sulky — 93 9 152 136

S. Quartet of pinkos changed heartless times (2 wds.) — 49 95 4 61 138 13 22 53

T. Second dwarf in for a shock — 32 6 90 164 110

U. Linette is about to qualify — 21 45 99 55 66 70 30

V. Right about, if split — 114 178 143 47

W. Waited for dwelling — 130 97 174 8 83

X. Oil ship, craft destroyed; it's in the deep (2 wds.) — 54 161 71 133 38 10 87 148 145 74 121 140

Y. Unusual tint surrounding turn of a type I sense — 122 106 89 35 127 77

Z. In the open, voter lay without a new alinement — 59 166 102 43 11 154 33

Z_1. Net wage could be satisfactory for old stronghold — 27 105 72 79 137 176 37

WORDS (grid)

1 F	2 L	3 K	4 S	5 H	6 T					
7 C	8 W	9 R	10 X	11 Z	12 K	13 S	14 L	15 F	16 K	
17 L	18 K	19 K	20 H	21 H	22 S	23 N	24 Q	25 O	26 A	
27 Z_1	28 J	29 F	30 T	31 L	32 T	33 Z	34 F	35 Y	36 I	
37 Z_1	38 X	39 O	40 J	41 N	42 M	43 Z	44 C	45 U	46 H	
47 V	48 M	49 S	50 Q	51 F	52 L	53 S	54 X	55 U		
56 G	57 Q	58 H	59 Z	60 F	61 S	62 A	63 D	64 G	65 K	
66 U	67 D	68 D	69 O	70 U	71 X	72 Z_1	73 A	74 X	75 F	
76 O	77 Y	78 B	79 Z_1	80 D	81 G	82 B	83 W	84 I		
85 F	86 B	87 B	88 E	89 Y	90 T	91 L	92 D	93 R	94 B	
95 S	96 E	97 W	98 B	99 U	100 E	101 A	102 Z	103 I		
104 O	105 Z_1	106 Y	107 G	108 G	109 N	110 T	111 O	112 K	113 I	
114 V	115 J	116 N	117 B	118 I	119 P	120 A	121 X	122 Y	123 G	124 O
125 E	126 M	127 Y	128 D	129 A	130 W	131 H	132 B	133 X		
134 J	135 B	136 R	137 Z_1	138 S	139 Q	140 X	141 D	142 N	143 V	
144 F	145 X	146 P	147 A	148 X	149 F	150 G	151 C	152 R		
153 G	154 Z	155 L	156 F	157 O	158 C	159 A	160 E	161 X	162 D	163 P
164 T	165 G	166 Z	167 A	168 E	169 D	170 A	171 I	172 B	173 G	
174 W	175 M	176 Z_1	177 P	178 V	179 K	180 I				

100

CLUES

A. Ease, lessen in intensity . . . .
B. Naked (3 wds.) . . . .
C. Ridiculed, gibed at . . . .
D. Aids for infirmity . . . .
E. Most accessible . . . .
F. Cause to grow pale . . . .
G. Blister gas used in WWI . . . .
H. Pleasure out of the ordinary . . . .
I. Game of chance . . . .
J. 1843 philosophical work by Kierkegaard (hyph.) . . .
K. Sudden sharp pain in the intercostal muscles . . .
L. "When we have ___ this mortal coil" (2 wds., "Hamlet") . . .
M. Distort . . . .
N. Addictions . . . .
O. Aspiration . . . .
P. Some blues . . . .
Q. Chub, perhaps . . . .
R. Cotton fabric made waterproof . . . .
S. Obliterated (2 wds.) . . . .
T. Unpleasant, offensive . . . .
U. Embarrassed; docile, meek . . . .
V. Weak, silly, puerile . . . .
W. Consequence, result . . . .
X. Eng. dramatist-novelist (1567–1601; "The Unfortunate Traveler") . . .
Y. "When I'm ___": Beatles song (hyph.) . . . .
Z. Strongly affected with dread, veneration, wonder, etc. . . .
Z₁. Compliant, submissive . . . .

WORDS

Clue	Numbers
A	133 40 103 192 123 184 65 28
B	114 122 166 59 109 4 26 47 200
C	156 94 208 138 83 72 194
D	79 68 5 148 27 2 210 126
E	158 12 74 39 155 121 69 89
F	147 80 95 34 62 8 33 134
G	96 53 60 125 180 107 76 132
H	63 78 87 199 162 205
I	108 84 202 188 142 207 93
J	176 48 120 16 190 11 195 23
K	41 117 73 1 49 189
L	75 91 145 46 174 56 7 25 31 66 85
M	171 161 57 135 157
N	149 64 71 50 185 136
O	51 42 101 163 13 67 17 104
P	54 144 20 151
Q	206 127 128 182 21 35 88 146 167
R	116 137 124 143 44 36 198 183
S	99 102 175 141 150 154 24 37 70
T	29 105 140 209 19 129 164 3 196 9 52
U	170 106 165 92 86 22 187 131
V	10 118 186 115 152 139 197 18
W	178 173 130 81 38 30 119 98 203
X	193 168 58 113 181
Y	14 112 110 169 160 201 45 179 77
Z	43 15 204 32 90 6 172 177 191
Z₁	100 61 159 97 82 153 111 55

Grid

1 K	2 D	3 T	4 B	5 D	6 Z	7 L	8 F	9 T		
10 V	11 J	12 E	13 O	14 Y	15 Z	16 J	17 O	18 V	19 T	
20 P	21 Q	22 U	23 J	24 S	25 L	26 B	27 D	28 A	29 T	
30 W	31 L	32 Z	33 F	34 F	35 Q	36 R	37 S	38 W		
39 E	40 A	41 K	42 O	43 Z	44 R	45 Y	46 L	47 B	48 J	49 K
50 N	51 O	52 T	53 G	54 P	55 Z₁	56 L	57 M	58 X	59 B	
60 G	61 Z₁	62 F	63 H	64 N	65 A	66 L	67 O	68 D	69 E	
70 S	71 N	72 C	73 K	74 E	75 L	76 G	77 Y	78 H	79 D	
80 F	81 W	82 Z₁	83 C	84 I	85 L	86 U	87 H	88 Q		
89 E	90 Z	91 L	92 U	93 I	94 C	95 F	96 G	97 Z₁		
98 W	99 S	100 Z₁	101 O	102 S	103 A	104 O	105 T	106 U	107 G	
108 I	109 B	110 Y	111 Z₁	112 Y	113 X	114 B	115 V	116 R		
117 K	118 V	119 W	120 J	121 E	122 B	123 A	124 R	125 G	126 D	127 Q
128 Q	129 T	130 W	131 U	132 G	133 A	134 F	135 M	136 N		
137 R	138 C	139 V	140 T	141 S	142 I	143 R	144 P	145 L		
146 Q	147 F	148 D	149 N	150 S	151 P	152 V	153 Z₁	154 S		
155 E	156 C	157 M	158 D	159 Z₁	160 Y	161 M	162 H	163 O	164 T	
165 U	166 B	167 Q	168 X	169 Y	170 U	171 M	172 Z	173 W	174 L	
175 S	176 J	177 Z	178 W	179 Y	180 G	181 X	182 Q	183 R	184 A	
185 N	186 V	187 U	188 I	189 K	190 J	191 Z	192 A	193 X		
194 C	195 J	196 T	197 V	198 R	199 H	200 B	201 Y	202 I		
203 W	204 Z	205 H	206 Q	207 I	208 C	209 T	210 D			

101

Grid

1 N	2 L	3 U	4 J	5 R	6 Q	7 A				
8 G	9 L	10 O	11 J	12 K	13 D	14 T	15 E	16 Q	17 R	18 U
19 S	20 M	21 A	22 L	23 Y	24 P	25 S	26 X	27 I	28 P	29 A
30 F	31 V	32 L	33 X	34 V	35 E	36 H	37 L	38 Q		
39 A	40 Y	41 C	42 V	43 N	44 S	45 V	46 L	47 W	48 U	
49 R	50 H	51 D	52 E	53 B	54 K	55 V	56 C	57 I	58 D	
59 L	60 M	61 Y	62 F	63 K	64 B	65 Q	66 J	67 M	68 H	
69 T	70 G	71 A	72 L	73 P	74 J	75 C	76 X	77 E	78 B	
79 F	80 B	81 Y	82 N	83 B	84 U	85 O	86 E	87 Q		
88 F	89 K	90 N	91 T	92 G	93 M	94 I	95 Q	96 B		
97 X	98 T	99 M	100 J	101 F	102 D	103 U	104 X	105 T	106 F	
107 D	108 S	109 W	110 R	111 B	112 P	113 M	114 N	115 O	116 T	117 Q
118 U	119 V	120 H	121 U	122 I	123 R	124 Q	125 B	126 D		
127 I	128 Q	129 U	130 X	131 R	132 F	133 X	134 E	135 Y	136 T	
137 V	138 G	139 X	140 S	141 K	142 R	143 I	144 U	145 W	146 G	147 Y
148 P	149 O	150 Q	151 T	152 I	153 R	154 J	155 S	156 B	157 C	
158 D	159 X	160 S	161 U	162 W	163 Q	164 D	165 K	166 E	167 B	
168 O	169 S	170 H	171 Q	172 G	173 A	174 B	175 N	176 L		
177 X	178 E	179 W	180 X	181 H	182 A	183 A	184 D	185 N		
186 L	187 P	188 R	189 E	190 P	191 O	192 L	193 S	194 R		
195 C	196 H	197 O	198 F	199 V	200 W	201 J	202 P	203 B		
204 Y	205 I	206 K	207 E	208 O	209 U					

WORDS

A Fit for use as a dwelling — 29 182 131 39 21 173 71 183 7

B Suddenly, unexpectedly (4 wds.) — 83 96 111 167 203 53 156 78 174 125 80 64

C Homeless wanderers — 195 157 41 56 75

D Jursidiction — 164 51 107 58 102 13 184 158 126

E Carefree; boisterous; hearty — 134 35 178 207 77 166 86 189 52 15

F Allow for exaggeration, as in a statement — 79 198 106 101 62 132 30 88

G Silly nonsense — 172 138 92 70 146 8

H Overwhelm with amazement — 196 181 170 50 68 120 36

I Permanent rules, laws — 127 94 152 122 27 57 143 205

J Wearisome — 4 201 154 100 11 74 66

K Roman name for Dionysus — 141 206 165 63 89 12 54

L Ceramics — 59 2 192 176 22 46 9 37 186 32 72

M Tax, duty — 20 67 60 113 93 99

N London prison torn down in 1902 — 114 185 1 43 175 82 90

O Pleasantly kind; heavens! — 191 197 85 10 208 149 168 115

P Remarkably good or lively; very — 24 190 148 28 202 112 187 73

Q Charitable — 16 95 117 87 6 171 65 150 124 128 38 163

R Highly pleasing to the senses, esp. taste or smell — 188 194 142 5 49 153 123 110 17

S Observant; considerate — 140 25 155 19 169 44 108 160 193

T Town in NE Va., site of battles of Bull Run — 91 136 105 14 151 116 98 69

U Compulsion, execution — 161 18 103 121 3 48 118 84 209 129 144

V Type of space endeavor — 119 34 31 42 137 45 55 199

W Emulates Demosthenes — 145 162 47 109 179 200

X Provocative; piquant, lively — 104 139 177 159 26 130 76 133 180 97 33

Y Delay; temporary relief — 61 135 147 81 204 40 23

102

CLUES

A 1921 waltz by Ryan and Violinsky (3 wds. followed by WORD O)
B Convulsed with laughter (2 wds.)
C ___ Tales: Five novels by J.F. Cooper
D Large Old World plovers
E Madness
F "And sang it ___ / Around, beneath, above" (3 wds.; Bridges, "I Made Another Song")
G Noxious effusions, foreboding atmosphere
H Tender of animals on display
I Personally (3 wds.)
J Prophet under David and Solomon (I Kings 1:34)
K Mt. ___: volcanic peak in the Cascade Range, Calif.
L Flanks; teams
M Very perceptive (hyph.)
N Torn, frayed, dowdy
O See WORD A (2 wds.)
P "Stars in the purple dusk above the ___" (Aiken, "Senlin. Morning Song")
Q Alone, solitary
R Welsh poet (1914–53, "Adventures in the Skin Trade")
S 1928 song by Shapiro, Campbell, and Connelly (4 wds.)
T Women's sleepwear
U Prod, spur, coaxer, one who provokes with schemes, ideas, etc.
V "That he can make / Figs out of ___ silk from bristles" (Tennyson, "Last Tournament")
W Defeating, surmounting
X Supple, pliant
Y Good-looking (4 wds.)
Z Gathered, put together
Z1 Withstanding, opposing
Z2 Historical period that followed the ...

WORDS

Clue	Numbers
A	17 82 69 40 49 44 67 232 21 12 65 222 233 177 210 105 225
B	78 151 5 103 20 50 60 15 227 166
C	123 113 34 26 146 99 241 132 226 59 156 22 48 234 80
D	141 4 240 100 207 190 160 179
E	45 92 25 167 79 171 202 144
F	107 119 23 85 142 73 122 16 184 168
G	129 181 205 170 188 121
H	143 208 174 149 131 120 63 195 214
I	9 182 41 101 37 223 76 220 89 125
J	30 231 46 139 221 13
K	165 219 84 136 216 38
L	133 87 57 189 10
M	161 72 185 238 169 75 102 66 112
N	108 117 191 58 53
O	43 147 229 11 186 29
P	228 91 111 173 145 42 163 70
Q	183 93 64 36 237 81 135 194
R	153 217 94 62 235 88
S	115 95 150 154 242 198 106 201 19
T	8 128 159 51 196 203 83 114
U	152 213 162 96 130 24
V	138 180 1 32 124 211 109 110
W	158 204 47 33 61 192 197 134 14
X	157 97 2 104 126
Y	218 164 137 243 7 209 31 230 55 178 199 140 172
Z	193 71 3 212 86 118 77 52 28
Z1	175 56 239 90 236 6 224 148 206
Z2	... 116 200 127 25 98 176 68 18 27 155 215 74

Grid

Cell(clue) across each row
1 V · 2 X · 3 Z · 4 D · 5 B · 6 Z1 · 7 Y
8 T · 9 I · 10 L · 11 O · 12 A · 13 J · 14 W · 15 B · 16 F · 17 A
18 Z2 · 19 S · 20 B · 21 A · 22 C · 23 F · 24 U · 25 E · 26 C · 27 Z2 · 28 Z
29 O · 30 J · 31 Y · 32 V · 33 W · 34 C · 35 Z2 · 36 Q · 37 I · 38 K
39 W · 40 A · 41 I · 42 P · 43 O · 44 A · 45 E · 46 J · 47 W
48 C · 49 A · 50 B · 51 T · 52 Z · 53 N · 54 Z2 · 55 Y · 56 Z1 · 57 L
58 N · 59 C · 60 B · 61 W · 62 R · 63 H · 64 Q · 65 A · 66 M
67 A · 68 Z2 · 69 A · 70 P · 71 Z · 72 M · 73 F · 74 Z2 · 75 M · 76 I
77 Z · 78 B · 79 E · 80 C · 81 Q · 82 A · 83 T · 84 K · 85 F · 86 Z
87 L · 88 R · 89 I · 90 Z1 · 91 P · 92 E · 93 Q · 94 R · 95 S · 96 U · 97 X
98 Z2 · 99 C · 100 D · 101 I · 102 M · 103 B · 104 X · 105 A · 106 S
107 F · 108 N · 109 V · 110 V · 111 P · 112 M · 113 C · 114 T · 115 S · 116 Z2
117 N · 118 Z · 119 F · 120 H · 121 G · 122 F · 123 C · 124 V · 125 I · 126 X
127 Z2 · 128 T · 129 G · 130 U · 131 H · 132 C · 133 L · 134 W · 135 Q · 136 K · 137 Y
138 V · 139 J · 140 Y · 141 D · 142 F · 143 H · 144 E · 145 P · 146 C
147 O · 148 Z1 · 149 H · 150 S · 151 B · 152 U · 153 R · 154 S · 155 Z2 · 156 C
157 X · 158 W · 159 T · 160 D · 161 M · 162 U · 163 P · 164 Y · 165 K · 166 B · 167 E
168 F · 169 M · 170 G · 171 E · 172 Y · 173 P · 174 H · 175 Z1 · 176 Z2
177 A · 178 Y · 179 D · 180 V · 181 G · 182 I · 183 Q · 184 F · 185 M · 186 O
187 Z2 · 188 G · 189 L · 190 D · 191 N · 192 W · 193 Z · 194 Q · 195 H · 196 T
197 W · 198 S · 199 Y · 200 Z2 · 201 S · 202 E · 203 T · 204 W · 205 G · 206 Z1 · 207 D
208 H · 209 Y · 210 A · 211 V · 212 Z · 213 U · 214 H · 215 Z2 · 216 K · 217 R
218 Y · 219 K · 220 I · 221 J · 222 A · 223 I · 224 Z1 · 225 A · 226 C · 227 B
228 P · 229 O · 230 Y · 231 J · 232 A · 233 A · 234 C · 235 R · 236 Z1
237 Q · 238 M · 239 Z1 · 240 D · 241 C · 242 S · 243 Y

103

CLUES / WORDS

A Intricate, tough question (2 wds.) · · · — 33 106 119 28 17 197 203 142 67 164 19 177 86

B Pressured to meet a deadline (3 wds.) — 90 163 175 98 82 53 173 47 64 57 15

C S American shrub whose root is used as a tonic and also to color port wine — 148 192 85 93 169 117 108

D Pedagogue — 52 92 63 191 168 115 139

E Brave, gallant — 60 36 153 113 196 41 183 27

F Compound eye — 89 80 135 34 110 14 116 35

G Hold it! Take it easy! (3 wds.) — 137 81 186 44 77 121 129 111 132

H "Broadway Joe," former Jet — 170 147 3 136 200 144

I Credits, debits, etc. — 156 179 76 199 71 79 184

J Apache Indian chief; paratroopers' battle cry — 210 141 146 176 37 109 189 94

K The three principles of classical drama — 74 46 208 26 20 195 91

L "Death, whene'er he call, / Must call ___," (2 wds.; Gilbert, "Yeomen of the Guard") — 181 105 50 143 45 40 151

M Man's name, from Hebrew meaning "without honor" — 193 118 88 96 207 24 131

N Province in E Canada — 78 22 38 104 31 150 194 84 127 161 209 171

O Double — 204 122 56 155 190 8 162 97 4

P Hymn — 100 130 160 133 65 112

Q Volatile petroleum distillate used as a solvent, fuel, etc. — 70 125 159 201 95 187 25

R Fr. painter-sculptor-engraver (1832–83) who illustrated "The Divine Comedy," "Don Quixote," The Bible, etc. — 152 32 182 145

S City in E Rhineland-Palatinate, Germany, where Luther was condemned as a heretic — 66 138 123 206 72

T Zeus assumed his form and seduced his wife, Alcmena — 158 68 10 30 166 180 62 9 149 43

U 1953 biblical epic, the first film in CinemaScope (2 wds.) — 124 39 83 58 2 49 174

V 1873 Trollope novel (2 wds. after "The") — 188 205 75 185 69 99 134 16 154 48 120 18 5 140 172

W ___ the Devil, sixth duke of Normandie, father of William the Conqueror — 114 29 23 202 101 13

X Dejected, dispirited — 42 103 61 126 12 167 54 7 102

Y Malicious burning — 51 11 178 198 87

Z 1934 play by Sidney Howard, based on Paul De Kruif's "Microbe Hunters" (2 wds.) — 55 128 165 107 6 1 73 59 157 21

Grid (cell number = clue letter)

1 Z	2 U	3 H	4 O	5 V	6 Z	7 X	8 O	9 T	10 T
11 Y	12 X	13 W	14 F	15 B	16 V	17 A	18 V	19 A	20 K
21 Z	22 N	23 W	24 M	25 Q	26 K	27 K	28 A	29 W	30 T
31 N	32 R	33 A	34 F	35 F	36 E	37 J	38 N	39 U	40 L
41 E	42 X	43 T	44 G	45 L	46 K	47 B	48 V	49 U	50 L
51 Y	52 D	53 B	54 X	55 Z	56 O	57 B	58 U	59 Z	60 E
61 X	62 T	63 D	64 B	65 P	66 S	67 A	68 T	69 V	70 Q
71 I	72 S	73 Z	74 K	75 V	76 I	77 G	78 N	79 I	80 F
81 G	82 B	83 U	84 N	85 C	86 A	87 Y	88 M	89 F	90 B
91 K	92 D	93 C	94 J	95 Q	96 M	97 O	98 B	99 V	100 P
101 W	102 X	103 X	104 N	105 L	106 A	107 Z	108 C	109 J	110 F
111 G	112 P	113 E	114 W	115 D	116 F	117 C	118 M	119 A	120 V
121 G	122 O	123 S	124 U	125 Q	126 X	127 N	128 Z	129 G	130 P
131 M	132 G	133 P	134 V	135 F	136 H	137 G	138 S	139 D	140 V
141 J	142 A	143 L	144 H	145 R	146 J	147 H	148 C	149 T	150 N
151 L	152 R	153 E	154 V	155 O	156 I	157 Z	158 T	159 Q	160 P
161 N	162 O	163 B	164 A	165 Z	166 T	167 X	168 D	169 C	170 H
171 N	172 V	173 B	174 U	175 B	176 J	177 A	178 Y	179 I	180 T
181 L	182 R	183 E	184 I	185 V	186 G	187 Q	188 V	189 J	190 O
191 D	192 C	193 M	194 N	195 K	196 E	197 A	198 Y	199 I	200 H
201 Q	202 W	203 A	204 O	205 V	206 S	207 M	208 K	209 N	210 J

104

CLUES

A. Gibberish, nonsense — 89 11 24 152 96 199 62 93 181 197 31

B. Alan Shepard, John Glenn, etc. — 155 75 92 106 191 160 33 144 138 213

C. 1945 John Steinbeck novel (2 wds.) — 76 119 158 32 128 37 5 111 173 104

D. Statement of the market price of a commodity — 129 87 198 186 46 172 80 40 171

E. Absolute, complete, thoroughgoing, unrelieved — 176 7 168 117 154 13 216 137 12 219 73

F. "Be not her maid, since she is ——," says Romeo — 19 174 114 159 72 210 16

G. Type of theatrical company — 3 135 109 97 156

H. Puffer, sometimes toxic — 36 187 162 147 20 6 29 48

I. Painters, sculptors, musicians, dancers, actors, etc. — 196 64 47 188 143 203 126

J. Skiff, perhaps — 41 209 200 88 68 182 95

K. Robin Hood of Mexico, who's been played by Douglas Fairbanks, Tyrone Power, Clayton Moore et al. — 118 170 18 149 105

L. All-inclusive — 130 123 15 189 61 201 69 23 35

M. Whickers — 183 153 121 82 136 108

N. Rorqual inhabiting all seas (2 wds.) — 86 49 57 205 98 4 25 85

O. Sense — 113 2 51 110 131 71

P. Fixed firmly, secured — 139 122 148 45 165 39

Q. One who trifles flirtatiously — 194 218 1 103 125 81 107 90 22 180 127

R. Lacking in reticence or restraint; unconfined — 67 185 167 78 26

S. Perplexing — 21 44 74 59 220 102 161 214 91

T. Queen of England, 1702–14 — 38 54 179 65

U. Peachy, swell, sharp, slick — 215 43 94 55 142

V. Impoverished — 134 190 79 83 34 27 212 14 63

W. Mahimahi; dorado; cetacean; Flipper, e.g. — 150 178 116 42 208 202 58

X. Dried root of a South American plant, used as an emetic — 206 17 157 112 53 145

Y. Lifts, erects — 132 140 100 193 70 151

Z. Earthwork for protection against enemy fire — 177 99 211 50 204 184 66 84 169 195 141 163

Z_1. Old Welsh six-stringed instrument — 166 192 60 120 10

Z_2. "But ——, and amiable words / And courtliness" (3 wds.; Tennyson, "Guinevere") — 217 133 30 101 56 146 115 175 52 207 164 28 77 | 8 124 9

GRID

```
Row  1:  1Q   2O   3G   4N   5C   6H   7E
Row  2:  8Z2  9Z2  10Z1 11A  12E  13E  14V  15L  16F
Row  3:  17X  18K  19F  20H  21S  22Q  23L  24A  25N  26R
Row  4:  27V  28Z2 29H  30Z2 31A  32C  33B  34V  35L
Row  5:  36H  37C  38T  39P  40D  41J  42W  43U  44S
Row  6:  45P  46D  47I  48H  49N  50Z  51O  52Z2 53X  54T
Row  7:  55U  56Z2 57N  58W  59S  60Z1 61L  62A  63V  64I
Row  8:  65T  66Z  67R  68J  69L  70Y  71O  72F  73E
Row  9:  74S  75B  76C  77Z2 78R  79V  80D  81Q  82M  83V  84Z
Row 10:  85N  86N  87D  88J  89A  90Q  91S  92B  93A  94U
Row 11:  95J  96A  97G  98N  99Z  100Y 101Z2 102S 103Q 104C
Row 12:  105K 106B 107Q 108M 109G 110O 111C 112X 113O 114F
Row 13:  115Z2 116W 117E 118K 119C 120Z1 121M 122P 123Q 124Z2 125Q
Row 14:  126I 127Q 128C 129D 130L 131O 132Y 133Z2 134V 135G
Row 15:  136M 137E 138B 139P 140Y 141Z 142U 143I 144B 145X
Row 16:  146Z2 147H 148P 149K 150W 151Y 152A 153M 154E
Row 17:  155B 156G 157X 158C 159F 160B 161S 162H 163Z 164Z2
Row 18:  165P 166Z1 167R 168E 169Z 170K 171D 172D 173C 174F
Row 19:  175Z2 176E 177Z 178W 179T 180Q 181A 182J 183M 184Z
Row 20:  185R 186D 187H 188I 189L 190V 191B 192Z1 193Y
Row 21:  194Q 195Z 196I 197A 198D 199A 200J 201L 202W 203I
Row 22:  204Z 205N 206X 207Z2 208W 209J 210F 211Z 212V 213B
Row 23:  214S 215U 216E 217Z2 218Q 219E 220S
```

105

WORDS

A 197 199 90 39 175 145 151
B 77 153 91 15 33 203
C 173 2 26 200 54 99
D 69 22 130 179 148 106
E 49 202 147 172 165 80 60 125 154 98 30 131 118
F 121 160 107 23 74 1 70 181
G 87 185 117 46 143 68 137 174 95 167
H 139 66 76 10 161 110
I 11 119 188 21 182 78 126 64 195
J 109 159 97 32 65 104 81 16 86 28 186 138
K 187 5 62 36 162 27 73 20 31
L 29 193 112 35 132 142 155 84 17
M 9 196 51 4 94 163 75 12 47 178 180 156
N 56 19 141 105 158 25
O 157 100 83 93 189 34 123 140
P 133 50 124 103 184 170 38 8 45 71 43
Q 128 122 120 13 37 164 3 190 116
R 114 149 183 72 59
S 201 92 152 40 113 115 168 134 52
T 108 150 198 144 57 14 48
U 53 79 58 67 169 194
V 44 102 111 177 63
W 157 61 88 85 191 166 96 18 135 24
X 146 192 7 42 136 55
Y 171 129 176 127 89 41 6 82

CLUES

A. Shoots (2 wds.)

B. Fleeced, swindled (2 wds.)

C. Make excessive demands on

D. Street fight between teenage gangs

E. Region of lower Egypt occupied by Israelites before the Exodus

F. Descent, lineage

G. "Storied ___ richly dight" (Milton, "Il Penseroso")

H. Based on weak evidence (hyph.)

I. Am. actor, Oscar-winner for "Save the Tiger," 1973

J. Exercises, instructions; punishments

K. Fr. painter, etcher (1836–1902) who did watercolor Bible illustrations

L. Thick soup or stew of vegetables or meat

M. Charge with a responsibility

N. Boy, lad, in Ireland

O. Makes complete or perfect (2 wds.)

P. Shield on which a coat of arms is depicted

Q. Take, appropriate, esp. without permission

R. Muscle, sinew

S. Pitifully ineffectual person, closely related to a schlemiel

T. Frogs, toads, salamanders, etc.

U. River, SE Scotland, flowing to the Tweed

V. Astonished, amazed; dazed

W. Claim, positive statement

X. Fictional Mississippi county created by Wm. Faulkner

Y. Line with a hard coating

Z. Suicidal gamble (2 wds.)

WORDS

A. 155 48 130 144 8 22 135 68

B. 95 3 46 77 194 164 131 26 11 149

C. 58 205 199 4 145 51 21

D. 148 191 114 99 52 85

E. 39 113 60 74 168 19

F. 75 187 1 35 195 182 28 206 14 170

G. 76 197 32 96 147 41 33

H. 186 196 108 18 67 27 167 184 163 204

I. 62 109 128 103 45 7

J. 192 100 172 43 17 140 44

K. 79 50 207 88 6 72

L. 2 179 65 116 125 91 188 69 107 81

M. 30 106 141 127 180 165 16

N. 152 129 136 162 93 54 178

O. 15 166 126 133 176 84 98 90 123

P. 104 115 64 143 124 49 29 80 134 189

Q. 71 181 185 38 57

R. 111 160 63 86 24

S. 55 183 118 121 78 110 70

T. 42 5 13 150 66 198 119 137 154 190

U. 151 36 209 31 174 156

V. 10 193 139 59 23 61 171

W. 87 210 25 177 200 53 20 173 159

X. 40 102 132 138 201 12 117 97 153 146 92 157 169

Y. 208 175 101 142 83 94 37

Z. 47 105 9 89 56 203 120 112 82 122 202 158 34 73 161

DIAGRAM

	1 F	2 L	3 B	4 C	5 T	6 K	7 I	8 A	9 Z	10 V
11 B	12 X	13 T	14 F	15 O	16 M	17 J	18 H	19 E	20 W	
21 C	22 A	23 V	24 R	25 W	26 B	27 H	28 F	29 P	30 M	31 U
32 G	33 G	34 Z	35 F	36 U	37 Y	38 Q	39 E	40 X	41 G	
42 T	43 J	44 J	45 I	46 B	47 Z	48 A	49 P	50 K	51 C	
52 D	53 W	54 N	55 S	56 Z	57 Q	58 C	59 V	60 E		
61 V	62 I	63 R	64 P	65 L	66 T	67 H	68 A	69 L	70 S	71 Q
72 K	73 Z	74 E	75 F	76 G	77 B	78 S	79 K	80 P		
81 L	82 X	83 Y	84 O	85 D	86 R	87 W	88 K	89 Z	90 O	
91 L	92 X	93 N	94 Y	95 B	96 G	97 X	98 O	99 D	100 J	
101 Y	102 X	103 I	104 P	105 Z	106 M	107 L	108 H	109 I	110 S	
111 R	112 Z	113 E	114 D	115 P	116 L	117 X	118 S	119 T	120 Z	
121 S	122 Z	123 O	124 P	125 L	126 O	127 M	128 I	129 N	130 A	131 B
132 X	133 O	134 P	135 A	136 N	137 T	138 X	139 V	140 J		
141 M	142 Y	143 P	144 A	145 C	146 X	147 G	148 D	149 B	150 T	151 U
152 N	153 U	154 T	155 A	156 U	157 X	158 Z	159 W	160 R		
161 Z	162 N	163 H	164 B	165 M	166 O	167 H	168 E	169 X		
170 F	171 V	172 J	173 W	174 U	175 Y	176 O	177 W	178 N	179 L	
180 M	181 Q	182 F	183 S	184 H	185 Q	186 H	187 F	188 L	189 P	190 T
191 D	192 D	193 V	194 B	195 F	196 H	197 G	198 T	199 C	200 W	201 X
202 Z	203 Z	204 H	205 D	206 F	207 K	208 Y	209 U	210 W		

107

WORDS

CLUES

A Discharge, outburst 35 131 182 107 67 123 17 172 196 168 55

B Mentally, in one's noodle (3 wds.) . . 22 83 86 127 201 45 121 62 192 16 174 8 197 94

C Mayor of N.Y.C., 1926–32 . . . . . . 191 122 162 200 90 4

D Muslim pilgrimage to Mecca 58 92 158 117

E Vastly, enormously, wonderfully (4 wds.) 181 135 53 66 43 30 57 156 163

F Tidbits, nothings, bagatelles . . . 146 11 84 73 138 160 70 106 76 95 48 89

G 15th-cen. English morality play . . 10 34 74 169 105 159 69 29

H Labored 170 31 12 42 3 130

I Shuddering fear, strong aversion . . 50 65 152 183 63 104

J Picture mentally 33 161 167 113 186 6 118 85

K Stiff-growing, erect zinnia of Mexico (hyph.) . . 37 132 119 203 20 193 26 112 128 80 101 39 64 144

L Positively, definitely 190 115 98 87 153 19 102 82 100 141 71 93

M Orchestration 108 189 18 81 27 179 185 38 140 157 99

N On all sides (3 wds.) 75 184 24 176 68 136 40 14 198 188 32 114

O Mantel, e.g. 7 125 61 148 44

P African insectivore also called potamogale (2 wds.) . . 171 175 124 111 120 41 52 60 5 46

Q In all honesty, to tell the truth . . 139 134 166 49 96 110 155

R Constructive worker 187 154 177 195 77 1

S Margaret ____ : Eng. novelist (1828–97; "Miss Marjoriebanks") . . 88 137 28 202 47 147 15 150

T Extremely wicked 145 23 164 103 129 149 13 133 199

U Lump, blob, little bit 91 56 109 143 72 9

V Canines 59 116 78 194 21 51 142 173

W Filled up again 36 151 79 165 97 178 25 54 2 126 180

Grid (cell number / clue letter)

1 R	2 W	3 H	4 C	5 P	6 J	7 O	8 B	9 U	10 G	11 F	12 H
13 T	14 N	15 S	16 B								
17 A	18 M	19 L	20 K	21 V	22 B	23 T	24 N	25 W	26 K		
27 M	28 S	29 G	30 E	31 H	32 N	33 J	34 G	35 A	36 W		
37 K	38 M	39 K	40 N	41 P	42 H	43 E	44 O	45 B			
46 P	47 S	48 F	49 Q	50 I	51 V	52 P	53 E	54 W			
55 A	56 U	57 E	58 D	59 V	60 P	61 O	62 B	63 I	64 K		
65 I	66 E	67 A	68 N	69 G	70 F	71 L	72 U	73 F			
74 G	75 N	76 F	77 R	78 V	79 W	80 K	81 M	82 L	83 B		
84 F	85 J	86 B	87 L	88 S	89 F	90 C	91 U	92 D			
93 L	94 B	95 F	96 Q	97 W	98 L	99 M	100 L				
101 K	102 L	103 T	104 I	105 G	106 F	107 A	108 M	109 U	110 Q		
111 P	112 K	113 J	114 N	115 L	116 V	117 D	118 J	119 K			
120 P	121 B	122 C	123 A	124 P	125 O	126 W	127 B	128 K	129 K		
130 H	131 A	132 K	133 T	134 Q	135 E	136 N	137 S	138 F			
139 Q	140 M	141 L	142 V	143 U	144 K	145 T	146 F	147 S			
148 O	149 T	150 S	151 W	152 I	153 L	154 R	155 Q	156 E	157 M	158 D	
159 G	160 F	161 J	162 C	163 E	164 T	165 W	166 Q	167 J	168 A		
169 G	170 H	171 P	172 A	173 V	174 B	175 P	176 N	177 R			
178 W	179 M	180 W	181 E	182 A	183 I	184 N	185 M	186 J	187 R		
188 N	189 M	190 L	191 C	192 B	193 K	194 V	195 R	196 A	197 B		
198 N	199 T	200 C	201 B	202 S	203 K						

108

CLUES

A John (dull), Annie (mixed up) play (4 wds.) . . . 63 68 103 126 86 4 131 90 165 11 80 109

B Esoteric aspect of war can engage one . . . 78 72 59 35 142 152

C Broken clay quoit breeds blather . . . 118 138 170 14 61 99 147 36 110

D Author had Mary shot—shot! (2 wds.) . . . 113 100 137 10 71 143 60 179 53 150 81

E Folly, if mad about spies with authori-zation . . . 9 183 51 29 92 117 12 46 88 149

F Flower of Hindustani leafage . . . 83 48 25 169

G Irritant: a rather brassy section . . . 175 102 22 47 130 185 177

H New chances scare them badly . . . 57 43 107 172 155 8 65 121 114

I Sounds like you might be classy . . . 77

J Within, Mae switched his club . . . 101 23 89 31 167 56

K Whomped, perhaps, by unruly beau, pent . . . 24 96 145 163 66 154 171 136

L Classes or castes holding some of WORD V . . . 184 70 159 112 153

M Records shot at hanging . . . 186 127 67 73 50 133 97 176

N I'm undefiled, or corrupt . . . 20 140 162 187 139 135

O Repairman has short chapter in cin-ema, mysteriously . . . 146 111 160 34 106 91 174 30

P Captivates nut with clumsy snatch . . . 7 168 27 116 158 44 94 18

Q Crazily quibble with love for one second—that's not straightforward . . . 21 6 173 181 85 39 119

R Off pie? Quit jumping around, Pet! (3 wds.) . . . 144 58 2 151 105 42 122 38 82 189

S French historian of certain epochs . . . 76 17 124 188 49

T It being the core portion of nincom-poops (hyph.) . . . 120 74 41 16 115 1 54 182

U Consumed a teen on a roll . . . 157 40 64 166 15

V Health's bad East and West in crea-tures we'd like to save (2 wds.) . . . 33 3 26 156 55 45 79 84 123

W A hot shot pledge . . . 52 141 164 95

X With pains, ill at heart, bounder dis-plays a weak spot (2 wds.) . . . 87 75 19 98 148 28 161 178 134 93 37 129

Y Measures of riotous noise in unstable minds . . . 132 108 180 32 62 104 128 69 125 5

WORDS

Grid (cell number and clue letter):

1 T	2 R	3 V	4 A	5 Y											
6 Q	7 P	8 H	9 E	10 D	11 A	■	12 E	13 A	■	14 C	15 U				
16 T	17 S	18 P	19 X	20 N	21 Q	22 G	23 J	24 K	25 F	26 V					
27 P	28 X	29 E	30 O	31 J	32 Y	33 V	34 O	35 B	36 C						
37 X	38 R	39 Q	40 U	41 T	42 R	43 H	44 P	45 V	46 E	47 G					
48 F	49 S	50 M	51 E	52 W	53 D	54 T	55 V	56 J							
57 H	58 R	59 B	60 D	61 C	62 Y	63 A	64 U	65 H	66 K						
67 M	68 A	69 Y	70 L	71 D	72 B	73 M	74 T	75 X							
76 S	77 I	78 B	79 V	80 A	81 D	82 R	83 G	84 V	85 Q	86 A					
87 X	88 E	89 J	90 A	91 O	92 E	93 X	94 P	95 W	96 K						
97 M	98 X	99 C	100 D	101 J	102 G	103 A	104 Y	105 R							
106 O	107 H	108 Y	109 A	110 C	111 O	112 L	113 D	114 H	115 T						
116 P	117 E	118 C	119 Q	120 T	121 H	122 R	123 V	124 S							
125 Y	126 A	127 M	128 Y	129 X	130 G	131 A	132 Y	133 M							
134 X	135 N	136 K	137 D	138 C	139 N	140 N	141 W	142 B	143 D						
144 R	145 K	146 O	147 C	148 X	149 E	150 D	151 R	152 B	153 L						
154 K	155 H	156 V	157 U	158 P	159 L	160 O	161 X	162 N	163 K						
164 W	165 A	166 U	167 J	168 P	169 F	170 C	171 K	172 H	173 Q						
174 O	175 G	176 M	177 G	178 X	179 D	■	180 Y	181 Q	182 T						
183 E	184 L	185 G	186 M	187 N	188 S	189 R									

109

Grid

1	2	3	4	5	6	7	8	9	10	11
1 L	2 R	3 I	■	4 K	5 G	6 F	7 W	8 X	9 D	10 M
11 S	12 G	13 O	14 F	15 I	16 E	17 W	18 O	■	19 P	20 L
21 U	22 O	23 H	24 X	25 A	26 V	27 R	■	■	28 S	29 C
30 T	31 Q	32 J	33 B	34 I	35 U	36 F	37 O	38 N	39 G	40 A
41 C	42 H	43 K	44 D	45 M	46 R	47 W	48 J	■	49 X	50 V
51 S	52 U	53 M	54 J	55 W	56 D	57 Q	58 F	■	59 M	60 N
61 Q	62 L	63 C	64 V	65 O	66 P	67 W	■	■	68 Q	69 S
70 H	71 O	72 J	73 L	74 T	75 O	76 I	77 R	■	78 P	79 M
80 I	81 A	82 I	83 K	84 G	85 N	86 Q	■	■	87 W	88 H
89 O	90 P	91 M	92 U	93 T	94 I	95 Q	96 P	■	97 L	98 O
99 N	100 I	101 A	102 M	103 E	104 G	105 K	106 Q	■	107 S	108 J
109 R	110 V	111 P	112 X	113 I	114 E	115 U	116 O	117 V	118 T	119 B
120 N	121 A	122 B	123 I	124 K	125 R	126 X	■	■	127 M	128 J
129 A	130 E	131 Q	132 V	133 R	134 O	135 P	136 H	137 F	138 N	139 H
140 X	141 C	142 U	143 M	144 F	145 P	146 Q	147 T	■	148 L	149 O
150 N	151 G	152 T	153 C	154 W	155 F	156 B	■	■	157 C	158 N
159 U	160 Q	161 C	162 A	163 D	164 S	165 L	■	■	166 G	167 F
168 M	169 N	170 M	171 F	172 I	173 T	174 K	175 G	■	176 R	177 H
178 C	179 L	180 W	181 I	182 A	183 S	184 L	185 N	■	186 X	187 W

CLUES

A Loss of feeling
81 40 121 162 25 182 129 101

B Word-play
122 33 156 119

C Policy of equal trade with all nations (2 wds.)
153 178 29 161 141 63 157 41

D One who is condescending or overbearing to others
9 56 163 44

E Sepulchre
130 114 16 103

F Nonplussed, baffled
171 36 155 144 58 137 167 6 14

G Accustomed, used; suited
84 175 39 104 166 151 12 5

H Bane, thorn in the flesh; goddess of divine retribution, daughter of Erebus and Nyx
70 139 88 42 177 23 136

I Special uses to which something is put
82 94 172 100 113 181 123 3 80 15 76 34

J Readily changeable, transitory
48 32 54 72 108 128

K Slovenly
4 83 105 124 43 174

L Capable of being piled in orderly fashion
73 184 148 97 165 1 62 179 20

M "___ house are many mansions" (3 wds.; John 14:2)
170 59 143 45 10 91 168 127 102 79 53

N "The time has been my senses would have cooled / To hear a ___" (hyph.; "Macbeth")
38 120 60 85 158 169 185 138 150 99 65

O "So shines a ___ naughty world," says Portia (4 wds.; "Merchant of Venice")
71 89 18 149 116 98 13 22 37 134 75

P Extended musical composition with a more or less dramatic text
145 19 96 135 78 90 111 66

Q Undertaken on behalf of only one faction
131 57 31 95 160 106 86 146 61 68

R Withstood
125 109 46 176 2 27 133 77

S Natives of Norman or Tulsa, e.g.
183 164 69 51 107 11 28

T Getting on
147 173 152 118 30 74 93

U Land of Tripoli and Tyre
35 52 159 21 115 142 92

V Magic, sorcery
110 50 117 132 64 26

W Redolence, effluvium
154 187 180 7 55 17 87 47 67

X Long seats
24 49 8 126 140 186 112

110

CLUES

A. Coat; complete

B. Escorts, leads, directs

C. Not likely to arouse excitement or to catch fire

D. Thou-shalt-not (hyph.)

E. Unwilling to submit to authority

F. Substance used to relieve nasal congestion

G. Amusement park ride featuring a steep incline (hyph.)

H. "Say 'a grave-maker': ___ that he makes last till doomsday" (2 wds., "Hamlet")

I. Art once thought to be belly-talk

J. Unmanly

K. Lizette Woodworth ___: Am. poet (1856–1935; "Years")

L. Tender, generous in spirit (hyph.)

M. Satirical 1872 Samuel Butler novel

N. Have a youthful fling at reckless behavior (4 wds.)

O. Infamy

P. Hassle, hubbub, fuss

Q. Resentment; transgression; crime

R. Urban sections inhabited primarily by members of a minority group

S. "The tree could bear no more. / But ___" (3 wds., followed by WORD W, Frost, "Birches")

T. Clothes, equips, provides

U. Low-grade paper made from wood pulp

V. "The ___ are wholesome; then no planets strike" ("Hamlet")

W. See WORD S (4 wds.)

X. Undergoes, endures, stands

Y. Exclamation of boredom, weariness, etc. (hyph.)

WORDS

A. 106 192 187 24 6 73

B. 200 155 46 164 22 136

C. 31 152 115 50 67 107 10 129 163 169 198 97 17 93

D. 37 162 206 9

E. 186 103 25 168 143 205 153 104 5 26 135 84 91

F. 183 184 4 139 87 165 132 56 86

G. 126 215 76 60 99 188 210 134 95 20 43 137 36 128

H. 224 151 96 167 42 122 202 23 64

I. 191 69 176 57 16 30 62 161 199 79 11 150 123

J. 66 51 208 21 39 221 111 156 181 193

K. 77 102 63 178 114

L. 130 78 72 203 121 108 47 41 19 147 18

M. 144 92 101 226 13 34 222

N. 44 124 100 119 2 173 197 131 105 160 49 71 216 145 214

O. 179 174 61 109 189 159 171 54 81 194

P. 90 27 207 190 211

Q. 225 89 7 219 180 70 40

R. 223 29 201 3 196 228 175 68

S. 158 213 218 58 55 83 1 212 113 45 15 142

T. 53 82 177 170 14 118

U. 48 110 146 116 217 125 195 157 154

V. 149 204 140 85 28 12

W. 141 94 172 80 59 112 33 117 133 185 209 220

X. 166 74 52 120 98 35 65

Y. 227 148 127 32 182 138 8

Grid

1 S	2 N	3 R	4 F	5 E	6 A	7 Q	8 Y	9 D	10 C
11 I	12 V	13 M	14 T	15 S	16 I	17 C	18 L	19 L	20 G
21 J	22 B	23 H	24 A	25 E	26 E	27 P	28 V	29 R	30 I
31 C	32 Y	33 W	34 M	35 X	36 G	37 D	38 O	39 J	40 Q
41 L	42 H	43 G	44 N	45 S	46 B	47 L	48 U	49 N	50 C
51 J	52 X	53 T	54 O	55 S	56 F	57 I	58 S	59 W	60 G
61 O	62 I	63 K	64 H	65 X	66 J	67 C	68 R	69 I	70 Q
71 N	72 L	73 A	74 X	75 O	76 G	77 K	78 L	79 I	80 W
81 O	82 T	83 S	84 E	85 V	86 F	87 F	88 O	89 Q	90 P
91 E	92 M	93 C	94 W	95 G	96 H	97 C	98 X	99 G	100 N
101 M	102 K	103 E	104 E	105 N	106 A	107 C	108 L	109 O	110 U
111 J	112 W	113 S	114 K	115 C	116 U	117 W	118 T	119 N	120 X
121 L	122 H	123 I	124 N	125 U	126 G	127 Y	128 G	129 C	130 L
131 N	132 F	133 W	134 G	135 E	136 B	137 G	138 Y	139 F	140 V
141 W	142 S	143 E	144 M	145 N	146 U	147 L	148 Y	149 V	150 I
151 H	152 C	153 E	154 U	155 B	156 J	157 U	158 S	159 O	160 N
161 I	162 D	163 C	164 B	165 F	166 X	167 H	168 E	169 C	170 T
171 O	172 W	173 N	174 O	175 R	176 I	177 T	178 K	179 O	180 Q
181 J	182 Y	183 F	184 F	185 W	186 E	187 A	188 G	189 O	190 P
191 I	192 A	193 J	194 O	195 U	196 R	197 N	198 C	199 I	200 B
201 R	202 H	203 L	204 V	205 E	206 D	207 P	208 J	209 W	210 G
211 P	212 S	213 S	214 N	215 G	216 N	217 U	218 S	219 Q	220 W
221 J	222 M	223 R	224 H	225 Q	226 M	227 Y	228 R		

111

Grid

#											
1 G	2 X	3 R	4 Y	5 A	6 H	7 U					
8 S	9 S	10 H	11 D	12 A	13 A	14 R	15 I	16 Z₁			
17 M	18 B	19 Y	20 Q	21 V	22 W	23 Q	24 I	25 M	26 W	27 B	
28 B	29 N	30 W	31 U	32 F	33 V	34 A	35 D	36 H			
37 C	38 B	39 Z₁	40 Z	41 M	42 Y	43 V	44 G	45 K	46 E	47 Z	
48 N	49 N	50 O	51 B	52 K	53 L	54 V	55 O	56 Y	57 M		
58 E	59 B	60 G	61 E	62 Z₁	63 Y	64 Q	65 B	66 W	67 A		
68 O	69 O	70 Z	71 E	72 T	73 W	74 X	75 C	76 P			
77 R	78 Z₁	79 M	80 Z	81 Y	82 J	83 A	84 Z₁				
85 J	86 G	87 S	88 M	89 E	90 I	91 C	92 N	93 L	94 Q		
95 D	96 H	97 F	98 V	99 Z	100 P	101 Z	102 G	103 D			
104 A	105 E	106 U	107 G	108 Q	109 S	110 W	111 U	112 N	113 K		
114 E	115 Q	116 H	117 W	118 Q	119 F	120 Y	121 C	122 X	123 H		
124 T	125 Z	126 W	127 J	128 A	129 Y	130 M	131 A	132 Z₁	133 W		
134 K	135 R	136 D	137 U	138 V	139 Z	140 H	141 R	142 F	143 C	144 V	
145 M	146 V	147 B	148 Z₁	149 V	150 R	151 E	152 Y	153 C			
154 R	155 U	156 W	157 I	158 R	159 A	160 O	161 L	162 H	163 C		
164 X	165 E	166 E	167 T	168 D	169 U	170 G	171 T	172 Q			
173 U	174 A	175 X	176 Q	177 A	178 O	179 X	180 V	181 W	182 U		
183 Y	184 Q	185 O	186 G	187 E	188 G	189 E	190 T	191 W	192 O		
193 Z₁	194 O	195 P	196 R	197 T	198 U	199 Y	200 C	201 L			
202 J	203 L	204 Z₁	205 M	206 Z₁	207 V						

CLUES

A Negligence 12 67 104 159 177 5 83 128 174 131 34

B Volcanic mountain peak in the Cascade Range . . . 65 27 18 147 38 51 59

C With Freud, author of 1933 book "Why War?" . . . 143 163 153 200 37 91 121 75

D He played Mr. Bridge in a 1990 film . . . 95 136 103 11 35 168

E Study of plant lore and agricultural customs . . . 166 46 61 151 189 89 71 187 58 114 105

F Officer killed leading Negro troops against Ft. Wagner, Charleston, S.C. . . . 32 119 97 142

G Medicine that thins the blood . . . 186 1 60 86 188 44 102 107 170

H Wife of Socrates . . . 116 10 36 123 6 162 96 140

I Claim on property to satisfy an obligation . . . 90 15 157 24

J River formed by the Allegheny and Monongahela . . . 202 85 127 82

K Prospect, scene . . . 52 45 113 134

L Upper regions of space . . . 203 201 93 53 161

M Covenant, esp. between God and humans . . . 25 41 130 205 88 17 57 145 79

N Vow . . . 29 48 92 112

O Very nervous or excitable (hyph.) . . . 178 69 68 185 49 160 55 194 192

P Keen, eager . . . 23 195 100 76

Q Pertaining to a pair of stamps printed with one of them inverted (hyph.) . . . 108 176 184 115 64 94 118 20 172

R Plant living within another, as a parasite . . . 3 158 154 150 77 135 14 141 196

S Arbitrary decree by one in authority . . . 9 109 8 87

T Rhythmic dance of Cuba . . . 197 171 72 124 190 167

U Without a blemish . . . 106 173 111 155 137 31 182 7 198 50 169

V Constrict closely . . . 21 180 149 146 43 98 138 54 33 207 144

W On-off device (2 wds.) . . . 117 191 22 181 110 133 126 30 66 73 156 26

X One-horse, 2-wheeled carriage . . . 175 2 74 179 122 164

Y Cloyingly charming . . . 199 120 28 129 63 19 4 152 42 81 183 56

Z London literary society, 1700–1720, to which Addison & Steele belonged (hyph. & wd.) . . . 99 80 101 165 125 70 47 13 40 139

Z₁ Self-possession, aplomb . . . 62 39 78 204 16 148 132 206 84 193

112

CLUES

A. Upright rough stone monolith 57 52 39 117 65 17

B. "Although the ___, they're quite impervious to heat" (3 wds.; Coward, "Mad Dogs and Englishmen") 96 146 139 162 80 14 182 27 105 49 86 15 42 150 71 55

C. Texan whose eyes "sparkle like the dew" in a 1955 song (2 wds.) 136 34 1 161 67 47 148 97 11

D. 1924 Rene Clair film 43 138 128 36 156 109 116 145

E. Mature, ready 177 88 45 173

F. Nonessential 87 38 44 4 59 100

G. Form a recess 75 95 40 23 115 171

H. Muffed, fluffed, screwed up 153 131 73 92

I. Henry IV's 1598 decree that gave some freedom to the Huguenots (3 wds.) 93 32 48 76 70 111 166 13 119 133 163 141 159

J. Overlook, slight, ignore 127 130 24 135 118 112 90

K. Assembled, mustered, rounded up 81 181 35 185 106 18 56 158 165 31

L. Most up-to-date 83 19 147 26 186 3

M. 1858 Ivan Goncharov novel 126 140 33 41 10 9 85

N. 1902 winner of Nobel Prize in Literature (full name) 172 104 155 108 134 16 123 64 183 149 29 5 2 180

O. Spirit of a people 58 103 164 125 69

P. Belgian port 176 157 142 122 63 98

Q. Gain, profit, take 74 62 53 22 68 178

R. Round bit for a horse 61 101 82 151 170 8

S. William ___: T. Roosevelt's Secretary of War (2 wds.) 129 167 143 99 25 66 21 160 120 102

T. Understanding 132 20 72 144 137 152 28 89

U. 1786 William Beckford novel 110 184 154 107 94

V. Nullifidians, infidels 168 12 30 124 6 37 175

W. Tempted 179 50 91 114 169 54 121

X. Iris . . . .

Y. Hamlet's late "fellow of infinite jest, of most excellent fancy" 7 84 79 60 51 113

Diagram

	1	2	3	4	5	6	7
	1 C	2 N	3 L	4 F	5 N	6 V	7 Y
8	8 R	9 M	10 M	11 C	12 X	13 I	14 B	15 B	16 N
17	17 A	18 K	19 K	20 T	21 S	22 Q	23 G	24 J	25 S	26 L
27	27 B	28 T	29 N	30 X	31 K	32 I	33 M	34 C	35 K	36 D
37	37 V	38 F	39 A	40 G	41 M	42 B	43 D	44 F	45 E	46 E
47	47 C	48 I	49 B	50 T	51 Y	52 A	53 Q	54 W	55 B	56 K
57	57 A	58 O	59 F	60 Y	61 R	62 R	63 P	64 N	65 A	66 S	67 C
68	68 Q	69 O	70 I	71 B	72 V	73 H	74 Q	75 G	76 I	77 X
78	78 C	79 Y	80 B	81 K	82 R	83 L	84 Y	85 M	86 B	87 F	88 E
89	89 T	90 J	91 W	92 H	93 I	94 U	95 G	96 B	97 C	98 P	99 S
100	100 F	101 R	102 S	103 O	104 N	105 B	106 K	107 U	108 N
109	109 D	110 U	111 I	112 J	113 Y	114 W	115 G	116 D	117 A	118 K
119	119 I	120 S	121 W	122 P	123 N	124 V	125 O	126 M	127 J	128 D
129	129 S	130 J	131 H	132 T	133 I	134 N	135 J	136 C	137 T	138 D
139	139 B	140 M	141 I	142 P	143 S	144 T	145 D	146 B	147 L	148 C
149	149 N	150 B	151 R	152 T	153 H	154 U	155 N	156 D	157 P	158 K	159 I
160	160 S	161 C	162 B	163 I	164 O	165 K	166 I	167 S	168 V
169	169 W	170 R	171 G	172 N	173 E	174 X	175 V	176 P	177 E	178 Q	179 W
180	180 N	181 K	182 B	183 N	184 U	185 K	186 L

113

Grid

1 M	2 Q	3 J	4 E	5 O	6 L	7 I	8 S			
9 L	10 T	11 N	12 S	13 U	14 Q	15 N	16 H	17 D		
18 G	19 P	20 R	21 W	22 K	23 L	24 E	25 G	26 S		
27 T	28 B	29 N	30 P	31 T	32 O	33 P	34 C	35 L		
36 Q	37 J	38 G	39 I	40 G	41 R	42 W	43 J	44 I	45 C	
46 F	47 P	48 T	49 M	50 K	51 J	52 R	53 B	54 T	55 G	
56 T	57 P	58 V	59 M	60 A	61 B	62 S	63 R	64 L		
65 A	66 K	67 M	68 T	69 F	70 C	71 P	72 J	73 O	74 A	75 G
76 V	77 B	78 E	79 Q	80 W	81 D	82 B	83 N	84 S		
85 R	86 K	87 V	88 E	89 N	90 U	91 A	92 G	93 B		
94 L	95 B	96 K	97 A	98 U	99 O	100 W	101 N	102 Q	103 L	104 M
105 Q	106 O	107 W	108 E	109 R	110 M	111 V	112 U	113 C	114 J	115 N
116 V	117 B	118 F	119 M	120 G	121 L	122 I	123 H	124 U		
125 G	126 M	127 A	128 Q	129 U	130 I	131 H	132 F	133 L	134 H	
135 T	136 C	137 G	138 F	139 F	140 O	141 K	142 J	143 V	144 U	
145 U	146 A	147 T	148 O	149 N	150 C	151 I	152 D	153 C		
154 R	155 J	156 E	157 G	158 P	159 A	160 W	161 S	162 F	163 D	
164 V	165 M	166 E	167 G	168 U	169 O	170 E	171 D	172 V		
173 V	174 K	175 W	176 A	177 J	178 S	179 G				

CLUES / WORDS

A First three of six famous last words
127 97 91 176 159 65 146 74 60

B "Stars in the purple dusk above the ___" (Aiken, "Senlin: A Biography")
117 95 82 93 53 28 61 77

C Extreme in degree, strength, or quality
34 70 113 136 150 45 153

D Sauciness, impudence
163 152 81 17 171

E Perturbed, excited
170 88 108 4 166 24 78 156

F Piers
139 118 46 138 162 132 69

G Four opening words of Henley's "Invictus"
92 157 120 25 38 55 18 179 167 137 40 75 125

H Late stage of epidemic encephalitis
131 123 16 134

I Escape, as from punishment (2 wds.)
7 122 151 130 39 44

J Hypersensitive or pathological reactions
37 177 155 114 51 142 3 43 72

K Belief; whim
96 50 174 86 22 141

L Competitors for the America's Cup
9 103 94 121 23 35 133 64 6

M Conceal (as, e.g., a flaw)
1 126 110 104 67 49 119 165 59

N Collateral or derived descendant
15 83 29 115 11 89 149 101

O "One murder made a villain, / ___ a hero" (O. Henry, "Death")
169 5 148 32 140 99 106 73

P Humiliated
30 57 47 19 158 71 33

Q Liquid petroleum derivative used as a solvent and cleaning fluid
79 105 128 14 36 102 2

R Bestows abundantly
52 109 154 63 85 41 20

S Muffs, misses
84 62 26 8 161 12 178

T Most probable or plausible
147 56 135 48 31 54 27 68 10

U Position of control or advantage (2 wds.)
90 13 145 144 98 129 112 124 168

V Boiling; very enthusiastic
172 116 164 111 143 173 76 87 58

W Causing to fall; spreading beyond limits
80 175 160 66 100 42 107 21

	1	K3	H4	F5	L6	E7	P8	K
9	S10 Q11	12 I13	L14	O15	J16	E17	D18	T
19 S20	21 K22	D23 R24	F	25	Q26	O27	G	
28 P29 O30	C	31 J32	A	33 U34	P35	L	36	D
37 S38 R39	Q	40 K41	C42 J43	U	44	T45	R46	S
47 V48 K49	T50 U51	Q52	O	53 V54	M55	J56	H	
57 B58 U59	R	60 Q61	T62 V63	U	64	Q65	A	
66 I67 M68	O	69 A70	C71 S72	I73	O74	B75	K76	F
77 C78 R79	V80 M81	Q82	B83 U84	P	85	K86	V	
87 I	88 K89	N90 J91	B92	C	93	K94	B95	N96 R
97 O	98 F99	G100 L101	K102 C103	J104	H105	B106	B107	V
108 A109 V110	E	111 A112	B113 F114	U115	M116	P		
117 L118 O119	P120 R	121	N122 J123	C124	V	125	A	
126 G127 I128	T129 K130	V131 H	132	S133	M134	G135	B136	F
137 D138 K139	C140 Q141	E142	143	H144	C145	D146	E	
147 Q148 S149	N150 K151	I152 J153	U	154	A155	C		
156 S157 Q158	B159 E160	C161 N162	U163	D164	Q165	G		
166 R167 R168	B169 K	170	T171 P172	D173	L174	C175	N	
176 A177 E178	Q179 V180	181	F182	V183	S184	G185	D	
186 J187 N188	M189 U190	I191 K192	G193	H194	195	T196	R	
197 A	198 B199	J200 D201	F	202	M203	S204	G205	D206 F
207 C208	F209 U210	E211 P212	S213	B214	Q			

CLUES

A Last word; certainty (2 wds.) . . . . .
B Gr. scholar (c 275–c 195 B.C.) credited with measuring circumference of the earth . . . . . .
C Determined by external rather than personal norms (hyph.) . . . . . .
D Bronc-busters and wranglers, e.g. (2 wds.) . . . . . .
E 1952 Johnny Mercer rewrite of a 1907 Paul Lincke song (hyph.) . . .
F Rejoicing . . . .
G Enclosure, as of a fortified place . . .
H Restraints, tethers . . . .
I Not exact . . . .
J Geological fault with a low dip and a large slip . . . .
K Walter De La Mare calls clouds "bright ___" (3 wds., "England") . . .
L Place for sideshows at a carnival; group of U.S. islets in the N Pacific
M Complex, intricate . . . .
N Iowa city on the Mississippi . . . . .
O Quickness; killing (var. sp.) . . . . . .
P Fr. priest (1624–1709), confessor to Louis XIV (2 wds.) . . . . . .
Q Exam demand for a short composition (2 wds.) . . . . . .
R Hostile, ill-disposed . . . .
S 1909 H.G. Wells novel (2 wds.) . . . .
T Basis of sashimi (2 wds.) . . . .
U Severe censure . . . .
V Common category of second-hand clothing (hyph.) . . . .

WORDS

A	111	32	69	125	187	176	138	197	65	154	108			
B	82	158	74	198	94	135	57	168	112	106	91	213		
C	160	104	155	207	92	140	144	41	123	174	70	77	30	
D	185	205	137	36	163	22	200	145	172	17				
E	146	16	177	110	6	142	210	159						
F	136	208	98	206	201	181	24	4	76	113				
G	126	99	204	184	165	134	193	27						
H	3	194	105	131	56	20	143							
I	12	180	151	127	101	72	66	191	87					
J	42	90	152	186	55	199	122	15	103	31				
K	75	129	21	139	102	85	150	40	8	192	48	2	88	93 169
L	13	173	100	117	5	35								
M	54	80	202	133	115	189	11	67						
N	149	175	121	161	188	95	89							
O	97	118	52	14	29	68	73	26						
P	119	34	211	28	7	171	84	116						
Q	214	164	60	147	51	64	178	39	25	141	157	10	81	
R	38	23	120	59	78	196	96	45	166	167				
S	71	183	148	19	156	46	203	9	212	132	37			
T	170	61	49	195	18	128	44							
U	1	58	50	83	162	190	33	209	43	63	153	114		
V	86	47	130	107	62	79	124	109	53	182	179			

115

Acrostic puzzle grid (white squares shown as *number·clue-letter*):

1 A	2 G	3 M	4 D	5 J	6 C	7 E				
8 T	9 I	10 L	11 V	12 E	13 T	14 L	15 C	16 C	17 U	
18 H	19 E	20 V	21 M	22 G	23 B	24 K	25 G	26 U	27 M	
28 S	29 Q	30 I	31 E	32 Q	33 C	34 A	35 P	36 E		
37 Q	38 O	39 F	40 H	41 G	42 B	43 M	44 T	45 F	46 K	47 D
48 S	49 C	50 J	51 E	52 F	53 P	54 B	55 O	56 T	57 J	
58 G	59 E	60 F	61 N	62 R	63 R	64 P	65 F	66 Q	67 V	
68 S	69 F	70 L	71 H	72 K	73 S	74 E	75 M	76 K	77 H	78 T
79 F	80 C	81 T	82 M	83 Q	84 D	85 R	86 J	87 P	88 R	
89 I	90 V	91 M	92 I	93 U	94 I	95 D	96 T	97 R		
98 I	99 H	100 J	101 G	102 H	103 P	104 N	105 B	106 A	107 K	
108 T	109 E	110 J	111 A	112 M	113 P	114 J	115 E	116 U	117 D	
118 B	119 U	120 M	121 L	122 D	123 I	124 H	125 P	126 F		
127 E	128 U	129 I	130 V	131 O	132 Q	133 G	134 U	135 L	136 C	
137 E	138 J	139 D	140 J	141 B	142 F	143 H	144 P	145 K	146 M	
147 N	148 D	149 M	150 L	151 N	152 S	153 S	154 V	155 M		
156 H	157 P	158 O	159 A	160 F	161 K	162 U	163 B	164 G	165 O	
166 T	167 O	168 U	169 I	170 S	171 J	172 H	173 O	174 G		
175 V	176 E	177 S	178 T	179 K	180 D	181 U	182 A			

CLUES

A "Like sunrise from the sea, / —— arose" (Shelley, "Hellas") · · · · · ·
34 182 111 159 1 106

B "Be ——; a golden bridge / Is for a flying enemy" (2 wds.; Byron, "The Deformed Transformed")
54 163 118 23 42 105 141

C Eng. mathematician and natural philosopher (1642–1727; "Opticks")
15 6 136 49 80 33

D Gr. philosopher, fl. c 300 B.C.
180 4 139 84 47 122 95 117 148

E One who drops things · · · · · · · · ·
115 74 127 19 176 12 31 137 51 109 59 7 36

F Henry James novel (2 wds. after "The") · · · · · ·
39 69 45 160 126 60 52 142 79 65

G Classical nag, married to Socrates · ·
174 2 101 58 25 41 164 133 22

H Game involving small plastic disks · ·
143 77 16 102 40 71 124 18 172 99 156

I Emanation · · · · · · · · · · ·
169 30 92 129 89 123 9 98 94

J Sharp knocking sound (hyph.) · · · · · ·
5 114 57 171 86 100 140 138 50 110

K Urges · · · · · · · · · · · · ·
107 179 161 145 76 72 46 24

L Former duchy in West Germany; type of golf match · · · · · ·
135 70 10 121 150 14

M 1965 hit play by Neil Simon, 1968 film (3 wds.) · · · · · ·
3 21 27 120 82 155 146 91 43 149 75 112

N Nymph loved by Pan and Narcissus · ·
61 151 147 104

O E.W. Hornung's gentleman thief · · · ·
38 131 55 158 165 173 167

P One who mumbles · · · · · · · · ·
144 53 87 125 113 157 35 103 64

Q Duty · · · · · · · · · · · · · ·
32 83 132 29 66 37

R Conspicuous hairnet · · · · · · · ·
63 85 97 88 62

S Pennsylvania-Dutch dish · · · · · ·
28 170 177 153 73 48 68 152

T Hints · · · · · · · · · · · · · ·
178 108 78 8 56 44 81 13 166 96

U For the most part (3 wds.) · · · · · ·
116 181 119 168 162 17 93 26 128 134

V Petroleum; petroleum distillate used as a solvent · · · · · · · · · · ·
154 67 175 130 90 20 11

Grid

1 G	2 Q	3 P	4 G	5 X	6 E	7 H				
8 G	9 T	10 D	11 H	12 C	13 R	14 F	15 T	16 M	17 E	
18 V	19 S	20 X	21 A	22 F	23 N	24 L	25 P	26 Q		
27 D	28 B	29 I	30 X	31 N	32 Q	33 S	34 R	35 J	36 R	
37 C	38 I	39 H	40 B	41 U	42 T	43 Q	44 N	45 L	46 R	47 O
48 F	49 G	50 I	51 B	52 V	53 W	54 D	55 T	56 H		
57 J	58 R	59 U	60 P	61 G	62 B	63 I	64 M	65 X		
66 R	67 H	68 C	69 U	70 I	71 N	72 S	73 K	74 L	75 S	
76 A	77 Q	78 U	79 M	80 X	81 B	82 K	83 R	84 O	85 A	
86 K	87 P	88 C	89 E	90 S	91 T	92 G	93 U	94 B		
95 F	96 A	97 K	98 O	99 D	100 R	101 I	102 J	103 I		
104 Q	105 E	106 C	107 X	108 D	109 J	110 I	111 V	112 S	113 T	114 G
115 O	116 N	117 A	118 L	119 M	120 B	121 R	122 F	123 P		
124 L	125 V	126 I	127 G	128 K	129 E	130 D	131 H	132 O	133 Q	134 C
135 S	136 U	137 P	138 L	139 E	140 L	141 I	142 N	143 H		
144 Q	145 P	146 I	147 N	148 F	149 B	150 C	151 C	152 W	153 K	
154 V	155 J	156 O	157 W	158 R	159 Q	160 A	161 Q	162 P		
163 G	164 H	165 T	166 J	167 P	168 W	169 U	170 B	171 N		
172 W	173 V	174 O	175 D	176 C	177 G	178 E	179 F	180 M	181 J	
182 C	183 K	184 J	185 V	186 X	187 S	188 E				

CLUES

A. Eng. Arctic explorer (1584–1622)
B. Tightened economy
C. Boisterous, rowdy play
D. Mourns, laments
E. Supporter; sticking
F. Took turns
G. State positively
H. Historical novel by Henryk Sienkiewicz (2 wds.)
I. Low-lying shrubbery in a forest
J. Basic, natural
K. Comfort
L. Liturgical prayer in Judaism
M. Eng. satirist (1567–1601; "The Unfortunate Traveler")
N. Protective garments
O. Fr. poet and dramatist (1868–1918; "Cyrano de Bergerac")
P. "A much more respectable bird" than the one "chosen as the representative of our country," said Franklin (2 wds.)
Q. Willful, obstinate
R. Great weariness
S. Eng. portrait painter (1723–92), first president of the Royal Academy
T. Arctic cetacean, the male of which has a tusk
U. Busy, occupied, pledged
V. Devil, deuce; Eng. novelist (1812–70)
W. Gaze with exultation or malicious pleasure
X. O.T. prophet who saw powerful and marvelous visions

WORDS

A. 76 21 160 96 85 117
B. 28 40 81 94 51 149 120 62 170
C. 106 176 134 151 182 37 88 12 150 68
D. 175 108 27 54 10 99 130
E. 89 17 105 129 6 178 188 139
F. 22 95 122 48 179 148 14
G. 4 49 8 114 177 92 127 163 1 61
H. 11 143 39 67 131 56 7 164
I. 110 103 70 141 38 126 101 146 50 29 63
J. 102 35 109 155 184 181 166 57
K. 97 183 86 73 82 153 128
L. 74 45 118 124 24 138 140
M. 16 79 119 180 64
N. 171 147 71 31 116 44 23 142
O. 132 98 47 84 174 156 115
P. 87 145 167 162 137 60 25 3 123
Q. 2 26 161 159 32 104 77 133 144 43
R. 34 121 58 66 83 46 36 13 100 158
S. 72 33 75 135 187 19 112 90
T. 55 15 113 91 42 165 9
U. 78 69 41 93 169 59 136
V. 154 185 18 173 125 111 52
W. 168 172 152 157 53
X. 107 186 30 80 5 20 65

117

The grid consists of numbered cells, each bearing a clue-reference letter. Cell numbers 1–182 carry the following clue letters:

Cell	1	2	3	4	5	6	7	8	9	10
Letter	H	M	T	B	M	I	C	G	H	E
Cell	11	12	13	14	15	16	17	18	19	20
Letter	N	C	Q	B	S	A	E	C	A	O
Cell	21	22	23	24	25	26	27	28	29	30
Letter	S	K	T	I	X	I	A	M	E	I
Cell	31	32	33	34	35	36	37	38	39	40
Letter	T	S	Z	R	E	V	Q	G	Q	W
Cell	41	42	43	44	45	46	47	48	49	50
Letter	O	U	S	I	X	C	K	X	V	D
Cell	51	52	53	54	55	56	57	58	59	60
Letter	J	J	T	M	F	L	U	F	E	Z
Cell	61	62	63	64	65	66	67	68	69	70
Letter	W	T	V	A	J	W	N	E	V	N
Cell	71	72	73	74	75	76	77	78	79	80
Letter	O	C	J	U	G	Z	C	Q	R	F
Cell	81	82	83	84	85	86	87	88	89	90
Letter	T	B	K	S	Y	U	O	L	X	W
Cell	91	92	93	94	95	96	97	98	99	100
Letter	F	Z	D	R	G	K	M	J	H	V
Cell	101	102	103	104	105	106	107	108	109	110
Letter	I	U	N	D	M	A	P	Y	H	Z
Cell	111	112	113	114	115	116	117	118	119	120
Letter	U	C	I	G	P	G	U	P	W	V
Cell	121	122	123	124	125	126	127	128	129	130
Letter	O	J	H	L	U	R	Y	T	P	A
Cell	131	132	133	134	135	136	137	138	139	140
Letter	J	M	V	Z	U	D	M	O	J	I
Cell	141	142	143	144	145	146	147	148	149	150
Letter	W	Y	H	Y	A	H	N	Y	V	N
Cell	151	152	153	154	155	156	157	158	159	160
Letter	Z	A	G	A	Z	Z	W	Y	J	V
Cell	161	162	163	164	165	166	167	168	169	170
Letter	B	L	X	S	F	T	Q	K	X	E
Cell	171	172	173	174	175	176	177	178	179	180
Letter	H	N	A	F	S	Q	S	D	W	N
Cell	181	182								
Letter	X	F								

CLUES

A 19th-cen. terrorist · · · · · · · · · · · · · · · · · · 152 145 173 154 27 106 64 130 16 19

B Death notice · 161 4 82 14

C Bug by repeating embarrassing stuff (3 wds.) · · · · · · · · · · · · · · · · · 18 77 72 112 7 12 46

D Disease caused by a paramyxovirus · · · · · 104 93 50 178 136

E Dimwit, dolt · 68 17 59 10 35 29 170

F Cataract, avalanche · · · · · · · · · · · · · · · · · 174 55 58 182 91 165 80

G Small dog resembling a greyhound · · · · · · 116 114 8 95 38 75 153

H Acuteness of mental discernment, wisdom · 9 109 146 143 99 171 1 123

I Giving rise to, originating · · · · · · · · · · · · · 44 30 24 101 140 6 26 113

J Ger. dramatist (1862–1946; "Before Dawn," "Rose Bernd") · · · · · · · · · · 139 73 98 51 52 122 131 159 65

K Throw into disorder · · · · · · · · · · · · · · · · 22 83 47 168 96

L Am. Sec. of State, 1961–69 · · · · · · · · · · 56 162 124 88

M Limited to two options (hyph.) · · · · · · · · 105 137 132 2 54 5 28 97

N Swimming · 172 103 150 70 11 180 67 147

O "Stephen Sly and old John Naps of ___" ("Taming of the Shrew") · · · · · · · · · · 138 71 41 20 87 121

P Adman's word indicating non-filling or non-fattening · · · · · · · · · · · · · · · · · 118 107 115 129

Q Divulge, reveal · · · · · · · · · · · · · · · · · · · 37 78 13 39 167 176

R Jerk, dimwit · 34 126 94 79

S Get along congenially (3 wds.) · · · · · · · · 15 43 84 177 164 175 21 32

T Vision · 31 166 3 23 128 62 53 81

U Native or inhabitant of Connecticut · · · · 102 86 125 111 117 74 57 135 42

V Barrelhouse jazz · · · · · · · · · · · · · · · · · · 69 49 133 120 149 160 100 63 36

W What Lilli Marlene stood underneath (with "The") · · · · · · · · · · · · · · · · · · 119 61 40 179 157 141 90 66

X 1917 song by Ballard MacDonald and James F. Hanley · · · · · · · · · · · · · · · · 25 181 48 89 45 163 169

Y One who mocks and ridicules · · · · · · · · · 144 108 148 127 142 158 85

Z Narrow and rigid in opinion, inflexible · · 134 151 92 155 60 156 33 110 76

Grid

1	2	W3	A4	Q5	R6	C7	H8	K
9 W	10 R11	Q12 Y	13	E14	M15	F16	T17	U18 R
19 G	20	J21 K	22 K23	F24	W25	N26	H27	F
28 E29	I30 L	31	E32 Z33	34	X35	D36	M37	N
38 E	39 P40	U41	42 Q43	H44	P45	S46	Z
47 U48	R49 D50	Z	51 Q	52	D53	G54	F55	T
56 X	57	S58	T59	J60	61	T62	H63	K64 Y65	L
66 O67	P68 W69	M	70 Z71	W72 Y73	74	Z75	N
76	B77	G78	C79 N80	L	81	A82	G83	S84	P85	C
86	S87 Y88	R	89 X	90	L91	B92	Z93	H94	S
95 Q	96 O97	I98	E	99 R	100	H101	Z102	N
103 J104	C105 G106	M107	N108	B109	I110	111 V112	F
113 T114	N115 C	116	Q117	O118	N119	M120 V	121	F122	Q
123 W124	A125 K	126	Y127	E128	T129	R130	U131	J132	J
133 M134	N135	O136	D137	G	138	D139	T140	P141	N142	E
143 A	144 P145	S	146 M147	K148	H149	Y150	S151	S152	R
153 H154	G155	J156	157	B158	A159	Z160	L
163 B164	V	165 G	166	I167	K168	L169	E170	171 V
172 B173	L174	E	175 O	176	Z177	Y178	A

CLUES

WORDS

A. Belvedere 178 124 158 143 81 3

B. Napolitano's motherland 157 76 172 91 108 163

C. Am. playwright (1906–63; "Waiting for Lefty") 78 6 115 104 85

D. Leafy shelter 138 35 52 49 136

E. Suckled (hyph.) 13 142 127 28 38 170 31 174 98

F. Definitely out of favor (2 wds.) 121 112 27 54 15 149 23

G. Planet Earth barrier 165 82 169 53 137 73 77 154 19 105

H. Not-too-profitable building 148 93 62 100 7 43 26 153

I. Pater familias of Sydney Smith's comic-strip Gump family 97 109 166 29

J. Eng. political scientist (1893–1950; "Karl Marx," "Communism") 132 155 103 59 20

K. Judicial investigations 167 21 63 147 60 125 22 8

L. Gave counsel 90 160 173 65 30 80 168

M. Uniform color (2 wds.) 36 106 119 133 146 156 14 69

N. Orphanage alternatives (2 wds.) 75 141 79 102 134 33 114 118 107 37 25

O. Shocked 135 110 96 175 66 117

P. Offended 144 67 140 39 84 44

Q. Narrow strip of land 51 95 122 11 42 4 116

R. Soaped 5 99 10 48 129 152 18 88

S. Brit. volunteer cavalry force 94 151 45 57 86 83 41 145

T. Stringed instrument bridge 16 162 61 128 58 55 139 113

U. Imprecation 40 131 47 17

V. Wise and wordly preceder 111 164 171 120 130

W. Submissive salutation 9 24 2 68 71 123

X. Footnote abbr. 1 34 89 56

Y. Loonybin 87 64 161 150 177 72 126 12

Z. Type of jacket stuffing (2 wds.) 46 101 32 70 159 176 74 92 50

119

CLUES

A Indebted ....

B Arouse to high passion ....

C Lowest tier of a four-tiered hull (2 wds.) ....

D "The wind blows over the ___" (followed by WORD E; Yeats, "Land of Heart's Desire") ....

E See WORD D (2 wds.) ....

F Those who refute or deny ....

G "Her hair that lay along her back was ___" (4 wds.; Rossetti, "The Blessed Damozel") ....

H What gardeners, ditchers, and grave-diggers hold up, according to the First Clown in "Hamlet" (2 wds.) ....

I Denial ....

J Thunderous, earthshaking ....

K Upper part of a ship's stern ....

L Editor of this quotation's source; one who exhibits a show-dog or trains a fighter ....

M Poll time (2 wds.) ....

N "Come, and trip it as ye go / On the light ___" (2 wds.; Milton, "L'Allegro") ....

O Northernmost town on Lake Tangan-yika ....

P Informs; cautions beforehand (2 wds.) ....

Q Not merited ....

R Echo, pulse, throb ....

S Delicacy from a Dutch dairy (2 wds.) ....

T Free, unconfined (3 wds.) ....

U Former colonial federation in SE Asia (2 wds.) ....

V 1860 George Eliot novel (4 wds. after "The") ....

W Stir to action ....

X Armistice year (2 wds.) ....

WORDS

A 4 159 2 114 234 155 76 129

B 226 42 198 127 168 196 156

C 197 99 150 14 161 50 181 74 66

D 13 203 147 51 188 111

E 190 95 125 46 228 195 208

F 81 174 61 67 31 88 121 139 223 77

G 235 205 7 120 236 69 166 28 16 183 134 162 169 82 149 194 54 214

H 18 158 112 140 38 72 173 222 56 25 109 185 154 104 123

I 204 30 225 32 163 122 152 62

J 231 221 53 87 37 191 200 33 138

K 48 90 193 108 115 63 211 24

L 209 219 187 29 210 202 132

M 141 45 177 23 124 128 118 233 92 110 189

N 146 133 175 27 206 85 179 75 44 35 57 96

O 43 105 22 89 12 58 207 39

P 153 6 170 116 47 94 98

Q 5 137 217 230 17 126 19 220 80 34

R 182 239 160 68 227 165 78 3

S 117 8 131 40 176 79 84 216 144 192

T 100 142 229 103 151 65 107 86 71 164

U 201 97 171 10 15 180 49 70 60 26 238 113 224 91 136

V 101 9 199 167 145 21 143 218 73 212 64 186 178 157

W 172 135 232 148 52 106

X 83 93 59 130 102 215 213 237 41 184 11 36 1 55 20 119

120

	1	I2	P3	N4	H5	O6	R7	M8	J9	G10 A
11 V	12 K13	L14	C15	U16	S17	O18	F	19	A20	D21 U
22	L23	C24	P25	X26	I	27	G28	U29	D30	P31 N
32	I33	F34	P35	D36	R37	Y	38	V39	Y40	T41 H
42 X	43	A44	J45	G	46	T47	Q	48	H49	F50 C
51	B52	P53	U	54	U55	K56	H57	P58	59	Y60 X
61	K62	G63	F64	U65	B	66	B67	T68	X69	P70 H71 J
72	Z73	E74	S75	76	W77	J78	Y79	R80	L81	U82 Q
83	M84	K85	V	86	S87	O88	I89	F	90	W91 E92 U
93	F94	V95	K96	97	Q98	P	99	R100	G101	B
102 P103	W104	J105	E106	N	107	L108	Y	109	F110	M111 D
112	L113	Y114	B115	Q116	V117	Z	118	Y119	G120	E121 D122 N
123 C124	H125	Z	126	C127	L128	G	129	V130	N131	T132 B
133	Z134	G135	P	136	U137	I	138	G139	F140	D141 I
142 W143	Q144	Y145	K146	V	147	K	148	V149	R150	J151 T
152	C153	N154	P155	Q156	S157	I158	A159	H160	Y161 M	162 P
163	I164	T165	W166	X167	C168	O169	S	170	B171	Q172 P
173	G174	C175	F176	B177	J178	E179	W180	A181	O182 Y	

121

CLUES

A. U.S. general who succeeded MacArthur in Philippines command in 1942

B. "I mind that I ___ my neighbour's wife to sin the deadly sin" (Kipling, "Tomlinson")

C. Faulkner's Mississippi county

D. Musical comedy star (1909–84; "Girl Crazy," "Annie Get Your Gun"; full name)

E. Purple or violet quartz, used as a gemstone

F. Tornado, whirlwind

G. Sleepwalker

H. Heartbeat disturbance

I. Astringent fruit that is sweet and edible when ripe

J. Remote (hyph.)

K. Stiff strips used in manicuring; nail files (2 wds.)

L. "Have no more profit of ___ / Than those that walk" (3 wds., "Love's Labour's Lost")

M. Satan (2 wds.)

N. In progress, advancing; expected (3 wds.)

O. "I'll not answer that: / But say it is my ___: is it answered?" says Shylock

P. "With my cross-bow ___" (4 wds., "The Ancient Mariner")

Q. River in N France flowing to the English Channel

R. Favor, aid, succor

S. Covered or surrounded with foliage

T. Covered the inside of (as clothing)

U. Powerful downward tennis stroke (2 wds.)

V. Sight; perception; apparition

W. 1894 George Moore novel (2 wds.)

X. Shields; fortifies; protects

WORDS

A. 79 83 222 39 10 157 57 212 178 132

B. 149 80 105 3 214 116 162 111

C. 38 158 33 24 63 69 67 143 113 177 163 139 77

D. 91 226 229 138 45 216 99 196 37 134 211

E. 145 125 203 85 22 217 34 27

F. 124 60 174 112 65 17 95

G. 108 126 62 224 164 159 30 40 197 73 96 68

H. 94 44 123 190 107 146 137 184 151 23

I. 218 93 150 47 207 205 53 101 20

J. 74 192 180 223 167 189 119 106 182 109 7

K. 170 193 87 202 213 2 35 185 209 100 72

L. 173 144 59 188 18 220 86 11 191 147 135 104 114 1 6 28 136 48

M. 58 13 19 36 210 128 75 155

N. 171 110 21 76 227 187 70 230

O. 98 215 175 129 9 50

P. 179 78 120 140 88 12 56 176 204 130 208 52 97 14 8 148 84

Q. 206 31 153 231 121

R. 42 154 172 127 89 181 82 115

S. 103 152 194 32 55 51 169 232 131

T. 165 117 64 46 49

U. 183 102 195 228 66 225 5 201 54 41 122 26 161

V. 16 4 200 168 61 142

W. 29 199 118 133 15 141 92 219 160 166 81 71

X. 25 198 156 43 186 90 221

122

Diagram

The numbered cells (with their clue-letter labels) in reading order, by row:

Row	Cells
1	1(W) 2(O) 3(R) 4(F) 5(S) 6(W) 7(X) 8(S) 9(I) 10(X)
2	11(J) 12(X) 13(N) 14(D) 15(W) 16(P) 17(Y) 18(A) 19(H) 20(J)
3	21(W) 22(Q) 23(X) 24(I) 25(O) 26(H) 27(K) 28(A) 29(Y) 30(P)
4	31(S) 32(L) 33(B) 34(C) 35(H) 36(G) 37(S) 38(F) 39(G)
5	40(B) 41(Z) 42(I) 43(C) 44(R) 45(U) 46(S) 47(M) 48(H) 49(D)
6	50(Y) 51(S) 52(I) 53(G) 54(G) 55(S) 56(B) 57(L) 58(P)
7	59(F) 60(J) 61(B) 62(Y) 63(A) 64(T) 65(V) 66(R) 67(D) 68(W) 69(N)
8	70(J) 71(P) 72(H) 73(S) 74(L) 75(E) 76(T) 77(R) 78(E)
9	79(Z) 80(Q) 81(S) 82(Y) 83(K) 84(O) 85(R) 86(U) 87(J) 88(D)
10	89(E) 90(D) 91(D) 92(B) 93(F) 94(I) 95(S) 96(C) 97(R)
11	98(Q) 99(X) 100(H) 101(C) 102(M) 103(O) 104(Z) 105(R) 106(L) 107(I)
12	108(J) 109(Z) 110(X) 111(R) 112(H) 113(W) 114(A) 115(T) 116(N)
13	117(F) 118(V) 119(A) 120(P) 121(X) 122(C) 123(B) 124(J) 125(O) 126(V)
14	127(P) 128(J) 129(D) 130(Q) 131(R) 132(U) 133(G) 134(S) 135(F)
15	136(Z) 137(T) 138(O) 139(J) 140(N) 141(E) 142(S) 143(U) 144(S) 145(V) 146(F)
16	147(G) 148(S) 149(H) 150(R) 151(K) 152(C) 153(H) 154(H) 155(N)
17	156(E) 157(J) 158(J) 159(S) 160(B) 161(U) 162(H) 163(I) 164(M) 165(G)
18	166(A) 167(N) 168(K) 169(Y) 170(B) 171(M) 172(T) 173(H) 174(M) 175(Q)
19	176(X) 177(S) 178(I) 179(C) 180(Y) 181(W) 182(P) 183(W) 184(E) 185(G) 186(S)
20	187(H) 188(Y) 189(M) 190(K) 191(U) 192(C) 193(O) 194(P) 195(Z) 196(D)
21	197(Q) 198(F) 199(R) 200(E) 201(C) 202(N) 203(Y) 204(N) 205(D) 206(P) 207(K)
22	208(R) 209(T) 210(S) 211(X) 212(E) 213(W) 214(X) 215(J) 216(L)

CLUES

A. Much ado about nothing? 114 63 166 28 18 119

B. One upon whom a payment is imposed 61 170 123 56 40 33 92 160

C. Like Conan Doyle's "League" or Lucy 152 201 192 122 96 179 101 34 43

D. Site of the Magna Carta's signing 88 196 129 90 49 91 205 14 67

E. Excite one's curiosity; banking term . . . 89 141 200 156 184 212 78 75

F. "Written After ___ from Sestos to Abydos" (Lord Byron) . . . 198 135 38 146 4 117 93 59

G. L. Frank Baum character; noise made by "My Grandfather's Clock" (hyph.) . . . 39 147 185 165 54 36 133 53

H. Bugliosi book; hasty confusion (hyph.) . . . 162 100 19 187 154 26 149 153 173 112 72 35 48

I. Cause great weight loss 24 178 9 52 42 107 94 163

J. Montana's neighbor; 1954 Alan Ladd film 108 87 157 124 128 158 70 139 215 11 20 60

K. Quechuan 27 168 190 151 207 83

L. Gringo reata 106 74 57 216 32

M. Not "the real McCoy" 164 47 102 189 171 174

N. High social rank; idealistic condition 13 167 204 140 202 69 116 155

O. Polo period 138 2 125 84 103 193 25

P. Packing material 71 194 182 30 127 206 58 120 16

Q. Eccentricity 98 130 22 197 80 175

R. "That's nonsense!" (hyph.) 131 199 208 66 111 44 85 77 97 150 105 3

S. "Still ___ blows the cold wind," says Edgar (3 wds., "King Lear") . . . 148 186 81 177 46 142 159 31 73 134 95 51 8 210 55 5 144 37

T. Household, abode 76 209 115 64 137 172

U. Eradicate, expunge 191 45 143 132 161 86

V. Give up, forfeit; fail 126 145 118 65

W. Observant, devoted 183 113 6 15 21 1 181 68 213

X. "___ be bloody or be nothing worth," says Hamlet (2 wds.) . . . 99 214 23 7 12 110 176 211 121 10

Y. One who flits aimlessly from one thing to another . . . 50 82 180 62 169 188 17 29 203

Z. Raucous cry; complain 79 195 104 136 41 109

123

CLUES / **WORDS**

A Provided 150 193 84 93 124 67 31 2 158

B Formal approval 100 103 22 161 149 179 80 42 48 191 143 68

C Satisfying desire 134 181 192 157 35 41

D Slavering 19 58 125 34 165 101

E "The heavens forbid / But that our ___ and comforts should increase," says Desdemona ("Othello") 72 162 62 17 94

F Scabs, as from burns 23 145 86 131 50 9 114

G Germany's armed forces, collectively 130 63 115 190 44 20 177 95 79

H Pertaining to points of equal radiation intensity in a contaminated area 154 73 169 24 15 128 88

I Distrustful 182 144 118 77 91 167 116 69 148 10

J Speech sound 21 7 32 172 176

K In an indiscriminate manner 122 52 112 168 180 82

L Flattery; candy 111 18 25 107 36

M Structural system composed of braced frames 139 27 184 194 40 175 136 49 92 12 105

N Shifty, cagey 171 70 11 138 96 98 61

O Holy Communion 174 5 160 81 129 75 110 38 30

P Type of protective covering 14 45 123

Q Castigating, attacking 28 97 186 4 159 120 113 155 187

R Wharf laborer, circus laborer 87 132 108 173 6 119 151 106 37 147

S Coarse twilled woolen cloth with a cotton warp 59 39 16 55 13 166

T Quality or state of being worthless, useless, or generally inferior 90 46 127 170 135 137 43 99 60 117

U "___ / 'I,' says the Quarterly" (4 wds., Byron poem of July, 1821) . . 3 53 57 85 51 133 102 71 141 156 26 183 29 47 76 89 178 146

V Declare 74 121 189 56

W Using an organization's own staff and resources rather than outside facilities (hyph.) 54 64 65 83 152 164 140

X A voiding or rendering inoperative . . 126 163 33 188 142 1 66 104 78 153 185 8 109

■	■	1 X	2 A	3 U	■	4 Q	5 O	6 R	7 J	8 X	9 F
10 I	■	11 N	12 M	13 S	■	14 P	15 H	16 S	17 E	■	18 L
19 D	20 G	21 J	22 B	23 F	24 H	■	25 L	26 U	27 M	■	28 Q
29 U	30 O	31 A	32 J	33 X	34 D	35 C	36 L	■	37 R	38 O	39 S
■	40 M	41 C	42 B	43 T	■	44 G	45 P	46 T	47 U	■	48 B
49 M	50 F	51 U	52 K	■	53 U	54 W	55 S	■	56 V	57 U	58 D
59 S	60 T	■	61 N	62 E	63 G	64 W	■	65 W	66 X	67 A	■
68 B	69 I	70 N	71 U	72 E	73 H	■	74 V	75 O	76 U	■	77 I
78 X	79 G	80 B	81 O	82 K	83 W	84 A	85 U	■	86 F	87 R	88 H
89 U	90 T	91 I	92 M	93 A	94 E	■	95 G	96 N	97 Q	■	98 N
99 T	100 B	101 D	■	102 U	103 B	104 X	105 M	■	106 R	107 L	■
108 R	109 X	110 O	111 L	112 K	■	113 Q	114 F	■	115 G	116 I	117 T
■	118 I	119 R	120 Q	121 V	122 K	123 P	124 A	125 D	126 X	■	127 T
128 H	■	129 O	■	130 G	131 F	132 R	133 U	134 C	■	135 T	136 M
■	137 T	138 N	■	139 M	140 W	141 U	142 X	143 B	144 I	145 F	■
146 U	147 R	148 I	149 B	150 A	■	151 R	152 W	153 X	■	154 H	155 Q
156 U	157 C	158 A	159 Q	160 O	161 B	162 E	163 X	164 W	165 D	166 S	■
■	167 I	168 K	169 H	170 T	171 N	172 J	■	173 R	174 O	175 M	176 J
177 G	178 U	179 B	180 K	181 C	182 I	■	183 U	184 M	■	185 X	186 Q
■	187 Q	188 X	189 V	190 G	191 B	192 C	193 A	194 M	■	■	■

CLUES

A. Restraints, checks — 117 5 100 173 72 97 93 12 183 84 114

B. European crows; swindles — 105 128 153 3 27

C. Defeat, subjugate — 43 134 95 111 54 31 48 116

D. Spotless, undefiled — 150 178 57 53 118 112 73 47 169 138

E. Ornamental recesses in a wall — 98 94 52 149 131 166

F. Wearing away by persistent nibbling; vexing, plaguing — 122 171 71 115 29 164 16

G. Open statement of affirmation — 2 30 36 179 58 70

H. Ranunculaceous herb with large, showy flowers — 136 25 163 125 49

I. Russian seaport on the Don, near the Sea of Azov — 17 187 162 168 35 67

J. Morbid secretion of sperm whales, used in perfumery — 68 127 50 65 26 33 89 170 139

K. Sport that prompted the founding of the Water Club of Cork Harbor in 1720 — 15 77 156 24 11 167 174 185

L. Alienate — 104 55 86 137 161 182 6 9

M. Gabs incessantly (2 wds.) — 148 66 23 129 28 83 151 61 41

N. Attaches securely — 62 107 8 184 101 19 40

O. Chiefly aquatic insectivore, Potamogale velox, of W Africa (2 wds.) — 22 78 99 81 141 135 193 191 46 38

P. Arbiters, judges — 82 140 87 113 34 177 106 181

Q. Am. comedian (1892–1957) often in "another fine mess" in film comedies (full name) — 88 158 110 142 74 159 176 124 45 20 102

R. Am. poet (1819–92; "Song of Myself") — 133 130 155 92 195 18 59

S. Irish patriot (1778–1803) — 56 21 37 42 1

T. Small cup or mug — 108 186 145 96 4 32

U. Large, powerful, short-haired dog — 14 7 75 175 69 189 146

V. 1605 comedy by Chapman, Jonson, and Marston (2 wds.) — 44 180 165 109 80 39 154 126 64 190 194

W. Having no weak points or openings — 10 143 132 152 91 172 119 63

X. 1940 Nelson Eddy–Jeannette MacDonald film (2 wds.) — 144 76 103 120 147 85 13

Y. 1933 Harbach-Kern song from "Roberta" — 60 160 90 192 51 123 188 157 121 79

WORDS / GRID

Cell	Cell	Cell	Cell	Cell	Cell	Cell	Cell	Cell	Cell	Cell
1 S	2 G	3 B	4 T	5 A	6 L	7 U	8 N			
9 L	10 W	11 K	12 A	13 X	14 U	15 K	16 F	17 I		
18 R	19 N	20 Q	21 S	22 O	23 M	24 K	25 H	26 J	27 B	28 M
29 F	30 G	31 C	32 T	33 J	34 P	35 I	36 G	37 S	38 O	
39 V	40 N	41 M	42 S	43 C	44 V	45 Q	46 O	47 D	48 C	
49 H	50 J	51 Y	52 E	53 D	54 C	55 L	56 S	57 D	58 G	
59 R	60 Y	61 M	62 N	63 W	64 V	65 J	66 M	67 I		
68 J	69 U	70 G	71 F	72 A	73 D	74 Q	75 U	76 X	77 K	78 O
79 Y	80 V	81 O	82 P	83 M	84 A	85 X	86 L	87 P		
88 Q	89 J	90 Y	91 W	92 R	93 A	94 E	95 C	96 T	97 A	
98 E	99 O	100 A	101 N	102 Q	103 X	104 L	105 B	106 P		
107 N	108 T	109 V	110 Q	111 C	112 D	113 P	114 A	115 F	116 C	117 A
118 D	119 W	120 X	121 Y	122 F	123 Y	124 Q	125 H	126 V	127 J	
128 B	129 M	130 R	131 E	132 W	133 R	134 C	135 O	136 H	137 L	
138 D	139 J	140 P	141 O	142 Q	143 W	144 X	145 T	146 U	147 X	148 M
149 E	150 D	151 M	152 W	153 B	154 V	155 R	156 K	157 Y	158 Q	
159 Q	160 Y	161 L	162 I	163 H	164 F	165 V	166 E	167 K	168 I	169 D
170 J	171 F	172 W	173 A	174 K	175 U	176 Q	177 P	178 D		
179 G	180 V	181 P	182 L	183 A	184 N	185 K	186 T	187 I	188 Y	
189 U	190 V	191 O	192 Y	193 O	194 V	195 R				

125

CLUES

A. Vulnerable feature (2 wds.) — 204 151 199 126 185 113 77 50 94 18 219

B. Like most stained-glass windows, e.g. — 181 107 120 63 133 31

C. Third book of the Pentateuch — 145 105 183 43 138 6 125 24 177

D. Disagreeable vapors from decaying matter — 159 2 187 32 191 103 58 144 220

E. Cleared; caught — 89 170 95 202 200 208

F. "Till a feeble cheer ___ / To our cheering sent us back" (2 wds.; Campbell, "Battle of the Baltic") — 194 203 39 87 157 134 10

G. Home circle; fireside — 96 37 163 213 59 13

H. Device on a harpsichord producing the effect of a distant sound (2 wds.) — 124 169 136 114 35 36 51 82

I. Fall to in the mess hall (2 wds.) — 173 80 70 46 165 150 12 8

J. Of a chance, better than even (hyph.) — 100 130 5 140 44 23

K. The floating in air of heavier-than-air bodies, as in spiritualism and magic — 153 55 40 193 128 3 198 1 88 91

L. City on Lake Winnebago — 176 42 215 76 117 11 161

M. Move in a circular orbit — 48 84 156 186 38 71 216

N. Vehement, acting with headlong energy — 41 179 121 102 190 4 14 164 34

O. Biscuit rusk also called Brussels biscuit — 61 22 78 86 147 172 210 141

P. 1934 Cole Porter musical (2 wds.) — 197 110 195 131 65 72 27 93 19 207 129 57

Q. Seesaw (hyph.) — 211 167 184 206 148 192 116 26 99 79 119 201

R. Next in relation, directly connected — 75 28 69 137 52 109 127 154 90

S. In bum shape; not working (3 wds.) — 21 152 149 178 217 142 15 189 111 174

T. Dopes, simpletons — 85 166 30 205 218 180 54

U. Gave — 146 112 45 81 175 7 98

V. Ornament — 62 188 101 115 143 92 108 73 20

W. Bully — 171 123 212 106 118 33 16 67

X. Sympathetic critical essay — 68 83 25 196 53 9 155 66 135 29 209 168

Y. Smarten up — 64 60 214 104 17 97 160 182

Z. "The ___'s a gentleman" (Kipling, "Oonts") — 49 74 162 122 132 139 56 158

WORDS

126

Grid

1 U	2 K	3 H	4 H	5 Y	6 T	7 S
8 B	9 P	10 O	11 D	12 R	13 V	14 Z	15 Z	16 I	17 E
18 R	19 B	20 X	21 E	22 H	23 S	24 T	25 Q	26 C	27 L
28 O	29 P	30 K	31 Z	32 Y	33 B	34 K	35 G	36 J	37 M
38 D	39 V	40 M	41 R	42 N	43 A	44 W	45 S	46 H
47 D	48 T	49 C	50 Y	51 W	52 W	53 F	54 R	55 H	56 P
57 G	58 K	59 K	60 L	61 C	62 T	63 T	64 R	65 R	66 O
67 K	68 J	69 Z	70 I	71 F	72 Z	73 L	74 L	75 D
76 N	77 A	78 J	79 K	80 I	81 F	82 C	83 Y	84 Y
85 C	86 V	87 E	88 B	89 W	90 M	91 G	92 W	93 L	94 J
95 P	96 Q	97 Z	98 B	99 F	100 H	101 E	102 X	103 S
104 Y	105 U	106 C	107 F	108 Y	109 F	110 U	111 J	112 A	113 Q
114 E	115 W	116 Y	117 K	118 A	119 K	120 G	121 Q	122 T
123 A	124 V	125 S	126 C	127 P	128 B	129 D	130 M	131 X	132 S	133 N
134 M	135 Q	136 O	137 L	138 E	139 L	140 B	141 N	142 X
143 U	144 O	145 L	146 N	147 I	148 P	149 D	150 B	151 E	152 O
153 I	154 S	155 V	156 M	157 S	158 H	159 Q	160 I	161 U	162 X
163 I	164 E	165 Z	166 O	167 H	168 S	169 C	170 M	171 U	172 A
173 T	174 U	175 A	176 L	177 Y	178 J	179 W	180 S	181 G	182 V	183 X
184 E	185 X	186 K	187 V	188 U	189 N

CLUES

	Clue	Words
A	Mild tonic or stimulant.	112 77 43 118 175 123 172
B	Famous people.	150 8 88 140 33 98 19 128
C	Totality of infinite time.	106 85 82 126 169 26 49 61
D	Women's close-fitting hats.	129 38 75 47 149 11
E	Emotional.	87 21 138 17 151 184 114 164 101
F	Dolt.	53 109 71 107 99 81
G	Ferment.	91 120 181 57 35
H	In a servile manner.	22 100 46 3 55 4 158 167
I	Raised.	16 147 160 80 153 163 70
J	Pronounced.	111 178 78 36 68 94 52
K	Baseball (sl.).	2 117 186 58 67 119 34 30 79
L	Extent of projection, as a boat's bow.	73 145 139 60 93 137 27 176
M	Idler, ne'er-do-well.	40 90 130 156 37 170 134
N	Nominal.	189 146 65 76 133 42 141
O	With spirit and vigor.	66 152 59 166 28 10 144 136
P	Weirdly.	29 56 9 127 148 95
Q	Australian marsupial.	96 25 113 135 159 121
R	Moral significance.	54 12 41 64 18
S	Intellectually pretentious.	45 125 23 154 168 180 103 7 132 157
T	Gad.	74 6 173 62 24 48 122
U	Peace pipes.	105 171 174 143 161 188 1 110
V	Alarm.	155 63 39 124 13 187 86 182
W	Dolt.	51 179 115 89 44 92
X	Blathers.	131 185 142 102 20 183 162
Y	Rouse; make fretful.	177 32 104 83 108 50 116 5
Z	Most filthy.	72 31 69 15 97 165 14 84

127

Grid

1 A	2 Z₁	3 X	4 Z₁	5 B	6 C	7 F	8 T	9 I		
10 H	11 G	12 B	13 F	14 J	15 N	16 H	17 Q	18 C	19 I	
20 E	21 K	22 R	23 M	24 T	25 G	26 D	27 F	28 Y	29 L	
30 Z₁	31 T	32 S	33 H	34 M	35 G	36 K	37 B	38 O	39 S	
40 M	41 L	42 G	43 J	44 W	45 H	46 N	47 V	48 I	49 O	50 P
51 K	52 Z	53 U	54 U	55 V	56 H	57 U	58 T	59 P	60 R	
61 D	62 S	63 M	64 W	65 J	66 Z₁	67 N	68 A	69 B	70 H	
71 T	72 F	73 H	74 Z	75 D	76 D	77 X	78 J	79 Q		
80 P	81 V	82 Z₁	83 K	84 Z	85 Q	86 F	87 Y	88 B	89 K	
90 V	91 D	92 K	93 H	94 E	95 I	96 H	97 O	98 Q	99 M	
100 V	101 E	102 P	103 B	104 Z₁	105 Z₁	106 A	107 R	108 F		
109 S	110 E	111 Z₁	112 K	113 M	114 O	115 B	116 X	117 L	118 Y	
119 K	120 V	121 Z	122 X	123 W	124 S	125 A	126 P	127 U	128 E	129 W
130 A	131 T	132 U	133 Y	134 B	135 G	136 F	137 N	138 D		
139 R	140 Q	141 Y	142 H	143 W	144 A	145 H	146 U	147 Z₁	148 B	149 E
150 M	151 D	152 R	153 O	154 I	155 J	156 U	157 O	158 Q		
159 L	160 G	161 F	162 S	163 C	164 P	165 R	166 V	167 I	168 J	
169 W	170 X	171 U	172 V	173 Y	174 S	175 C	176 X	177 G	178 I	
179 S	180 F	181 Y	182 A	183 E	184 Y	185 B	186 G	187 Q		
188 C	189 V	190 P	191 X	192 L	193 U	194 B	195 D	196 C		

CLUES / WORDS

A Othello says his eyes "Drop tears as fast as the ___ trees / Their medicinal gum" — 182 144 130 125 68 1 106

B Meaning — 37 69 115 185 194 5 88 103 148 12 134

C Eng. poet (1849–1903; "England, My England") — 6 196 163 18 188 175

D Understanding — 138 195 151 61 26 76 75 91

E Minister (1844–1930) known for such metatheses as "kinquering congs" — 94 128 110 149 183 101 20

F Without premeditation — 108 86 13 136 180 72 161 7 27

G Smartest — 177 25 42 186 35 11 160 135

H Walkers — 145 96 73 56 16 46 33 142 93 70 10

I Severely criticized — 95 48 9 154 167 19 178

J Spiny anteater — 78 14 168 65 43 155

K Ohio valley Indians — 119 51 83 89 21 92 112 36

L Destroy — 41 117 29 192 159

M Dropping off — 63 99 113 150 40 34 23

N Plate in a suit of armor — 67 15 46 137

O Trojan hero — 114 157 49 153 38 97

P Nonsense — 59 50 190 102 80 126 164

Q Frustrates — 17 187 158 79 140 98 85

R "Lord" who propagandized for the Nazis (hyph.) — 107 22 60 152 139 165

S Forbade — 32 174 179 162 124 109 62 39

T Concealed difficulties or disadvantages — 131 71 31 8 24 58

U "Gentlemen always seem to ___ blondes" (Anita Loos) — 171 127 156 146 53 57 132 193 54

V Based on experience — 81 172 120 47 100 166 90 55 189

W Man plays such fantastic tricks "As make the ___ weep," ("Measure for Measure") — 64 44 169 143 129 123

X Rump (2 wds.) — 191 176 3 77 170 122 116

Y Sovereign; commanding; august — 184 28 181 118 87 133 173 141

Z Wet place in a dry clime — 121 84 52 74

Z₁ Teller — 2 4 66 111 82 105 30 104 147

128

The grid (enumerated squares, letter-coded):

7 L	8 K9	A10	Y11 U		1	E2	O3	X4	F	5	H6 Q
	18 A19	T20	E21 M22	L	12 E13	X14	R15	I	16	G17 C
27 Q28	C29	J30	P	31 I	32 Q	23	A24	Y25	W	26 M
37 R38	N39	F40	W	41 I	42 G43	F44	H45	R46 K	33 G34	K35	V36 H
47 F48	U	49	P 50	Y51	J	52 M53	T 54	T 55	O56 K
57 C58	M59	V60	Y61	G	62 D63	I 64	Q	65 B
66 N67	I 68	O69	C70	S 71 Q	72 V73	J 74	B 75	P 76 Q
77 R	78 Q79	J 80	U81	B	82 S83	C	84	V85 O
86 B87	U	88	V 89	C	90	O91	L92	S 93	J 94 Y
95 M96	H97	T 98	C 99	U100	G101	X102 F	103 A104	M105 D
106 I	107 C108	W	109 B	110 S	111 N112 Q	113 H114	A115 B
116 A117	E118	N119	D120 Y	121 L	122 P	123 D	124 J
125 W126	T127	128 R	129 D	130 V	131 U	132 B	133 Q	134 X	135 I
136 P	137 L	138 X	139 Q	140 Y	141 O	142 W	143 G	144 V	145 H	146 T
147 M	148 E	149 B	150 J	151 T	152 A	153 U	154 I	155 X	156 V
157 E	158 O	159 H	160 S	161 C	162 E	163 F	164 A	165 R	166 N
167 W168	U169	L170	Q171	J	172 Q	173 W	174 E	175 K	176 D
177 V178	K179	180 V	181 B	182 A	183 T	184 E	185 R	186 L
187 U188	I189	O	190 Q	191 N	192 Y	193 M194	V195	U196 H
197 W	198 U	199 X	200 F	201 X	202 W	203 G	204 O	205 M	206 C
207 S	208 E	209 P	210 D	211 A	212 R	

WORDS / CLUES

A Digression as an address to someone not present.
9 103 164 182 23 18 152 116 114 211

B Hermann Goering's pride and joy.
86 181 132 81 109 149 74 65 115

C Its cap. is Abidjan (2 wds.)
69 28 89 57 17 206 83 98 161 107

D Saw.
119 105 129 210 62 123 176

E Some have-not nations (2 wds.)
162 148 184 1 157 117 20 174

F Seat of the papacy during the "Babylonian Captivity"
200 47 163 102 4 43 39

G Base, mean.
100 33 61 203 143 16 42

H Opposed by contrary proof
44 196 5 159 145 188 96 36

I Fancy word for an article of soul food
135 63 53 154 188 127 67 15 31 106 41

J Transgressed
51 124 73 29 150 171 79 93

K Indolent
34 8 175 178 56 46

L Insect named for its sound.
169 91 121 186 21 137 7 22

M Comforter
58 193 147 21 52 95 104 26 205

N D. Hoffman's transvestite
111 191 66 179 166 38 118

O Musket predecessor.
2 85 141 158 204 68 90 55 189

P Racing-shell crews
136 75 49 122 209 30

Q "Monkey terrier".
27 133 78 170 71 190 172 32 139 76 112 64

R Boer War siege.
212 14 185 77 37 128 165 45

S Mechanical contrivance
160 92 146 151 54 19 97 183 207

T Fortification.
126 146 151 11 198 48 99

U Conjurer, magician
187 87 80 130 144 177 84 88 59 35 156

V Union
194 72 130 180 144 197 173 25 134 3 155

W "Samson ____" (Milton)
167 40 125 101 13 199 134 50 94

X They were reputedly gay.
201 138 101 13 199 134 50 94

Y To a small degree.
120 192 10 60 24 140 50 94

CLUES

A Hero of the Texas Revolution (1796–1836), killed at the Alamo

B Manual, notebook

C Spiritually significant or symbolic

D Popular assembly of anc. Athens

E Bombed, stoned, plastered

F Strong, sweet wine, originally from Greece

G Storms, charges

H Most modern

I Municipal borough on the Sow River, England; Izaak Walton's birthplace

J Volume having pages of the largest size

K Sturdy breed of western saddle horses

L Mah-jongg pieces

M Qualifying races

N Bunk, hooey

O Discomposed, shaken

P Reversible fabric woven with patterns

Q Leap during which a dancer crosses his feet while in the air

R Palace of the Moorish kings in Granada

S Inordinate greed

T Drifts along

U Escort, comrade

V Biased

W Snub, be snooty toward (hyph.)

X Pale yellow; very brittle; omelet residue

Y Sightseer, tourist

WORDS

A	82	159	177	128	16					
B	153	51	6	12	68	110	38	162	135	121 96
C	19	101	39	176	7	143				
D	70	63	149	29	173	47	117	20		
E	172	66	35	79	184	75				
F	126	168	15	118	141	133	181			
G	1	26	175	119	158	150	89			
H	183	48	53	32	60	14				
I	59	142	30	136	36	41	95	11		
J	103	46	33	91	78					
K	109	77	31	86	24	52	130	76	114	
L	115	140	45	3	107					
M	67	72	174	156	50					
N	97	81	10	129	42	34	157			
O	155	13	99	43	73	58	25			
P	132	144	4	90	17	64				
Q	178	2	124	134	93	44	138	56	65	
R	94	55	22	170	145	85	139	148		
S	87	154	80	102	137	125	169	71		
T	54	100	182	88	151	69				
U	8	104	61	164	112	49	83	21	167	
V	108	186	179	92	28	122	9	74	152	160 18
W	27	111	123	163	37	5	180			
X	105	113	165	98	116	23	161	120		
Y	84	62	171	147	146	106	131	127	40	57

130

CLUES

A. Shakespearean sleepwalker (2 wds.)
B. Race course S of London (2 wds.)
C. Outfitted with a 3-electrode semiconductor device
D. Nocturnal benefactor for small children (2 wds.)
E. See WORD G (3 wds.)
F. U.S. institution established in 1836 to encourage inventiveness (2 wds.)
G. 1942 book by C. O. Skinner and E. Kimbrough (3 wds. followed by WORD E)
H. Small bomb
I. Indian prince or king
J. Book of the Old Testament
K. Playboy Club waitresses
L. Not applicable.
M. Food
N. Horses that don't win, place, or show (hyph.)
O. Immense number
P. Material useful in attack or defense.
Q. Eng. actor who won an Oscar for "Separate Tables" (1958)
R. Stronger; more resistant
S. Grub found at the roots of the Australian acacia; chief food of the marsupial mole
T. Grasshoppers, locusts, crickets, etc.
U. Made thinner
V. Fabled solution to a Parisian bread famine (4 wds.)
W. Athenian orator and statesman (348?-322 B.C.)

WORDS

A. 138 148 110 11 29 69 74 3 51 122 192
B. 37 115 118 211 104 113 198 18 27 147
C. 23 67 116 42 5 168 179 160 96 19 130 181 220
D. 83 91 59 107 201 199 25 54 187 38
E. 63 33 114 80 126 66 106 142 47 108 58
F. 100 209 68 137 7 200 176 196 212 131 21 170
G. 119 13 182 214 45 139 24 167 173 194 87 219 202
H. 156 102 73 135 95 31 8
I. 136 62 32 39 204
J. 165 203 14 143 157 17 124 53 64 180 43 178
K. 216 60 154 2 184 56 82
L. —
M. 81 183 128 141 149 121 44 177 16 20
N. 36 134 103 158 78 92 26 217 40
O. 101 132 10 79 35 218 210 28
P. 84 133 207 30 153 57
Q. 205 152 61 4 125 88 77 1 12 109
R. 166 206 86 99 112
S. 9 140 34 72 98 144 197 52
T. 171 195 191 127 123 94 162 97 188
U. 186 161 90 93 85 76 213 105 190 155
V. 169 71 46 146 159 6 48 50 55 150 49 65 22 111 208 193 129 174 175 15 145 164
W. 41 75 120 189 117 163 172 89 215 70

131

Grid (reading order; each cell shows number and answer-letter)

1 I	2 D	3 R	4 F	5 J	6 D	7 D	8 Y	9 V		
10 Q	11 O	12 F	13 Z	14 Y	15 Z₁	16 B	17 X	18 N	19 Z₂	
20 W	21 L	22 A	23 Y	24 E	25 P	26 M	27 G	28 C	29 A	
30 Q	31 C	32 X	33 H	34 F	35 R	36 K	37 C	38 Z₁	39 C	
40 H	41 V	42 I	43 L	44 D	45 T	46 Y	47 N	48 P		
49 S	50 Z₂	51 G	52 O	53 C	54 P	55 Y	56 T	57 S	58 Q	
59 N	60 L	61 W	62 F	63 K	64 E	65 V	66 H	67 Z	68 A	
69 W	70 E	71 Z₂	72 O	73 K	74 A	75 I	76 Z₁	77 R	78 Q	
79 S	80 Z	81 A	82 V	83 J	84 Y	85 B	86 Z	87 G	88 C	
89 O	90 B	91 J	92 X	93 K	94 S	95 Z	96 F	97 R	98 D	99 Y
100 G	101 H	102 J	103 B	104 Q	105 Y	106 E	107 V	108 W	109 C	
110 S	111 L	112 J	113 I	114 J	115 U	116 L	117 Z₁	118 P		
119 V	120 A	121 W	122 G	123 R	124 S	125 F	126 I	127 K	128 J	129 T
130 F	131 C	132 Q	133 B	134 S	135 C	136 M	137 T	138 J	139 X	
140 Z	141 G	142 B	143 U	144 J	145 I	146 J	147 O	148 U	149 T	
150 Z₂	151 P	152 V	153 T	154 Y	155 F	156 W	157 I	158 D		
159 M	160 Z₁	161 V	162 O	163 J	164 Z₂	165 Y	166 E	167 I	168 E	
169 U	170 W	171 J	172 M	173 K	174 Z₁	175 S	176 B	177 Z₂		
178 D	179 V	180 T	181 W	182 K	183 U	184 G	185 R	186 S	187 N	
188 D	189 B	190 Z	191 E	192 C	193 X	194 G	195 J	196 O	197 D	198 F
199 K	200 Z₁	201 R	202 Z₂	203 B	204 Z₁	205 G	206 Z	207 O		
208 R	209 N	210 M	211 W	212 P	213 T	214 E	215 F	216 O		
217 G	218 U	219 H	220 I	221 L	222 P	223 I	224 R	225 V	226 D	

CLUES

A Rules, principles . . . .
B Long, trumpet-shaped drinking glass with a bulb at the closed end (hyph.)
C Rule considered as derived from right reason and held as ethically binding (2 wds.)
D Greatly frightened . . . .
E Most convenient . . . .
F Resident . . . .
G Copying secretary . . . .
H Barrier, boundary, protection . . .
I One who has withdrawn from his native country
J Nonspecific, vague, general . . . .
K Sorcerer, wizard . . . .
L Flee, slip out, leak . . . .
M Permission; farewell . . . .
N Struck; killed . . . .
O Exposed to loss or injury . . . . .
P Insoluble yellow coloring matter of some flowers
Q Flips, throws . . . .
R Disparity, unevenness . . . . . .
S Apparently self-contradictory propositions
T Movie outline . . . .
U Diabolically wicked persons . . . .
V Involving perpendiculars . . . . .
W Position of honor or special trust (2 wds.)
X Plasterlike preparation as a surface for painting
Y Present before one's eyes (3 wds.) .
Z Taking an irregular course . . . .
Z₁ Attempt that has little chance of success (2 wds.)
Z₂ Dismissed (2 wds.) . . . .

WORDS

A 81 120 22 68 74 29
B 203 189 90 85 103 133 176 142 16
C 131 53 88 31 37 109 135 28 39 192
D 158 226 98 197 44 178 6 188 2
E 214 168 24 70 106 166 191 64
F 198 62 125 130 96 34 4 215 12 155
G 87 51 217 100 205 122 194 184 27 141
H 33 219 40 101 66
I 113 220 145 223 75 167 126 1 42 157
J 146 138 195 163 171 144 91 128 114 102 83 112 5
K 93 127 63 73 182 173 36 199
L 21 60 221 111 116 43
M 136 210 26 159 172
N 59 187 18 209 47
O 196 147 207 11 7 162 89 72 52 216
P 48 212 151 25 222 118 54
Q 104 58 132 30 78 10
R 201 77 35 208 123 3 224 185 97
S 124 134 57 49 110 186 79 94 175
T 213 56 129 45 180 149 137 153
U 148 183 143 115 169 218
V 161 179 152 65 82 225 9 107 41 119
W 69 61 108 211 20 156 170 181 121
X 139 92 17 32 193
Y 99 84 46 165 23 154 8 14 55 105
Z 206 140 95 67 86 80 190 13
Z₁ 15 204 174 200 38 117 76 160
Z₂ 50 71 177 164 150 19 202

133

The grid (each cell shows its number and clue letter):

1 U	2 K	3 Z	4 U	5 T						
6 A	7 I	8 E	9 B	10 X	11 H	12 J	13 T	14 Q	15 L	16 V
17 I	18 F	19 C	20 G	21 E	22 Q	23 R	24 D	25 Y	26 B	
27 O	28 Z	29 H	30 B	31 E	32 S	33 F	34 Q	35 X	36 R	
37 B	38 H	39 F	40 Z	41 K	42 T	43 B	44 O	45 E	46 T	
47 K	48 Y	49 M	50 X	51 H	52 U	53 B	54 W	55 P	56 K	
57 F	58 V	59 U	60 C	61 E	62 R	63 D	64 L	65 Y	66 S	67 C
68 X	69 B	70 Q	71 K	72 E	73 A	74 U	75 D	76 M	77 P	78 J
79 I	80 J	81 W	82 C	83 N	84 F	85 A	86 U	87 R		
88 O	89 G	90 T	91 Q	92 A	93 H	94 D	95 K	96 T	97 B	
98 C	99 F	100 A	101 J	102 M	103 X	104 L	105 G	106 S	107 M	
108 N	109 P	110 L	111 R	112 I	113 F	114 Z	115 L	116 E	117 T	
118 E	119 U	120 D	121 S	122 J	123 I	124 A	125 Y	126 V	127 S	128 K
129 C	130 U	131 N	132 I	133 G	134 T	135 B	136 F	137 M	138 D	139 O
140 S	141 F	142 B	143 Z	144 W	145 Z	146 L	147 B	148 A	149 X	150 K
151 L	152 H	153 K	154 G	155 I	156 J	157 T	158 J	159 C	160 F	
161 I	162 H	163 Y	164 M	165 Y	166 F	167 B	168 Z	169 O	170 W	171 G
172 Q	173 Z	174 K	175 X	176 O	177 B	178 F	179 S	180 N	181 V	
182 A	183 Q	184 R	185 J	186 E	187 P	188 K	189 V	190 G	191 Z	
192 X	193 T	194 W	195 J	196 F	197 K	198 N	199 F	200 C		
201 Y	202 B	203 X	204 S	205 C	206 W					

CLUES

A Courteous, polite
B Pliant; susceptible
C "Open the old cigar box, get me a ___" (2 wds.; Kipling, "The Betrothed")
D Blades, shivs
E Rendered groggy, as by anesthetic
F Stiff-growing composite plant of Mexico (hyph.)
G Alarms; ugly or ridiculous persons or things
H Administrative divisions of Yorkshire, Eng.
I Outflow
J Having keen vision (hyph.)
K Handicap
L Eng. churchman (1808–92), Cardinal in the Roman Catholic Church
M Tests, analyzes
N Boob, dolt, sap
O Cheap, cheesy
P White Rhine wine (chiefly Brit.); pawn
Q Palestinian sect (fl. 2nd cen. B.C.-2nd cen. A.D.) characterized by asceticism and celibacy
R Beginnings; originals
S Checked, slowed down
T Not to be desired
U Bilious; cross; having a sour disposition
V Doubles, pairs
W "To draw ___ to ride, and speak the truth" (2 wds.; Byron, "Don Juan")
X Cheerful sign, promising glimmer (3 wds.)
Y Avoids, shuns
Z Passes the summer

WORDS

A 85 182 92 100 6 73 148 124
B 37 142 147 97 26 43 53 69 30 135 167 177 9 202
C 159 67 129 60 19 205 98 82 200
D 120 94 75 63 24 138
E 72 61 21 118 8 45 31 186 116
F 196 178 99 160 57 141 33 39 113 166 199 84 136 18
G 105 89 154 190 133 20 171
H 162 93 29 152 38 51 11
I 17 132 79 161 7 155 112 123
J 78 195 156 122 12 158 80 185 101
K 56 188 150 128 71 153 41 2 47 197 95 174
L 146 64 15 115 110 104 151
M 137 76 164 107 49 102
N 83 131 108 198 180
O 88 27 44 169 139 176
P 77 55 109 187
Q 172 34 70 14 91 22 183
R 36 87 23 111 62 184
S 204 106 140 121 66 127 32 179
T 90 46 193 42 13 134 96 117 157 5
U 130 52 74 86 119 1 59 4
V 16 181 58 189 126
W 144 206 170 54 81 194
X 175 103 10 50 68 192 35 203 149
Y 125 65 165 201 163 25 48
Z 28 168 191 40 173 114 3 145 143

CLUES

A — "Can ___, except they be agreed?"
(3 wds.; Amos 3:3) 186 191 124 21 145 40 93 104 37 219 121 148 159 2 24

B — Furnishing with equipment 187 105 158 154 125 190 152 58 205 184

C — NASA guidance group (2 wds.) 198 92 161 103 177 109 175 38 153 168 136 35 140 112

D — Ignis fatuus; illusion (hyph.) 133 174 157 91 209 86 188 142 12 99 29 1

E — Liberal, generous, magnanimous 171 207 97 89 185 134 218 32 20 57

F — Nickname for William Joyce, WW II Nazi propagandist (wd. & hyph.) 182 34 146 214 216 13 81 101 194 70

G — Oxymoronic term for booze 107 88 43 166 15 56 11 78 67

H — Spectacle, show 80 27 87 162 141 183 18 189 49 119

I — Softens, makes more palatable 170 144 135 75 94 79 199 163 181 7

J — "The Vamp of Savannah" who poured water on a drowning man (hyph. & wd.) 55 204 3 122 77 41 192 98 8 156 129 96 111 213 84 73 53

K — U.S. Air Force Base in S Calif., proving ground for military aircraft 203 138 52 44 208 151 116

L — Frightened, nervous, shy 196 62 42 172 28 36 22

M — Decline to testify (3 wds.) 217 178 202 23 176 137 47 16 155 210 68 106 59 180

N — Electrified, startled into sudden activity 90 5 132 65 17 19 197 164 26 169

O — Pastoral people of S Africa; Khoikhoi 48 118 45 95 66 128 123 85 69

P — Memorable Duke Ellington composition (4 wds.) 76 149 25 39 102 61 31 71 179 114 130 201 143

Q — "Country Justice" appearing in "Henry IV, Part II" and "The Merry Wives of Windsor" 14 9 167 131 113 54 60

R — Armado "draweth out the thread of his verbosity finer than ___ of his argument," says Holofernes (2 wds., "Love's Labour's Lost") 30 4 64 72 215 82 117 173 51

S — Honorable, straightforward 212 6 193 200 127 150 120 147 74 100

T — Suppurated 33 115 83 63 46 110 160 206

U — Aircraft carriers 108 165 10 139 126 211 195 50

135

WORDS / CLUES

A Sticky, tenacious — 168 117 85 195 74 29 99 7

B Beach promenade — 44 25 131 183 114 86 77 13 158

C Mountain range of the Balkan Peninsula — 151 56 125 204 94 137 15

D Temporal incongruity — 156 95 182 196 32 101 23 51 119 193 27

E Theories — 121 169 20 175 202 72 170 152 76 129

F Firedogs — 98 174 165 47 194 105 80 9

G Bartender — 181 59 140 149 199 66 166 50 16 31

H Hung around — 75 41 106 120 179 189 83 111

I Encroach — 145 143 26 112 79 127 35 118

J Thrush noted for the male's melodious song — 11 161 93 178 64 1 191 103 115 155 153

K Delighted, bewitched — 157 52 150 42 49 104 128

L Intermittently (3 wds.) — 176 65 2 12 78 192 186 97

M Dictionary — 198 46 60 54 71 33 92

N Functional disorders — 4 87 126 18 197 40 113 84

O Painful — 102 201 90 171

P Loosed — 67 70 146 91 53 38

Q Swarm, horde — 177 36 187 142 110 89

R Tapered pillar — 10 154 200 82 141 185 133

S Agitator, streetfighter, barroom scrapper — 188 167 160 144 138 203 68

T Exemption from penalty — 88 136 6 109 24 69 57 123

U Proposed — 135 81 61 107 162 28 14

V "___ and sapphires in the mud / Clot the bedded axle-tree" (Eliot, "Burnt Norton") — 55 48 180 45 22 148

W Mother of Zeus. Poseidon et al. — 132 108 63 96

X Stressed — 43 17 134 100 164 37 62 130

Y Punctuation pair — 124 3 8 139 116 122 147 39 58 172 30

Z Japanese verse — 159 190 19 184 34

Z_1 Something that causes ferment — 5 73 163 173 21

Grid

1 J	2 L	3 Y	4 N	5 Z_1	6 T	7 A	8 Y			
9 F	10 R	11 J	12 L	13 B	14 U	15 C	16 G	17 X	18 N	19 Z
20 E	21 Z_1	22 Z_1	23 D	24 T	25 B	26 I	27 D	28 U		
29 A	30 Y	31 G	32 D	33 M	34 Z	35 I	36 Q	37 X	38 P	
39 Y	40 N	41 H	42 K	43 X	44 B	45 V	46 M	47 F	48 V	
49 K	50 G	51 D	52 K	53 P	54 M	55 V	56 C	57 T		
58 Y	59 G	60 M	61 U	62 X	63 W	64 J	65 L	66 G	67 P	
68 S	69 T	70 P	71 M	72 E	73 Z_1	74 A	75 H	76 E	77 B	
78 L	79 I	80 F	81 U	82 R	83 H	84 N	85 A	86 B		
87 N	88 T	89 Q	90 O	91 P	92 M	93 J	94 C	95 D	96 W	
97 L	98 F	99 A	100 X	101 D	102 O	103 J	104 K	105 F	106 H	
107 U	108 W	109 T	110 Q	111 H	112 I	113 N	114 B	115 J	116 Y	
117 A	118 I	119 D	120 H	121 E	122 Y	123 T	124 Y	125 C	126 N	
127 I	128 K	129 E	130 X	131 B	132 W	133 R	134 X	135 U	136 T	
137 C	138 S	139 Y	140 G	141 R	142 Q	143 I	144 S	145 I	146 P	147 Y
148 V	149 G	150 K	151 C	152 E	153 J	154 R	155 J	156 C	157 K	
158 B	159 Z	160 S	161 J	162 U	163 Z_1	164 X	165 F	166 G		
167 S	168 A	169 E	170 E	171 O	172 Y	173 Z_1	174 F	175 E		
176 L	177 Q	178 J	179 H	180 V	181 G	182 D	183 B	184 Z	185 R	
186 L	187 Q	188 S	189 H	190 Z	191 J	192 L	193 D	194 F	195 A	
196 D	197 N	198 M	199 G	200 R	201 O	202 E	203 S	204 C		

Grid

The numbered squares (with their clue-letters) read, row by row:

1 S	2 L	3 R	4 T	5 P	6 C	7 O	8 M			
9 L	10 V	11 N	12 I	13 L	14 N	15 F	16 P	17 V	18 S	
19 B	20 Q	21 L	22 P	23 N	24 J	25 O	26 R	27 L	28 F	
29 H	30 G	31 S	32 J	33 K	34 D	35 I	36 M	37 X		
38 A	39 D	40 H	41 S	42 E	43 U	44 P	45 M	46 F		
47 J	48 P	49 L	50 F	51 U	52 B	53 B	54 Q	55 B		
56 T	57 P	58 H	59 Q	60 O	61 M	62 S	63 F	64 V	65 O	66 C
67 X	68 X	69 D	70 A	71 W	72 E	73 U	74 K	75 A		
76 A	77 R	78 X	79 I	80 J	81 N	82 E	83 Q	84 I	85 F	
86 C	87 T	88 H	89 P	90 A	91 O	92 X	93 A	94 B		
95 R	96 I	97 O	98 J	99 T	100 W	101 P	102 F	103 B	104 N	
105 M	106 I	107 I	108 L	109 V	110 X	111 L	112 X	113 K	114 H	
115 S	116 Q	117 G	118 Q	119 K	120 X	121 T	122 V	123 K		
124 H	125 N	126 J	127 I	128 K	129 G	130 C	131 O	132 K	133 S	
134 I	135 G	136 P	137 H	138 B	139 F	140 S	141 F	142 G	143 X	
144 C	145 Q	146 R	147 J	148 E	149 B	150 A	151 H	152 O	153 P	
154 Q	155 O	156 A	157 F	158 J	159 J	160 C	161 B	162 K		
163 H	164 D	165 E	166 H	167 M	168 L	169 K	170 W	171 N	172 Q	173 R
174 I	175 V	176 X	177 B	178 E	179 H	180 G	181 Q	182 T	183 U	
184 N	185 H	186 E	187 Q	188 G	189 D	190 N	191 P	192 S	193 K	
194 T	195 G	196 B	197 J	198 O	199 S	200 D				

CLUES

A Officer followed by three-fourths of the town, most of the people

B Urchin gets eastern Greek letter, leading to modern confusion

C Wharf is collapsing, yielding sashimi (2 wds.)

D Put aside easy bridge hand

E Say true mixing occurs where river meets sea

F Robin's mom in institution

G Troubled by bugs in party by editor

H Marines hide pets

I Went and gave in sinister fashion (hyph.)

J It's all over! First lady takes train, and we must go around her

K Beast makes company go back in river—so right to go back!

L Tosses plans

M Poor ole Dad is drunk

N Right of writer with "it"? Yes.

O Playwright sets one before legendary forest

P Thin cape results in prejudice

Q Dance on ship or play this

R Results from very loud soapy mixtures

S Excitement when U.S. anthem is ordered

T Provides Air Force with Model Ts, perhaps

U Philosopher blows up tank

V Mean to do in time, finish at last

W Beery actor had answer to excessive precipitation

X My amusing construction of athletic facility

WORDS

A 156 38 93 76 70 150 90 75

B 94 177 196 19 138 53 161 52 103 55

C 86 160 149 130 66 6 144

D 164 189 200 39 69 34 108

E 72 148 42 178 186 82 165

F 15 50 28 157 141 63 46 102 85 139

G 142 117 188 129 180 195 30 135

H 88 124 137 151 29 40 166 163 185 58 114 179

I 65 84 96 12 35 107 134 174 127 106

J 197 80 32 147 24 126 159 158 98 47

K 74 123 132 33 162 113 169 128 193 119

L 49 13 2 111 9 168 21 27

M 105 36 61 8 167 45

N 81 14 11 184 104 23 190 171 125

O 7 60 152 97 131 25 155 91 198

P 101 16 191 57 22 153 44 5 136 48

Q 20 154 59 187 54 172 181 145 116 118 83 89

R 3 26 173 146 95 77 68

S 133 140 1 18 62 192 41 199 115 31

T 56 194 121 87 4 182 99

U 51 43 73 183

V 175 10 122 64 17 109

W 170 100 79 71

X 143 110 37 78 112 176 120 67 92

137

Acrostic puzzle grid (rotated). Cell-to-clue assignments, reconstructed from the Words list (each cell shows a number and the letter of the word it belongs to):

1–6	P N X E I M
7–16	J S B T Y V X B W F
17–24	D Q F W R T G G
25–34	B V A U O N E H L B
35–45	K C A J U Y E A B V L
46–55	V T D G Q O C U X H
56–65	P M Q K G U X B A T
66–76	C J N T A G L H D B W
77–85	K V Q D U E W E G
86–95	K F J I R A P N W A
96–105	M K E W D N A K V Q
106–114	E M L I W F S J P
115–123	B M H L P J I L F
124–133	J S B O L X W Y A H
134–143	X W Y A H S O C R X
144–153	G P F R N U Y I B V
154–162	M Y I H J Y Y W T
163–172	H D C S K F P O J O
173–182	K I O Y T Q B P Q G
183–188	S R D L K C

CLUES

A "The rapture of the ___" (2 wds.; Meredith, "The Thrush in February")

B Eager for wealth

C Muslim chiefs

D Strong fabric used esp. in covering mattresses

E 1955 translation of Ehrenburg novel about life under Stalin (2 wds.)

F Browbeaten, abject

G Fade away

H Son of Gilead and a harlot (Judges 11:1)

I Leading character of John Lyly's *Anatomy of Wit*

J Most commendable

K Eng. poet and playwright (1837–1909, *Atalanta in Calydon*)

L Outlined

M "___ an unfelt sorrow is an office / Which the false man does easy" (2 wds., *Macbeth*)

N Rosalind's lover (*As You Like It*)

O Enliven, renovate

P Vigorous, enthusiastic

Q Norse explorer, fl. 880

R Uncultivated, untilled, unsown

S Hand on hip

T Ornamental plume; style, verve

U Practical; coarse, unrefined

V Rope used for pulling a sail along a boom, yard, etc.

W Want, need, distress

X Extravagant, excessive

Y Advocacy; marriage

WORDS

A 129 70 137 42 27 102 91 37 133 95 64

B 115 152 25 34 126 9 14 63 43 75 179

C 52 165 141 36 188 66

D 80 74 164 185 48 100 17

E 106 98 41 31 84 82 4

F 87 123 111 168 19 146 16

G 24 49 182 71 85 144 60 23

H 55 73 138 132 157 32 163 117

I 5 89 174 109 151 121 156

J 7 88 124 113 158 67 38 120 171

K 86 103 59 167 77 187 97 35 173

L 128 186 33 108 72 45 118 122

M 116 96 57 6 107 154

N 101 131 148 2 68 30 93

O 51 29 170 175 127 140 172

P 1 169 56 180 114 145 119 92

Q 18 181 58 178 79 105 50

R 21 184 90 147 130 142

S 8 112 166 125 183 139

T 177 65 47 10 69 22 162

U 61 53 39 28 81 149

V 12 46 44 153 104 26 78

W 135 161 110 94 76 83 20 99 15

X 54 143 13 62 134 3

Y 159 40 160 176 136 150 155 11

138

CLUES

A. Heritage, inheritance 123 208 12 39 42 220 131 139 144 217

B. Book by Louisa May Alcott (3 wds.) . . . 28 21 197 189 64 166 207 13 161 154 32 222 44 121

C. Pouring, coming down cats and dogs (2 wds.) 114 19 196 138 46 181 202 31 141 4 61 211 204 173 151 71 53

D. ___ flower: flower of the genus Scabiosa . . . 162 137 29 92 63 77 45 98 50 34

E. They fired "the shot heard round the world," said Emerson (2 wds.) . . . 194 108 214 2 136 15 23 120 155 171 25 59 97 96 192 146

F. Mythological characters in a tale of unrequited love (3 wds.) . . . 221 133 18 7 33 190 158 209 70 101 11 110 199 86 60 40

G. Sown; in tournaments, arranged so that the best players don't meet in the early rounds . . . 206 72 184 223 145 107

H. Am. author (1889-1970), creator of Perry Mason (full name) . . . 130 3 127 90 57 112 134 99 56 180 224 210 14 26 188 20 75 82

I. Vegetables used for flavoring . . . 191 111 195 95 102 149 125 87 213

J. Adder's-tongue (2 wds.) 193 37 185 94 172 200 119 153 218 169 163 159 74

K. Supple rod; changeover; movable rail for shunting . . . 135 6 126 35 17 183

L. Am. statesman-lawyer, Nobel Peace Prize, 1912 (full name) . . . 16 103 116 179 122 89 201 88 182

M. Oxygenation of the body by respiration 164 52 8 215 128 157 80 117

N. Floral hip (2 wds.) 49 203 140 156 79 167 113 73 85

O. Gardens of plants trimmed in fantastic shapes . . . 58 54 48 205 186 81 216 115 10

P. Type of country dance 93 84 100 68 168 178 142

Q. Supple rod 41 212 62 129 1

R. Ornamental Eastern Orthodox roof structures (2 wds.) . . . 152 106 55 83 67 177 38 47 198 219

S. Turning, as on an axis; type of pool game . . . 187 109 143 91 118 148 27 176

T. Island off SE Mass. (2 wds.) . . . 69 175 132 170 5 105 104 51 43 165 22 78 66 36 174

U. Dashiell Hammett's private eye (full name) . . . 24 160 9 124 150 76 30 65

139

CLUES

A "He lies white-faced and still in the ___." (Whitman, "Reconciliation") · · · · · ·

B Sea of ___, arm of the Pacific, W of Kamchatka Peninsula · · · · · · · · ·

C Popular embroidery figures (2 wds.) · ·

D Lower in rank or station: second-rate · ·

E Wanting · · · · · · · · · · · · · ·

F 1936 Astaire-Rogers film (2 wds.) · · ·

G At hand · · · · · · · · · · · · · ·

H Lower jawbone · · · · · · · · · · ·

I Daughter of Zeus and Demeter, abducted by Pluto · · · · · · · · · · ·

J Neglected child: urchin (2 wds.) · · · ·

K S Am. revolutionary leader (1720?-1801) first president of Chile · · · · ·

L Talked on at length, scolded (Brit. sl.) · · · · · · · · · · · · · · ·

M Belief, doctrine · · · · · · · · · · ·

N Toasts · · · · · · · · · · · · · · ·

O Factor, part, constituent · · · · · · ·

P Latest · · · · · · · · · · · · · · ·

Q Pacific atoll, major WW II fleet anchorage · · · · · · · · · · · · ·

R "The Destruction of ___." by Lord Byron · · · · · · · · · · · · · ·

S A bursting inward · · · · · · · · · ·

T Discussing, dealing with, doctoring · ·

U "Why, I will see thee ___." says Brutus (3 wds., "Julius Caesar") · · ·

V FDR's program of which the NRA, the AAA, and the TVA were components (2 wds.) · · · · · · · · · · · · · ·

W "___ him, I say, quite from your memory," says Mrs. Malaprop ("The Rivals") · · · · · · · · · · · · ·

X Terrify · · · · · · · · · · · · · · ·

WORDS

Clue	Word (cell numbers)
A	167 71 187 177 61 105
B	188 87 55 133 151 38 103
C	77 199 143 160 56 41 84 18 3 164 62 82 10 68
D	172 16 70 148 189 136 128 100
E	89 67 40 51 154
F	11 39 200 53 80 123 88 34 190
G	47 101 170 13 86 186 162 137
H	135 111 129 203 26 45 179 175
I	65 152 20 142 75 197 94 7 122 83
J	174 126 157 120 95 117 31 168 102 185
K	91 19 146 17 106 127 79 198
L	36 150 54 130 171 72 166 163
M	108 144 182 99 118
N	115 159 180 96 30 119 48
O	35 145 42 158 193 64 139
P	110 22 32 173 183 60 134 156 69 191
Q	44 14 107 74 192 52
R	194 21 181 98 57 132 49 124 66 104 147
S	121 58 109 76 4 29 15 131 27
T	37 5 73 116 8 196 113 28
U	141 81 43 9 112 153 97 1 138 6 195 202 125
V	25 50 140 184 59 161 176
W	85 46 201 169 114 24 2 12 93 33
X	63 155 92 149 78 90 165 23

Grid

1	U2	W3	C4	S5	6 U
7 I	8 T	U9	C10	F11	W12	G13	Q14	Q15	S16 D
17 K	C18	K19	K20	I21	R22	P23	X24	W25	V26	H27 S
28 T	S29	N30	J31	J32	W33	W34	F35	O36	L37	H38 B
39 F	E40	C41	O42	U43	Q44	H45	W46	W47	G48 N
49 R	V50	E51	Q52	Q53	L54	L55	B56	57 R
58 S	V59	P60	A61	C62	C63	X64	65	I66	E67	E68 C
69 P	D70	A71	L72	T73	Q74	I75	S76	S77	C78	X79 K
80 F	U81	C82	I83	C84	W85	W86	G87	F88	F89 E
90 X	K91	X92	W93	I94	J95	N96	N97	U98 R
99 M	D100	G101	J102	B103	R104	A105	A106	Q107	Q108 M
S109	P110	H111	H112	T113	W114	N115	N116	T117 J
118 M	N119	J120	S121	I122	F123	R124	R125	J126	K127	K128 D
129 H	L130	S131	R132	B133	P134	H135	H136	D137 G
138 U	O139	V140	U141	I142	C143	M144	M145	K146	K147 R
148 D	X149	X150	L151	I152	B153	U154	X155	X156	P157	J158 O
159 N	V160	V161	V162	G163	C164	X165	X166	167 A
168 J	J169	G170	L171	D172	D173	J174	H175	V176	V177 A
178 U	H179	N180	R181	M182	P183	P184	A185	G186	A187	A188 B
189 D	F190	P191	Q192	O193	R194	U195	T196	T197
198 K	C199	F200	W201	U202	U203 H

CLUES

A Bucket of bolts, tin lizzie · · · · · · · 148 51 15 41 77 162 164 59 30 132

B Briefly (2 wds.) · · · · · · · · · · · 119 35 115 146 75 90 158

C Small, snug place · · · · · · 99 11 166 39 112 42 54 22 37

D Port of Kiungshan, Kwangtung prov., China · · · · · 130 154 3 65 187 29

E Eng. actor-director-producer (*In Which We Serve, Gandhi*) · 184 7 150 93 141 194 56 173 60 107 103 181

F Requital; recompense for evil action 80 91 170 69 121 106 175 88 13 144 47

G Uncertain · · · · · · · · · · 52 87 174 46 25 76 9

H Crowded around · · · · · · · · 92 86 189 79 104 117

I Being prepared (3 wds.) · · · · · · 72 94 176 50 1 57 23 199 185 44

J One with short arms and low pockets 196 116 193 20 89 67 152 38

K Point, horn of the moon, e.g. · · · · · 4 136 183 55

L Dope fiend · · · · · · · · · · · 100 165 19 16 167 84 160

M Ugandan town on Lake Victoria · · 131 102 120 66 188 85 43

N Watch · · · · · · · · · · · · · 111 33 124 45 142 159 5

O Relaxes, eases (2 wds.) · · · · · · 70 156 12 149 97 2

P Good luck! Bon voyage! · · · · · · 83 127 36 157 26 133 58 71

Q Teeny (hyph.) · · · · · · · · 113 180 125 28 32 191 108 49 40

R Most affectionate · · · · · · · · · 143 109 123 95 182 105 153

S "See——o' battle lour" (2 wds.; Burns, "Scots Wha Hae") · · · · · · · 197 27 62 188 134 178 114 145

T Pleasant refuges from the ordinary, annoying, or difficult · · · · · · · · 140 101 31 186 122

U Joyous, merry · · · · · · · · · · 126 6 163 171 21 61 190

V Made much ado about trifles · · · 177 34 135 98 118 78

W Spell, charm; magic ceremony · · · 81 192 74 137 155 129 17 14 48 68 53

X Am. astronomer (1732–96), successor to Franklin as pres. of the American Philosophical Society · · · · · 128 139 64 73 198 110 151 96 8 24 169

Y Adventurous spirit, energy; *Star Trek* starship · · · · · · · · · · · 195 82 18 172 63 10 179 161 138 147

141

Grid

Row	Cells (number · clue-letter)
1–	1 J · 2 Z · 3 K · 4 J · 5 M
6–	6 A · 7 G · 8 I · 9 L · 10 P · 11 H · 12 X · 13 K · 14 M · 15 O
16–	16 Z₂ · 17 I · 18 X · 19 L · 20 G · 21 S · 22 K · 23 P · 24 C · 25 W
26–	26 B · 27 C · 28 Z₁ · 29 J · 30 D · 31 L · 32 T · 33 V · 34 G
35–	35 L · 36 A · 37 E · 38 D · 39 U · 40 J · 41 N · 42 J · 43 Q · 44 D
45–	45 S · 46 K · 47 O · 48 A · 49 Q · 50 M · 51 R · 52 Z₁ · 53 N
54–	54 J · 55 Z · 56 F · 57 L · 58 E · 59 K · 60 P · 61 H · 62 G · 63 D · 64 Z
65–	65 V · 66 C · 67 K · 68 E · 69 Q · 70 Z₂ · 71 Z₁ · 72 Y · 73 D
74–	74 A · 75 Z · 76 T · 77 P · 78 G · 79 L · 80 C · 81 W · 82 N · 83 M
84–	84 G · 85 Z · 86 R · 87 B · 88 V · 89 Y · 90 S · 91 S · 92 B · 93 F
94–	94 N · 95 M · 96 X · 97 G · 98 H · 99 R · 100 L · 101 A · 102 X
103–	103 F · 104 Q · 105 J · 106 R · 107 V · 108 H · 109 W · 110 E · 111 T
112–	112 M · 113 R · 114 Q · 115 L · 116 N · 117 L · 118 I · 119 J · 120 W
121–	121 Z₁ · 122 Z₂ · 123 R · 124 F · 125 S · 126 Z · 127 E · 128 W · 129 N · 130 V
131–	131 C · 132 V · 133 K · 134 N · 135 X · 136 S · 137 L · 138 Z₁ · 139 T · 140 P
141–	141 K · 142 Y · 143 M · 144 F · 145 H · 146 S · 147 Y · 148 Z₁ · 149 L · 150 R · 151 T
152–	152 O · 153 K · 154 Z · 155 C · 156 Z₁ · 157 O · 158 C · 159 B · 160 X · 161 Y
162–	162 E · 163 H · 164 Z · 165 J · 166 C · 167 Z₂ · 168 Q · 169 Y · 170 L · 171 N
172–	172 P · 173 U · 174 W · 175 C · 176 A · 177 I · 178 N · 179 Z · 180 Z₁ · 181 H
182–	182 F · 183 F · 184 U · 185 V · 186 S · 187 T · 188 M · 189 F · 190 Z₁
191–	191 G · 192 U · 193 J · 194 C · 195 B · 196 H · 197 E · 198 R · 199 D · 200 Z₁ · 201 N
202–	202 Z · 203 J · 204 O · 205 F · 206 R · 207 F · 208 E · 209 R · 210 I
211–	211 V · 212 H · 213 I · 214 P · 215 Z₂ · 216 V · 217 W · 218 Q · 219 K
220–	220 P · 221 M · 222 X · 223 D · 224 C

CLUES

A. Special aptitude · · · · · · · · · · 74 6 101 176 36 48

B. River that joins the Saône at Lyons · 26 92 159 87 195

C. Chufa (2 wds.) · · · · · · · · · · 80 155 66 194 175 131 158 166 27 24 224

D. Reasonably to be expected · · · · · 223 38 73 199 30 63 44

E. Appeal, plea · · · · · · · · · · 197 162 58 208 127 68 110 37

F. Magnetic charm · · · · · · · · · 56 182 183 205 124 207 103 144 93 189

G. Delicacy, niceness; fine-drawn distinction · · 7 34 97 84 20 62 191 78

H. First name, WORD J · · · · · 181 145 163 108 196 11 98 61 212

I. Irascible; requiring caution · · · · 8 17 118 213 210 177

J. Ger. composer and teacher (1854–1921; "Hansel und Gretel") · · · 42 165 29 4 193 40 105 1 203 119 54

K. Dugout, as a trench or ditch, perhaps · 133 13 59 219 22 3 67 141 46 153

L. 1933 Kenneth Roberts novel (3 wds.) · 35 115 79 100 149 170 9 137 31 19 117 57

M. Adorn, ornament · · · · · · · 143 112 50 188 5 95 14 83 221

N. Greedy · · · · · · · · · · 53 178 134 82 201 41 171 129 94 116

O. Eng. metaphysical poet (1572–1631; "The Bait," "Love's Deity") · · 157 204 47 15 152

P. Fortune, chance · · · · · · · · 214 10 220 23 77 60 172 140

Q. Letting fly; untying · · · · · · · 69 104 49 114 43 168 218

R. Excessively busy · · · · · · · · 106 198 113 51 99 123 209 150 206 86

S. Inappropriate · · · · · · · · · 125 186 91 90 21 146 136 45

T. Greg Louganis's sport · · · · · · 76 139 187 111 32 151

U. Fr. dramatist, poet, and novelist (1802–85; "Le Roi s'amuse," "Ruy Blas") · · 192 39 173 184

V. Power, jurisdiction · · · · · · · 211 130 33 216 65 132 185 107 88

W. Mischievous; improper · · · · · 109 81 217 25 120 174 128

X. Roundabout; not straightforward · · 96 102 160 222 12 18 135

Y. Dull, stupid, stolid · · · · · · · 169 89 142 161 72 147

Z. Carnal, sensual (3 wds.) · · · · · 202 55 154 164 179 2 64 75 126 85

Z₁. To all appearances · · · · · · 28 200 190 52 156 138 71 121 148 180

Z₂. Its capital is Nairobi · · · · · · 70 122 215 16 167

WORDS

142

Grid

1	2	3	4	5	6	7	8	9		
1	Z2	X3	B4	Y5	E6	■7	F8	O9	D	
10	P11	A12	Y13	I14	L15	U16	V17	J18	19	I20 Q
21	Y22	E23	N24	H25	K■	26	G27	I28	Q29	T30 W31 E
32 D	■	33	L34	T35	I36	C37	H■	38	F39	V 40 G
41	A42	E■	43	Z■	44	V45	P46	B47	J48	G49 K50 F
51	Q52	M53	A54	O55	K56	Y57	H58	G■	59	U60 K
61	R62	C63	W64	V65	O■	66	X67	E68	D■	69 W70 V
71	B72	U73	X74	J75	E76	L77	H78	D79	F80	Y81 T82 Q
83	Q84	U■	85	A86	G87	F■	88	D89	N90	E91 M
92	J93	T94	H95	Y96	Z97	E98	S99	C100	I■	101 B
102	P103	H■	104	N105	O106	B107	H108	P■	109	D110 V111 X
112	O113	P114	U115	S■	116	M117	Q■	118	Y119	V 120 O
121	C122	M123	X124	W125	H126	I■	127	C128	L■	129 P130 U
131	T132	L■	133	Z■	134	N135	M136	G137	H138	D139 V140 S
141	B142	R143	C■	144	Q145	R146	G147	S148	X149	N 150 X
151	C■	152	D153	A154	V155	Y■	156	C157	W■	158 U159 B
160	T161	P162	R163	H164	W165	S■	166	E167	A■	168 Z169 L
170	R171	O172	F173	S174	K175	N176	M■	177	Z178	C 179 T
180	L181	K■	182	F183	N■	184	I185	G186	R187	A188 F

CLUES

A Tranquil, quiet
B Seaside resort, extreme S Italy, devastated by Turks in 1480
C U.S. area known for religious fundamentalism (2 wds.)
D Form an opinion of, judge
E Villain of "The Three Musketeers"
F Tremulous, shaky
G Windward (naut.)
H Chaucer story of two clerks who take vengeance on the wife and daughter of the man who robbed them (2 wds. after The)
I Garbage can, in England (hyph.)
J Talk wildly
K Regard, consider
L Japanese Prime Minister between 1946 and 54
M Personification of the S Wind
N Very fine threadlike structure
O Structure enclosing our heart and lungs (2 wds.)
P Apprehension of the nature of a thing
Q Mixture of decaying organic substances
R "___ of Gaul," knight-errant, "the flower of chivalry"
S Pseudonym of Friedrich Von Hardenberg (1772–1801)
T College in Baltimore
U Smothered, in music
V Native of Nagasaki, e.g.
W Builder of the Trojan horse
X Make mild or kind; enrich; soften
Y Emperor of Mexico, 1822–23
Z Ruler of a Shan state, Burma

WORDS

A 41 53 11 85 167 153 187
B 159 71 106 3 141 101 46
C 36 99 156 143 178 127 151 121 62
D 88 109 138 78 152 9 32 68
E 97 75 22 67 42 90 166 5 31
F 79 38 182 7 172 87 50 188
G 185 26 58 40 136 86 48 146
H 57 94 125 163 24 107 37 137 77 103
I 126 35 19 13 184 27 100
J 92 17 47 74
K 60 25 55 49 181 174
L 128 169 180 132 14 33 76
M 91 135 176 116 122 52
N 104 23 149 6 134 175 89 183
O 8 105 120 112 54 65 171
P 113 10 129 45 161 102 108
Q 51 117 144 20 83 82 28
R 142 170 145 186 162 61
S 165 140 147 98 18 173 115
T 93 34 179 131 29 81 160
U 72 59 15 130 158 84 114
V 64 139 110 44 70 16 119 154 39
W 164 69 157 63 30 124
X 123 150 111 148 66 2 73
Y 12 155 56 4 118 80 95 21
Z 168 133 1 96 177 43

143

CLUES

A. Alarm clocks, e.g. · · · · · · · · · ·
B. 1935 Sinclair Lewis novel (4 wds.) · ·
C. Remnant · · · · · · · · · · · · · ·
D. Relaxes · · · · · · · · · · · · · ·
E. Essential nature, spirituality · · · ·
F. Dipsomaniacs · · · · · · · · · · ·
G. Sept. 29 (2 wds.) · · · · · · · · · ·
H. Prescience · · · · · · · · · · · · ·
I. Precisions · · · · · · · · · · · · ·
J. Sweet William (2 wds.) · · · · · · ·
K. Longhand reporters · · · · · · · · ·
L. Rose-scented snuff · · · · · · · · ·
M. Of feeling · · · · · · · · · · · · ·
N. Compulsions · · · · · · · · · · · ·
O. Disjoin · · · · · · · · · · · · · ·
P. Producing a loud noise · · · · · · ·
Q. Have or spare the price of · · · · ·
R. Holly · · · · · · · · · · · · · · ·
S. Mental creativity · · · · · · · · · ·
T. Modernity · · · · · · · · · · · · ·
U. Wearing gauntlets, e.g. · · · · · · ·
V. Norm · · · · · · · · · · · · · · · ·
W. Young hares · · · · · · · · · · · · ·
X. Harmless · · · · · · · · · · · · · ·
Y. Prolix · · · · · · · · · · · · · · ·
Z. Development · · · · · · · · · · · · ·

WORDS

A. 197 167 37 114 176 88 143 191
B. 149 14 118 135 188 82 166 1 98 195 175 227 85 51 109 117
C. 185 211 2 39 80 138 77 230
D. 203 126 196 171 161 90 224
E. 6 43 116 30 152 96 103 130 36 205
F. 25 164 221 12 208 170 5 35 18 178
G. 154 101 207 174 159 49 92 29 74 65 218 33 28
H. 106 46 55 4 31 215 102 173 131 198 147 181 157
I. 93 22 73 206 156 68 11 122 142 115
J. 45 155 100 123 105 84 172 163 10 165
K. 112 209 60 16 8 128 86 184 67 40 34 204
L. 169 58 189 158 21 136 202 38
M. 226 162 81 124 41 69 217 50 95
N. 180 190 232 199 63 153 111 76
O. 129 146 210 229 125
P. 200 42 75 20 225 222 148 97 177 70
Q. 187 216 91 119 160 194
R. 48 144 64 183 231 7
S. 99 53 140 228 89 120 182 23 223 214 13
T. 220 56 78 59 32 121 104
U. 145 17 44 87 151 57
V. 192 113 83 212 19 47 79
W. 27 219 141 133 62 72 94 110
X. 186 52 193 137 213 108 9 24 134
Y. 132 61 15 71 201 233 3
Z. 139 150 107 26 127 66 179 54 168

Solution Grid

1 M	2 K	3 E	4 B	5 F	6 U	7 O	8 R	9 X	■	■
10 F	11 U	12 C	■	13 V	14 E	15 M	16 P	17 K	18 I	■
19 A	20 T	21 H	22 D	■	23 E	24 W	25 X	26 F	27 T	28 K
29 X	30 N	31 U	32 B	■	33 W	34 A	35 Y	36 S	37 F	38 X
39 J	40 D	41 Y	42 T	43 R	44 P	45 T	46 W	47 F	48 R	49 U
50 A	51 M	52 J	53 H	54 E	55 Q	56 O	57 T	58 G	59 S	60 E
61 N	62 D	■	63 G	64 F	65 V	■	66 H	67 A	68 M	69 Q
70 R	71 E	72 O	73 L	74 K	75 P	76 H	77 J	78 C	79 G	80 Y
81 W	82 U	83 I	84 A	85 F	86 P	87 E	88 J	89 A	90 B	91 M
92 F	93 W	94 Y	95 D	96 G	97 G	98 P	99 B	100 K	101 A	■
102 J	103 T	104 V	105 Q	106 G	107 F	108 C	109 M	110 J	111 A	112 I
113 V	114 Y	■	115 Q	116 N	117 D	118 B	■	119 O	120 V	121 T
122 R	123 W	124 J	125 D	126 N	■	127 W	128 O	129 R	130 C	131 X
132 P	133 T	134 G	135 L	136 N	■	137 M	138 P	139 G	140 Q	141 T
142 B	143 U	144 S	145 W	146 Q	147 R	148 H	149 O	150 P	151 U	■
152 Q	153 A	■	154 R	155 F	156 C	157 L	158 I	159 G	160 V	161 N
162 R	163 U	■	164 W	165 O	166 I	167 E	168 B	169 S	170 Q	■
171 L	172 U	173 C	174 T	175 D	176 O	177 T	178 V	179 R	180 J	181 C
182 L	183 A	184 T	185 N	186 H	187 R	188 L	189 S	190 F	191 P	■
192 Q	193 F	194 C	195 J	196 E	197 A	198 D	199 Y	200 X	201 B	202 L
203 I	204 S	■	205 I	206 T	207 B	208 J	209 V	210 C	■	■

CLUES

A Slicked up, in full feather (hyph.) . . .
B Planned, plotted (2 wds.) . . . .
C Tormented, in great pain . . . .
D Obscure; incapable of being specified .
E Disfigurement of fruit . . . .
F "___ correction is his own worst enemy" (3 wds.; Prov. 15:32, New Eng. Bible)
G U.S. polar explorer (1880–1951) . . . .
H Reconnoiters . . . .
I Dialects . . . .
J Has, at final tally (3 wds.) . . . .
K Indian prince . . . .
L Ended; everywhere (2 wds.) . . . .
M Identified wrongly . . . .
N Hero of Gide's "The Counterfeiters" . .
O Shape crudely (hyph.) . . . .
P Not capable of being obliterated . . . .
Q Visiting (2 wds.) . . . .
R Belonging; incident (to) . . . .
S Sconce, bean, conk . . . .
T French pres., June 1894–Jan. 1895 (hyph.)
U Where to find Fremantle, Newcastle, and Perth . . . .
V Exalted, noble; raised up . . . .
W Imitation marble . . . .
X Suitable for farming . . . .
Y Rise against constituted authority . . . .

WORDS

A 67 111 19 34 84 197 89 50 101 183 153
B 90 4 118 142 201 32 207 168 99
C 108 194 130 78 181 12 210 156 173
D 175 198 117 95 62 125 40 22
E 3 196 87 60 54 23 14 71 167
F 155 92 10 64 47 5 85 37 193 190 107 26
G 139 106 58 96 97 134 79 63 159
H 148 53 186 21 66 76
I 158 166 83 205 18 203 112
J 102 124 110 77 39 195 208 52 180 88
K 28 2 17 74 100
L 135 202 188 157 182 171 73
M 1 109 91 51 137 68 15
N 185 126 30 61 116 161 136
O 119 128 149 176 7 165 72 56
P 98 138 86 44 150 191 132 75 16
Q 115 140 55 170 105 152 69 146 192
R 162 187 179 8 43 48 70 147 122 129 154
S 169 144 36 204 59 189
T 177 27 141 174 121 57 103 184 45 206 20 42 133
U 172 82 163 6 143 151 31 49 11
V 120 13 160 104 178 209 65 113
W 164 145 24 46 93 123 81 127 33
X 38 9 131 29 200 25
Y 80 114 94 35 199 41

145

Grid (each cell shows its number and clue-letter, in reading order by row):

1 D	2 J	3 Q	4 C	5 C	6 X	7 H	8 Y	9 U			
10 J	11 U	12 T	13 L	14 E	15 Q	16 K	17 T	18 G	19 O		
20 V	21 U	22 N	23 M	24 J	25 H	26 E	27 V	28 S	29 F		
30 U	31 L	32 T	33 U	34 F	35 B	36 M	37 A	38 Q	39 D		
40 A	41 J	42 T	43 Z	44 L	45 M	46 I	47 S	48 M	49 N		
50 L	51 R	52 H	53 F	54 Y	55 T	56 F	57 W	58 G	59 O	60 K	
61 V	62 L	63 E	64 A	65 C	66 Z	67 M	68 T	69 N	70 Q		
71 X	72 A	73 Z	74 R	75 C	76 D	77 H	78 A	79 E			
80 N	81 S	82 V	83 Q	84 O	85 C	86 Z	87 U	88 Y	89 P	90 R	
91 O	92 U	93 Z	94 J	95 W	96 A	97 W	98 C	99 I	100 L		
101 W	102 G	103 H	104 G	105 R	106 C	107 J	108 E	109 K	110 L		
111 A	112 D	113 T	114 Y	115 L	116 G	117 S	118 Q	119 D	120 C	121 E	
122 P	123 O	124 I	125 N	126 S	127 Q	128 T	129 K	130 Y	131 U		
132 D	133 B	134 M	135 O	136 T	137 D	138 I	139 B	140 R			
141 Q	142 C	143 G	144 I	145 B	146 J	147 U	148 E	149 O	150 B		
151 L	152 G	153 M	154 Y	155 V	156 U	157 P	158 O	159 T			
160 T	161 W	162 C	163 A	164 E	165 X	166 W	167 D	168 J	169 X		
170 E	171 F	172 R	173 A	174 I	175 Z	176 M	177 P	178 U			
179 X	180 D	181 A	182 A	183 P	184 M	185 L	186 J				

CLUES

A Menelaus's wife, abducted by Paris (3 wds.) — 78 111 163 72 40 64 181 182 37 96 173

B Vows — 139 133 35 145 150

C Sloppily (hyph.) — 65 75 85 142 98 120 5 162 106 4

D Rubber center of the U.S. (2 wds.) — 39 137 167 1 76 119 132 112 180

E Very rare, choice, arcane — 108 170 14 148 164 26 121 63 79

F Joints, holes, dumps; gin mills — 171 34 53 56 29

G Deep, narrow ravines — 102 18 143 152 104 116 58

H Characteristic of Greece; part of a house — 25 77 7 52 103

I Putrid, foul; miserable — 46 99 174 144 124 138

J Conditioned or determined by something else — 107 186 10 24 2 41 146 168 94

K Hawaiian goose — 60 129 16 109

L Fan — 185 110 115 44 100 31 151 50 62 13

M Gets back, regains — 48 36 134 184 67 45 23 176 153

N Essential piece of jai alai equipment — 125 49 80 69 22

O Hubbub, ruckus — 19 84 158 123 149 91 59 135

P "Yours is the ___ and everything that's in it" (Kipling, "If") — 122 177 89 157 183

Q It. operatic soprano (1913–) — 141 3 83 127 118 70 38 15

R Cheap, cheesy, inferior (hyph.) — 74 140 90 172 105 51

S With absolute, disdainful aloofness — 28 47 117 126 81

T Shipbuilding center at the mouth of the James River, VA (2 wds.) — 113 159 32 55 42 128 17 68 136 160 12

U Juice of Malaysian trees, used in dental cement, golf balls, etc. (hyph.) — 178 92 30 131 156 147 9 33 87 21 11

V Major concern of Thomas Bulfinch — 82 20 27 155 61

W Surmises, gathers, draws conclusions — 161 101 97 166 57 95

X Strength, courage; audacity — 6 169 71 165 179

Y Low intellectual or moral condition — 130 54 88 154 8 114

Z Rat, stoolie, fink — 73 66 86 43 93 175

CLUES

A Issue; a first might be prized 207 39 122 19 59 101 174

B Flower heard as a snappy cat 159 4 57 143 37 24 92 151 197

C What rabbits inhabit 109 173 181 139 97 12 117

D Become thin or fine 113 33 45 90 42 104 79 2 132

E Cuddly doll (2 wds.) 121 51 199 136 32 185 44 17 36 163 112

F Pipe conveying rainwater to the ground 52 161 154 168 5 172 138 34 140

G Unit of intensity of light 187 192 25 9 14 201

H Whale of the genus Megaptera . . 61 22 126 16 83 155 180 10

I Unseemly 124 98 160 28 48 116 193 107 85 176

J Launch at Cape Kennedy, e.g. (hyph.) 206 186 15 6 130 137 21

K Casey Jones's workplace 23 103 73 177 63 40 99 1 89 47

L One who cherishes noble principles 88 91 203 183 31 11 66 86

M Grooved-billed bird 30 71 108 26 110 50

N Machine for clearing wintry walks (2 wds.) 146 119 170 41 43 77 134 3 158 35

O Siberian sled dog 115 67 64 167 194 149 13

P Without dissent 65 135 196 80 166 75 84 178 169 114 20

Q Canadian province 165 129 147 87 76 62 111 198 60 205 152 175

R One who cracks cryptography . . . 38 182 58 164 128 195 179

S Pashto 127 94 70 46 8 150

T Milfoil 145 53 105 18 29 162

U Rogue, knave 188 54 49 102 82 189 144 202

V Hired for exclusive use 100 141 123 96 125 78 204 153 81

W Port in N Israel 157 74 190 93 118

X Narrow strip connecting larger entities 200 106 191 7 184 56 156

Y Kind of lizard or railroad car 133 55 171 68 120 95

Z Nymph who became a laurel tree . . 69 72 27 148 131 142

WORDS

147

Grid

■	1 F	2 J	3 E	4 L	5 H	■	6 I	7 J	■	8 V
9 H	10 B	11 Q	12 K	13 D	14 P	15 L	16 H	17 U	18 B	19 O
20 T	■	21 K	22 E	23 Q	24 N	■	25 I	26 J	27 G	28 C
29 K	30 E	31 H	■	32 A	33 E	34 A	35 Q	36 N	37 P	38 R
39 H	40 T	41 Q	42 N	43 A	■	44 E	45 G	46 R	47 E	
48 B	49 A	50 V	51 M	52 K	53 E	54 P	55 O	56 D	57 M	58 C
59 H	60 T	61 F	62 B	63 F	■	64 O	65 F	66 J	67 R	
68 K	69 C	70 L	71 I	72 T	73 P	74 J	■	75 B	76 P	77 K
78 U	79 E	80 A	81 Q	82 N	83 U	84 H	85 T	■	86 C	87 K
88 Q	89 G	90 P	91 L	■	92 D	93 U	94 R	95 F	■	96 H	97 R
98 A	99 L	100 S	101 G	102 D	103 T	104 F	105 K	106 R	107 R	
108 M	109 I	110 V	111 U	112 K	113 G	114 S	115 H	116 F	117 I	
118 D	119 A	120 H	121 U	122 C	123 Q	■	124 O	125 P	126 S	127 A
128 B	129 G	130 Q	131 K	132 F	133 C	134 C	135 L	136 F		
137 J	138 R	139 E	140 E	141 S	142 B	143 V	144 M	145 Q	146 A	147 I
148 F	149 L	150 T	151 P	152 U	153 C	154 I	■	155 B	156 H	
157 U	158 M	159 D	160 M	161 H	162 L	163 D	164 O	165 N		
166 J	167 H	168 E	169 T	170 I	171 D	■	172 I	173 R	174 C	175 P
176 L	177 G	178 S	179 D	180 F	181 E	182 O	183 P	■	184 U	
185 B	186 A	187 I	188 O	189 P	190 R	191 V	192 K	193 T	194 L	
195 G	196 R	197 Q	198 C	199 J	200 D	201 S	202 J	203 H	204 T	
205 F	206 L	207 A	208 O	209 R	210 D	211 Q	212 S	213 C		

CLUES

A Transports; deprives of self-control by exciting the feelings (2 wds.)
119 146 127 98 32 207 43 80 34 49 186

B Ambitious, self-seeking person
75 48 185 155 142 62 128 10 18

C Type of illegal daily lottery (2 wds.)
69 174 134 28 122 86 213 58 198 153 133

D Female branch of a family or descent (2 wds.)
179 200 118 163 102 13 92 159 56 171 210

E Without limit; endlessly
140 181 139 22 79 53 3 33 44 47 168 30

F Body politic; federation of former colonies
205 180 136 95 116 63 1 104 65 148 61 132

G Narrative poem by Keats; youth loved by the goddess Selene
101 45 27 177 113 89 129 195

H "We few, we happy few, we ——" (3 wds.;"Henry V")
167 9 203 115 96 84 39 16 59 156 161 5 120 31

I Alternating motion of the sea (3 wds.)
154 147 172 187 170 109 117 71 25 6

J Utterly debauched persons
66 202 199 137 2 7 26 166 74

K Pretentiousness, ostentation, imposingness
77 105 112 192 12 68 29 52 87 131 21

L Flagrantly, glaringly, shockingly
176 70 206 162 91 194 135 15 99 4 149

M More trim or tidy
57 51 158 160 108 144

N Shrimplike crustaceans, food for some whales
42 24 36 82 165

O Language of Orwell's "1984"
188 19 208 124 64 182 164 55

P Pretentious display
14 183 125 175 90 37 54 73 189 151 76

Q Old World songbirds, often kept as pets
211 197 23 81 130 145 123 41 35 11 88

R Applies oneself, goes to it (2 wds.)
67 209 97 190 196 173 38 106 46 94 107 138

S Reduces in strength or spirit
100 178 126 212 114 141 201

T Broke, lacking pecuniary resources (3 wds.)
169 40 103 72 85 150 60 20 204 193

U Suits, sweaters, topcoats, etc.
78 83 17 111 93 157 121 184 152

V Athenian statesman known for severity of his laws
8 110 143 50 191

148

Grid

Each numbered square with its clue letter:

1 U	2 G	3 P	4 F	5 E	6 I	7 V	8 M	9 F	10 B
11 K	12 N	13 L	14 Q	15 S	16 P	17 C	18 I	19 A	20 M
21 B	22 H	23 I	24 M	25 E	26 R	27 S	28 K	29 G	30 E
31 K	32 B	33 L	34 D	35 J	36 E	37 M	38 B	39 W	40 L
41 H	42 A	43 I	44 G	45 T	46 E	47 C	48 H	49 R	50 N
51 C	52 U	53 V	54 R	55 Q	56 L	57 C	58 V	59 P	60 F
61 C	62 T	63 V	64 B	65 G	66 U	67 L	68 C	69 K	70 W
71 N	72 G	73 P	74 B	75 N	76 K	77 O	78 M	79 H	80 D
81 Q	82 S	83 H	84 I	85 O	86 J	87 I	88 U	89 B	90 D
91 S	92 G	93 F	94 G	95 C	96 L	97 F	98 V	99 C	100 H
101 L	102 Q	103 R	104 U	105 A	106 C	107 V	108 W	109 C	110 B
111 P	112 H	113 J	114 R	115 H	116 T	117 E	118 G	119 S	120 B
121 Q	122 O	123 F	124 U	125 D	126 A	127 B	128 C	129 W	130 K
131 V	132 P	133 M	134 F	135 W	136 D	137 U	138 S	139 B	140 R
141 T	142 N	143 I	144 Q	145 B	146 V	147 V	148 C	149 M	150 O
151 T	152 N	153 C	154 I	155 J	156 U	157 L	158 C	159 J	160 J
161 A	162 C	163 G	164 T	165 V	166 R	167 W	168 Q	169 D	170 C
171 V	172 R	173 I	174 J	175 H	176 W	177 U	178 M	179 B	180 G
181 V	182 C	183 B	184 J	185 D	186 I	187 S	188 A	189 O	190 D
191 R	192 U	193 V	194 U	195 P	196 M	197 C	198 U	199 S	200 M
201 K	202 J	203 M	204 D	205 O	206 S	207 B	208 H	209 Q	210 F
211 C	212 N								

CLUES

A. Bird of prey

B. Stuck-up, condescending, uppity (4 wds.)

C. 1916 song by Goetz, Young, and Wendling, from "Robinson Crusoe, Jr." (4 wds.)

D. Presumably, they are among those who love not wisely, but too well

E. 11th letter of the Greek alphabet

F. Early bicycle, also called a penny-farthing

G. Ready to commit some mischief (4 wds.)

H. Neutral territory between combatants; area of anomalous, ambiguous, indefinite character (hyph.)

I. Equivalent in significance

J. Malice; filth; obscenity

K. Fashionable health food (2 wds.)

L. Most fatigued

M. Presbyterian clergyman (1723–94), b. Scotland, pres. of the College of New Jersey (later Princeton), 1768–94

N. Hireling, ruffian; mercenary

O. Property

P. Filled

Q. Tangles, as in a net

R. Bore up under

S. Competent, capable, economical

T. Derelict, lax, neglectful

U. Diverting, amusing

V. 1st and last name of Senators' pitcher (1887–1946) also known as "The Big Train"

W. Distinguished, prominent

WORDS

A. 19 42 126 105 161 188

B. 74 89 10 120 127 38 207 145 64 179 32 110 139 183 21

C. 61 182 211 99 153 68 148 57 47 106 197 128 51 17 170 109 95 162 158

D. 169 90 80 136 204 190 34 185 125

E. 36 117 30 46 5 25

F. 134 9 123 210 4 97 60 93

G. 44 72 2 94 118 29 92 180 65 163

H. 79 175 115 208 41 112 100 83 48 22

I. 23 18 154 43 186 173 143 87 84 6

J. 113 35 155 86 202 184 174 160 159

K. 69 76 31 201 28 130 11

L. 157 101 40 96 56 33 67 13

M. 178 78 196 24 37 133 149 8 203 200 20

N. 142 152 212 71 50 12 75

O. 205 85 77 189 150 122

P. 73 111 132 16 3 59 195

Q. 14 209 81 144 102 55 121 168

R. 54 103 114 49 140 26 172 166 191

S. 138 187 27 119 206 15 82 91 199

T. 45 116 151 62 164 141

U. 177 198 137 52 88 192 124 1 104 156 66 194

V. 181 107 131 146 58 53 147 193 165 98 171 7 63

W. 167 39 129 135 70 176 108

149

CLUES

A. "The very casques / That did ____" (3 wds. followed by WORD G; "Henry V")
B. Open boat used in loading and unloading ships
C. Intuitive, perceptive
D. Old-time paving materials
E. Represent in raised ornamentation; decorate (a surface) in relief
F. In the low countries, a local annual outdoor fair
G. See WORD A (2 wds.)
H. With great vigor, determination, and vehemence (3 wds.)
I. Hard aromatic seed, used grated as a spice, as in eggnog
J. On ____: In a desperate position, close to defeat (2 wds.)
K. Slang term for a baseball
L. Arousing, calling forth; producing or suggesting, as through artistry
M. Violent escape of air, steam, etc.; lavish party
N. Giddy, talkative person
O. Not expressly stated; absolute, total
P. Biological catalysts, as pepsin, essential to fermentation
Q. Propitious eras; happy days (2 wds.)
R. As much as one wants to see; beauty, pip, humdinger
S. 1905 song by Alex Rogers and Bert Williams
T. More comfortable
U. Exult
V. Humiliated; embarrassed
W. Attack of nervousness (2 wds.)
X. Ducked, doused, dipped, sunk
Y. Consequence, issue, final product
Z. Kidney stone

WORDS

A. 52 183 197 158 167 101 188 120 143 45 194 137 68 82
B. 139 10 208 219 35 125 66
C. 210 100 113 72 159 127 138 7 76 39
D. 74 59 204 166 116 131 87 153 36 69 173 162
E. 86 186 193 114 142 73
F. 172 5 98 23 110 203 147
G. 102 70 1 182 20 33 212 154 108 171 216
H. 145 30 107 51 155 115 81 181 215 218 32 190 168 19
I. 77 177 144 106 135 25
J. 174 26 99 55 128 209 150 67
K. 94 196 85 111 41 213 133 126 140
L. 34 134 217 93 63 163 24 42 148
M. 37 201 54 132 75 3 47
N. 61 11 198 44 96 43 84 141 187 50
O. 180 122 15 92 199 104 206 78
P. 165 22 124 103 221 83 175
Q. 179 117 91 97 57 40 156 189 136
R. 65 80 29 60 191 12
S. 207 90 118 185 178 58
T. 220 161 2 56 151 184
U. 195 17 53 105 8 88 214
V. 170 149 49 46 14 146 64
W. 211 71 38 176 123 112 200 205 79 18
X. 13 192 152 62 6 130 160 31
Y. 121 129 48 9 21 169 202
Z. 109 157 4 89 16 119 28 95 27 164

Diagram

1 G	2 T	3 M	4 Z	5 F	6 X	7 C	8 U	9 U	10 B	11 N
12 R	13 X	14 V	15 O	16 Z	17 U	18 W	19 H	20 G	21 Y	22 B
23 F	24 L	25 I	26 J	27 Z	28 Z	29 R	30 H	31 X		
32 H	33 G	34 L	35 B	36 D	37 M	38 W	39 C	40 Q	41 K	
42 L	43 N	44 N	45 A	46 V	47 M	48 Y	49 V	50 N		
51 H	52 A	53 U	54 M	55 J	56 T	57 Q	58 S	59 D	60 R	
61 N	62 X	63 L	64 V	65 R	66 B	67 J	68 A	69 D	70 G	
71 W	72 C	73 E	74 D	75 M	76 C	77 I	78 O	79 W	80 R	
81 H	82 A	83 P	84 N	85 K	86 E	87 D	88 U	89 Z	90 S	91 O
92 O	93 L	94 K	95 Z	96 N	97 Q	98 F	99 J	100 C	101 A	
102 G	103 P	104 O	105 U	106 I	107 H	108 G	109 Z	110 F	111 K	112 W
113 C	114 E	115 H	116 D	117 Q	118 S	119 Z	120 A	121 Y	122 O	
123 W	124 P	125 B	126 K	127 C	128 J	129 Y	130 X	131 D	132 M	133 K
134 L	135 I	136 Q	137 A	138 C	139 B	140 K	141 N	142 E	143 A	
144 I	145 H	146 V	147 F	148 L	149 V	150 J	151 T	152 X		
153 D	154 G	155 H	156 Q	157 Z	158 A	159 C	160 X	161 T	162 D	
163 L	164 Z	165 P	166 D	167 A	168 H	169 Y	170 V	171 G		
172 F	173 D	174 J	175 P	176 W	177 I	178 S	179 Q	180 O	181 H	182 G
183 A	184 T	185 S	186 E	187 N	188 A	189 Q	190 H	191 R		
192 X	193 E	194 A	195 U	196 K	197 A	198 N	199 O	200 W	201 M	
202 Y	203 F	204 D	205 W	206 O	207 S	208 B	209 J	210 C	211 W	
212 G	213 K	214 U	215 H	216 G	217 L	218 H	219 B	220 T	221 P	

150

Grid

(Acrostic diagram — each square shows its cell number and the letter of the clue it belongs to. Black squares separate the words of the quotation.)

1 G	2 Y	3 W	4 S	5 Z₁	6 C				
7 Y	8 R	9 Q	10 R	11 V	12 N	13 Y	14 P	15 B	
16 L	17 O	18 Z	19 K	20 U	21 V	22 R	23 H	24 X	
25 C	26 Z₁	27 U	28 T	29 R	30 A	31 Y	32 T	33 Q	34 U
35 R	36 M	37 L	38 G	39 R	40 Z₁	41 J	42 O	43 H	
44 D	45 Q	46 R	47 I	48 S	49 F	50 A	51 P	52 Y	53 K
54 J	55 I	56 F	57 H	58 G	59 E	60 X	61 Z	62 Z₁	
63 N	64 W	65 S	66 H	67 D	68 G	69 B	70 V	71 U	72 P
73 Y	74 G	75 H	76 V	77 A	78 X	79 D	80 E	81 Y	82 N
83 A	84 I	85 V	86 A	87 G	88 T	89 A	90 S	91 L	92 H
93 B	94 Z₁	95 E	96 Q	97 J	98 P	99 F	100 Q	101 J	102 X
103 Y	104 O	105 H	106 J	107 Y	108 D	109 M	110 H	111 Z	112 C
113 N	114 Y	115 U	116 O	117 L	118 C	119 S	120 I	121 Y	122 O
123 Y	124 M	125 X	126 T	127 S	128 M	129 Y	130 U	131 U	
132 O	133 G	134 A	135 P	136 D	137 Z₁	138 F	139 W	140 A	141 R
142 Q	143 H	144 Y	145 A	146 S	147 P	148 A	149 V	150 Q	
151 Z	152 L	153 Y	154 C	155 Z₁	156 H	157 U	158 B	159 G	160 C
161 F	162 Y	163 K	164 W	165 U	166 S	167 E	168 U	169 T	
170 H	171 A	172 C	173 F	174 E	175 O	176 A	177 U	178 A	179 J
180 Z	181 N	182 T	183 S	184 A	185 W	186 D	187 A	188 J	
189 G	190 Y	191 X	192 F	193 Y	194 K				

CLUES

A Adage for a conservative consumer (4 wds.) 30 187 50 171 89 178 86 134 145 184 140 83 176 77 148

B Chancy 158 69 15 93

C Detests 112 118 25 160 172 154 6

D Dutch-born Am. airplane designer (1890–1939) 44 108 136 79 67 186

E Indian prince 174 167 80 59 95

F Resistance to change of motion or direction 99 138 173 49 56 161 192

G Great reptiles 58 74 159 189 1 38 87 68 133

H Faculty of making happy chance finds 75 57 92 23 66 105 170 156 143 110 43

I Mince, chop small 120 84 55 47

J Hires; interlocks 54 97 188 106 179 101 41

K With breakfast on face, perhaps . . . 19 53 163 194

L Was overly fond 37 117 152 91 16

M Slap; edge of gauntlet 124 109 128 36

N Slip-knotted rope 181 113 82 12 63

O State, early scene of the civil rights movement 17 122 104 116 132 42 175

P Stew of meat and vegetables 147 135 98 14 51 72

Q Not straightforward . . . 150 142 45 33 96 100 9

R Biblical monster (Job 40:15) . . . 10 141 22 29 39 35 46 8

S Composed in an exaggerated, flowery style 146 90 65 166 4 183 127 119 48

T Alternates 182 88 28 169 32 126

U "Doubt thou —— fire" (3 wds., "Hamlet") 34 131 115 20 27 157 130 168 177 71 165

V Eng. philosopher (1588–1679; "Leviathan") 149 70 85 76 11 21

W Embroidered garment for an ancient Hebrew priest . . . 3 64 164 139 185

X Abases; brings down; looks angry . . . 191 78 24 125 102 60

Y Where the poet wants to read verses to his love (3 wds., "Omar Khayyam") 81 162 193 121 114 190 144 129 7 153 13 73 103 107 31 123 52 2

Z Brooch; short film scene with a big star . . . 111 61 18 180 151

Z₁ Name important to Oscar Wilde . . . 137 5 155 62 40 26 94

151

CLUES

A Finally (3 wds.) . . . .

B Type of door lock (2 wds.) . . . . .

C Spouse (2 wds.) . . . .

D Arne's drunken father (Bjornson, "Arne") . . . .

E Wild fruit, Prunus americana (2 wds.) . . . .

F Very small fraction . . . .

G Minister or priest performing a religious service . . . .

H Subordinate . . . .

I Divide (a word) into sound segments

J Pure, innocent (hyph.) . . . .

K Teensy (hyph.) . . . .

L Shoe sole trimmed and sewn very close to the upper (2 wds.) . . . . .

M Water-soluble adhesive product of the acacia (2 wds.) . . . .

N Soccer forward (2 wds.) . . . .

O Through successive possession by a number of people (4 wds.) . . . . . .

P Shrub, Styrax grandifolia (2 wds.) .

Q Duty payable in goods or services instead of money (3 wds.) . . . . . .

R Careless, unaware . . . .

S Soldier from Nepal (var. sp.) . . . .

T Slanderer . . . .

U Surpass in crying . . . .

V Pain, indisposition . . . .

W Dwelling made of skins, etc. (var. sp.) . . . .

WORDS

Clue	Letters
A	46 155 91 14 198 10 56 82 117
B	111 116 31 210 133 123 131 90 142 5
C	156 122 164 110 86 67 205 54 176
D	25 37 99 74
E	140 124 213 107 141 115 12 182 3 76
F	187 147 113 138 152 26 105 59 204
G	75 93 160 84 47 6 144 184 121
H	64 173 65 211 196 119 11 62 139
I	151 162 212 191 201 136 44 92 95
J	168 1 146 178 66 89 128 41 209
K	186 78 167 108 32 23 102 83 40
L	190 33 73 22 77 169 18 43 135
M	98 88 114 85 15 126 63 145 174 101 24
N	130 21 39 4 192 51 149 61 172 103 134 158
O	52 171 175 94 118 154 148 36 112 159 20 35 17 58
P	13 161 81 38 53 19 195 50 166 153 188 203 45 170 181 9
Q	106 71 132 79 64 96 165 57 125
R	60 30 177 87 72 185 189 8 70
S	109 208 199 150 193 28 183
T	179 16 129 48 100 29 206 97 202
U	157 137 207 163 197 180 2
V	49 120 200 80 69 127 27
W	34 104 143 7 68 194

152

Grid (cells numbered 1–180, each with its word-letter):

1	H2	T3	W	4	L5	A6	U7	P8	N9	O10 · C
11	E12	A · 13	R14	D15	B16	K17	W18	X19		M
20	I21	T22	G23	X24	D · 25	X26	V27	A28	M29	J
30	K31	P32	R33	L · 34	B35	G36	T · 37	B38	Q39	M
40	H41	P42	O43	F44	I · 45	O46	C47	N48	D49	I50 · A
51	X52	U53	P54	H55	F56	S · 57	V58	59	I60 · S	
61	G62	K · 63	H64	M65	X66	F67	D68	W69	J70	L71 · N
72	E73	R74	K75	B · 76	D77	A · 78	N79	B80 · U		
81	W82	V83	I84	H85	Q86	F87	O88	N · 89	B90	P91 · V
92	S93	F94	M95	W · 96	V97	J · 98	J99	X100 · W		
101	Q102	I103	T104	G105	O106	N · 107	N108	A109	F110	M111 · Q
112	A113	N · 114	O115	J116	L · 117	C118	T119	U120 · I		
121	Q122	B123	H124	L125	S · 126	K127	L · 128	W129	Q130 · V	
131	F132	D133	C134	S135	G136	I · 137	B138	P139	L · 140	J
141	X · 142	D143	J144	F145	H146	C147	T148	E149	G150	A151 · U
152	S153	B · 154	F155	D156	J157	R158	M · 159	G160	P161 · L	
162	D163	V · 164	G165	N166	H167	M · 168	C169	R170	J171 · A	
172	S173	D174	B175	L · 176	D177	M178	P179	R180 · L		

CLUES

A Pertaining to exciting emotion

B European thrush with a russet back and buff to white underparts

C Nimbly

D Rogue

E Former name of Tokyo

F England's deepest lake, SW of Keswick (2 wds.)

G Large (chiefly Brit. sl.)

H Ultimate, final

I Likely to occur at any moment now

J Maze

K Modulations, as of voice, e.g.

L Am. historian (1916–70) Pulitzer Prizes 1956 and 1963

M Public walkway

N Short work of fiction

O Wards off

P Garrote

Q Disquiet

R Smart, jaunty

S Piled up

T Suds

U "Good my ___ of virtue, answer me," says the Clown to Olivia ("Twelfth Night")

V Mean, base

W Japanese girdle ornament

X Propriety

WORDS

A 112 77 12 108 50 150 5 171 27

B 137 122 75 79 34 15 58 37 89 153 174

C 46 133 117 168 146 10

D 67 48 176 24 14 155 173 132 142 76 162

E 148 72 11

F 131 109 43 144 154 93 55 66 86

G 164 35 159 149 22 104 61 135

H 145 84 123 54 1 63 40 166

I 102 20 59 83 49 136 120 44

J 156 170 140 97 29 98 143 69 115

K 30 126 74 16 62

L 4 161 127 180 33 70 175 139 116 124

M 39 158 110 167 177 64 28 94 19

N 71 8 47 165 107 106 78 113 88

O 45 105 42 9 114 87

P 41 31 90 138 7 178 160 53

Q 101 129 38 85 111 121

R 169 32 157 73 13 179

S 60 92 152 56 125 172 134

T 147 21 103 2 36 118

U 52 119 151 6 80

V 57 163 82 130 96 26 91

W 17 95 100 68 81 128 3

X 65 51 18 23 99 25 141

153

CLUES

WORDS

A 1954 Danny Kaye film (3 wds.) . . . . .
186 152 67 125 114 76 174 104 37 7 44

B Split, make tracks . . . .
83 128 92 35 161 192 1 173

C Hepcat, jazzbo . . . .
53 172 87 31 61 196 140 84 190

D "He sinks ____ with bubbling groan"
(3 wds.; Byron, "Childe Harold") . . . .
12 200 189 86 150 126 157 28 134 95 40 33

E Furloughs; tabletop sections . . . . . .
5 180 78 145 109 115

F Basic . . . .
191 55 81 9 164 30 110 105 178 46

G Chicken, craven coward, gutless wonder (hyph.) . . . .
89 148 16 42 187 72 168 62 103 54 66

H Brazen, contemptuous . . . .
199 60 65 10 147 175 143 182

I Slopes, hillsides . . . .
108 163 112 36 137

J Wrong . . . .
93 135 98 71 120 39 90 20 6

K Sleeveless outer vestment of the cele-
brant at Mass . . . .
57 22 15 160 73 179 101 177

L Luanda is its capital . . . .
102 113 69 26 100 132

M "As my poor father used to say / In
1863, / Once people start on all this
Art / Good-bye, ____" (A.P. Herbert,
"Lines for a Worthy Person") . . . . .
131 19 183 181 25 119 32 99 3

N Principal city of the Ruhr River valley
153 63 167 138 156

O Ohio port on Lake Erie . . . .
198 133 111 11 122 18 68 24 64

P One who adds spoken commentary . .
38 159 82 51 17 130 13 70

Q One who exacts satisfaction, as on
another's behalf . . . .
146 176 52 14 165 4 195

R Not properly suited . . . .
91 123 2 184 34

S "Charms strike ____, but merit wins
the soul" (2 wds.; Pope, "Rape of the
Lock") . . . .
170 58 162 107 171 121 48 94

T Dines not wisely but too well . . . . .
41 118 8 127 136 142 80 154

U Rider who was joined by Revere and
Prescott on the storied "midnight
ride" . . . .
88 59 85 194 141

V Turns, opportunity for action . . . . .
117 149 139 43 75 166 129

W Am. clergyman, author, educator
(1752–1817) a leader of the Connecticut Wits . . . .
124 27 151 116 96 79

X Lop off, remove . . . .
155 77 74 169 193 45 50 158

Y Borrow without intent to repay . . . .
185 49 144 197 29

Z Formal agreement . . . .
21 188 97 23 47 56

Grid

1 Q	2 F	3 B	4 H	5 U	6 R	7 V	8 S	9 Q	10 F
11 N	■	12 F	13 U	14 V	15 N	16 J	17 U	18 H	19 B
20 G	21 A	22 T	23 M	24 J	25 D	26 N	27 E	28 Q	29 J
30 T	31 E	32 G	33 V	34 D	35 I	36 S	37 O	38 D	39 J
40 H	41 O	42 F	43 H	44 N	45 G	46 P	47 A	48 B	49 U
50 F	51 M	52 Q	53 K	54 B	55 U	56 A	57 M	58 G	59 Q
60 V	61 D	62 J	■	63 C	64 I	65 K	66 C	67 M	68 K
■	69 I	70 K	71 O	72 T	73 F	74 A	75 R	76 E	77 H
78 B	79 J	80 R	81 L	82 G	83 S	84 E	85 M	86 C	■
87 M	88 O	89 J	90 D	91 S	92 R	93 K	94 C	95 U	96 V
97 I	98 V	99 E	■	100 G	101 L	102 I	103 S	104 A	105 A
106 P	107 N	108 J	■	109 N	110 F	111 P	112 A	113 M	114 U
115 G	116 V	117 K	118 C	119 H	120 B	121 T	122 Q	123 M	124 I
■	125 P	126 M	127 Q	128 K	129 L	130 P	131 H	132 C	133 J
134 E	135 B	136 N	137 N	138 M	139 K	140 P	141 O	■	■
142 M	143 Q	144 J	145 E	146 C	147 U	148 T	149 Q	150 N	151 L
152 P	153 F	■	154 M	155 H	156 F	157 P	158 B	159 O	160 N
161 T	162 S	163 M	164 A	165 R	166 B	167 Q	168 E	169 U	170 T
171 R	172 K	173 G	174 Q	175 U	■	176 C	177 L	178 F	179 V

CLUES

A Where "Chinese" Gordon was killed

B "I would not be ___ for thousands," said Nelson at the battle of Copenhagen

C Comes forth, originates

D In India, moutain passes or places of cremation

E Violet or purple gemstone

F Deepest; farthest down

G Flat, upper part of the stern of a vessel

H What small families might have for Easter dinner (2 wds.)

I Preserve from decay; make fragrant

J Picture in shades of one color

K Fabric with curly fur-like pile

L Guilt; disgrace

M Type of informal, non-alcoholic social gathering (2 wds.)

N Site of an infamous Southern California killing (2 wds.)

O Organic remnant; old fogy

P Doctrine of the millennial return of Christ to reign on earth

Q William Dean Howell's father, e.g. (2 wds.)

R City in Lombardy, birthplace of Vergil (2 wds.)

S Bamboozled, hoodwinked, duped

T Clumsy, inconvenient

U What the freshest Christmas trees are (2 wds.)

V Amaze; stagger; stun

WORDS

A 104 74 21 164 56 47 112 105

B 3 54 120 158 48 166 135 19 78

C 94 118 146 176 63 132 86 66

D 61 90 25 38 34

E 84 134 145 76 31 168 27 99

F 110 153 73 2 178 50 12 10 42 156

G 82 173 20 115 58 100 32 45

H 40 18 4 43 77 119 131 155

I 35 69 97 102 124 64

J 144 29 16 133 24 62 89 39 79 108

K 68 93 172 117 70 128 139 65 53

L 81 129 151 101 177

M 85 126 87 138 23 163 67 123 154 142 51 113 57

N 44 136 109 137 26 11 15 160 150 107

O 37 88 71 141 41 159

P 152 157 140 46 130 106 111 125

Q 59 28 143 52 149 9 122 174 1 167 127

R 92 6 171 165 80 75

S 83 91 103 36 8 162

T 161 121 72 30 170 22 148

U 147 49 17 95 55 114 5 169 13 175

V 7 60 33 96 116 98 14 179

155

CLUES

		1 G	2 W	3 N	4	5 L	6 T	7 E
8 D	9 O	10 N	11 N	12 P	13 M	14 C	15	16 X	17 U	18 A
19 P	20 P	21 N	22 O	23 V	24 V	25 I	26 M	27 X
28 V		29 I	30 C	31 C	32 U	33 O	34 L	35 J	36 P	37 A
38 R	39 N	40 E	41 P	42 U	43 N	44 L	45 L	46 S	47 O	48 T
49 B	50 C	51 K	52 K	53 M	54 E	55 A	56 A	57	58 B
59 D	60 D	61 I	62 U	63 G	64 G	65 N	66 M	67	68 O	69 L
70 P	71 E	72 G	73 I	74 J	75 V	76 V	77 R	78 I	79 C
80 O	81 O	82 K	83 X	84	85 R	86 T	87 C	88 D	89 P
90 F	91 U	92 O	93 K	94 M	95 N	96 N	97 F	98 D	99 S
100 V	101 P	102 R	103 D	104 E	105 L	106 C	107 M	108 X	109 K	U
110 F	111 V	112 E	113 Q	114 P	115 M	116 U	117 G	118 W	119 T	120 A
121 H	122 M	123 E	124 X	125 J	126 I		127 Q	128 P	129 R
130 E	131 L	132 B	133 K	134 F	135 S	136 O	137 L	138 F	139 S	140 V
141 J	142 G	143 C	144 A	145 L	146 V	147 O	148 Q	149 O
150 X	151 A	152 P	153 M	154 O	155 I	156 H	157 W	158 U	159 K	160 F
161 L	162 O	163 K	164 U	165 B	166 F	167 C	168 W	169 D	170 O
171 U	172 H	173 S	174 B	175 J	176 R	177 X	178 K	179 S	180 R
181 O	182 Q	183 E	184 H	185 A	186 D	187 W	188 E	189 V
190 O	191 S	192 R	193 K	194 Q	195 A	196 E

156

CLUES

A With a reflective, forlorn aspect . . . .
B "Language was not powerful enough to describe the ___", (2 wds.; Dickens, "Nicholas Nickleby")
C Honoring, having great respect for (3 wds.) . . . .
D Lit out, beat it, skedaddled (2 wds.) . . . .
E Bare facts (2 wds.) . . . .
F Spain and Portugal . . . .
G "When all aloud the wind doth blow / And coughing ___", (4 wds., "Love's Labour's Lost")
H Designation of the period of the reign of Hirohito . . . .
I Plant of the genus Alcea, of the mallow family . . . .
J In a weird, uncanny way . . . .
K Feeling of great happiness or confidence . . . .
L Argumentative . . . .
M "I should have fatted all the region kites / With ___," says Hamlet (2 wds.) . . . .
N 1932 Marx Bros. film (2 wds.) . . . . . .
O King Arthur's magic sword . . . .
P Easy-money transportation (2 wds.) . . . .
Q The eating of raw meat . . . .
R Censure, reproach, blame . . . .
S Graphic, outlined . . . .
T 1941 Triple Crown–winning racehorse . . .
U Big brass interpretation (hyph.) . . . . . .
V Cadenced . . . .
W Symbol of dullness . . . .

WORDS

Clue	Letters/Numbers
A	203 143 223 189 91 82 76 55 95
B	109 179 113 27 220 2 43 128 15 145 163 195 30 75 81 173
C	56 96 151 185 154 9 16 90 162 205 135
D	92 63 199 149 172 133 1 191
E	120 41 99 94 140 79 160
F	101 117 66 217 204 200
G	5 119 196 108 184 215 141 71 74 52 169 130 78 144 21 147 137 60 159
H	62 134 39 153 118
I	73 84 58 142 194 213 35 168 22
J	121 107 98 219 164 61
K	103 69 192 111 70 127 6 208
L	19 225 193 89 97 166 57 155 178 211 152 161
M	110 206 222 174 7 170 129 125 93 10 64 104 212 46 186
N	156 8 88 115 23 210 20 183 102 139 126 29 224
O	87 48 123 33 209 167 181 12 177
P	190 24 105 65 67 175 51 112 165 226
Q	53 171 44 83 100 176 227 114 218
R	132 216 182 124 11 26 150
S	86 136 77 180 47 31 221 37 148 138 146 106
T	85 198 157 42 122 13 59 50 80
U	25 68 45 131 4 207 34 17 202
V	14 49 187 38 40 3 54 28
W	32 214 197 201 116 72 188 158 36 18

Grid (cells by row: number–letter)

Row	Cells
1	1-D 2-B 3-V 4-U 5-G 6-K 7-M 8-N
9	9-C 10-M 11-R 12-O 13-T 14-V 15-B 16-C 17-U 18-W
19	19-L 20-N 21-G 22-I 23-N 24-P 25-U 26-R 27-B 28-V
29	29-N 30-B 31-S 32-W 33-O 34-U 35-I 36-W 37-S
38	38-V 39-H 40-V 41-E 42-U 43-B 44-Q 45-U 46-M 47-S
48	48-O 49-V 50-T 51-P 52-G 53-Q 54-V 55-A 56-C
57	57-L 58-I 59-T 60-G 61-J 62-H 63-D 64-M 65-P 66-F
67	67-P 68-U 69-K 70-K 71-G 72-W 73-I 74-G 75-B
76	76-A 77-S 78-G 79-E 80-T 81-B 82-A 83-Q 84-I 85-T
86	86-S 87-O 88-N 89-L 90-C 91-A 92-D 93-M 94-E 95-A
96	96-C 97-L 98-J 99-E 100-Q 101-F 102-N 103-K 104-M 105-P
106	106-S 107-J 108-G 109-B 110-M 111-K 112-P 113-B 114-Q
115	115-N 116-W 117-F 118-H 119-G 120-E 121-J 122-U 123-O 124-R
125	125-M 126-N 127-K 128-B 129-M 130-G 131-U 132-R 133-D 134-H
135	135-C 136-S 137-G 138-S 139-N 140-E 141-G 142-I 143-A
144	144-G 145-B 146-S 147-G 148-S 149-D 150-R 151-C 152-L
153	153-H 154-C 155-L 156-N 157-T 158-W 159-G 160-E 161-L
162	162-C 163-B 164-J 165-P 166-L 167-O 168-I 169-G 170-M 171-Q
172	172-D 173-B 174-M 175-P 176-Q 177-O 178-L 179-B 180-S 181-O
182	182-R 183-N 184-G 185-C 186-M 187-U 188-W 189-A 190-P 191-D
192	192-K 193-L 194-I 195-B 196-G 197-W 198-T 199-D 200-F 201-W
202	202-U 203-A 204-F 205-C 206-M 207-U 208-K 209-O 210-N
211	211-L 212-M 213-I 214-W 215-G 216-R 217-F 218-Q 219-J 220-B
221	221-S 222-M 223-A 224-N 225-L 226-P 227-Q

CLUES

A. Romantically naive, sentimentally innocent (hyph.) 70 45 76 58 24 121 18 125

B. Filled with sudden horror 161 150 84 127 135 141

C. 1939 comedy starring Melvyn Douglas and Greta Garbo 60 90 162 129 23 64 80 13 173

D. Unfinished, rudimentary 100 94 54 167 143 97 171 106

E. Devotee, fan 4 115 170 139 154 73 92 177 14 101

F. Colorless vesicant used in chemical warfare 57 136 19 175 166 15 3 69

G. Thin cotton fabric woven with a stripe or check of heavier yarn 158 179 120 164 42 78

H. 1894 George Moore novel (2 wds.) 133 142 82 105 63 25 34 102 28 184 17 32

I. Passes off or inserts wrongfully 2 56 7 47 138 38

J. The Foul Fiend, The Deuce, Lucifer (2 wds.) 33 181 137 172 140 62 152 88

K. Bacchanalian cry 50 183 48 145

L. Instant; importance or consequence 49 72 122 43 112 22

M. Entrancing; mystic, oracular 114 68 131 55 123 91

N. Receives enthusiastically; eats or drinks (2 wds.) 41 52 130 71 27 110

O. "And the lean ___ went to sleep" (Praed, "The Vicar") 77 157 8 113 83 35

P. Most gross, corpulent, or rich 6 59 146 119 67 134 79

Q. Winning, winsome; cuddly 156 39 66 36 26 74 99

R. 1925 Sinclair Lewis novel 81 5 169 109 10 95 159 107 116 147

S. Expressing denial; prohibitory; minus 53 12 16 93 104 148 98 160

T. Exaggerates in telling stories; overstates (3 wds.) 61 132 40 126 89 174 117 9 51 168 124 96 20 182 29

U. 1605 comedy by G. Chapman, Jonson, and J. Marston (2 wds.) 11 1 103 151 176 118 108 163 87 75 85

V. Plays or frolics boisterously 44 153 144 86 31

W. Very thin person; emaciation (3 wds.) 178 37 111 149 30 180 46 155 65 165 21 128

WORDS / GRID

	1	2	3	4	5	6	7	8	9	
		U2	I3	F4	E5	R	P7	I8	O9	T
10	R11	U12	S13	C14	E15	F16	S17	H18	A19	F
20	T21	W22	L23	C24	A25	■	H26	Q27	N28	H
29	T30	W31	V32	H33	J34	H35	O36	Q37	■	W
38	I39	Q40	T41	N42	G43	L44	V45	A46	■47	I
48	K49	L50	K51	T52	N53	S54	D55	M56	I57	F58 A
59	P60	C61	T62	J63	H64	C65	W66	Q67	P68	M
69	F70	A71	N72	L73	E74	Q75	U76	A77	O78	G
79	P80	C81	R82	H83	O84	B85	V86	V87	■	U
88	J89	T90	C91	M92	E93	S94	D95	R96	T97	D98 S
99	Q100	D101	E102	H103	U104	S105	H106	D107	■	R
108	U109	R110	N111	W112	L113	O114	M115	E116	R117	T
118	U119	P120	G121	A122	L123	M124	T125	A126	■	T
127	B128	W129	C130	N131	M132	T133	H134	P135	B136	F137 J
138	I139	E140	J141	B142	H143	D144	V145	K146	P147	R
148	S149	W150	B151	U152	J153	V154	E155	W156	Q157	O158 G
159	R160	S161	B162	C163	U164	G165	W166	■	■	F
167	D168	T169	R170	E171	D172	J173	C174	T175	■	F
176	U177	E178	W179	G180	W181	J182	T183	K184	■	H

158

CLUES

A. "She is / The queen of ___ and cream" ("The Winter's Tale") . .

B. Peruvian author (1833–1919; "Knights of the Cape"; full name)

C. Exceed in violence, outrage, or extravagance (hyph.)

D. "We have ___ and he is us" (3 wds.; Walt Kelly, "Pogo")

E. Term for the web in Mary Howitt's "The Spider and the Fly"

F. Made a solemn declaration to establish a fact

G. Legendary Celtic poet, traditionally an old blind man

H. Reporters . . . .

I. Kafka's tale of transformation (2 wds.)

J. Eruptive skin disease . . . . . .

K. Valley of the upper Inn River, Switzerland

L. Dizzy, frivolous . . . .

M. Self-reliant enterprise . . . . . .

N. Fr. entomologist and author (1823–1915, "Life of the Spider") . . . .

O. Principally, the Malay Archipelago (2 wds.) . . . . . .

P. Frequently . . . .

Q. Followers of, e.g., Elizabeth Cady Stanton

R. Gov. William Bradford started it . .

S. Small falcon; activity pursued for relaxation . . . .

T. 1953 song by Carl Sigman & Robert Maxwell (2 wds.)

U. "Verbal fencing match" much used in classical drama

V. Musingly thoughtful . . . .

W. Sweet Betsy from Pike crossed the wide prairies with him . . . . .

X. What Ben Franklin said were certain (3 wds.) . . . . .

Y. Elevated condition, high rank . . .

Z. Having many branches . . . . . .

WORDS

A. 101 187 35 163 207
B. 188 97 124 108 179 63 153 161 47 167 147 3
C. 210 117 145 55 129 31 190 105
D. 12 193 70 192 125 86 82 135 158 77 132
E. 195 102 65 28 186 15
F. 48 29 191 30 162 185 69 155 45
G. 17 160 137 100 111 211
H. 127 5 156 221 154 144 139
I. 87 2 215 10 180 24 121 189 171 165 61 20 58 106 67 218
J. 157 119 4 21 198
K. 104 93 51 150 204 1 41 72
L. 214 95 94 219 103 75 201 126 73 7 52
M. 113 182 199 39 92 25 174 84 122 220
N. 18 23 13 109 64
O. 175 37 54 79 146 98 216 134 46 6
P. 114 59 83 27 159 80 168 133 183 60
Q. 205 196 131 49 203 32 38 112 173
R. 96 81 212 9 91 66 42 53 200 138 44 128
S. 155 156 157 116 151
T. 148 213 26 19 40 130 76
U. 57 107 62 140 88 36 149 172 118 143 71 206
V. 68 141 50 16 209 110 123
W. 217 169 164
X. 99 170 178 74 120 78 90 136 142 43 194 8 177
Y. 14 22 89 115 56 197 152 34
Z. 176 202 85 181 166 11

159

CLUES

A. Revealing 13 118 18 2 40 150 166 77 71 172

B. "The utmost I can do for him [Lord Littleton] is to consider him as a respectable ___" (Chesterfield) 158 56 177 129 4 148 105 59 89

C. Park in E England (2 wds.) 143 30 84 115 99 23 86 196 15 20 137 189

D. Joint; short, double-breasted jacket 144 83 179 55 11 88

E. "The Cardinal Lord ___ of Rheims" (Barham, "The Jackdaw of Rheims") 28 171 82 27 155 163 110 9 103 42

F. Sino-Tibetan language 197 21 132 147 125 51

G. Disheartened 188 174 1 135 100 123 91 79

H. Out of alignment (hyph.) 181 95 102 192 43 53 157 107 134

I. Type of baton-twirler 64 198 108 41 161 124 12 8 183

J. Extensive tract of uncultivated land 106 101 186 200 3

K. 1908 Arnold Bennett novel (3 wds. after *The*) 193 153 139 182 117 69 98 46 5 109 72 128

L. Of an indefinitely large number in succession: Var. 136 58 116 96 34 63 85 19

M. Arcadian nymph who was transformed into a reed 159 154 168 113 112 81

N. Tied (hyph.) 37 162 68 76 26 176 6 180 191 187

O. She metamorphosed into a laurel tree 44 73 170 146 78 94

P. Not fitting or suitable 67 175 47 92 122

Q. Shown facing forward without a neck (Heraldry) 145 52 33 156 173 90 39 66

R. 1940 Robert Sherwood play (5 wds.) 74 31 169 104 138 195 190 49 10 184 152 133 22 87 7 61 165 178 126

S. Go from place to place 62 142 185 114 80 57 70 35 14

T. Irritate, vex 167 60 17 121 141 36

U. County, N Scotland 199 45 25 50 164

V. Brother of Moses 111 151 93 131 194

W. Restoration 97 160 38 140 48 32 120

X. Warning of possible danger (2 wds.) 201 65 29 119 16 130 24 75 149 127 54

WORDS (grid, by row)

Cells (number·clue)
1·G 2·A 3·J 4·B 5·K 6·N 7·R
9·E 10·R 11·D 12·I 13·A 14·S 15·C 16·X 17·T
18·A 19·L 20·C 21·F 22·R 23·C 24·X 25·U 26·N 27·E
28·E 29·X 30·C 31·R 32·W 33·Q 34·L 35·S 36·T 37·N
38·W 39·Q 40·A 41·I 42·E 43·H 44·O 45·U 46·K 47·P
48·W 49·R 50·U 51·F 52·Q 53·H 54·X 55·D 56·B 57·S
58·L 59·B 60·T 61·R 62·S 63·L 64·I 65·X
66·Q 67·P 68·N 69·K 70·S 71·A 72·K 73·O 74·R 75·X 76·N
77·A 78·O 79·G 80·S 81·M 82·E 83·D 84·C 85·L
86·C 87·R 88·D 89·B 90·Q 91·G 92·P 93·V 94·O 95·H
96·L 97·W 98·K 99·C 100·G 101·J 102·H 103·E 104·R 105·B
106·J 107·H 108·I 109·K 110·E 111·V 112·M 113·M
114·S 115·C 116·L 117·K 118·A 119·X 120·W 121·T 122·P 123·G 124·I
125·F 126·R 127·X 128·K 129·B 130·X 131·V 132·F 133·R
134·H 135·G 136·L 137·C 138·R 139·K 140·W 141·T 142·S 143·C
144·D 145·Q 146·O 147·F 148·B 149·X 150·A 151·V 152·R 153·K 154·M
155·E 156·Q 157·H 158·B 159·M 160·W 161·I 162·N 163·E 164·U 165·R
166·A 167·T 168·M 169·R 170·O 171·E 172·A 173·Q 174·G 175·P
176·N 177·B 178·R 179·D 180·N 181·H 182·K 183·I 184·R
185·S 186·J 187·N 188·G 189·C 190·R 191·N 192·H 193·K
194·V 195·R 196·C 197·F 198·I 199·U 200·J 201·X

160

CLUES

A. Marquise de ——: mistress of Louis XIV
B. Manage; furnish
C. City, W Ukraine, Russia
D. Supporter, follower
E. Horrid, loathsome (Scot. & N Eng.)
F. Deeply engrossed; transported with emotion
G. Secluded place for meditation and study (2 wds.)
H. Reddish dye used for silks and in microscopy
I. Hair-piece, "rug"
J. James Whitcomb Riley, "The —— Poet"
K. Red, reddish; blushing
L. Zealous Am. Revolutionary soldier (1736–96) who summarily executed a group of loyalists; his surname thus became a verb
M. Ancient calculator
N. Arranged compactly
O. Cog; fondness or taste for
P. Urban district, Cumberland, Eng., where Coleridge and Southey each lived for a time
Q. Persons recently admitted to a club, sect, or the like
R. Brief interlude from work (2 wds.)
S. Scottish mountains containing the highest peak in Great Britain
T. Matter; cram
U. Paris's wife, abandoned for Helen
V. Meets with
W. Highwayman, e.g.
X. Engaged
Y. Reddish brown pigment
Z. Branch of the military art
Z₁. River flowing from Turkey to the Persian Gulf

WORDS

Clue	Numbers
A	37 19 174 10 97 159 60 128 122
B	69 110 152 125 12 171
C	141 172 38 7
D	74 103 140 33 57 64 4 120
E	115 56 179 151 109 94
F	138 91 116 54
G	149 143 158 155 76 30 26 126 89 48
H	178 169 17 36 44
I	150 137 176 162 32 135
J	27 68 15 42 121 3 112
K	41 161 11 134 24 106 127 16 168 175
L	130 98 157 49 31
M	47 88 62 21 59 77
N	34 119 22 1 73 6
O	105 58 40 20 2
P	35 13 78 136 43 90 63
Q	80 18 104 87 53 66 85 173 117
R	129 164 146 50 25 111 148 84
S	123 163 170 29 72 86 5 102 156
T	93 95 160 132 52
U	108 118 145 100 65 133
V	99 147 9 71 114
W	113 124 131 46 153
X	79 144 70 154 14
Y	101 23 67 166 75
Z	82 51 39 142 167 61 28 107 45
Z₁	8 92 81 96 177 55 139 83 165

Diagram (cell number · clue letter, in reading order)

1 N	2 O	3 J	4 D	5 S	6 N	7 C				
8 Z₁	9 V	10 A	11 K	12 B	13 P	14 X	15 J	16 K	17 H	
18 Q	19 A	20 O	21 M	22 N	23 Y	24 K	25 R	26 G		
27 J	28 Z	29 S	30 G	31 L	32 I	33 D	34 N	35 P	36 H	
37 A	38 C	39 Z	40 O	41 K	42 J	43 P	44 H	45 Z		
46 W	47 M	48 G	49 L	50 R	51 Z	52 T	53 Q	54 F		
55 Z₁	56 E	57 D	58 O	59 M	60 A	61 Z	62 M	63 P	64 D	
65 U	66 Q	67 Y	68 J	69 B	70 X	71 V	72 S	73 N	74 D	
75 Y	76 G	77 M	78 P	79 X	80 Q	81 Z₁	82 Z	83 Z₁	84 R	
85 Q	86 S	87 Q	88 M	89 G	90 P	91 F	92 Z₁	93 T	94 E	
95 T	96 Z₁	97 A	98 L	99 V	100 U	101 Y	102 S	103 D		
104 Q	105 O	106 K	107 Z	108 U	109 E	110 B	111 R	112 J	113 W	114 V
115 E	116 F	117 Q	118 U	119 N	120 D	121 J	122 A	123 S	124 W	
125 B	126 G	127 K	128 A	129 R	130 L	131 W	132 T	133 U		
134 K	135 I	136 P	137 I	138 F	139 Z₁	140 D	141 C	142 Z	143 G	
144 X	145 U	146 R	147 V	148 R	149 G	150 I	151 E	152 B		
153 W	154 X	155 G	156 S	157 L	158 G	159 A	160 T	161 K	162 I	
163 S	164 R	165 Z₁	166 Y	167 Z	168 K	169 H	170 S	171 B	172 C	
173 Q	174 A	175 K	176 I	177 Z₁	178 H	179 E				

161

CLUES

A Confection made from almonds and egg whites · · · · · · · · · — 23 56 177 66 25 107 137 16

B Natural, of the essence · · · · · · · · · — 29 88 136 120 153 98 62 172

C Alarm bell · · · · · · · · · — 169 145 5 85 38 30

D Surrendered · · · · · · · · · — 60 93 90 49 63

E Dreadful, horrible · · · · · · · · · — 2 83 36 179 57 123 18

F Heightened, augmented · · · · · · · · · — 133 157 6 180 110 160 14 148

G 1920 Harbach-Hirsch song from "Mary" (2 wds. after *The*) — 88 7 13 84 71 22 182 126

H Added a little liquor to · · · · · · · · · — 9 47 79 45 34

I Atticlike space, upper story · · · · · — 115 158 122 58

J Card game played with 32 cards · · · — 72 41 125 11 21 173

K Fixed firmly · · · · · · · · · — 149 105 82 44 144 94 42 111

L One who is habitually negative · · · · · · — 129 156 46 50 109 96 168 181

M Gradually, slowly (3 wds.) · · · · · · · — 59 33 171 151 73 178 117 162 52 97

N Sicken · · · · · · · · · — 166 67 27 4 24 12 118 161

O "When the light wave lisps, '___'" (Browning, "Cleon") · · · · · · — 143 131 76 170 54 32

P Resort town of N New Mexico · · · · · — 69 81 102 139

Q Exaggerated; cooked too long · · · · — 128 92 152 75 112 176 28 106

R Cleverly amusing · · · · · · · · · — 116 127 135 1 65

S Turn over for safekeeping · · · · · · · — 35 124 108 86 113 10 43

T One of the sons of "Simon, a Cyrenian" (Mark 15:21) · · · · · · — 39 87 26 51 154

U Not liked (3 wds.) · · · · · · · · · — 140 19 160 15 175 103 61 37 164 80

V Results, products, consequences · · — 159 99 78 104 138 134

W Canned, sacked · · · · · · · · · — 95 8 91 40 148 167

X Terrified, horrified · · · · · · · · · — 130 163 53 77 101 147

Y Rammed · · · · · · · · · — 64 165 119 31 142 100

Z Mayfly · · · · · · · · · — 89 20 55 3 141 17 48 70 121

Z₁ Shining; clear; rational — 114 74 155 132 174

WORDS / GRID

(Cells in reading order — number with clue letter; ■ = black square)

Row 1: 1-R 2-E 3-Z 4-N 5-C 6-F 7-G 8-W 9-H 10-S ■
Row 2: 11-J 12-N 13-G 14-F 15-U 16-A 17-Z 18-E 19-U 20-Z
Row 3: 21-J 22-G 23-A 24-N 25-A 26-T 27-N 28-Q 29-B 30-C
Row 4: 31-Y 32-O 33-M 34-H 35-S 36-E 37-U 38-C 39-T 40-W 41-J
Row 5: 42-K 43-S 44-K 45-H 46-L 47-H 48-Z 49-D 50-L
Row 6: 51-T 52-M 53-X 54-O 55-Z 56-A 57-E 58-I 59-M 60-D
Row 7: 61-U 62-B 63-D 64-Y 65-R 66-A 67-N 68-B 69-P 70-Z 71-G
Row 8: 72-J 73-M 74-Z₁ 75-Q 76-O 77-X 78-V 79-H 80-U 81-P 82-K
Row 9: 83-E 84-G 85-C 86-S 87-T 88-G 89-Z 90-D 91-W 92-Q
Row 10: 93-D 94-K 95-W 96-L 97-M 98-B 99-V 100-Y 101-X
Row 11: 102-P 103-U 104-V 105-K 106-Q 107-A 108-S 109-L 110-F 111-K
Row 12: 112-Q 113-S 114-Z₁ 115-I 116-R 117-M 118-N 119-Y 120-B 121-Z
Row 13: 122-I 123-E 124-S 125-J 126-G 127-R 128-Q 129-L 130-X 131-O 132-Z₁
Row 14: 133-F 134-V 135-R 136-B 137-A 138-V 139-P 140-U 141-Z 142-Y
Row 15: 143-O 144-K 145-C 146-W 147-X 148-F 149-K 150-U 151-M 152-Q
Row 16: 153-B 154-T 155-Z₁ 156-L 157-F 158-I 159-V 160-F 161-N 162-M
Row 17: 163-X 164-U 165-Y 166-N 167-W 168-L 169-C 170-O 171-M 172-B
Row 18: 173-J 174-Z₁ 175-U 176-Q 177-A 178-M 179-E 180-F 181-L 182-G

162

Grid

1 L	2 H	3 C	4 G	5 O	6 F	7 Y	8 R		
9 N	10 C	11 G	12 W	13 M	14 Z	15 Y	16 U	17 C	18 X
19 P	20 G	21 B	22 Z1	23 K	24 Z	25 G	26 U		
27 H	28 Q	29 H	30 U	31 A	32 V	33 Y	34 S	35 W	36 E
37 R	38 L	39 G	40 T	41 K	42 J	43 O	44 F	45 W	46 E
47 N	48 Z2	49 F	50 P	51 L	52 T	53 L	54 H	55 W	
56 M	57 F	58 G	59 X	60 E	61 K	62 X	63 I	64 G	
65 J	66 U	67 Q	68 L	69 G	70 R	71 Y	72 C	73 A	74 D
75 Z1	76 Q	77 B	78 J	79 L	80 I	81 H	82 Y	83 R	84 U
85 Q	86 N	87 B	88 V	89 S	90 D	91 W	92 G	93 C	94 P
95 K	96 Z1	97 S	98 Z2	99 B	100 Y	101 Z2	102 P	103 E	
104 Q	105 H	106 A	107 F	108 W	109 O	110 A	111 D	112 C	113 J
114 S	115 I	116 K	117 H	118 Z	119 H	120 B	121 C	122 F	123 D
124 Q	125 E	126 M	127 Z2	128 Z1	129 A	130 V	131 M	132 Q	
133 L	134 G	135 H	136 I	137 V	138 U	139 Z2	140 Z2	141 S	142 H
143 V	144 I	145 J	146 G	147 C	148 J	149 P	150 Z2	151 Z1	152 B
153 R	154 X	155 B	156 E	157 T	158 S	159 M	160 J		
161 V	162 G	163 A	164 Z	165 T	166 O	167 Z	168 P	169 E	170 N
171 G	172 B	173 D	174 I	175 G	176 S	177 B	178 V	179 U	
180 W	181 A	182 L	183 F	184 E	185 U	186 A	187 D	188 R	189 D
190 O	191 E	192 C	193 B	194 U	195 O	196 K	197 H	198 N	199 B
200 C	201 I	202 L	203 G	204 P	205 Y	206 D	207 B	208 A	
209 V	210 V	211 T	212 U	213 R	214 Q	215 W			

CLUES

WORDS

A Having a desire to do harm — 31 181 73 110 186 129 208 163 106

B See WORD G (3 wds.) — 207 77 120 177 21 99 172 155 152 193 199 87

C One of the Lake Poets — 112 147 17 200 192 93 72 121 3 10

D Position; outlook — 189 173 123 74 111 206 90 187

E Chimney corner — 125 103 60 191 46 156 184 169 36

F Sail; direct one's course — 57 6 183 107 134 122 49 44

G "___ and a time to every purpose under the heaven" (Eccl. 3:1; 4 wds. after WORD B) — 146 175 69 171 4 58 203 39 20 11 25 64 162 92

H Pretentious, haughty — 135 81 54 119 2 29 142 117 197 27 105

I "Like a rich jewel in an ___ ear" ("Romeo and Juliet") — 144 136 115 63 174 201 80

J Equivocal, wavering in opinion — 145 78 65 113 148 42 160

K Entirely, altogether (2 wds.) — 61 196 95 116 23 41

L Weaken, make slender or fine — 1 79 68 53 38 133 202 182 51

M River flowing from SE Switzerland to the North Sea — 126 131 159 56 13

N Incensed, angry — 47 170 198 9 86

O Mountain peak in Colorado — 195 190 166 109 5 43

P Japanese dish of raw fish — 168 102 204 50 94 149 19

Q Cream, oyster, e.g. (hyph.) — 132 214 124 28 85 104 67 76

R Overheated, as a body — 188 37 153 70 213 8 83

S Transversely, across — 141 34 97 158 176 89 114

T Fatuous person, fool (Brit. dial.) — 165 157 52 40 211

U ___ point of the turning world" (3 wds.; Eliot, "Triumphal March") — 16 179 26 138 66 30 84 185 194 212

V Temporary expedient or substitute — 210 88 143 178 137 161 32 209 130

W Sticky, gluey — 35 108 180 91 12 55 45 215

X Eagerly enthusiastic, loony, screwy — 59 154 62 18

Y Dregs of a half-smoked pipe — 82 205 100 71 7 15 33

Z Type of antiknock fluid — 167 118 24 14 164

Z1 Herbaceous twining plant — 75 22 128 151 96

Z2 Rave, make a fuss, bubble over — 139 48 140 101 150 127 98

163

Grid

1 W	2 A	3 S	4 F	5 M	6 J	7 Y	8 V			
9 R	10 A	11 N	12 F	13 M	14 J	15 H	16 X	17 L		
18 O	19 K	20 R	21 J	22 F	23 D	24 Y	25 G	26 K	27 J	28 I
29 S	30 F	31 E	32 J	33 A	34 I	35 P	36 G	37 J	38 O	
39 E	40 S	41 T	42 W	43 M	44 S	45 I	46 Q	47 D		
48 G	49 B	50 S	51 A	52 Q	53 Y	54 O	55 O	56 F	57 B	
58 A	59 H	60 D	61 S	62 D	63 W	64 B	65 L	66 M		
67 T	68 P	69 K	70 R	71 Y	72 Y	73 G	74 Y	75 T		
76 I	77 P	78 V	79 R	80 G	81 H	82 B	83 S	84 D	85 F	86 W
87 K	88 A	89 J	90 N	91 I	92 J	93 N	94 W	95 F	96 S	97 S
98 I	99 U	100 L	101 S	102 V	103 K	104 I	105 C	106 S	107 G	
108 L	109 P	110 D	111 I	112 C	113 W	114 L	115 D	116 E	117 N	
118 H	119 Y	120 E	121 K	122 O	123 X	124 V	125 B	126 W	127 R	
128 A	129 G	130 L	131 M	132 B	133 S	134 H	135 Y	136 Y	137 R	
138 G	139 O	140 H	141 F	142 Y	143 V	144 E	145 T	146 K	147 X	148 M
149 N	150 S	151 E	152 L	153 U	154 B	155 E	156 W	157 T		
158 T	159 U	160 J	161 O	162 M	163 S	164 X	165 Y	166 R	167 B	
168 J	169 W	170 C	171 A	172 Y	173 F	174 N	175 C	176 U	177 Q	
178 V	179 H	180 J	181 L	182 A	183 I	184 C	185 P			

CLUES

A Redolent annual weed of California
B Fishing port of N Scotland
C Industrial suburb of Chicago
D Blameworthy (2 wds.)
E Vestibule leading to the nave of a church
F Citizen of Reykjavik, e.g.
G Early TV show featuring Edward R. Murrow (3 wds.)
H Loss of memory
I Plant whose rhizomes yield a nutritious starch
J "I'll tickle your ___" ("Henry IV, Part 2," II:2)
K Of dark complexion
L Poet satirized as "Grosvenor" by W.S. Gilbert in "Patience"
M One no longer popular or effective (hyph.)
N Dichroic blue mineral also called cordierite
O Snuggle, cuddle
P Haunts or overruns in a troublesome manner
Q Bird's beak
R Am. lyricist (1886–1941; "Yes, Sir! That's My Baby"; full name)
S Novel by E.A. Braithwaite (4 wds.)
T Chorus girl or boy, e.g.
U Mother of Zeus
V Apparatus representing the solar system
W Belonging to the elm family
X Gr. goddess of the earth
Y Plant growing in water or wet ground

WORDS

A 58 88 182 2 51 10 171 33 128
B 82 167 57 132 154 125 64 49
C 184 170 112 175 105 73
D 115 60 110 62 23 84 47
E 39 155 120 31 144 151 116
F 85 95 4 173 22 30 141 56 12
G 72 80 107 129 25 138 48 36
H 179 81 118 140 15 59 134
I 104 183 34 45 98 111 28 76 91
J 27 37 180 14 6 160 21 168 92 32 89
K 146 103 121 19 69 87 26
L 114 181 152 65 55 17 108 130 100
M 162 43 5 131 13 66 148
N 174 117 93 90 149 11
O 122 18 38 161 139 54
P 136 77 68 35 109 185 97
Q 46 52 177
R 79 9 166 20 137 70 127
S 83 29 44 163 101 61 50 106 150 3 40 133 96
T 75 145 67 158 157 41
U 153 99 176 159
V 8 143 178 102 124 78
W 1 156 113 94 86 42 169 126 63
X 164 16 147 123
Y 53 119 172 135 71 74 165 7 24 142

CLUES

	Clue	Word numbers
A	Scum, refuse	120 107 202 195 181
B	Pretense	50 102 193 86 145 125 206 121 97 161 233
C	Schlemiel	222 69 17 25 23 99 40
D	Inexpedient, injudicious	179 7 157 116 79 44 85 54 134
E	Venturesome, resourceful	101 151 49 169 154 211 30 177 196 130 190 65
F	Bumpkins, boors	205 26 218 147 201
G	Unmercifully, adamantly	104 62 199 186 43 71 126 58 13 48 166 210
H	Haughty; tending to domineer	189 207 231 12 29 150 223 170 64 93 153
I	1,200-mile-long Russian river flowing to the Sea of Azov	159 19 143
J	Is wide open	144 155 16 52 113
K	Summer	68 118 217 34 168 197 39 158
L	Wealth	96 31 1 122 208 214
M	Binding; rigorous	117 56 209 148 70 140 92 128 183
N	Home for foundlings; type of Christmas tableau	180 227 119 131 164 11
O	Inaugural vows (3 wds.)	18 60 163 185 235 221 187 192 160 173 142 109 87
P	1939 Ernst Lubitsch film	81 220 24 141 27 91 14 230 127
Q	Frozen Arctic plain	200 42 55 22 100 132
R	Handbook, manual	76 88 114 2 216 137 15 47 146 175 37
S	"And maiden virtue rudely ———" (Shakespeare, Sonnet 66)	133 45 110 3 105 174 84 191 165 226
T	Clumsy ships	219 198 10 112
U	Eagerly interested	41 229 178 139 95 171 111 33 53 184 82 5
V	"Call in thy ——— there, tie up thy fears" (hyph.; Herbert, "The Collar")	225 167 36 51 135 236 72 123 182 75
W	Assignations	89 162 80 108 32 156
X	Cattlemen, e.g.	212 77 74 138 6 21 188 204
Y	(Followed by WORD Z) 1932 song by Mack Gordon and Harry Revel	136 224 38 106 4 203 98 73 129 90
Z	See WORD Y (3 wds.)	94 66 234 57 124 115 59 46 9 20 103 172 83
Z₁	Queen Mab's "chariot is an empty ———" (hyph., "Romeo and Juliet")	28 194 149 63 176 35 228 215
Z₂	Greek herald in "The Iliad"	152 67 8 232 61 213 78

Diagram (cell number : clue-letter)

Row (1–6): 1 L · 2 R · 3 S · 4 Y · 5 U · 6 X
Row (7–17): 7 D · 8 Z₂ · 9 Z · 10 T · 11 N · 12 H · 13 G · 14 P · 15 R · 16 J · 17 C
Row (18–27): 18 O · 19 I · 20 Z · 21 X · 22 Q · 23 C · 24 P · 25 C · 26 F · 27 P
Row (28–37): 28 Z₁ · 29 H · 30 E · 31 L · 32 W · 33 U · 34 K · 35 Z₁ · 36 V · 37 R
Row (38–47): 38 Y · 39 K · 40 C · 41 U · 42 Q · 43 G · 44 D · 45 S · 46 Z · 47 R
Row (48–56): 48 G · 49 E · 50 B · 51 V · 52 J · 53 U · 54 D · 55 Q · 56 M
Row (57–66): 57 Z · 58 G · 59 Z · 60 O · 61 Z₂ · 62 G · 63 Z₁ · 64 H · 65 E · 66 Z
Row (67–76): 67 Z₂ · 68 K · 69 C · 70 M · 71 G · 72 V · 73 Y · 74 X · 75 V · 76 R
Row (77–87): 77 X · 78 Z₂ · 79 D · 80 W · 81 P · 82 U · 83 Z · 84 S · 85 D · 86 B · 87 O
Row (88–98): 88 R · 89 W · 90 Y · 91 P · 92 M · 93 H · 94 Z · 95 U · 96 L · 97 B · 98 Y
Row (99–108): 99 C · 100 Q · 101 E · 102 B · 103 Z · 104 G · 105 S · 106 Y · 107 A · 108 A
Row (109–120): 109 O · 110 S · 111 U · 112 T · 113 J · 114 R · 115 Z · 116 D · 117 M · 118 K · 119 N · 120 A
Row (121–130): 121 B · 122 L · 123 V · 124 Z · 125 B · 126 G · 127 P · 128 M · 129 Y · 130 E
Row (131–139): 131 N · 132 Q · 133 S · 134 D · 135 V · 136 Y · 137 R · 138 X · 139 U
Row (140–150): 140 M · 141 P · 142 O · 143 I · 144 J · 145 B · 146 R · 147 F · 148 M · 149 Z₁ · 150 H
Row (151–160): 151 E · 152 Z₂ · 153 H · 154 E · 155 J · 156 W · 157 D · 158 K · 159 I · 160 O
Row (161–170): 161 B · 162 W · 163 O · 164 N · 165 S · 166 G · 167 V · 168 K · 169 E · 170 H
Row (171–180): 171 U · 172 Z · 173 O · 174 S · 175 R · 176 Z₁ · 177 E · 178 U · 179 D · 180 N
Row (181–189): 181 A · 182 V · 183 M · 184 U · 185 O · 186 G · 187 O · 188 X · 189 H
Row (190–199): 190 E · 191 S · 192 O · 193 B · 194 Z₁ · 195 A · 196 E · 197 K · 198 T · 199 G
Row (200–209): 200 Q · 201 F · 202 A · 203 Y · 204 X · 205 B · 206 H · 207 H · 208 L · 209 M
Row (210–220): 210 G · 211 E · 212 X · 213 Z₂ · 214 L · 215 Z₁ · 216 R · 217 K · 218 F · 219 T · 220 P
Row (221–230): 221 O · 222 C · 223 H · 224 Y · 225 V · 226 S · 227 N · 228 Z₁ · 229 U · 230 P
Row (231–236): 231 H · 232 Z₂ · 233 B · 234 Z · 235 O · 236 V

165

CLUES

WORDS

A Where Odin and the spirits of dead heroes feast on mead and boar's meat
96 186 77 27 140 20 160 107

B Deceptive, misleading
36 2 21 76 151 5 119 179 145 64 62

C One of a 19th-cent. group opposed to manufacturing machinery
91 152 80 53 65 18 116

D Improved by supplementing or enriching
177 45 153 117 42 109

E Near
130 78 90 105 95 1 43 128

F Walked pompously
182 99 124 13 6 149 71 141

G Look disapprovingly
89 115 92 35 162

H Odoriferous
193 97 148 168 61 14 49 129

I Impart knowledge
157 185 70 165 163 44 32 87 37

J Last name of football Hall-of-Famer "Bronko"
59 17 50 30 171 188 67 178

K Battle, fight against
28 111 47 131 143 170

L Act of forcible ejection (hyph.)
16 181 104 73 54 139 29

M Cunning, sly, deceitful
26 190 135 123 11 102

N Alert, sharp, hep, hip, ready (3 wds.)
88 57 15 84 114 69 176 187 132

O Depriving of courage or confidence
189 25 52 74 46 154 174 8 146

P Meddle, pry
108 150 4 24

Q Oppressively hot
166 161 23 41 72 173

R Attributed; alluded
86 133 22 58 98 12 125 113

S Competitor for, e.g., the America's Cup
122 68 175 167 60 138 81 85 126

T Jacks; scoundrels
94 66 172 156 137 158

U Hugeness
48 142 121 101 93 7 155 183 34

V Lofty
10 159 164 38 33 56 112 191

W Pariah; shipwrecked person
127 51 39 136 40 110 19 82

X Devotion to pleasure
118 79 63 9 31 184 106 55

Y Humbug, nonsense
103 194 147 120 3 83 100

Z Connecticut, the ___ State
144 169 180 134 192 75

166

CLUES

A One of the Anisoptera 110 156 134 69 37 28 188 117 139

B Terrible; solemnly impressive 97 129 55 67 124

C Puck's mother ''was a ____ of my order,'' says Titania (''Midsummer Night's Dream'') 74 112 152 173 189 161 2

D Neglect 57 65 1 176 113 18 178 111 125 43 166

E Fit together neatly 122 130 184 154 41 9 95 31 84 118

F 1666 Moliere comedy (after ''The'') 88 121 175 168 19 146 105 94 138 99 70

G Dissonance, racket 58 190 5 187 12 83 167 23 11

H Edible skim-milk curds (2 wds.) 29 54 44 42 64 119 104 85 133 108 62 79 34

I Remove from a mount 120 10 47 30 131 15 59

J Ambiguous, doubtful, as a sort of compliment (hyph.) 109 100 81 53 6 71 126 136 78 137

K Hide fakery 103 14 150 158 40 115 170 46 82 60 106

L Comedy ____ (social satire; 2 wds.) 180 56 3 183 32 90 165 36 147

M Offense 4 92 35 142 75 179 144

N Talkative 49 160 13 135 38 76 101 141 128

O Thumbs 114 16 155 96 61 45 27 151 127 8

P Oedipus' birthplace 172 33 123 143 25 171

Q Wrestled playfully 191 116 163 66 107 153 80 174 52 149 73

R Improbability 157 98 63 22 132 51 26 177 182 89 140 17

S Hodgepodge 164 169 21 50 87 68 48 181 145 159

T Supplementary materials 7 102 148 93 186 181 24 185 162

U Confection of sugar paste 72 86 77 39 91 20

WORDS (grid)

1 D	2 C	3 L	4 M	5 G	6 J	7 T	8 O		
9 E	10 I	11 G	12 G	13 N	14 K	15 I	16 O	17 R	18 D
19 F	20 U	21 S	22 R	23 G	24 T	25 P	26 R	27 O	28 A
29 H	30 I	31 E	32 L	33 P	34 H	35 M	36 L	37 A	38 N
39 U	40 K	41 E	42 H	43 D	44 H	45 O	46 K	47 I	
48 T	49 N	50 S	51 R	52 Q	53 J	54 H	55 B	56 L	57 D
58 G	59 I	60 K	61 O	62 H	63 R	64 H	65 D	66 Q	67 B
68 S	69 A	70 F	71 J	72 U	73 Q	74 C	75 M	76 N	77 U
78 J	79 H	80 Q	81 J	82 K	83 G	84 E	85 H	86 U	87 S
88 F	89 R	90 L	91 U	92 M	93 T	94 F	95 E	96 O	97 B
98 R	99 F	100 J	101 N	102 T	103 K	104 H	105 F	106 K	107 Q
108 H	109 J	110 A	111 D	112 C	113 D	114 O	115 K	116 Q	
117 A	118 E	119 H	120 I	121 F	122 E	123 P	124 B	125 D	126 J
127 O	128 N	129 B	130 E	131 I	132 R	133 H	134 A	135 N	136 J
137 J	138 F	139 A	140 R	141 N	142 M	143 P	144 M	145 S	146 F
147 L	148 T	149 Q	150 K	151 O	152 C	153 Q	154 E	155 O	
156 A	157 R	158 K	159 S	160 N	161 C	162 T	163 Q	164 S	165 L
166 D	167 G	168 F	169 S	170 K	171 P	172 P	173 C	174 Q	175 F
176 D	177 R	178 D	179 M	180 L	181 S	182 R	183 L	184 E	
185 T	186 T	187 G	188 A	189 C	190 G	191 Q			

167

CLUES

A Not easy to please . . . . — 95 126 77 54 11 188 115 51 136 43

B Reasonableness . . . . — 34 7 116 60 23 165 90 168 100 105 5

C Comely . . . . — 139 179 107 86 29 1 64 185 176 71

D Terms comprising a set or system . . . — 91 153 6 58 40 124 83 164 69 85 13 45

E Expertise (hyph.) . . . . — 25 183 33 172 10 63 46

F Nephew to King Arthur . . . . — 81 42 113 120 182 61

G Ficus elastica, of the mulberry family (2 wds.) . . . . — 149 16 50 74 177 111 163 129 47 80 84

H Majesty, excellence . . . . — 103 146 123 134 175 32 160 28 109 56 119

I Long, loose garment . . . . — 44 24 128 73 4 102 145 162 78

J "I asked a thief to steal me ___" (2 wds.; Blake, "I Asked a Thief") . . — 118 141 31 173 161 65

K Entangled . . . . — 30 68 57 158 9 114

L Boorish, oafish, indelicate . . . . . . — 110 178 148 140 12

M Sir Walter Scott's estate . . . . — 35 21 67 112 62 48 157 20 17 147

N Having a notched edge or sawlike teeth . . . . — 101 66 144 137 171 53 41 92

O Cut, outlined, delineated . . . . — 14 135 127 108 169 166

P "O, call back ___ bid time return," says Salisbury ("Richard II") . . . . . — 27 186 3 150 97 143 8 130 174

Q Type of bit, with rings on the ends . . — 121 18 49 184 96 37 151

R One of the three useful things taught by antique Persians in addition to "to ride and speak the truth" (4 wds.; Byron, "Don Juan") . . . . — 15 156 89 131 2 170 155 99 138 36 55 117

S Priest's garment of blue, gold, purple, and fine twined linen (Ex. 28:6) . . . — 38 104 159 39 98

T "Dark and true and tender is the ___" (Tennyson, "The Princess") . . . . . . — 87 75 72 125 180

U Basse-Terre and Grande-Terre, in the Leeward Islands . . . . — 132 52 142 152 82 187 94 154 59 88

V Sold abroad . . . . — 181 76 122 106 22 19 79 93

W ___ Bank, South of the Seine, Paris . . — 26 133 167 70

WORDS

1 C	2 R	3 P	4 I	5 B	6 D	7 B	8 P
9 K	10 E	11 A	12 L	13 D	14 O	15 R	16 G	17 M	18 Q
19 V	20 M	21 M	22 V	23 B	24 I	25 E	26 W	27 P	28 H
29 C	30 K	31 J	32 H	33 E	34 B	35 M	36 R	37 Q	38 S
39 S	40 D	41 N	42 F	43 A	44 I	45 D	46 E
47 G	48 M	49 Q	50 G	51 A	52 U	53 N	54 A	55 R
56 H	57 K	58 D	59 U	60 B	61 F	62 M	63 E	64 C	65 J
66 N	67 M	68 K	69 D	70 W	71 C	72 T	73 I	74 G	75 T
76 V	77 A	78 I	79 V	80 G	81 F	82 U	83 D	84 G	85 D
86 C	87 T	88 U	89 R	90 B	91 D	92 N	93 V	94 U	95 A
96 Q	97 P	98 S	99 R	100 B	101 N	102 I	103 H	104 S
105 B	106 V	107 C	108 O	109 H	110 L	111 G	112 M	113 F	114 K
115 A	116 B	117 R	118 J	119 H	120 F	121 Q	122 V
123 H	124 D	125 T	126 A	127 O	128 I	129 G	130 P	131 R	132 U	133 W
134 H	135 O	136 A	137 N	138 R	139 C	140 L	141 J	142 U	143 P
144 N	145 I	146 H	147 M	148 L	149 G	150 P	151 Q	152 U	153 D
154 U	155 R	156 R	157 M	158 K	159 S	160 H	161 J	162 I
163 G	164 D	165 B	166 O	167 W	168 B	169 O	170 R	171 N
172 E	173 J	174 P	175 H	176 C	177 G	178 L	179 C	180 T	181 V
182 F	183 E	184 Q	185 C	186 P	187 U	188 A

CLUES

A. Sharpens

B. Lifeless

C. Bay SW of Dorset

D. Easy Street, clover (3 wds. after "the")

E. Arabian camel

F. Release, open

G. Intensified by sympathetic vibration

H. Dutch city on the Rhine

I. 1941 Bob Hope film (4 wds.)

J. Family on whom Thyestes laid a curse (4 wds.)

K. Kantian principle (2 wds.)

L. With care and diligence

M. Admonition

N. Compassionate (hyph.)

O. Dictatorship or absolute monarchy, e.g.

P. Governor of Michigan, 1963–69

Q. "The times should cease / ___ year would make the world away" (2 wds.; Shakespeare, Sonnet xi)

R. Henry Percy's earldom in "Henry IV"

S. Anger, pique

T. Roman military hero; Shakespearean play

U. Precursor

V. Clefts, splits

W. Go-between

X. Arrangement of parts

Y. Irish poet (1779–1852; "Irish Melodies"; "Lalla Rookh"; full name)

WORDS

A. 144 192 111 30 44

B. 24 11 23 238 140

C. 109 53 154 185

D. 225 31 108 56 148 213 84 101 92 15 155

E. 136 167 208 17 153 74 199 87 226

F. 178 205 241 117 176 151 79 105

G. 58 102 210 51 135 89 162 41

H. 124 232 189 22 76 194

I. 187 34 54 47 164 125 20 132 231 227 157 249 114 21 244 59 211 2

J. 95 116 156 242 64 170 36 229 212 67 80 1 14 133 72 230

K. 113 29 248 43 216 18 171 145 123 197 60 48 198 219 234 63 70 118 173 98

L. 104 196 174 27 143 209 45 149 96 222 78 122

M. 243 206 228 159 119 179 175 115 188 83 235

N. 49 120 46 169 147 180 10 81 191 88 236

O. 13 38 200 97 181 158 195 9 245

P. 138 240 65 73 217 131

Q. 168 203 103 146 126 75 237 61 12 184 86 215 66

R. 112 202 25 165 71 247 177 221 4 52 130 204 90 62

S. 129 220 91 190 172 141 107

T. 224 182 39 207 142 163 16 32 110 8

U. 55 161 100 35 223 183 33 166 69

V. 6 42 94 28 139

W. 40 19 5 93 201 160 3 77 106 99 128 57

X. 239 50 186 134 37 218 7 26 193

Y. 150 152 214 121 127 82 85 246 68 233 137

Grid

1 J	2 I	3 W	4 R	5 W	6 V	7 X	8 T	9 O	10 N	11 B
12 Q	13 O	14 J	15 D	16 T	17 E	18 K	19 W	20 I		
21 I	22 H	23 B	24 B	25 R	26 X	27 L	28 V	29 K	30 A	31 D
32 T	33 U	34 I	35 U	36 J	37 X	38 O	39 T	40 W	41 G	42 V
43 K	44 A	45 L	46 N	47 I	48 K	49 N	50 X	51 G	52 R	
53 C	54 I	55 U	56 D	57 W	58 G	59 I	60 K	61 Q	62 R	63 K
64 J	65 P	66 Q	67 J	68 Y	69 U	70 K				
71 R	72 J	73 P	74 E	75 Q	76 H	77 W	78 L	79 F	80 J	81 N
82 Y	83 M	84 D	85 Y	86 Q	87 E	88 N	89 G	90 R		
91 S	92 D	93 W	94 V	95 J	96 L	97 O	98 K	99 W		
100 U	101 D	102 G	103 Q	104 L	105 F	106 W	107 S	108 D	109 C	
110 T	111 A	112 R	113 K	114 I	115 M	116 J	117 F	118 K	119 M	
120 N	121 Y	122 L	123 K	124 H	125 I	126 Q	127 Y	128 W	129 S	
130 R	131 P	132 I	133 J	134 X	135 G	136 E	137 Y	138 P	139 V	
140 B	141 S	142 T	143 L	144 A	145 K	146 Q	147 N	148 D	149 L	150 Y
151 F	152 Y	153 E	154 C	155 D	156 J	157 I	158 O	159 M		
160 W	161 U	162 G	163 T	164 I	165 R	166 U	167 E	168 Q	169 N	170 J
171 K	172 S	173 K	174 L	175 M	176 F	177 R	178 F	179 M		
180 N	181 O	182 T	183 U	184 Q	185 C	186 X	187 I	188 M	189 H	190 S
191 N	192 A	193 X	194 H	195 O	196 L	197 K	198 K	199 E		
200 O	201 W	202 R	203 Q	204 R	205 F	206 M	207 T	208 E	209 L	
210 G	211 I	212 J	213 D	214 Y	215 Q	216 K	217 P	218 X		
219 K	220 S	221 R	222 L	223 U	224 T	225 D	226 E	227 I	228 M	229 J
230 J	231 I	232 H	233 Y	234 K	235 M	236 N	237 Q	238 B	239 X	
240 P	241 F	242 J	243 M	244 I	245 O	246 Y	247 R	248 K	249 I	

WORDS

CLUES

A Difficult to deal with · · · · · · · · · 12 84 125 43 112 96 90

B Without concern · · · · · · · · · 101 54 11 122 1 110 86 34 152 104

C Marilyn Monroe's last film (after *The*) · · · · · · · · · 61 133 97 149 4 20 121

D Imminent (2 wds.) · · · · · · · · · 167 92 78 102 46 150

E Not pure; bawdy · · · · · · · · · 136 24 53 109 159 147 64 31

F Come to or rouse again · · · · · · · · · 22 146 155 73 44 183 98 36

G Makes reparation · · · · · · · · · 85 15 95 134 66 144

H Slender, lithe · · · · · · · · · 165 7 117 153 174 83

I Miserable dwellings · · · · · · · · · 139 10 41 143 37 186

J Type of painted canvas · · · · · · · · · 23 184 89 124 70 2 50 76

K "Heathen heart that puts her trust / In ___ and iron shard" (2 wds.; Kipling, "Recessional") · · · · · · · · · 178 81 14 162 120 156 116 114 3 127 19

L Wrenches · · · · · · · · · 77 26 40 154 166 108

M Toasts · · · · · · · · · 27 105 60 103 173 9 68

N Giving offense · · · · · · · · · 177 164 99 56 93 74 51 130 67

O Calm · · · · · · · · · 80 42 107 140 29 163 17 38

P Staggers · · · · · · · · · 138 115 118 48 176 142 63

Q Navel-like · · · · · · · · · 169 13 137 18 49 132 47 182 157

R Disparaged; pursued and captured (2 wds.) · · · · · · · · · 65 172 59 141 151 8 52

S Type of Turkish saber · · · · · · · · · 128 106 75 71 135 30 33 181

T Scottish author (1828–97; "Salem Chapel") · · · · · · · · · 170 131 123 69 21 180 160 87

U Street vendors; coarse, scolding women · · · · · · · · · 39 161 126 82 32 62 57 28 45

V Got rid of, rejected (2 wds.) · · · · · · · · · 5 111 88 148 171 16 179 94

W Netted · · · · · · · · · 25 185 158 79 145 119 58 113

X Insect larva that eats wood · · · · · · · · · 6 72 168 35 129 175 91 55 100

Puzzle grid (each cell shows its sequence number and clue letter, in reading order):

1 X	2 D	3 J	4 C	5 M	6 R	7 A	8 X	9 Q	10 A	11 Q	12 O	13 K	14 H
15 B	16 F	17 E	18 V	19 E	20 U	21 S	22 Z	23 Y	24 F				
25 I	26 P	27 W	28 U	29 Y	30 B	31 J	32 O	33 K	34 N				
35 F	36 P	37 I	38 F	39 Z	40 G	41 Q	42 V	43 O					
44 B	45 V	46 V	47 E	48 P	49 N	50 S	51 L	52 M	53 W				
54 Z	55 O	56 F	57 N	58 I	59 R	60 Q	61 Y	62 E	63 P				
64 F	65 K	66 W	67 J	68 D	69 A	70 O	71 M	72 S					
73 C	74 X	75 P	76 G	77 V	78 O	79 V	80 T	81 D	82 G				
83 L	84 Q	85 X	86 L	87 Z	88 B	89 A	90 Q	91 P	92 R				
93 U	94 F	95 Y	96 G	97 M	98 X	99 S	100 J	101 A					
102 Y	103 D	104 F	105 N	106 S	107 O	108 W	109 A	110 R	111 D				
112 P	113 B	114 C	115 W	116 Y	117 E	118 V	119 L	120 G					
121 W	122 T	123 H	124 O	125 F	126 J	127 Z	128 Q	129 F	130 G				
131 B	132 V	133 D	134 A	135 O	136 S	137 U	138 B	139 C	140 N				
141 Z	142 D	143 L	144 B	145 J	146 M	147 Y	148 H	149 A	150 E				
151 Z	152 V	153 O	154 P	155 P	156 V	157 J	158 F	159 E	160 A				
161 I	162 Y	163 S	164 F	165 R	166 B	167 K	168 L	169 R	170 Q				
171 P	172 E	173 J	174 C	175 G	176 X	177 L	178 I	179 G	180 A				
181 O	182 D	183 B	184 Z	185 G	186 K	187 M	188 B	189 H	190 L				
191 T	192 Q	193 K	194 Y	195 P	196 X	197 Z	198 W	199 L	200 G				
201 T	202 J	203 L	204 S	205 I									

CLUES

A Nagging women, shrews · · · · · · · · ·
B Untidy heap, mess (2 wds.) · · · ·
C Caribbean belief system akin to Voo-doo · · · · · ·
D Quick, witty reply; wit · · · · · · ·
E "___ has she now, no force" (2 wds.; Wordsworth, "A Slumber Did My Spirit Seal") · ·
F Equivocate, apostasize · · · · ·
G Small pathological bony growth · ·
H Scent; nuzzle; pry; defeat narrowly · ·
I Australian marsupial resembling a small bear · · · · · · · · ·
J Off the cuff, spur-of-the-moment · · ·
K Dirty old man, e.g. · · · · · · · · ·
L Calumny, slander · · · · · · · · ·
M Shun, avoid · · · · · · · · · · · ·
N "...shall outlive this powerful ___" (Shakespeare, Sonnet lv) · · · ·
O Working of miracles; magic · · · · ·
P Bees, wasps, ants, etc. · · · · · ·
Q Incipient, rudimentary · · · · · ·
R Work of a writer, painter, or the like · ·
S Striped bass · · · · · · · · · · · ·
T Abominable Snowman · · · · · · · ·
U Probability, chance · · · · · · · ·
V Section of a European newspaper de-voted to light literature, etc. · · · ·
W Staggers, totters, sways abruptly · ·
X Huge · · · · · · · · · · · · · · · ·
Y Savage, fierce · · · · · · · · · · ·
Z Producing a desired result, capable, competent · · · · · · · · · · · ·

WORDS

A	160	89	134	149	109	10	7	180	101	69	
B	183	113	30	88	44	131	188	15	138	166	144
C	139	174	73	4	114						
D	142	2	133	68	103	182	111	81			
E	172	19	47	62	117	17	150	159			
F	64	158	24	16	35	38	104	129	125	164	94 56
G	76	82	130	120	40	185	200	175	96	179	
H	123	14	148	189							
I	25	58	178	161	37	205					
J	145	157	202	3	126	31	67	173	100		
K	13	193	33	65	167	186					
L	86	119	51	203	168	83	199	143	177	190	
M	52	5	146	97	187	71					
N	140	34	105	57	49						
O	181	153	135	32	55	12	70	107	78	124	43
P	36	75	155	171	112	195	48	91	154	63	26
Q	128	170	192	84	60	11	41	9	90		
R	169	92	165	110	59	6					
S	50	106	163	21	99	136	204	72			
T	80	201	191	122							
U	20	93	28	137							
V	118	79	77	46	42	18	132	152	156	45	
W	121	115	27	53	108	66	198				
X	1	196	176	98	74	8	85				
Y	61	162	116	23	194	147	95	102	29		
Z	197	22	151	39	141	54	87	127	184		

171

Grid (cell number · clue letter):

1 L	2 I	3 B	4 F	5 J	6 Q	7 U	8 V	9 Z	10 Q	
11 E	12 I	13 S	14 J	15 J	16 S	17 B	18 N	19 V	20 X	
21 J	22 W	23 N	24 P	25 O	26 I	27 S	28 H	29 E	30 F	
31 C	32 H	33 Y	34 D	35 F	36 F	37 L	38 A	39 P	40 X	
41 Y	42 F	43 M	44 I	45 H	46 N	47 G	48 D	49 Z	50 D	
51 F	52 W	53 U	54 O	55 B	56 T	57 A	58 D	59 O	60 M	
61 A	62 P	63 U	64 T	65 H	66 I	67 Q	68 V	69 Y	70 T	
71 O	72 L	73 Z	74 J	75 U	76 X	77 B	78 Z	79 W	80 K	
81 Z	82 S	83 R	84 D	85 C	86 K	87 Z	88 Q	89 M		
90 P	91 G	92 X	93 E	94 R	95 S	96 H	97 G	98 K		
99 Y	100 Q	101 G	102 H	103 X	104 Q	105 O	106 T	107 Q		
108 I	109 X	110 V	111 C	112 R	113 W	114 U	115 S	116 E	117 Y	118 L
119 A	120 U	121 I	122 Z	123 W	124 T	125 K	126 H	127 X	128 G	129 E
130 S	131 D	132 J	133 W	134 P	135 L	136 Y	137 N	138 K	139 M	
140 B	141 Q	142 V	143 Z	144 Y	145 S	146 U	147 D	148 Q		
149 B	150 U	151 H	152 I	153 E	154 F	155 V	156 Y	157 P		
158 Q	159 P	160 F	161 U	162 V	163 D	164 W	165 P	166 H	167 M	168 O
169 Q	170 E	171 B	172 Z	173 F	174 T	175 F	176 Z	177 D		
178 U	179 O	180 F	181 X	182 I	183 W	184 X	185 N	186 S	187 J	
188 U	189 R	190 Q	191 H	192 D	193 F	194 K	195 U	196 V	197 X	
198 C	199 U	200 V	201 P	202 Z	203 L	204 E	205 D	206 A	207 F	
208 J	209 H	210 M	211 S	212 A	213 E	214 Z	215 R	216 S	217 I	
218 L	219 Q	220 N	221 A	222 T	223 I	224 I	225 Z	226 U	227 R	

CLUES

A 1788 Mozart symphony · · · · · · · · · · 61 206 38 57 119 221 212

B Maladroit · · · · · · · · · · · · · · · · 77 140 3 171 149 55 17

C "Liebster Jesu, ___ Verlangen"; Bach Cantata 32 · · · · · · · · · 85 31 111 198

D Began · · · · · · · · · · · · · · · · · · 163 48 192 84 34 177 205 50 58 131 147

E Short operatic aria · · · · · · · · · · · 116 204 11 170 213 93 129 29 153

F He said, "My name means the shape I am" (full name) · · · · · · · · · · · 30 42 207 51 154 173 193 4 160 36 180 175

G Flag · · · · · · · · · · · · · · · · · · · 35 101 97 47 128 91

H Impressionistic suite by Manuel de Falla (3 wds. followed by WORD U) · · · · 209 126 102 32 151 28 45 65 96 191 166

I Abnormal protrusion of the eyeballs · · 182 217 2 108 224 223 152 12 44 121 26 66

J Constrictor appreciated by farmers (2 wds.) · · · · · · · · · · · · · · · · 187 208 21 5 132 15 14 74

K Rapid rhythmic beat · · · · · · · · · · 125 86 194 80 138 98

L Publicity release · · · · · · · · · · · · 1 37 118 203 72 135 218

M Strain · · · · · · · · · · · · · · · · · · 210 139 60 89 167 43

N One of Wagner's giants in "Das Rheingold" · · · · · · · · · · · · · · 18 23 220 46 137 185

O Beauties · · · · · · · · · · · · · · · · 71 105 59 179 168 25 54

P Parquet in a theatre · · · · · · · · · · 90 201 24 165 39 157 134 159 62

Q "I had rather be a dog, ___ than such a Roman" (4 wds., "Julius Caesar") · · 6 10 169 67 158 219 190 88 107 148 141 100 104

R Craving · · · · · · · · · · · · · · · · 112 227 189 83 215 94

S Eng. composer who set Byron's "Hebrew Melodies" to music (full name) · · 216 27 211 82 13 115 145 186 130 95 16

T Anc. Arabian kingdom, S of Edom · · · 106 124 174 56 70 222 64

U See WORD H (3 wds.) · · · · · · · · 226 188 53 75 120 150 178 114 199 161 63 195 7 146

V Drudge (2 wds.) · · · · · · · · · · · · 162 19 142 196 155 200 8 110 68

W Scottish author (1828–97, "Salem Chapel") · · · · · · · · · · · · · · · 52 123 113 183 22 133 79 164

X 1959 Ionesco play · · · · · · · · · · · 40 181 103 127 184 92 197 20 109 76

Y Former gold coin of France (Wd. & contr.) · · · · · · · · · · · · · · · · 99 117 33 156 69 144 41 136

Z Welsh poet (1340–1400; 3 wds.) · · · 81 172 73 78 176 9 122 49 87 225 143 214 202

172

CLUES

A Science fiction king ("Dandelion Wine"; full name) . . . .
140 114 87 43 136 180 159 54 97 30 47

B Too severe to be endured . . . . . .
75 93 102 55 68 135 45 139 60 169 40

C Shift . . . .
149 2 158 85 70 13 104

D Chorus girls and boys, e.g. . . . . .
99 175 127 167 65 4 115

E Crafty, wily . . . .
32 143 154 28 1 18

F Atoned for . . . .
7 42 124 52 31 23 152 16

G Vague; questionable . . . .
69 128 39 92 34 49 105

H Scram! Shut up! (2 wds.) . . . . .
62 137 112 109 125 166 9 174

I Experienced . . . .
148 25 120 5 51 121 133 82 36

J Go back to . . . .
108 178 134 78 73 88 57

K Pondering, meditation . . . .
123 35 91 168 46 14 20 118 63 181

L Semicircular projection of Antarctica (2 wds.) . . . .
164 173 94 138 41 141 95 21 29 119 171

M Soviet city on the Lena River . . . .
126 160 117 8 116 153 76

N Odd or unusual happenings or creatures; side-show features . . . . . .
146 89 106 107 150 66

O Having an end in itself . . . .
100 56 58 67 37 22 74 162 6

P Besides (2 wds.) . . . .
84 80 33 59 38 79

Q "To an ___ Dying Young" (Housman poem) . . . .
53 98 103 132 155 110 61

R Bombed, stewed, pickled . . . . . .
131 96 145 156 90 163

S Blistering poison gas . . . .
113 24 165 130 161 15 176 142

T Exert influence reciprocally . . . . .
172 19 101 11 72 157 147 86 26

U German poet, dramatist, novelist (1749–1832) . . . .
17 27 71 10 151 170

V Bum's rush (hyph.) . . . .
177 77 50 179 3 111 44

W "Ask for me ___, and you shall find me a grave man," says Mercutio ("Romeo and Juliet") . . . .
144 122 64 83 12 81 48 129

	1 E	2 C	3 V		4 D	5 I	6 O	7 F	8 M	9 H	10 U
11 T	12 W		13 C	14 K	15 S	16 F		17 U	18 E	19 T	20 K
21 L	22 O	23 F	24 S	25 I		26 T	27 U	28 E		29 L	30 A
31 F		32 E	33 P	34 G	35 K	36 I		37 O	38 P		39 G
40 B		41 L	42 F	43 A	44 V	45 B	46 K		47 A	48 W	49 G
	50 V	51 I	52 F		53 Q	54 A	55 B	56 O	57 J		58 O
59 P		60 B	61 Q	62 H	63 K	64 W	65 D		66 N	67 O	68 B
69 G	70 C	71 U	72 T	73 J		74 O	75 B	76 M	77 V		78 J
79 P		80 P	81 W		82 I	83 W	84 P		85 C	86 T	87 A
	88 J		89 N	90 R	91 K	92 G	93 B	94 L		95 L	96 R
97 A		98 Q	99 D	100 O	101 T		102 B	103 Q	104 C	105 G	106 N
	107 N	108 J	109 H		110 Q	111 V	112 H		113 S	114 A	115 D
116 M		117 M	118 K	119 L	120 I		121 I	122 W	123 K	124 F	125 H
	126 M	127 D	128 G		129 W	130 S	131 R	132 Q		133 I	134 J
135 B	136 A		137 H	138 L	139 B	140 A		141 L	142 S	143 E	144 W
	145 R	146 N		147 T	148 I	149 C	150 N		151 U	152 F	
153 M	154 E	155 S	156 R	157 T	158 C	159 A		160 M	161 S	162 O	163 R
164 L		165 S	166 H		167 D	168 K	169 B	170 U	171 L		172 T
173 L	174 H	175 D		176 S	177 V	178 J		179 V	180 A	181 K	

173

CLUES

A. Rattled, discombobulated (2 wds.) .... `4 88 27 131 170 44 13`

B. "The Sun Also Rises" heroine (first name) .... `106 42 22 117 64`

C. "Stars in the purple dusk above the ___," (Aiken, "Morning Song") .... `132 107 41 33 52 50 43 120`

D. Confident, self-assured .... `135 19 112 123 94 110 151 162`

E. "If it would but apprehend ___," (2 wds.; "A Midsummer Night's Dream") .... `49 168 130 89 114 2 72`

F. Am. weapons inventor (1826–85) .... `100 74 98 169 128 150 155 133 59`

G. Crowding about noisily .... `111 31 166 118 143 97 153`

H. Am. poet indicted for treason (1885–1972; "Hugh Selwyn Mauberley," "Cantos"; full name) .... `81 138 16 84 92 57 3 78 9`

I. Disobedient; improper .... `102 77 28 141 21 163 119`

J. Last name, WORD B .... `70 65 11 149 39 26`

K. Fetid, stinking .... `152 34 101 29 67 91 48`

L. Children's game, a predecessor of baseball (3 wds.) .... `38 66 58 15 85 62 76 148 87`

M. Deprive of color .... `147 5 129 99 137 161`

N. Refuse .... `126 96 25 10 105 1`

O. Movingly expressive .... `69 86 159 134 108 18 61 56`

P. Sharply explosive stroke on a snare drum (2 wds.) .... `146 125 156 71 164 53 68`

Q. Unmoving, quiescent .... `116 20 122 8 83`

R. Very appetizing in appearance or aroma (hyph.) .... `144 93 160 109 37 23 55 80 136 35 63 121 103`

S. Asseverate, depose .... `60 124 14 47 158 54`

T. Hamadryads, oreads, etc. .... `140 73 17 46 30 104`

U. Customary .... `7 40 75 24 82`

V. Distribute in shares .... `157 45 32 12 51 95 139 145 113`

W. Pharos .... `167 90 127 142 79 154 6 115 36 165`

WORDS — GRID

1 N	2 E	3 H		4 A	5 M	6 W	7 U	8 Q	9 H	
10 N	11 J	12 V	13 A	14 S	15 L	16 H	17 T	18 O		
19 D	20 Q	21 I	22 B	23 R	24 U	25 N	26 J	27 A		
28 I	29 K	30 T	31 G	32 V	33 C	34 K	35 R	36 W		
37 R	38 L	39 J	40 U	41 C	42 B	43 C	44 A	45 V	46 T	
47 S	48 K	49 E	50 C	51 V	52 C	53 P	54 S	55 R	56 R	
57 H	58 H	59 F	60 S	61 O	62 L	63 R	64 B	65 J		
66 L	67 K	68 P	69 O	70 J	71 P	72 E	73 T	74 F	75 U	
76 L	77 I	78 H	79 W	80 R	81 R	82 H	83 Q	84 H		
85 L	86 O	87 L	88 A	89 E	90 W	91 K	92 H	93 R	94 R	
95 V	96 N	97 G	98 F	99 M	100 F	101 K	102 I	103 R	104 T	
105 N	106 B	107 C	108 O	109 R	110 D	111 G	112 D	113 V		
114 E	115 W	116 Q	117 B	118 G	119 I	120 C	121 R	122 Q	123 D	
124 S	125 P	126 N	127 W	128 F	129 M	130 E	131 A	132 C		
133 F	134 O	135 D	136 R	137 M	138 H	139 V	140 T	141 I	142 W	143 G
144 R	145 V	146 P	147 M	148 L	149 J	150 F	151 D	152 K	153 G	
154 W	155 F	156 P	157 V	158 S	159 O	160 R	161 M	162 D		
163 I	164 P	165 W	166 G	167 W	168 E	169 F	170 A			

174

CLUES

A. Outlaws

B. Finessed

C. Lambastes, blisters; razzes, rides

D. Apollo and Poseidon, e.g.

E. Diversion

F. Up-to-date

G. Talks persistently and tiresomely

H. Most cherished or cherishing

I. Item of carry-on luggage (2 wds.)

J. Hawk

K. Eng. water dog with a thick, oily coat.

L. Entrancing

M. Famous published piscator (1593–1683; full name)

N. Ski lodge specialty

O. Observation

P. Reason

Q. Island ceded by N.Y. to Mass. in 1692

R. Comic strip started in the '30s by Lee Falk and Ray Moore (2 wds.)

S. Manifestation of a god

T. Making something new of materials already used, esp. in writing

U. Fabulous; untrue

V. Lampblack mixed with size or glue (2 wds.)

W. Depressing

X. King of Corinth condemned to eternal rock-rolling in hell

Y. "A little touch of Harry ____," (3 wds., "Henry V")

Z. Stereotypical friendly British appellation (2 wds.)

Z_1. Town in N Israel

Z_2. Deceptive, evasive

WORDS

Clue	Cell numbers
A	97 162 54 76 20 62 6
B	92 98 171 217 214 224 1 159 201
C	197 222 135 165 23 90
D	127 64 199 208
E	211 83 65 193 177 128 46 152 202 114 3 16 155
F	210 13 181 173 95 28
G	149 41 70 14 157 33 161
H	108 120 22 179 130 134 203
I	85 58 183 184 45 124 72 220 107 11 207
J	55 27 126 143
K	30 35 69 122 103 81 109 5 25 21
L	4 144 26 53 119 71 205 78 154
M	125 175 218 68 206 187 75 48 91 15 57
N	150 100 50 19 49
O	142 52 101 44 196 17
P	82 185 137 37 47 139 189 194 66
Q	63 34 145 212 223 174 168 102 164
R	219 74 94 158 2 133 10 43 209 111
S	169 31 105 93 192 176 182 73
T	40 59 156 160 138 172 61 89 84
U	121 38 29 129 200 42 9 166
V	24 163 186 167 147 180 12 141
W	116 77 170 146 56 136 140 148 86
X	178 8 198 18 131 188 115 106
Y	51 153 123 67 32 190 117 216 36 80
Z	112 204 60 118 221 104 39
Z_1	215 87 195 96 110 132 191 151
Z_2	7 213 88 113 99 79

Grid (cell number + clue letter, in reading order)

1 B	2 R	3 E	4 L	5 K	6 A	7 Z_2	8 X			
9 U	10 R	11 I	12 V	13 F	14 G	15 M	16 E	17 O	18 X	
19 N	20 A	21 K	22 H	23 C	24 V	25 K	26 L	27 J	28 F	
29 U	30 K	31 S	32 Y	33 G	34 Q	35 K	36 Y	37 P	38 U	
39 Z	40 T	41 G	42 U	43 R	44 O	45 I	46 E	47 P	48 M	49 N
50 N	51 Y	52 O	53 L	54 A	55 J	56 W	57 M	58 I	59 T	60 Z
61 T	62 A	63 Q	64 D	65 E	66 P	67 Y	68 M	69 K		
70 G	71 L	72 I	73 S	74 R	75 M	76 A	77 W	78 L		
79 Z_2	80 Y	81 K	82 P	83 E	84 T	85 I	86 W	87 Z_1	88 Z_2	89 T
90 C	91 M	92 B	93 S	94 R	95 F	96 Z_1	97 A	98 B	99 Z_2	
100 N	101 O	102 Q	103 K	104 Z	105 S	106 X	107 I			
108 H	109 K	110 Z_1	111 R	112 Z	113 Z_2	114 E	115 X	116 W	117 Y	
118 Z	119 L	120 H	121 U	122 K	123 Y	124 I	125 M	126 J	127 D	
128 E	129 U	130 H	131 X	132 Z_1	133 R	134 H	135 C	136 W	137 P	138 T
139 P	140 W	141 V	142 O	143 J	144 L	145 Q	146 W	147 V		
148 W	149 G	150 N	151 Z_1	152 E	153 Y	154 L	155 E	156 T	157 G	
158 R	159 B	160 T	161 G	162 A	163 V	164 Q	165 C	166 U	167 V	168 Q
169 S	170 W	171 B	172 T	173 F	174 Q	175 M	176 S	177 E	178 X	
179 H	180 V	181 F	182 S	183 I	184 I	185 P	186 V	187 M		
188 X	189 P	190 Y	191 Z_1	192 S	193 E	194 P	195 Z_1	196 O	197 C	
198 X	199 D	200 U	201 B	202 E	203 H	204 Z	205 L	206 M	207 I	
208 D	209 R	210 D	211 E	212 Q	213 Z_2	214 B	215 Z_1	216 Y	217 B	
218 M	219 R	220 I	221 Z	222 C	223 Q	224 B				

175

WORDS / CLUES

A Downgrade — 37 110 29 200 175 120

B Pithy saying — 106 181 81 148 78 34 101 128

C Type of peak — 121 54 1 90 168

D Instantly (6 wds.) — 127 134 184 117 2 73 100 115 111 24 80 47 177 40 76 59

E Fault, culpability — 4 129 164 9 163 95 33

F Implore — 75 173 204 145 162 63 87 130 72 53 32 132

G Vicissitudes (3 wds.) — 25 155 140 14 68 97

H Unspoken — 178 126 19 196 187

I Clear, shining — 125 193 44 49 139 21 93 85

J "___ and tongues a-talking / Make the rough road easy walking" (2 wds.; Housman, "A Shropshire Lad, 49") — 96 6 48 141 30 56 203 182 60 26

K Inordinate greed — 153 16 94 131 191 61 77 45

L "___, the slave, and the liberticide" (2 wds.; Shelley, "Adonais") — 107 13 11 194 158 64 150 166 57

M He says, "Good-night, sweet prince" ("Hamlet") — 71 114 183 170 152 18 157

N He is summoned by Death in a 15th-cent. morality play — 31 10 43 22 195 172 118 143

O Bring; achieve; attain — 186 137 86 92 39

P "Son of the old moon-mountains ___" (Keats, "To the Nile") — 88 147 123 67 202 154 74

Q Higher, more stately — 52 185 8 89 133 69 28

R Feel disgust at; detest — 66 146 27 167 58 156

S Former earldom of SE France — 113 12 99 42 198 122

T Immediately — 151 102 201 104 161 108 138 38 188

U Blocks, frustrates — 70 144 176 20 83 149 169 119

V Take, acknowledge — 142 46 124 41 65 160

W 1916 D. W. Griffith film — 165 197 55 159 3 109 82 51 103 91 116

X Small wooded areas — 135 35 5 17 180 62

Y Postponed; inactive (3 wds.) — 190 174 50 105 84 15 179 189 136 199

Z Punctilios — 112 23 192 36 171 7 79 98

176

CLUES

A. Covenant . . . . $\overline{130}\ \overline{30}\ \overline{176}\ \overline{36}\ \overline{50}\ \overline{1}\ \overline{20}\ \overline{66}\ \overline{13}$

B. Answer . . . . $\overline{70}\ \overline{115}\ \overline{19}\ \overline{63}\ \overline{52}\ \overline{83}\ \overline{25}\ \overline{40}\ \overline{122}$

C. A daughter of Agamemnon and Clytemnestra . . . . $\overline{26}\ \overline{168}\ \overline{120}\ \overline{87}\ \overline{84}\ \overline{6}\ \overline{43}\ \overline{41}\ \overline{151}$

D. Place for research . . . . $\overline{166}\ \overline{28}\ \overline{86}\ \overline{145}\ \overline{75}\ \overline{46}\ \overline{22}\ \overline{80}\ \overline{104}\ \overline{132}$

E. Coniferous tree yielding a tough, durable wood . . . . $\overline{156}\ \overline{60}\ \overline{140}\ \overline{123}\ \overline{102}$

F. Relating to (3 wds.) . . . . $\overline{58}\ \overline{110}\ \overline{45}\ \overline{136}\ \overline{17}\ \overline{172}\ \overline{150}\ \overline{61}\ \overline{72}\ \overline{88}\ \overline{14}$

G. Conventional Hindu expression on meeting or parting . . . . . $\overline{134}\ \overline{167}\ \overline{49}\ \overline{85}\ \overline{165}\ \overline{149}\ \overline{113}$

H. Freed from attachment . . . . . . $\overline{90}\ \overline{125}\ \overline{37}\ \overline{170}\ \overline{29}\ \overline{135}\ \overline{155}\ \overline{111}$

I. Recounts . . . . $\overline{53}\ \overline{71}\ \overline{91}\ \overline{39}\ \overline{164}\ \overline{143}\ \overline{162}\ \overline{117}$

J. Stroke fondly . . . . $\overline{64}\ \overline{160}\ \overline{112}\ \overline{68}\ \overline{95}\ \overline{42}$

K. Excessive . . . . $\overline{82}\ \overline{24}\ \overline{76}\ \overline{8}\ \overline{97}\ \overline{148}\ \overline{159}\ \overline{65}\ \overline{154}\ \overline{139}$

L. Brinks . . . . $\overline{138}\ \overline{175}\ \overline{57}\ \overline{161}\ \overline{4}\ \overline{89}$

M. Gradually (3 wds.) . . . . $\overline{23}\ \overline{129}\ \overline{21}\ \overline{152}\ \overline{108}\ \overline{2}\ \overline{94}\ \overline{12}\ \overline{59}\ \overline{33}$

N. Assail with satire . . . . $\overline{131}\ \overline{7}\ \overline{55}\ \overline{174}\ \overline{163}\ \overline{119}\ \overline{101}$

O. Ropes . . . . $\overline{78}\ \overline{142}\ \overline{177}\ \overline{31}\ \overline{48}\ \overline{5}$

P. Looper . . . . $\overline{144}\ \overline{73}\ \overline{9}\ \overline{105}\ \overline{98}\ \overline{79}\ \overline{163}\ \overline{77}$

Q. Worker in a pub, e.g. . . . . $\overline{18}\ \overline{109}\ \overline{116}\ \overline{157}\ \overline{34}\ \overline{171}$

R. Tries; struggles . . . . $\overline{121}\ \overline{114}\ \overline{74}\ \overline{124}\ \overline{67}\ \overline{35}\ \overline{107}$

S. Town on the Clyde, W central Scotland . . . . $\overline{169}\ \overline{15}\ \overline{51}\ \overline{69}\ \overline{93}\ \overline{103}\ \overline{147}$

T. Two high cards lacking an intervening card . . . . $\overline{32}\ \overline{96}\ \overline{137}\ \overline{158}\ \overline{27}\ \overline{38}$

U. Prefecture of central Honshu, Japan, cap. Kanazawa . . . . . $\overline{133}\ \overline{141}\ \overline{10}\ \overline{173}\ \overline{81}\ \overline{128}\ \overline{47}\ \overline{54}$

V. Babylon's river . . . . $\overline{56}\ \overline{106}\ \overline{92}\ \overline{62}\ \overline{3}\ \overline{178}\ \overline{127}\ \overline{100}\ \overline{16}$

W. Beezer, beak . . . . $\overline{126}\ \overline{146}\ \overline{44}\ \overline{11}\ \overline{118}$

WORDS

(Diagram — each numbered cell carries its clue letter)

1 A	2 M	3 V	4 L	5 O	6 C	7 N	8 K	9 P	10 U
11 W	12 M	13 A	14 F	15 S	16 V	17 F	18 Q	19 B	20 A
21 M	22 D	23 M	24 K	25 B	26 C	27 T	28 D	29 H	30 A	31 O
32 T	33 M	34 Q	35 R	36 A	37 H	38 T	39 I	40 B
41 C	42 J	43 C	44 W	45 F	46 D	47 U	48 O	49 G
50 A	51 S	52 B	53 I	54 U	55 N	56 V	57 L	58 F	59 M
60 E	61 F	62 V	63 B	64 J	65 K	66 A	67 R	68 J
69 S	70 B	71 I	72 F	73 P	74 R	75 D	76 K	77 P	78 O
79 P	80 D	81 U	82 K	83 B	84 C	85 G	86 D	87 C	88 F
89 L	90 H	91 I	92 V	93 S	94 M	95 J	96 T	97 K	98 P
99 H	100 V	101 N	102 E	103 S	104 D	105 P	106 V	107 R	108 M
109 Q	110 F	111 H	112 J	113 G	114 R	115 B	116 Q	117 I	118 W
119 N	120 C	121 R	122 B	123 E	124 R	125 H	126 W	127 V	128 U
129 M	130 A	131 N	132 D	133 U	134 G	135 H	136 F	137 T	138 L
139 K	140 E	141 U	142 O	143 I	144 P	145 D	146 W	147 S	148 K	149 G
150 F	151 C	152 M	153 N	154 K	155 H	156 E	157 Q	158 T
159 K	160 J	161 L	162 I	163 P	164 I	165 G	166 D	167 G
168 C	169 S	170 H	171 Q	172 F	173 U	174 N	175 L	176 A	177 O	178 V

177

The diagram grid (cells shown as number + letter):

1 O	2 B	3 P	4 R	5 H	6 S	7 L	8 C	9 V		
10 X	11 F	12 E	13 X	14 K	15 Z	16 G	17 A	18 F	19 E	
20 V	21 T	22 P	23 M	24 R	25 W	26 J	27 Y	28 L	29 B	30 S
31 R	32 E	33 A	34 Q	35 W	36 P	37 S	38 V	39 R		
40 X	41 F	42 B	43 Q	44 L	45 K	46 Y	47 I	48 F	49 B	
50 Q	51 C	52 N	53 G	54 Q	55 U	56 F	57 W	58 K	59 B	
60 O	61 J	62 F	63 B	64 S	65 K	66 N	67 O	68 E	69 W	
70 H	71 X	72 C	73 I	74 Y	75 O	76 N	77 R	78 A	79 B	
80 L	81 F	82 E	83 H	84 O	85 Y	86 X	87 U	88 Q		
89 W	90 R	91 W	92 S	93 Q	94 B	95 E	96 R	97 A	98 N	
99 S	100 F	101 B	102 M	103 X	104 U	105 P	106 J	107 F	108 C	
109 J	110 X	111 T	112 A	113 N	114 E	115 D	116 R	117 T	118 P	
119 K	120 V	121 F	122 D	123 A	124 T	125 M	126 C	127 U	128 G	
129 D	130 F	131 Z	132 S	133 M	134 G	135 I	136 X	137 C	138 D	
139 T	140 U	141 A	142 K	143 D	144 C	145 I	146 K	147 L		
148 Q	149 J	150 E	151 Y	152 W	153 D	154 U	155 P	156 H		
157 O	158 F	159 A	160 Z	161 L	162 C	163 B	164 P	165 R		
166 C	167 L	168 Q	169 Z	170 F	171 O	172 V	173 Q	174 Q		
175 D	176 H	177 Z	178 L	179 V	180 A	181 B	182 S	183 H	184 E	
185 Z	186 A	187 U	188 V	189 H	190 M	191 G	192 S	193 J		

CLUES

A Halcyon 33 180 159 97 141 112 17 186 78 123

B Confess to; grant 42 63 94 181 2 49 29 163 101 79 59

C Throwing into confusion 137 162 8 51 166 144 72 126 108

D Chump, sap, boob 175 143 138 115 122 153 129

E Awkward, bungling 19 32 12 184 82 68 150 95 114

F This went with shoofly pie in the 1946 song by Gallop and Woods (3 wds.) 158 11 121 48 41 130 170 107 62 81 56 100 18

G Buttocks 191 128 53 134 16

H Petroleum distillate used as a solvent, fuel, etc. 176 70 189 183 156 83 5

I Extinct bird formerly inhabiting islands of the Indian Ocean . . . 135 73 145 47

J Bring in as a member; draft . . . 106 61 193 109 26 149

K U.S. Secretary of War 1862–67 . . 119 14 146 65 142 45 58

L Lambastes, gives what-for (2 wds.) 44 167 7 147 161 80 28 178

M Type of willow 125 133 23 190 102

N Corruptly mercenary 66 76 52 98 113

O Bunk 84 171 67 75 60 1 157

P Search vigorously through 36 118 164 22 155 3 105

Q "__ . . would, as his kind, grow mischievous, / And kill him __" (3 wds., "Julius Caesar") . . . 174 148 88 50 34 173 54 168 43 93

R Leader of the Southampton Insurrection (full name) 90 39 165 31 24 4 96 116 77

S Four-wheeled pleasure carriage with two inside and two outside seats 182 37 92 30 132 6 64 99 192

T Rings 111 21 117 139 124

U Old-World solanaceous herb with poisonous and narcotic properties 127 140 104 154 187 87 55

V Type of inscription 38 20 9 120 172 188 179

W Erred in judgment 25 57 69 91 89 35 152

X Make changes 103 110 10 136 40 13 71 86

Y "Wax-works weren't made to be looked at for nothing, __" (Carroll, "Through the Looking-Glass") 74 27 46 151 85

Z Thingummy, gismo 160 177 15 169 131 185

WORDS

CLUES

A Article of men's formal attire (2 wds.) 100 56 74 116 134 158 148 66 26 165 193

B "Spruce goose" recluse (full name) 153 112 115 200 183 167 2 214 128 75 25 185

C Rubbed out 60 161 27 90 39 144 140

D Horse opera hero's Indian pal . . . 22 119 111 107 76

E Touch me not! (2 wds.) 216 106 18 179 55 69 141 181

F Ugly 72 145 176 17 227 211 67 102 152

G Self-image lover (Gr. myth.) 127 138 34 118 68 124 133 231 170

H Power-driven forging tool (hyph.) 104 14 143 220 32 178 84 151 136

I Milk train, e.g. 41 126 12 135 92

J That sets forth or exhibits 13 21 31 218 155 85 206 125 97 50 64

K 10th letter of the Hebrew alphabet 192 230 35

L Bondage 210 29 173 197 63 160 174 83 150

M Achieved against odds (hyph.) . . 228 187 59 86 16 113 205 96

N Accent 130 186 199 120 82

O Dupes 207 226 91

P 17th-cen. British dramatist ("The Usurper", full name) . . . 87 81 94 6 88 47 108 209 131 36 57 223

Q Canadian province 80 3 77 171 225 23 9 121 204 162 53 202

R Am. inventor of the sewing machine (full name) 164 147 43 79 117 105 62 5 180

S Shofar (2 wds.) 142 101 219 110 78 40 24 222

T Very rarely (5 wds.) 54 159 61 233 169 166 95 190 189 172 114 19 149 194 201

U Useless 129 11 154 51 175 20 103 48 139 195

V Resides temporarily 28 213 71 182 10 98 46 7

W Cedes 93 123 58 42 38 1

X Got away unscathed (2 wds.) . . . 33 232 163 45 4 52 156 168 184 212 177

Y Hymn 8 70 15 122 30 137

Z Put (old material) in a new form . . 196 99 229 132 73 49

Z₁ Mountain range of New Mexico (3 wds.) 157 221 37 215 224 44 146 89 203 217 109 198 208 191

WORDS

179

WORDS

CLUES

Clue	Answer cells
A Empty tomb	129 35 11 117 199 148 141 87
B Ejected	42 158 198 74 128 51
C Lower	72 91 105 100 2 125
D Restrict or hem in	26 18 193 178 39 29 111 169
E Covenant; agreement	86 50 135 174 79 84 182 161 7
F Heard a case and rendered a decision	37 127 185 166 207 47 99 145 140 60 173
G Irritating	215 85 96 170 163 176 23 104 80 107
H Tenant farmer; type of pin	187 27 54 38 10 59
I Butler's utopia	4 14 94 1 76 214 41
J Fail	157 64 197 110 137 210 77
K Member of papal party in medieval Italy	66 68 186 56 124 144
L Arbor in Sp. Am. architecture	134 22 49 203 201 73
M Lighthouse of song	17 102 6 202 131 188 8 34 116
N Judicial investigation	109 204 165 196 121 179 113
O Wild strawberry (Fr., hyph.)	28 69 98 122 139 192 63 25 78 184 70 83 149
P Molly Malone, e.g.	136 168 112 181 150 195 162 130 36
Q Gracious custom among New Orleans merchants	115 95 13 172 160 167 58 146 153
R Superficially	46 200 212 90 53 43 9 108 114
S Kind of labor contract	191 71 126 20 82 106 31 156 93 89
T Husky	16 120 143 40 211 3 164
U Inspiring reverence	92 45 62 147 133 208 81
V Member of an ancient Persian religion	48 209 97 30 152 171 194 159 119
W Portrait, likeness	151 118 190 12 32 57
X Dimmer, e.g.	123 19 33 67 132 24 206 75
Y A Gilbert and Sullivan fairy	213 183 154 88 5 44 175 55
Z Mentioned	61 52 103 142 205
Z₁ Legal agent	15 21 180 189 138 177 101 155

Grid

Row	Cells (number·clue-letter)
1	1 I · 2 C · 3 T · 4 I · 5 Y · 6 M · 7 E · 8 M
2	9 R · 10 H · 11 A · 12 W · 13 Q · 14 I · 15 Z₁ · 16 T · 17 M · 18 D
3	19 X · 20 S · 21 Z₁ · 22 L · 23 G · 24 X · 25 O · 26 D · 27 H · 28 O
4	29 D · 30 V · 31 S · 32 W · 33 X · 34 M · 35 A · 36 P · 37 F · 38 H
5	39 D · 40 T · 41 I · 42 B · 43 R · 44 Y · 45 U · 46 R · 47 F
6	48 V · 49 L · 50 E · 51 B · 52 Z · 53 R · 54 H · 55 Y · 56 K · 57 W · 58 Q
7	59 H · 60 F · 61 Z · 62 U · 63 O · 64 J · 65 P · 66 K · 67 X · 68 K · 69 O
8	70 O · 71 S · 72 C · 73 L · 74 B · 75 X · 76 I · 77 J
9	78 O · 79 E · 80 G · 81 U · 82 S · 83 O · 84 E · 85 G · 86 E · 87 A
10	88 Y · 89 S · 90 R · 91 C · 92 U · 93 S · 94 I · 95 Q · 96 G
11	97 V · 98 O · 99 F · 100 C · 101 Z₁ · 102 M · 103 Z · 104 G · 105 C · 106 S
12	107 G · 108 R · 109 N · 110 J · 111 D · 112 P · 113 N · 114 R · 115 Q · 116 M
13	117 A · 118 W · 119 V · 120 T · 121 N · 122 O · 123 X · 124 K · 125 C
14	126 S · 127 F · 128 B · 129 A · 130 P · 131 M · 132 X · 133 U · 134 L · 135 E · 136 P
15	137 J · 138 Z₁ · 139 O · 140 F · 141 A · 142 Z · 143 T · 144 K · 145 F · 146 Q · 147 U
16	148 A · 149 O · 150 P · 151 W · 152 V · 153 Q · 154 Y · 155 Z₁ · 156 S
17	157 J · 158 B · 159 V · 160 Q · 161 E · 162 P · 163 G · 164 T · 165 N · 166 F · 167 Q
18	168 P · 169 D · 170 G · 171 V · 172 Q · 173 F · 174 E · 175 Y · 176 G · 177 Z₁
19	178 D · 179 N · 180 Z₁ · 181 P · 182 E · 183 Y · 184 O · 185 F · 186 K
20	187 H · 188 M · 189 Z₁ · 190 W · 191 S · 192 O · 193 D · 194 V · 195 P · 196 N
21	197 J · 198 B · 199 A · 200 R · 201 L · 202 M · 203 L · 204 N · 205 Z
22	206 X · 207 F · 208 U · 209 V · 210 J · 211 T · 212 R · 213 Y · 214 I · 215 G

180

CLUES

A. Techniques of classification — 172 199 237 14 37 171 123 193 231 74

B. Blurred effect often caused by strong back-lighting — 192 47 239 245 129 247 8 54

C. Mountains of the eastern U.S. — 155 201 211 208 46 225 187 78 179 119 25 95

D. Noisily; in an unruly way — 128 40 120 107 204 20 143 233 84 34

E. Sagging — 224 212 10 127 162 182 140 170 99

F. 1954 song by Carolyn Leigh and Johnny Richards (3 wds.) — 67 234 45 125 249 75 177 33 3 69 167 195

G. Natives of Papeete, e.g. — 217 51 28 13 105 97 79 248 161

H. Arena for equestrian events — 31 60 9 39 144 116 104 196 194 164

I. Of summer — 198 135 12 150 89 160 72

J. Liberate; deliver from sin — 139 221 17 64 108 165

K. Issue forth in bubbles — 90 151 57 103 7 220 26 190 44 55

L. Having a double propeller (naut.; hyph.) — 42 2 19 111 36 61 147 216 63

M. Reprimand — 130 6 158 235 117 230 207

N. Gangsters — 145 168 30 246 166 82 115 138 131 118

O. In these times — 114 56 178 203 133 124 76 232

P. U.S. nuclear physicist — 38 214 228 241 102 62 71 113 18 191 48

Q. Diagram of procedure (2 wds.) — 70 180 53 83 92 59 243 186 126

R. Saint-Exupéry's interplanetary traveler (3 wds.) — 240 215 16 159 142 77 175 181 153 200 229 29 87 109 219

S. Silver serving dishes — 137 110 5 85 24 58 101 238 41 185

T. Avoid — 96 68 149 163 183 27

U. Filled with disgust — 15 157 148 209 223 210 98 236 21

V. Equal, as in distance (3 wds.) — 66 32 112 136 91 174 23

W. Silent screen vamp (full name) — 141 173 88 205 93 49 188 218 134

X. Former name of JFK airport — 43 242 202 132 35 50 169 122

Y. On the winning side — 184 81 146 80 213 226 244 227 154 106 11 22 1 86

Z. Of high-ranking diplomacy (var.) — 206 65 197 121 4 52 73 94 100 152 156 176 189 222

WORDS / GRID

■	■	1 Y	2 L	3 F	4 Z	5 D	6 M	7 K	8 B	9 H	10 E
11 Y	12 I	13 G	14 A	15 U	16 R	17 J	18 P	19 L	20 D	21 U	22 Y
23 V	24 S	25 C	26 K	27 T	28 G	29 R	30 N	31 H	32 V	33 F	34 D
35 X	36 L	37 A	38 P	39 H	40 D	41 S	42 L	43 X	44 K	45 F	46 C
47 B	48 P	49 W	50 X	51 G	52 Z	53 Q	54 B	55 K	56 O	57 K	58 S
59 Q	60 H	61 L	62 P	63 L	64 J	65 Z	66 V	67 F	68 T	69 F	70 Q
71 P	72 I	73 Z	74 A	75 F	76 O	77 R	78 C	79 G	80 Y	81 Y	82 N
83 Q	84 D	85 S	86 Y	87 R	88 W	89 I	90 K	91 V	92 Q	93 W	94 Z
95 C	96 T	97 G	98 U	99 E	100 Z	101 S	102 P	103 K	104 H	105 G	106 Y
107 D	108 J	109 R	110 S	111 L	112 V	113 P	114 O	115 N	116 H	117 M	118 N
119 C	120 D	121 Z	122 X	123 A	124 O	125 F	126 Q	127 E	128 D	129 B	130 M
131 N	132 X	133 O	134 W	135 I	136 V	137 S	138 N	139 J	140 E	141 W	142 R
143 D	144 H	145 N	146 Y	147 L	148 U	149 T	150 I	151 K	152 Z	153 R	154 Y
155 C	156 Z	157 U	158 M	159 R	160 I	161 G	162 E	163 T	164 H	165 J	166 N
167 F	168 N	169 X	170 E	171 A	172 A	173 W	174 V	175 R	176 Z	177 F	178 O
179 C	180 Q	181 R	182 E	183 T	184 Y	185 S	186 Q	187 C	188 W	189 Z	190 K
191 P	192 B	193 A	194 H	195 F	196 H	197 Z	198 I	199 A	200 R	201 C	202 X
203 O	204 D	205 W	206 Z	207 M	208 C	209 U	210 U	211 C	212 E	213 Y	214 P
215 R	216 L	217 G	218 W	219 R	220 K	221 J	222 Z	223 U	224 E	225 C	226 Y
227 Y	228 P	229 R	230 M	231 A	232 O	233 D	234 F	235 M	236 U	237 A	238 S
239 B	240 R	241 P	242 X	243 Q	244 Y	245 B	246 N	247 B	248 G	249 F	■

181

CLUES

A Mutual exchange — 97 60 37 176 92 9 135 189 24 113 102

B Back of the skull — 159 110 44 121 187 167 85

C Naval construction battalion personnel — 128 82 139 64 107 147 156

D Gr. tragedian (479?–406? B.C., "Medea," "Electra") — 79 58 185 5 29 129 28 51 74

E Centaur whose poisoned tunic caused the death of Hercules — 50 73 56 17 141 16

F Large, silvery game fish of the western Atlantic — 105 8 126 1 103 61

G Gift to a beggar, e.g. — 138 14 116 23 134 160 151

H Set apart for a specific purpose — 87 12 122 173 35 100 186 117

I Pointed surgical knives — 30 114 3 131 22 47 72

J Change in the way of doing things — 184 94 101 111 59 155 170 34 45 25

K (Followed by WORD L) Laurence Sterne novel — 192 181 49 166 78 67 11 148

L See WORD K — 32 152 42 46 75 178

M Firmly stuffed cushion usable as a seat — 171 19 119 71 26 83 190

N Butler's utopia — 137 165 10 120 146 76 150

O Parts; assumed functions — 40 179 154 191 7

P Bristling, prickly — 169 20 106 149 133 31 145 153

Q Biased — 53 6 70 177 33 163 144

R Not among the first three to cross the finish line in a horse race, e.g. (4 wds.) — 188 180 18 125 158 84 86 93 43 98 90 66 162

S Large, slender, deep-sea game fish — 99 89 161 69 36 112

T True substance — 65 95 140 175 136 4 172

U Passerine birds of the northern hemisphere, having a showy crest — 13 164 80 124 62 174 68 108

V Stanley Cup sport — 183 57 39 127 132 91

W Space ship featured in "Star Trek" — 38 77 157 109 52 81 55 115 168 143

X Overly luxuriant, flagrant, stinking — 63 48 130 21

Y With the greatest of ease — 2 96 104 54 118 88 123 41 182 142 27 15

WORDS (grid)

1 F	2 Y	3 I	4 T	5 D	6 Q	7 O	8 F	9 A		
10 N	11 K	12 H	13 U	14 G	15 Y	16 E	17 E	18 R	19 M	
20 P	21 X	22 I	23 G	24 A	25 J	26 M	27 Y	28 D		
29 D	30 I	31 P	32 L	33 Q	34 J	35 H	36 S	37 A	38 W	
39 V	40 O	41 Y	42 L	43 R	44 B	45 J	46 L	47 I	48 X	49 K
50 E	51 D	52 W	53 Q	54 Y	55 W	56 E	57 V	58 D	59 J	
60 A	61 F	62 U	63 X	64 C	65 T	66 R	67 K	68 U	69 S	
70 Q	71 M	72 I	73 E	74 D	75 L	76 N	77 W	78 K	79 D	
80 U	81 W	82 C	83 M	84 R	85 B	86 R	87 H	88 Y	89 S	
90 R	91 V	92 A	93 R	94 J	95 T	96 Y	97 A	98 R	99 S	
100 H	101 J	102 Y	103 F	104 Y	105 F	106 P	107 C	108 U		
109 W	110 B	111 J	112 S	113 A	114 I	115 W	116 G	117 H	118 Y	119 M
120 N	121 B	122 H	123 Y	124 U	125 R	126 F	127 V	128 C		
129 D	130 X	131 I	132 V	133 P	134 G	135 A	136 T	137 N		
138 G	139 C	140 T	141 E	142 Y	143 W	144 Q	145 P	146 N	147 C	
148 K	149 P	150 N	151 G	152 L	153 P	154 O	155 J	156 C		
157 W	158 R	159 B	160 G	161 S	162 R	163 Q	164 U	165 N	166 K	
167 B	168 W	169 P	170 J	171 M	172 T	173 H	174 U	175 T		
176 A	177 Q	178 L	179 O	180 R	181 K	182 Y	183 V	184 J		
185 D	186 H	187 B	188 R	189 A	190 M	191 O	192 K			

182

CLUES

WORDS

A Hypodermic 145 194 135 8 182 185 146 149 168 116 128 159

B Am. civil engineer (1879–1965), designer of the George Washington, Hell Gate, and other bridges . . . 176 206 57 1 154 37

C Baubles; small ornaments or pieces of jewelry 35 74 7 22 188 42 190 107

D Gothic bishop (c.311–383), translator of the Bible into Gothic 157 199 93 17 80 48 184

E Fortifications 201 52 112 122 39 66 198 141

F Calm, impartial 118 45 193 142 161 31 179 36 151 18 186 79 24

G Ansate cross, Egyptian symbol of life 113 162 44 180

H One of the rare-earth elements 81 91 32 111 82 100 4

I Starts back, staggers back 6 192 76 148 133 28 158

J Joins up: engages in public service, esp. as a soldier 26 96 11 160 115 196 134

K One skilled in words 13 202 156 195 3 105 55 189 25

L "Your ___ is the only peace-maker" ("As You Like It") 65 64

M Am. polar explorer (1880–1951) . . 120 27 56 38 51 63 59 183 132

N Mass. town known for manufacture of toys 89 87 175 58 191 77 15 178 130 73

O "O well for the ___ boy, / That he shouts with his sister at play" (Tennyson, "Break, Break, Break") . . 131 119 62 33 95 20 174 85 147 29

P Second edition of a published work, e.g. 164 75 84 121 90 83 102

Q Where one is sent "up the river" from New York City 171 99 69 14 137 210 187 109

R Cap. of Kabardino-Balkar Republic, Russia 10 21 117 209 49 153 138

S One of a series of overlapping pieces forming a kind of skirt in plate armor 144 9 23 200

T 4203-meter peak in the Swiss Alps . 86 103 165 47 54 12 61 97 70 92 127 53 2

U Providing shade, shady; apt to take offense 136 152 101 94 34 16 124 166 30 50

V East Texas town, site of Stephen F. Austin State College 177 203 43 60 155 169 67 170 98 123 88

W Elementary particle having no charge 78 5 173 104 208 71 68

X Opera written for American diva Sybil Sanderson by Massenet in 1889 . . . . 110 126 150 172 163 140 40 143 46 204 207

Y Russ. historical painter (1844–1930) 125 106 41 197 114

Z Instructions, routines, programs, etc. for computers 205 181 19 129 72 108 167 139

183

CLUES

A. Mineral named for a German poet-dramatist-novelist-philosopher · · · · · ·
   167 109 160 141 96 79 92 154

B. "The ___ have holes, and the birds of the air have nests" (Matt. 8:20) · · · ·
   67 57 135 176 130

C. Wotan's pseudonym in "Siegfried" · · · · · · ·
   110 27 144 170 162 14 183 51

D. Rock in the North Sea, covered by water at high tide · · · · · · · · ·
   48 72 61 112 184 13 25 134

E. Small, arboreal Madagascans related to monkeys · · · · · · · · ·
   68 75 203 131 16 156

F. Reputed dwelling of a questionable monster (2 wds.) · · · · · · ·
   153 101 56 74 91 150 117 36

G. Prehistoric site in Wiltshire · · · · · · ·
   70 169 129 19 103 90 193 99 60

H. Historical work by Xenophon · · · · · ·
   54 88 196 200 106 35 113 155

I. High-pitched, piercing · · · · · · · ·
   187 147 41 165 65 26

J. 1854 Dickens novel (2 wds.) · · · · · · ·
   6 2 149 121 190 37 89 40 173

K. Purposes, designs · · · · · · · · · ·
   191 102 52 34 29 46 189 87 3 12

L. Queen of Egypt, aunt of Tutankhamen · · · · · · · ·
   139 202 45 126 108 159 85 55 97

M. Hypothetical land mass that split off to form S America · · · · · · · · ·
   107 194 83 115 93 18 171 69 137 104 33 127

N. Upside-down (hyph.) · · · · · · · ·
   146 77 136 174 120 111 186 58 84 4

O. Genus of yellow-flowered S African herbs · · · · · · ·
   168 100 47 124 114 8 179

P. Former kingdom of SW France and northern Spain · · · · · · ·
   158 63 123 80 11 177 188

Q. "Bach, interwoven / With ___ and Beethoven" (Gilbert, "The Mikado") · · · · · ·
   43 180 199 53 119

R. "My strength is as the strength of ten / Because ___" (4 wds.; Tennyson, "Sir Galahad") · · · ·
   42 20 133 82 31 59 125 7 145 175 116 198 172

S. Think, imagine, preconceive · · · · · · · ·
   151 32 122 94 21 17

T. Burrowing lagomorphs · · · · · · · ·
   161 140 182 30 28 128 152

U. Stellular reference mark · · · · · · ·
   138 105 73 66 86 157 192 9

V. Disdain, scorn · · · · · · · ·
   78 143 98 39 10 1 197 195

W. Children's rainwear or hiking gear (2 wds.) · · · · · · ·
   201 142 164 118 81 23 64 44 22 5 49

X. County in SE England · · · · · · ·
   148 163 181 15 24

Y. Upright bars or supports · · · · · · ·
   95 62 185 166 132 178 71 50 38 76

WORDS

(Diagram cell assignments — number : clue-letter)

No.	Ltr	No.	Ltr	No.	Ltr	No.	Ltr	No.	Ltr	No.	Ltr	No.	Ltr
1	V	30	T	59	R	88	H	117	F	146	N	175	R
2	J	31	R	60	G	89	J	118	W	147	I	176	B
3	K	32	S	61	D	90	G	119	Q	148	X	177	P
4	N	33	M	62	Y	91	F	120	N	149	J	178	Y
5	W	34	K	63	P	92	A	121	J	150	F	179	O
6	J	35	H	64	W	93	M	122	S	151	S	180	Q
7	R	36	F	65	I	94	S	123	P	152	T	181	X
8	O	37	J	66	U	95	Y	124	O	153	F	182	T
9	U	38	Y	67	B	96	A	125	R	154	A	183	C
10	V	39	V	68	E	97	L	126	L	155	H	184	D
11	P	40	J	69	M	98	V	127	M	156	E	185	Y
12	K	41	I	70	G	99	G	128	T	157	U	186	N
13	D	42	R	71	Y	100	O	129	G	158	P	187	I
14	C	43	Q	72	D	101	F	130	B	159	L	188	P
15	X	44	W	73	U	102	K	131	E	160	A	189	K
16	E	45	L	74	F	103	G	132	Y	161	T	190	J
17	S	46	K	75	E	104	M	133	R	162	C	191	K
18	M	47	O	76	Y	105	U	134	D	163	X	192	U
19	G	48	D	77	N	106	H	135	B	164	W	193	G
20	R	49	W	78	V	107	M	136	N	165	I	194	M
21	S	50	Y	79	A	108	L	137	M	166	Y	195	V
22	W	51	C	80	P	109	A	138	U	167	A	196	H
23	W	52	K	81	W	110	C	139	L	168	O	197	V
24	X	53	Q	82	R	111	N	140	T	169	G	198	R
25	D	54	H	83	M	112	D	141	A	170	C	199	Q
26	I	55	L	84	N	113	H	142	W	171	M	200	H
27	C	56	F	85	L	114	O	143	V	172	R	201	W
28	T	57	B	86	U	115	M	144	C	173	J	202	L
29	K	58	N	87	K	116	R	145	R	174	N	203	E

184

WORDS

A 97 226 40 59 149 162 72 13 7 83

B 87 223 188 232 117 137 176 170

C 183 66 233 118 178 53 90 172

D 49 200 76 150 75 225 86 181 156 215 168

E 22 195 158 70

F 26 146 94 57 10 186

G 190 145 60 175 135 33 199

H 116 219 20 126 184 207 35

I 230 74 105 45 134 216 3 198 127

J 206 173 19 50 5 80 100 11 84

K 125 140 21 30 122 227 154 142 93

L 82 39 131 151 136 14 147 91 203 4

M 48 194 208 69 224 120 191 58

N 77 98 17 44 73 204 185 119 182 211 12 34 6 166

O 104 189 214 63 139 18

P 99 187 110 148 217 174 62 129 24 64 167

Q 209 16 109 54 43 157 210 123 89 132 114 28 141 155

R 193 221 133 61 231 115 88 144

S 229 78 31 113 38 192 124 102 42 180 56 112 164 213 1 95 9 152 23

T 55 220 205 138 103 27 196 37 32 79 160 177

U 128 65 96 111 165 81 46 25

V 161 71 29 171 179 197 228 92 212 8

W 218 143 47 153 67

X 107 15 2 163 51 169

Y 68 202 108 130

Z 85 201 52 106 159 36 41 222 121 101

CLUES

A Wife of Uriah and David — 205 110 43 73 37 34 80 59 108

B Irritates or vexes the mind or spirit — 105 235 152 136 84 30 174

C Aquatic insectivore of W Africa (2 wds.) — 151 49 104 182 227 19 27 186 219 15

D 6th cent. B.C. Gr. poet, traditional father of Gr. tragedy — 61 168 188 229 97 113 239

E Mexican agave whose fiber is used for cordage — 189 202 121 11 230 60 185 18

F For shame! — 153 207 62

G Genus of soil bacteria — 204 178 124 117 55 48 164 144 199 150 13 95

H Kind of N American freshwater sucker — 101 139 176 4 64 81 24 39

I Muddle, mess (3 wds.) — 160 232 78 116 3 67 148 234 137 173 123 212

J Having regular flowers — 8 77 100 47 112 154 91 165 31

K Shipbuilding center on the Tyne, SE Northumberland, England — 142 126 63 224 1 114 221 7 54

L Form of carbon used as pencil-leads — 143 127 25 53 93 213 156 155

M Pertaining to biological classification — 172 71 217 210 75 206 40 141 237

N Generous (hyph.) — 74 79 102 162 20 200 130 146 236 131

O Dozed — 51 190 220 125 228 198

P Australian tree with fragrant white flowers, also called Victorian box — 218 32 233 41 128 10 68 120 57 183

Q Cargo, freight — 29 69 87 223 197 215

R Attached, affixed; added as a supplement — 85 222 98 138 14 203 46 36

S Son and successor of Saul (II Sam. 2-4) — 161 149 119 45 50 70 16 94 181 89

T Sojourned in the country; suspended from a British university — 111 194 82 134 158 180 23 88 122 133

U Agreement between nations — 99 109 92 38 72 166 17

V Drawing, alluring — 96 238 211 195 35 184 107 66 115

W American coot (2 wds.) — 147 226 42 135 216 86

X Insectivorous Old World tropical bird (hyph.) — 187 179 76 21 196 225 5 201

Y Casual eatery serving light meals — 2 231 214 26 157 90 193 58 52 175 167 33

Z Passage of a sailing ship as from the Cape of Good Hope to Australia (2 wds.) — 118 170 56 208 192 209 163 103 44 22 145

Z₁ "A slow and silent stream. / Lethe the ___ rolls" (3 wds., "Paradise Lost," Bk. II) — 171 177 191 169 6 129 9 83 106 140 28 12 132 65 159

ANSWERS

1
WILLIAM ZINSSER ON WRITING WELL

Taste chooses words that have originality, strength and precision; non-taste veers into the breezy vernacular of the alumni magazine's class notes where people in authority are the top brass or the powers that be. What . . . is wrong with "the top brass"? . . . it's better to call people . . . officials.

A What the hey!
B Intolerable
C Lighthouse
D Larboard
E Infiltrate
F Aesop
G Motes
H Zechariah
I Instate
J Nize Baby
K Sputters
L Scottish
M Entr'actes
N Rapport
O Oppressive
P Newport
Q Wherewithal
R Revery
S Insights
T Touches off
U Into a trance
V Neats
W Ghosts
X Watchword
Y Espionage
Z Lone Star State
Z_1 Love in Bloom

2
ROBERT F. MURPHY THE BODY SILENT

Contrary to popular fears, the overwhelming majority of people who enter hospitals come out not only alive, but also in better health than when they entered. What one loses in the hospital is not life but freedom of choice . . . passivity is complete.

A Rejection
B Off the wall
C Boorish
D Esthetic
E Reprieve
F Top-hole
G Fifth
H Mailer
I Unfeeling
J Rivals
K Piety
L Hatchet man
M Youth on the prow
N Too soon
O Hot plate
P Eyelashes
Q Boom Town
R Outlive
S Dreamboat
T Yen
U Speciality
V In dutch
W Lamppost
X Earth's
Y Nonsense
Z Trowel

3
(IAN) WHITCOMB (THE) BECKONING FAIRGROUND

Boogie's progressive beat . . . touched the mainstream . . . and . . . set America on a . . . craze that rolled right into the Second World War. . . . swingers like Tommy Dorsey scored instrumental hits . . . while the Andrews Sisters caught the war spirit with "The Boogie Woogie Bugle Boy of Company B."

A Whitehead
B Hollow
C Impetuosity
D Tobies
E Clipboard
F Original sin
G Monster
H Blowout
I Bovary
J Emerged
K Cabbage
L Kowtow
M Onslaught
N Nowadays
O Inchoate
P Necessary
Q Gothic
R Freezers
S Arrowsmith
T Itchweed
U Relished
V Grommet
W Resenting
X Orchestrate
Y Uttar Pradesh
Z Nighttime
Z_1 Desists

4
JOHN FINLATOR (THE) DRUGGED NATION

The rejection of the parental and acceptance of grandparental dress; the rejection of personal hygiene; the . . . acceptance of the road to the drug scene; the outward sophistication but inward ignorance are all expressions of youth asking . . . for understanding . . . and help.

A Jackson
B Opinionated
C Heine
D Naphtha
E Fat chance
F Indecision
G Northern
H Lecherous
I Arbitrate
J Trajectory
K Offended
L Repel
M Detested
N Rasselas
O Untoward
P Gangway
Q Griffon
R Escutcheon
S Doth protest
T Nightingale
U Applesauce
V Toe dancers
W Intercept
X Oxford Group
Y Nathan Hale

5
TOM STOPPARD: THE REAL THING

Words . . . They're innocent, neutral, precise, standing for this, describing that, meaning the other, so if you look after them you can build bridges across incomprehension and chaos. . . I don't think writers are sacred, but words are. They deserve respect.

A Turn around
B One's finger
C Motions
D Seedbed
E Trencher friend
F Orestes
G Pintado
H Pinkerton
I Accession
J Restrictive
K Dossiers
L Thresh
M Hayburner
N Edwards
O Rhythmic
P Esteem'd
Q Artichoke
R Landlubber
S Tiny Alice
T Hoosegow
U Ipso facto
V Night Watch
W Guaranty

6
BARBARA NOVAK: NATURE AND CULTURE

The artist's job, as a minority view saw it, was to get there first and document a doomed nature. Facing nature's inevitable decline, this task teems with ironies. Only when the colonist had cleared the forest and made it fit for "man's abode" could he approach the luxury of loving it.

A Blow off steam
B Affright
C Rattletrap
D Benjamin
E Avidity
F Racoon
G Aphids
H Nauseate
I Odious
J Voiced
K Almond
L Kosher
M Notched
N All the way
O Thomist
P Unchaste
Q Rubdown
R Estimate
S Athens
T Niceties
U Distinctly
V Chew the fat
W Unheard-of
X Loitering
Y Toadies
Z Unrewarding
Z₁ Roosevelt
Z₂ Extremities

7
HENRI TROYAT: IVAN THE TERRIBLE

Far away among the Tatars, the Khan of Kazan, learning of the birth of Ivan, told the Russian boyars who had come to visit him, "A sovereign has been born to you and he already has two teeth. With one, he will devour us; but with the other, he will devour you!"

A Hathaway
B Ehrlich
C Noshed
D Rotten
E Inability
F Thomas Mann
G Rowboat
H Out-and-out
I Yahoo
J Awful
K They shoved
L If I Were King
M Varnishes
N Amazed
O Nightshade
P To boot
Q Health
R Ekes out
S Thaw
T Evert
U Rehearsal
V Rub the wrong way
W Inverted
X Buffoon
Y Lavish
Z Elihu Root

8
(ROBERT) CLAIBORNE: OUR (MARVELOUS) NATIVE TONGUE

The Italian port of Ligorno (now Livorno) was long ago twisted into Leghorn—and gave its name to a breed of chicken and a kind of straw hat. Somewhat later, the jolly tars who manned H.M.S. Bellerophon, no experts in Greek mythology, christened her the Bully Ruffian.

A Chaps
B Longs
C Astrakhan
D Illogical
E Bookworm
F Off the bat
G Ridgway
H Needle
I Earth and sky
J On the spot
K Universal joint
L Roofs of gold
M Niger
N All the world
O Tightly
P Infernal machine
Q Voodoo
R Edwin Newman
S The wheat
T Oxymoron
U North Star
V Gale
W Umpteenth
X Ehrenbreitstein

9
(VICTOR) BORGE: MY FAVORITE INTERMISSIONS

Borodin was a gentle, kindly man, a general in the Russian Army, a famous chemist, and the original Absent-Minded Professor. Borodin was so absent-minded that he once walked out of his house in full military dress . . . complete with everything except his pants.

A Banns
B On the prowl
C Rascality
D Gams
E Expiation
F Mashed
G Yielded
H Flushed
I Anneal
J Veins
K Oleander
L Readied
M Immutable
N Twins
O Embank
P Incorrigible
Q Naughty Marietta
R Toff
S Enchant
T Rooked
U Moons
V Ipswich
W Slough
X Suite
Y Irish yew
Z Orphans of the
     Storm
Z₁ Nested
Z₂ Stands

10
ALICE (MARTIN) LESTER: SIX MEN OF SCIENCE

A gynecologist must be
Possessed of equanimity –
Not even stirred by Aphrodite
Enveloped in a silken nightie.

A paragon of poise and tact,
Yet scientifically exact!
Hippocrates to womankind–
A braver man you'll never find.

A Alleviate
B Landis
C Itty-bitty
D Cavern
E Empower
F Lapland
G Esquamate
H Scab
I Tease
J Effete
K Reins
L Snap up
M Inka Dinka Doo
N Xochimilco
O Missed
P Erythrophobia
Q Niggardly
R Outgoing
S Fast
T Soften
U Cope
V Intend
W Envy
X Notion
Y Crisp
Z Everyone

11
BRIAN O'DOHERTY: AMERICAN MASTERS

The mysteriousness of Hopper's pictures lies in the disparity between cause and effect. Sunlight falling across a floor amounts to an event, an empty street holds attention. How such scenes become important has engendered much critical speculation.

A Bender
B Rorschach
C Inherent
D Attention
E Nuncupative
F Out of the blue
G Dopes
H Occiput
I Hoofs
J Euhemerism
K Ringhals
L Tends
M Youghal
N Attest to
O Mossy
P Ettwein
Q Remiss
R Inception
S Calf
T Accord
U Newcastle
V Matchless
W Applause
X Steffens
Y To sin
Z Elapse
Z₁ Reminder
Z₂ Stygian

12
CHARLES CLEMENTS (M.D.): WITNESS TO WAR

It was in Fiji that I began seriously to consider studying medicine. The notion had been with me ever since Vietnam, where I felt the only positive roles were played by the medics and physicians and those pilots who rescued and ferried the wounded.

A Cinders
B Heady
C Attenuates
D Room Service
E Lippy
F Enchantment
G Sassy
H Coined
I Larch
J Endowed
K Maisie
L Nelpout
M Nitid
N The Tweed
O Sapajou
P Windy
Q Intensify
R The heights
S Nihilist
T Elbowroom
U Soirée
V Siddons
W Thy bride-bed
X Overweening
Y Whiff
Z Authentic
Z₁ Reviled

13

(JAMES J.) KILPATRICK:
THE WRITER'S ART

A redundant word is an unnecessary word. Considering the high price of newsprint and book stock, we ought to watch for redundancies and pluck them from our writing as if we were plucking ticks off a dog's back. Redundancies, like ticks, suck the blood from our prose.

A	Knock on Any	M	Edward the
	Door		Confessor
B	Isomere	N	Wedded
C	Ludicrous	O	Rufus
D	Peter Ibbetson	P	Infink
E	Autocratic	Q	Taking
F	Trumped up	R	Ensconced
G	Rockfish	S	Recalling
H	Inkpots	T	Science
I	Chow down	U	Awkward Age
J	Kung fu	V	Ralph Roister
K	Trafficking		Doister
L	Hogwash	W	Thumbs down

14

RONALD BLYTHE:
SHADES OF EMPIRE

Adventure was the nation's most popular reading, not crime or romance. The Empire was its adventure playground. But huge tracts of it were rough, lonely going, and, one way or another, the imperial gamesmen and women suffered a good deal.

(From *The Manchester Guardian Weekly* June 30, 1985)

A	Roughage	N	Heads off
B	Overwrought	O	Aggrieved
C	Narrow	P	Darrow
D	Aphrodite	Q	Endymion
E	Lap up	R	Stoic
F	Denote	S	Oatmeal
G	Brant	T	Fulminate
H	Latent	U	Euphemisms
I	Yearning	V	Monger
J	Totter	W	Panacea
K	Hones	X	Inundate
L	Eumenides	Y	Rodgers
M	Swallow	Z	Emunctory

15

J(ESSICA) MITFORD:
DAUGHTERS AND REBELS

"Is she one of us . . . ?" Grandmother used to ask . . . Mother would join mildly in our amusement at the outrageous question. Class was a delicate matter, a subject for intuition rather than conversation, one of those "borderline" subjects, deeply felt but never discussed.

A	James Earl Jones	O	Edulcorate
B	Moose	P	Richardson
C	Injuries	Q	Sowed
D	Tons	R	Arabesque
E	Foss	S	Nictitating
F	Out of kilter		membrane
G	Ranunculus	T	Dotty
H	Distort	U	Roundabout
I	Devote	V	Elusive
J	Ascent	W	Battery
K	Unwonted	X	Emolument
L	Gesso	Y	Louise
M	Half-hitch	Z	Sheepshead
N	Thrift		

16

(VIRGIL) THOMSON:
WHY COMPOSERS WRITE HOW

Appreciation teaching is not even a skill of any kind. It is on the level of Minimum Musicality . . . So your composer who sticks at it becomes an ex-composer and an embittered man. Always beware of ex-composers. Their one aim in life is to discourage the writing of music.

A	Tambour	N	Pieces of eight
B	Heft	O	One Alone
C	Ocarina	P	Soften
D	Molly	Q	Eustacia Vye
E	Screed	R	Risibilities
F	Okovanggo	S	Suns
G	Nimiety	T	Wombat
H	Wapiti	U	Riotous
I	Hemp	V	Intrinsic
J	Yspadaden	W	Tommies
	Penkawr	X	Extinction
K	Climax	Y	Hammers out
L	Oceanic	Z	Off one's rocker
M	Meshed	Z_1	Williams

17

IVOR RICHARD:
WE, THE BRITISH

Things have changed, and it is a common theme of readers' letters to Conservative newspapers that there has been a . . . "falling-off in standards" – but statistics can be interpreted in various ways, and Britain remains on the whole law-abiding.

A	Ironclad	M	Eiderdowns
B	Voracity	N	Tatters
C	On the mend	O	Halvah
D	Repeaters	P	Ebullient
E	Revealing	Q	Bastions
F	Ipswich	R	Rama
G	Chastens	S	Intense
H	Hobbes	T	Termagants
I	Adhesive	U	Inattention
J	Ragamuffins	V	Snapdragons
K	Daft	W	Habitations
L	Wretched wife		

18

B(ARRY) COMMONER:
THE CLOSING CIRCLE

Air pollution . . . is a reminder that our most celebrated technological advancements – the automobile, the jet plane, the power plant, industry in general, and indeed the modern city itself – are, in the environment, failures.

A	Berate	N	Lintel
B	Crispin	O	Orphic
C	Out of the blue	P	Steady
D	Mates	Q	Inigo Jones
E	Mettle	R	Neith
F	Oleander	S	Gilt
G	Narwhal	T	Crimped
H	Envious moon	U	Inferential
I	Ramadan	V	Red tape
J	Trite	W	Clutter
K	Haunts	X	Limed
L	Earthly	Y	Even-handed
M	Connote		

19

(ROMAIN) ROLLAND:
BEETHOVEN THE CREATOR

The empire of art, like that of action, belongs not to the subtle but to the strong – to him who dares to be himself and proclaim it imperially. The world follows him. The voice of Beethoven speaks for him: he is the emperor of the world of feeling.

A	Rhyme to death	N	Vermin
B	Ohthere	O	Elbowroom
C	Loot	P	Novelists
D	Lifts	Q	Throw off
E	Adroit	R	Homilies
F	Night-shriek	S	Eclipse
G	Dipper	T	Commonweal
H	Behest	U	Ruffle
I	Elopements	V	Eights
J	Efate	W	Atone
K	Took out	X	The bower
L	Hobbit	Y	Ophthalmic
M	Offal	Z	Right and left

20

LAURENCE BERGREEN:
JAMES AGEE

He befriended an "Irish politician" who gave him access to the Boston morgue and jail. While his Exeter classmates were at home learning about the stock market at their father's knee . . . James studied corpses and meditated on the fine line between the quick and the dead.

A	Loathed	N	Endearment
B	Antithesis	O	Euphemistic
C	Unpretentious	P	North-west
D	Retracted	Q	John-a-dreams
E	Eightball	R	Acquisitive
F	Necktie	S	Make a wish
G	Chamois	T	Ewe lamb
H	Ethics	U	Sheets
I	Backhanded	V	Adjoined
J	Endorsement	W	Ghetto
K	Rooked	X	Exhilarate
L	Go-between	Y	Enfilade
M	Raffish		

21
FARLEY MOWAT
MY FATHER'S SON

The opera was Aida and, though you enjoy that sort of thing, Mater, your son was not amused . . . The San Carlo Opera House is supposed to be the home of opera, but . . . Damned if I can get enthused by the vocal contortions and posturings that go on—and on and on.

A Fragonard
B Attempting
C Rejuvenation
D Laugh it up
E Entraps
F Youmans
G Monotonous
H On the one hand
I Woe
J Attends
K Toucan
L Moosehead
M Yeddo hawthorn
N Faded
O Apostrophe
P Tongue-lashing
Q Hassan
R Eustachio
S Redcoats
T Standout
U Soporific
V On the other
W Nobody's Baby

22
L. (EWIS) H. LAPHAM
(THE) IMPERIAL MASQUERADE

"The arts," Richard Nixon once said, his voice trembling with integrity (and his golfing companions cut in for a percentage), "provide the intangible qualities of grace, beauty, and spiritual fulfillment." . . . the Mobil Corporation couldn't have said it better.

A Leghorn
B Heftiest
C Lamprey
D Affable
E Poisoning
F Hotbed
G Actor
H Moonglow
I Insipid
J Mulch
K Phased
L Exhilarating
M Rabbit
N Inconclusive
O Attitude
P Lovage
Q Matterhorn
R Attrition
S Softens
T Quintilian
U Unburden
V Eighty
W Rapid-fire
X Agricola
Y Distinctive
Z Eccentric

23
EDWARD T. HALL
(THE) SILENT LANGUAGE

Complete lack of congruence occurs when everything is . . . out of phase . . . Lack of congruence in dress is always obvious and often humorous—witness the endless cartoons of natives wearing a loin cloth and a silk hat.

A English muffin
B Depicts
C Woven
D Anima
E Root cause
F Doorways
G Tocsin
H Heavy
I Aright
J Lockup
K Lubes
L Sloven
M Infect
N Luckiest
O Encroach
P Nearness
Q The flood
R Locus
S Act One
T No-show
U Garish
V Underfoot
W Askance
X Grown
Y Essential

24
(DON MIGUEL DE) UNAMUNO
(THE) TRAGIC SENSE OF LIFE

What differentiates man . . . is perhaps feeling rather than reason. I have seen a cat reason more often than laugh or weep. Perhaps it laughs or weeps within itself—but then perhaps within itself a crab solves equations of the second degree.

A Up in the air
B Nepenthe
C Arapahos
D Mischief
E Uproar
F Newspaper
G Oleander
H Teflon
I Rhett Butler
J Affidavit
K Gossamer wings
L Innocent
M Cleavage
N Sweet-heart
O Eighth note
P Nawab
Q Shipshape
R Earth
S On faith
T Fresh
U Losses
V Irish tweed
W Feasts
X Eloquent

25
RING LARDNER
TIPS ON HORSES

How often do you hear . . . parents order their kiddies to cut out the horse play. The answer is that a horse can't play nice like kittens or oxen or even wolfs, but has got to be ribald and rough in their sports as in everything else.

A Rotten apples
B Itinerant
C Newlywed
D Ghost
E Lands of
F Aphrodite
G Rockford
H Delirious
I Navy
J Ether
K Retired
L Taught
M In hot water
N Pharaoh
O Set-to
P On one's high horse
Q Nesbitt
R Houseboat
S Obituary
T Roaches
U Skinner
V Exclusively
W Skeet

26
(ANGELA) CARTER
(THE) LANGUAGE OF SISTERHOOD

Sisterhood . . . has a certain self-confidence about dismissing structured, patriarchal, authoritarian devices like syntax, grammar, and artistic form with a deprecating supercilious smile; they are part of the conspiracy to stifle Woman's Voice in its uniqueness.

A Catafalque
B Architectonics
C Riven
D Tombs
E Exfoliation
F Ridiculous
G Levitate
H Acharnians
I Niche
J Gruff
K Underwent
L Arrests
M Gratuity
N Echinoids
O Okinawa
P Fascist
Q Simmers
R Issued
S Sump
T Traction
U Epistolary
V Repents
W Harmed
X Ophiolatry
Y Oireachtas
Z Dismiss

27
HUMPHREY COBB
PATHS OF GLORY

Wars . . . They're part of life . . . There are lots worse things than war to my mind. For example, sitting on your tail in some bastard's office and making and counting his money for him. It takes a man to make a war, but a louse can make money.

A Hammerhead
B Uxorious
C Mantis
D Phantasm
E Himalayan
F Rake-off
G Eminent
H Yarrow
I Community
J Omei
K Batten down
L Balalaika
M Proctors
N Amanuensis
O Teasing
P Hawser
Q Strike off
R Orchestrate
S Fittest
T Gawking
U Lofted
V Ontology
W Rind
X Yemen

28
NATHAN SILVER
ARCHITECT TALK

Architect talk doesn't have to be accurate. Since it is primarily descriptive of looks, frequently it can't be. It achieves its results by using the language of the moment that signals certain things, and by going on at three times the necessary length.

A Narcolepsy
B Attribution
C Tightest
D Haggis
E Agave
F Nictate
G Static
H Intrinsic
I Lebanon
J Vividness
K Eleemosynary
L Refines
M Attacking
N Recent
O Chiggers
P Heath hen
Q Implicate
R Trotters
S Eyes to behold
T Cuttlefish
U Tongue
V Thatches
W Alfred Noyes
X Limbs
Y Kumquat

29

(ERIC) PARTRIDGE
SHAKESPEARE'S BAWDY

Shakespeare seems to have held … that … composition is superior to love-making as a means of satisfying the need for self-expression … almost equal to it as an anodyne to that loneliness with which all of us, but especially the … artistic … creators, are beset.

A Praiseworthy
B Apprehensive
C Rachel
D To shoot
E Reflections
F Ill omens
G Dorset
H Gossoon
I Essence
J Steamboat
K Hush of
L Afloat
M Kittenish
N Evening
O Suspicious
P Palatine
Q Emotes
R Askance
S Requital
T Estate
U Solemnity
V Battle-ax
W Ashram
X Whitefish
Y Distal
Z Yard-of-ale

30

E(DITH) WHARTON
THE AGE OF INNOCENCE

The Newport Archery Club … which had hitherto known no rival but croquet, was beginning to be discarded in favour of lawn-tennis; but the latter game was still considered too rough and inelegant for social occasions.

A Earthbound
B Wicked
C Hollow out
D Acquires
E Rupture
F Thriving
G On the ball
H New London
I Temblors
J Hawthorn
K Etches
L Arrive
M Gal
N Earwig
O Odds
P Fashioning
Q Insist
R Notion
S Nabob
T Old Guard
U Chewa
V Ecstasy
W Nectar
X Contact
Y Efficient

31

FRED MUSTARD STEWART
THE TITAN

Turkey had been cursed by rulers of dazzling ineptitude for centuries. … Sloth, drunkenness, mass murder … genocide, torture, fratricide, uxoricide, infanticide, gluttony—all vices had been worn out by the parade of Sultan-Caliphs … known as "God's Shadow on Earth."

A Fault-finding
B Redounds
C Extraordinary
D Delirious
E Maverick
F Unsuitable
G Schnoz
H Tocsin
I Answered
J Robbers
K Deduces
L So to bed
M Tarzan
N Enemies
O Whiffled
P Ares
Q Rocket
R Touching
S Tousled
T Hatchery
U Edward Kennedy
V Topic
W In the long run
X Truthfully
Y Appraises
Z Nougat

32

T.C. MCLUHAN
THE WAY OF THE EARTH

The ancient Greeks believed their homeland to be an extension of their bodies and spirit. The ground and self were considered one, a belief that sprang from deep love of country and the hallowed ancestral imperative that rooted and nourished the Greek spirit.

A Traipsed
B Cheered on
C Miffed
D Cottontail
E Libertine
F Unfounded
G Hearthstone
H Axolotl
I Nudes
J Tabasco
K Hook-nosed
L Enterprise
M Weeping
N A drop of water
O Ypsilanti
P Overbearing
Q Fiddleheads
R Teething
S Highest
T Evidenced
U Earth Mother
V Albemarle
W Revised
X Trenton
Y Hanker

33

JACQUES BARZUN
SIMPLE AND DIRECT

The very word *article* means a little joint, and the convenient size of *a* and *the*, as well as their frequency in print, show that their function is not negligible or their behavior hidden from view. Why, then, the misuse, particularly the wrong omission of *the?* The main reason is … captions and headlines.

A Jettison
B Air is delicate
C Chemist
D Quintessential
E Uther Pendragon
F Elderberry wine
G Swahili
H Bahamas
I Alioth
J Running off
K Zoo Story
L Unfinished
M Novitiate
N Svelte
O In the worst way
P Menthol
Q Pedant
R Liverish
S Entitles
T Anchovy pear
U Neith
V Doormat
W Dire
X In tow
Y Rhenish
Z Encroachment
Z₁ Chaffing
Z₂ The whole

34

(KATE) MOODY
GROWING UP ON TELEVISION

Cartoon violence does not represent a form of "artistic conflict." "It is carefully and deliberately used to play on the child's vulnerabilities, to get him or her to watch, and to lure the largest possible audience for the purpose of selling products.

A Morocco
B Off-putting
C Out of hand
D Daffodil
E Yalta
F Galleries
G Resolution
H Orpheus
I Wobble
J Introduce
K Nerds
L Garble
M Unhappy times
N Plaited
O Ostler
P Necessities
Q The death of
R Erratic
S Latches
T Ectophyte
U Ventral
V Illicit
W Soccer
X Intrusion
Y Overlord
Z Nestle

35

ANNE (RIVERS) SIDDONS
HEARTBREAK HOTEL

He switched on the radio: Elvis Presley, inevitably. … "Since muh baby lef' me, found a new place to dway-ull, uh!" "Heartbreak Hotel" had reached number one on the mercurial charts that May and it ran through the summer like a leitmotif.

A Aerie
B Naturally
C Nordhoff and Hall
D Empty
E Switch
F Infamy
G Dither
H Ducat
I Ovate
J Neith
K Steamed
L Hellenic
M Eweries
N Amish
O Rheum
P Thumbs
Q Booms
R Roth
S Enrapture
T Arch villain
U Knowledge
V Hebe
W Outback
X There beauty
Y Euchre
Z Lady Hamilton

36

C(HARLES) GRODIN
HOW I GET THROUGH LIFE

I've always been a little wary of people who make a lot of money from ways other than getting up and going to work. A guy who can make as much money in one phone call as another guy could in a lifetime of labor somehow makes me nervous.

A Compress
B Gallows humor
C Ran off
D Outlook
E Doubtful
F Impish
G Nefarious
H Homage
I Okinawa
J Womanly
K In the way
L Goethe
M Engage
N Takes away
O Typee
P Hammock
Q Recreant
R On view
S Uncle Sam
T Gave a damn
U Hoopoe
V Lenny
W Interminably
X Follow
Y Eyetooth

37
J(AMES) REDFIELD
(THE) CELESTINE PROPHECY

The plane jerked forward and taxied out to the runway. I closed my eyes and felt a mild dizziness as the big jet . . . lifted into a thick cloud cover. When we reached cruising altitude, I finally relaxed and drifted into sleep.

A Jezebel
B Rank
C Endorsed
D Dimwit
E Flax
F Inigo Jones
G Earache
H Little
I Descanted
J Cadillac
K Euthenist
L Listed
M Whip
N Erewhon

N Shifty
O Tiered
P Intuition
Q Nudge
R Edom
S Pickled
T Runway
U Outflow
V Prolix
W Hazarded
X Evidently
Y Chaffed
Z Yeats

38
ANNE (RIVERS) SIDDONS
HEARTBREAK HOTEL

In the old chifforobe that sheltered the ghosts of Mississippi lavender and dimity and satins and point d'esprit, the Atlanta cottons looked lost and perfunctory and rawly new, and seemed to hide themselves in shame in the . . . gloom.

A Amphora
B Neologism
C Ninepins
D Effortless
E Safety
F Intrinsic
G Dodds
H Disco
I Oddities
J Noodles
K Saddled
L Hind
M Ethel Waters

N Appointment
O Rimy
P To the chaps
Q Bevan
R Rattled
S Endive
T Aghast
U Kiln
V Hotshot
W On the way home
X Tufts
Y Enthral
Z Lamented

39
LARRY WILDE
THE GREAT COMEDIANS (TALK ABOUT COMEDY)

Since all are associated with the comic, you don't think of them in terms of good looks . . . yet . . . perhaps glamour queen Tina Louise said it best. "Anybody who doesn't love Jimmy Durante just doesn't have an eye for real beauty."

A Ladies
B Antrobus
C Replied
D Revels
E You Can't Take It
F With You
G Inhuman
H Lots
I Dismay
J Eyesore
K Tojo
L Handkerchief
M Emote
N Gath

O Ripe
P Enfold
Q A wolf
R The touch
S Coyote
T Osmosis
U Majesty
V Evade
W Daubs
X Intent
Y Algonquin
Z Nobody
Z₁ Smart

40
PAULA (J.) CAPLAN
THEY SAY YOU'RE CRAZY

As I know from my own practice, as well as from other therapists' and patients' reports, unless a therapist takes great care . . . to deal with these issues in depathologizing ways, simply being in therapy can tend to make the patient feel abnormal.

A Phratries
B Aroint
C Unclear
D Limpid
E Apposite
F Commits
G Athos
H Pettifog
I Letdown
J Argot
K Newts
L Titter
M Hits
N Eases

O Yawl
P Sharpen
Q Assistant
R Yoknapatawpha
S Yelp
T On the mend
U Uriah
V Remiss
W Elbe
X Cleft
Y Reflections
Z Awake and sing
Z₁ Zorba the Greek
Z₂ Yes-man

41
BERYL MARKHAM
WEST WITH THE NIGHT

Who doesn't look upward when searching for a name? Looking upward, what is there but the sky to see? And seeing it, how can the name or the hope be earthbound? Was there a horse named Pegasus that flew? Was there a horse with wings?

A Bruised
B Essen
C Ridges
D Youghal
E Looks
F Matte
G Ashamed
H Rebate
I Known
J Hangar
K Accost
L Mab
M Whip
N Erewhon

O Sedate
P Throughout
Q Wherewithal
R In the wind
S The heat
T Hawkes
U Toss off
V Heaped
W Earthenware
X Noose
Y Inept
Z Grownup
Z₁ Hawse
Z₂ Thrown

42
RACHEL (L.) CARSON
THE SEA AROUND US

In the sea, as on land, spring is a time for renewal of life. During the . . . months of winter in the temperate zones the surface waters have been absorbing the cold. Now the heavy water begins to sink, slipping down and replacing the warmer layers below.

A Reviews
B Ambivalent
C Chattels
D Howard
E Entwine
F Lippy
G Case
H Alacrity
I Rowboat
J Spanner
K Offense
L Newton
M Tinkers

N Hobble
O Embowed
P Swing shift
Q Ephemeral
R Affright the air
S Adherent
T Reprehend
U Utilize
V Nesting
W Drags on
X Unwholesome
Y Singsong

43
KAREN ARMSTRONG
A HISTORY OF GOD

The Christian God seemed a ferocious, primitive deity, who kept intervening . . . in human affairs . . . It was one thing to suggest that men of the caliber of Plato or Alexander the Great had been sons of a god, but a Jew who had died a disgraceful death . . . was quite another matter.

A Kefauver
B Afterword
C Rimini
D Extreme unction
E Nightie
F Adjacent
G Roundhead
H Meadows
I Swathed
J Tansies
K Rattrap
L Of the best
M Nifties
N Goodman

O Abash
P Heath
Q Incapable
R Straightened
S The highest
T Oviparous
U Ratchet
V Yellow dog
W Oatmeal
X Foregone
Y Gaud
Z Off-white
Z₁ Disquieting

44
RAY PARKER
RV HAVING FUN YET?

Ethel and I passed the time away reading paperbacks. After hours of the most rain we'd ever seen, I began hoping . . . the promoter who sold us on this "adventure" was also out somewhere in the wilderness, sopping wet and utterly miserable.

A Row, Row, Row
B Arbitrate
C Yellowweed
D Pests
E Allowed
F Resembled
G Kemp
H Empanada
I Rhenish
J Repetition
K Veins
L Headed

M Veep
N Ignorant
O Nuthouse
P Girth
Q Facetious
R Upstairs, Downstairs
S Nothingness
T Yarmouth
U Emphases
V The bees

45
C(YRA) MCFADDEN
THE SERIAL (A YEAR IN THE LIFE) OF MARIN (COUNTY)

Even though Harvey was into wine himself, he hated standing around trying to think of variations on "yeasty," "fruity," "stemmy," "chewy," "corky," "acidulous," etc. ... What the hell difference did it make? Wine was just so many sour grapes anyway.

A Carried away
B Move out
C Cutaway
D Famish
E A fish that talks
F Dewey
G Douse
H Eyesight
I Nimiety
J Ty
K Handy Andy
L Amity
M Lotte
N Endowment
O Rigidity
P Interject
Q Arapaho
R Lengths
S Overthrow
T Fun is fun
U Mushy
V Awfully
W Reckon
X Intercession
Y Nothing

46
(ANN) RICHARDS
STRAIGHT FROM THE HEART

Once, down Mariscal Canyon I was lying on a grassy bank looking up at the slit between the top of two canyon walls, and a peregrine falcon just darted and sailed back and forth across that little ribbon of light. If you ever feel religious or close to God, it's at a time like that.

A Substantial
B Tumult
C Unknown
D Asinine
E Rumble
F Tensile
G Chipping in
H Hermit
I Annoys
J Screws
K Emphasis
L Tissues
M Yew tree
N Rousseau
O Artiste
P Nessus
Q Niceties
R Youth nor age
S Ossify
T Fruits
U Wastebasket
V Obscene
W Rabbit
X Dissolution
Y Shebeen

47
STUART CHASE
(THE) TYRANNY OF WORDS

What a ... term is "business," especially in America! How is business?—not your business, but business-in-general. ... If there is not such entity as "business"—and ... we know there is not—it seems ... superfluous to be constantly taking its temperature.

A Roots
B Intellectual
C Crowded
D Hellbent
E Antigone
F Rafters
G Dawn of day
H Scoot
I Steadies
J Traditions
K Rapidity
L Anklebone
M Inflection
N Gadabout
O Hoisting
P Two-to-two
Q Fasting
R Rascality
S Olive Oyl
T Muskellunge
U Trajan
V Hankow
W Encephalograph
X Hack off
Y Estimable
Z Angelic
Z₁ Robes
Z₂ Trashy

48
SARA PARETSKY
GUARDIAN ANGEL

The local block development committee ... didn't much like the dogs. ... The Lab was the only purebred: the other four were mutts ranging in size from a large off-white Benji replica to something that looked like a walking gray earmuff.

A Skiffle
B Affright the air
C Refinement
D Adjunct
E Podunk
F Almost
G Remit
H Embraceable You
I Temple
J Seville
K Kazoo
L Yawl
M Gecko
N Upswing
O Abhor
P Ragtime
Q Ditch
R Immerse
S All Through the Night
T Noodle
U Attend
V Nether world
W Goof
X E.B. White
Y Locket

49
FRED (ALAN) WOLF
PARALLEL UNIVERSES

Einstein once said, "The most incomprehensible thing about the universe is that it is comprehensible." Well and good, for someone like Einstein to say. But for the rest of us mortals, it still looks incomprehensible, even to the brightest physicists.

A Fletcher
B Reese
C Entrapment
D Distinction
E Wresting
F Open book
G Limb
H Flash in the pan
I Possessive
J Abstemious
K Robin Hood
L Amity
M Lotte
N Luther
O Ethyl chloride
P Loseth his life
Q Unsettle
R Nesbitt
S Issuing
T Vision
U Emmett
V Regions
W Sheik
X Escharotic
Y Soon-to-be

50
(ANNIE) DILLARD
PILGRIM AT TINKER CREEK

I remember what the city has to offer: human companionship, major-league baseball, and a clatter of quickening stimulus like a rush from strong drugs ... I remember how you bide your time in the city, and think ... "next year ... I'll start living; next year ... I'll start my life."

A Daybreak
B Insurrection
C Lamb
D Lummox
E Acquisition
F Rajah
G Distaff
H Prism
I Inferential
J Loft
K Giggle
L Rent
M Imprudent
N Mews
O Attribute
P Thoroughly
Q Thatcher
R Immunity
S Nimble
T Knives
U Eyes of most unholy
V Rittenhouse
W Catamaran
X Rayleigh
Y Eyeshadow
Z Execrable
Z₁ Krill

51
STEPHANIE BRUSH
LIFE: A WARNING

Boys and men have the option of growing beards, sideburns, moustaches and eyebrows to cover ... skin ailments, but... ... For every year that a beard remains on your face, your actual chin will recede a full inch: and if you shave off a beard ... your own family will not recognize you.

A Scruffy
B Too young
C Eye for an eye
D Panorama
E Halfway
F Anchorage
G Numbs
H Immures
I Eventually
J Butchery
K Revocation
L Undeterred
M Scrawny
N Holozoic
O Layovers
P Indirectly
Q Fulfilled
R Edwardians
S Abase
T Waiver
U Affectionate
V Rhomboid
W Not so bad
X In the know
Y Nourishes
Z Gibbous

52
WALTER M. BORTZ (II, M.D.)
WE LIVE TOO SHORT (AND DIE TOO LONG)

Antidepressants are one of the few batches of prescriptions ... I really feel comfortable about because of the manifest good they provide to my older patients. It is wonderfully gratifying to see a person recapture his interest in being alive after he had previously lost the zest.

A Weirdest
B Assertively
C La Chaise
D Trouping
E Easter bonnet
F Redbreast
G Monopoly
H Buttonhole
I O'Hare
J Rachmaninoff
K The feet of
L Zuppa Inglese
M Wheedle
N Elvis Presley
O Latterday
P Incipient
Q Vitiate
R Emporia
S Toasty
T Outfitter
U Obsessed
V Self-effacing
W Husbandry
X Office
Y Roosters
Z Tightrope

53
(CAROL) TAVRIS
THE MISMEASURE OF WOMAN

The . . . women's movement has . . . opposed . . . policies that would . . . be female-specific, fearing these would be used against women's best interests. Their attitude reflects Mae West's . . . "Men are always trying to protect me . . . Can't imagine what from."

A Trotter
B Access
C Vigil
D Rights of Man
E Idyllic
F Stewed
G Testament
H Hee-haw
I Emit
J Macaw
K In soot I sleep
L Seeps
M Mews

N Establish
O Adept
P Sweetmeat
Q Unctuous
R Rabble
S Edwin
T Osteopathy
U Frenetic
V Wharf
W Offered
X Momentum
Y Agent Orange
Z Nepotism

54
J.R. POLE
(THE) LANGUAGE OF PRESIDENTS

Eisenhower was not responsible for the drift of his time, but his style reflected it with a nonchalant fidelity which encouraged loose writing and soft thinking in others; . . . Stevenson as . . . leader of a major party . . . set a tone to which others must at least reply.

A Jackanapes
B Ringalievio
C Paraffin
D On the whole
E London
F Eustachio
G Letts
H Antibody
I Nether
J Gushed
K Unhealthy
L At heart
M Got off

N Embolism
O On the rise
P Forensics
Q Position
R Rimshots
S Earthly
T Switch
U In the worst way
V Defects
W Edward Teller
X Nefertiti
Y Tissot
Z Strewn

55
ROBERT MACNEIL
WORDSTRUCK

I was . . . fascinated by radio. The summer I was ten, I took a . . . cardboard carton and made a shortwave . . . set by drawing dials and . . . switches all over the face. I spent hours . . . transmitting and receiving imaginary broadcasts . . . to planes and ships.

A Riddled
B Overthrow
C Barbarians
D Enhanced
E Rattail
F Twists
G Madagascar
H Amagansett
I Canadian Capers
J Naiad
K Evans
L Idiocy

M Loaded
N Wapiti
O Obstinate
P Roosters
Q Devils
R Swami
S Turn of the Screw
T Ragtag
U Unfinished Symphony
V Chemist
W Knobs

56
PHILIP SLATER
WEALTH ADDICTION

Advertising . . . has never tried to hide its effort to convince the public that every human need can be satisfied by buying something. You get health by buying drugs, doctors, breakfast foods and—when people begin to realize that "less is more"—diet books, diet foods, jogging equipment, exercycles, and whatnot.

A Peashooter
B Head of state
C Improve on
D Lee J. Cobb
E Idle hands
F Pettifog
G Sheheen
H Lip-synched
I Astonished
J The quick brown fox
K Edges out
L Rubberneck
M Wearing

N Effete snob
O Arouse
P Lavishing
Q The lazy dog
R Hasten
S Army guy
T Ditty bag
U Demigod
V Invective
W Chitterlings
X Teddy boy
Y Intersection
Z Outfitting
Z_1 Nostradamus

57
SIMON RAMO
(THE) BUSINESS OF SCIENCE

If you had been born in the West . . . and then moved to Schenectady, New York, chances are you . . . would develop a severe case of Californiaitis. This disease causes . . . extreme pain . . . and is an ailment for which the definitive cure, smog, had not yet been discovered.

A Severe
B In the line of fire
C Motive
D Outstrip
E Necessity
F Rosy
G Ah, Wilderness
H Midday
I Obadiah
J Bitchy
K Untrammeled
L Seedy
M Ichabod Crane

N Ninotchka
O Ennui
P Stood off
Q Sheen
R Othhere
S Feuded
T Swedes
U Chaise
V Invocation
W Encapsulate
X New wave
Y Code
Z Extravagance

58
JEREMY LEWIS
PLAYING FOR TIME

In those days, South Kensington was a land . . . populated by maiden aunts, dilapidated majors with watery eyes and damp, tobacco-stained moustaches, and ashen-faced City men who bore a strong resemblance to T.S. Eliot and went to work in black jackets and black-and-white striped trousers.

A Jack Sprat
B Entombed
C Rechecked
D Earnest
E Macadam
F Yonder window breaks
G Latched on
H Endowed
I Wordsworth
J In dispute
K Sweats out
L Panama hat

M Lilliput
N Are as goads
O Yacht basin
P Ink Spots
Q Nijinsky
R Glad-handed
S Factiousness
T Obtuse
U Rottenstone
V Tobacconist
W In the way
X Mandalay
Y Embattled

59
PETER VANSITTART
(IN) THE FIFTIES

Picasso was in full flood . . . during the Cold War he designed a dove of peace which decorated many Communist-directed peace conferences. The dove had originated in a pigeon, a gift from Matisse; 'peace' appropriated by Marxists as if it were their discovery.

A Philippic
B Endymion
C Trudges
D Expected
E Ring out old
F View with alarm
G Arrowhead
H Not so bad
I Surefire
J Ideas
K Tommies
L The goods
M Apostasy

N Rope dancer
O Top drawer
P The mission
Q Heading off
R Efface
S Forage
T Incapacity
U Flaccid
V The vices
W Ice-Cream
X Evince
Y Saddened

60
A(NNE) TAYLOR) FLEMING
MOTHERHOOD DEFERRED

When it seemed everything would work out, men would . . . be happy to share, . . . to be tender and relieved of their hefty bravado, everything turned muddy again and we confronted our own impotence. It was, said a friend of mine, like walking upstream on icebergs.

A Arrowsmith
B Fly-by-night
C Landau
D Echeverria
E Maiden
F Imbue
G Nasty
H Greensward
I Moved
J Oftentimes
K Twelve
L Honey-bee
M Effi Briest

N Revelation
O Hankow
P Opiate
Q Outwitting
R Dead end
S Duchy
T Enduring
U Famous
V Enthrone
W Reputed
X Reckoning
Y Elwood P. Dowd
Z Draw poker

61
V(ERMONT) ROYSTER
A PRIDE OF PREJUDICES

The dichotomy persists. . . . Casey Stengel, the Yankee philosopher, is barred from the fraternity of eggheads just because he garbles his grammar. And radio crooner Pat Boone dumbfounds teenagers when he graduates from Columbia University magna cum laude.

A Venerable
B Roughen
C Out of luck
D Years ago
E Shameless
F Thrashes out
G Esme
H Remind us
I Accredit
J Progging
K Rhodes
L Iceland
M Drought

N Effete
O Oyster Bay
P Foofaraw
Q Phantasm
R Rubbish
S Ephraim
T Jaundiced eye
U Untold
V Dreaming
W Instate
X Chemotherapy
Y Embarrassment
Z So Big

62
(VIRGIL) THOMSON
A VIRGIL THOMSON READER

The presence among us of Edith . . . Piaf . . . is a reminder . . . a very pleasant one, that the French chanson is an art form as traditional as the concert song. . . . Miss Piaf represents the art of the chansonniere at its most classical. . . . She is a great technician because her methods are of the simplest.

A Tartuffe
B Heloise
C Orchards
D Menton
E Sob sisters
F Offending
G Nastiest
H Affronts
I Vacate
J Irishman's heart
K Rehashing
L Gestate
M Heath

N Eastward
O Behemoth
P Rake's Progress
Q At thy window
R Sweatshop
S Steal away
T Rushmore
U Isle of Man
V Nefandous
W Gaud

O Tarmacadam
P Hearth
Q Oceana Roll
R Match
S Specify
T Ophthalmic
U Necessitates
V Recession
W Enthrone
X Amorphous
Y Decapitate
Z Ephesians
Z₁ Represents

N Lecithin

63
ERICA JONG
ANY WOMAN'S BLUES

I think of the scene last night in the bar. All the young pulchritude. . . . The difference between forty-four and twenty-two in a woman's life is not just a question of looks. I don't look worse than a twenty-two-year-old—but I know too much. I am less easily conned.

A Embellished
B Rationally
C Infinity
D Corwin
E Attention
F Jockey shorts
G Operation
H Not true
I Got funny
J Allotted
K Namesake
L Yawweed

M Whetstone
N Obsequious
O Matterhorn
P Affluent
Q Nut house
R Show-off
S Bottle
T Lowdown
U Unfinished
V Echo and a light
W Sticky wicket

64
ASHLEY MONTAGU
GROWING YOUNG

Before we became a watching society and learned to sequester ourselves from each other in the same room—the family would gather round the piano . . . and the whole family sang. No longer. Today, singing is for professionals.

A Ache
B Socialists
C Hams
D Layoff
E Eon
F Yahoo
G Marley
H One-sided
I Nice
J Traces
K Amphitheater
L Glow
M Undergrowth

N Golfers
O Resemble
P Offender
Q Withal
R In time
S Normal
T Gad
U Yeager
V Out of the question
W Underwent
X Noah's sons
Y Gaboon viper

65
BILL MAULDIN
THE BRASS RING

My parents were like France and Germany; peace for them was a pause between wars. He drank and roared; she sulked and clawed. He would threaten to blow his brains out and she would tell him it was a good idea. It was that sort of marriage.

A Bank Dick
B Infallible
C Leashed
D Leeward
E Meadow
F Arc de Triomphe
G Untoward
H Loewe
I Darwin
J Iced tea
K Narragansett
L Tuner

66
EZRA F. VOGEL
JAPAN AS NUMBER ONE

The elite bureaucrat enjoys a prestige that extends far beyond mere . . . acceptance of his authority. His family are buoyed by his status, share in his success. . . . provide him with support and recognize his extraordinary hours of work.

A Espied
B Zachariah
C Rhinestone
D Array
E Fishy
F Voracious
G Othere
H Ghetto
I Emery
J Limelight
K John the Baptist
L Artistry
M Prioress

N Abacus
O Necessary
P Aside
Q Sufi
R Noddy
S Unwary
T Mufti
U Buckets
V Eschew
W Roxie Hart
X Out of bounds
Y Nipper
Z Exacted

67
(KAMALA) MARKANDAYA
NECTAR IN A SIEVE

While the sun shines . . . and the fields are green and beautiful to the eye, and your husband sees beauty in you which no one has seen before, and you have a . . . roof over you and a sweet stirring in your body, what more can a woman ask for?

A Meathead
B Ayesha
C Ruinous
D Know
E Arduous
F Nashua
G Doff one's hat
H Athens
I Yeobright
J Anyhow
K Nearing
L Ennui

M Chiseler
N Teeny-weeny
O Afresh
P Rubbed off
Q Ironwood
R Nohow
S Arbuthnot
T Sesame seed
U In a stable
V Everyday
W Voyeur
X Elucidation

68
EDWARD T. HALL
(THE) SILENT LANGUAGE

Westerners tend to be impressed by big numbers. . . . The Japanese, however, have numbers that mean good luck, wealth, bankruptcy, and death. This fact complicates the Japanese telephone system. Good numbers bring a high price, unlucky ones are palmed off on foreigners.

A Eke out
B Defending
C Whickers
D Approbation
E Repeatedly
F Department
G The rooftops
H Hashbrowns
I Adjustment
J Levees
K Laughs off
L Scabbard
M Immelmann turn

N Lamprey
O Ejecting
P Northwest
Q The cheek
R Lesser
S Abeyance
T Nebbish
U Go-by
V Up-and-comers
W Achieve
X Gangsters
Y Euphonium

69
PETER SCHWED
HANGING IN THERE

Your security may be gone, but so is the dread of risking it . . . so why not . . . start thinking of how you're going to enjoy the rest of your life? You haven't a thing to lose and, very possibly for the first time . . . the world is your oyster.

A Panjandrum	N Nostrils		
B Eyebright	O Goo-goo eyes		
C Tryout	P In the works		
D Eyetooth	Q Nomo		
E Rossini	R Goofball		
F Stiffy	S Ironies		
G Cubit	T Nerve		
H History	U Tryst		
I Worth	V Hittite		
J Egotist	W Effuse		
K Dufy	X Rough out		
L Hawkish	Y Everyday		
M Andy Rooney			

70
(RICHARD) MITCHELL
THE GRAVES OF ACADEME

Idle chatter finds respectability . . . when it becomes Interpersonal Group Communication Methodology. Furthermore, while a course in writing needs only some paper and pencils, courses in communicology can generate some very impressive budgets.

A Might and main	N Almond
B Infusing	O Verbs
C Torrent	P Embower
D Ceremonious	Q Sweeten
E Hyssop	R Orchiectomy
F Environment	S Finite
G Lower	T Acceptance
H Limp	U Crispin
I Turbid	V Applesauce
J Hound	W Dimples
K Egregious	X Eschatology
L Guidon	Y Mersey
M Restore	Z Ecclesiolatry

71
(JACQUES) BARZUN
A WORD OR TWO BEFORE YOU GO

A language is not a mere device; it is a fund of embodied ideas, the first raw shape of poetry. Hence changes brought about by new forms and sounds in the web of its inner relations are as debatable as a piece of foreign policy or a bronze nude in a public square.

A Bouffant	O Worsen
B Audacious	P Old fashioned
C Rectitude	Q Babies
D Zephyr blows	R Entebbe
E Unfavorable	S Foeman
F Nephritic	T On the run
G Abrogate	U Rescind
H Weimar	V Effigies
I Openhanded	W Yearning
J Rancid	X Olaf I
K Decease	Y Ubiquity
L Omphalos	Z Grates
M Repeating	Z₁ Oases
N Tasso	

72
(LEO) ROSTEN
PASSIONS AND PREJUDICES

Dear friends confuse our discontent with disease and mistake simple displeasure for dark disturbance. . . . Few people have the gall to operate on your liver, but just as few show the slightest hesitancy about messing with your "unconscious."

A Riled	O Almost
B O'Shaughnessy	P Nefarious
C Suited	Q Debut
D Trust	R Pelvis
E Enfilade	S Resurrect
F Niveous	T Eisenstein
G Patch up	U John of Gaunt
H Arabia	V Unkempt
I Sweeney	W Drawbacks
J Sidh	X Igorot
K Idiot	Y Cartwheel
L Ormolu	Z Eye shadow
M Newel post	Z₁ Scotch
N Stiffs	

73
WALT KELLY
TEN (EVER-LOVIN' BLUE-EYED) YEARS WITH POGO

It's like the old question of whether or not a tree falling in the forest with no one around to hear it makes a noise. I don't understand completely, and I don't care to understand, the mechanics and physics of sound. I know that if it falls on me, I'll make a noise.

A Whisk off	N Eminence
B At the stars	O Armadillo
C Lacked	P Requisition
D Temptation	Q Shafted
E Knout	R Worthies
F Elimination	S Inclined
G Limned	T Touched off
H Litanies	U Heart and soul
I Yokels	V Parthenon
J Tenor	W On one's oath
K Edda	X Granted
L Nonsense	Y Out of this world
M Yacht	

74
CYRA MCFADDEN
RAIN OR SHINE

I was baptized as a Catholic at my own insistence. . . . I had undergone a conversion of epic proportions, complete with religious visions . . . from "The Song of Bernadette" and an inner voice announcing I was destined to be a saint.

A Callow	M Reacted
B You're the Top	N Awe-inspiring
C Raccoons	O Invitation
D Amplitude	P New wine
E Mechanic	Q Option
F Cosmic	R Reasons
G Fob off	S Stodge
H Aggressive	T Habitation
I Dido	U Innovation
J Debs	V Nastiest
K Ezra Pound	W Enshrine
L Nannies	

75
CAMILLE PAGLIA
SEXUAL PERSONAE

Paradoxically, assent to savage chthonian realities leads not to gloom but to humor . . . For life is not a tragedy but a comedy. Comedy is born of the clash between Apollo and Dionysus. Nature is always pulling the rug out from under our pompous ideals.

A Comfort	O Embassy
B Alloway	P Xanthic
C Mutt	Q Unusual
D Irish lord	R Auspicious
E Loon	S Lisle
F Laughing	T Pulchritude
G Etting	U Eustacia
H Psalter	V Roasts
I Almond tree	W Stood on
J Goober	X Over my dead body
K Loot	Y Nagy
L Inter	Z Apple of one's eye
M Adamant	Z₁ Earthbound
N Show-off	

76
MARK TWAIN
THE DAMNED HUMAN RACE

Man seems to be a rickety poor sort of a thing, any way you take him; a kind of British Museum of infirmities and inferiorities. He is always undergoing repairs. A machine that is as unreliable as he is would have no market.

A Mystifies	O Monkeys
B Apparel	P Nubia
C Kibosh	Q Embitter
D Tacky	R Diamond
E Washing	S Hookah
F Alewife	T Usher
G Infield	U Monstrous
H Nations	V Aerie
I Titi	W Nashe
J Hooves	X Runaway
K Either-or	Y Airlifts
L Damia	Z Certifies
M Augury	Z₁ Enigma
N	

77

P(AULA J.) CAPLAN
THEY SAY YOU'RE CRAZY

After all, there's so much talk about emotional problems and abnormality that many people wonder if they need help. If they don't feel particularly upset, they wonder if they may have problems they haven't recognized.

A Proffer
B Clobber
C Alekhine
D Petrillo
E Largo
F Applaud
G Now he is dead
H Tent
I Heavenly
J Entitlement
K Yeoman
L Shipmates
M Anthem
N Youthful
O Yacht basin
P Ophelia
Q Unfolded
R Revolted
S Empery
T Cowboy
U Rhythm
V Aftermath
W Zesty
X Yatter

78

(JAMES C.) NEELY, (M.D.)
GENDER (THE) MYTH OF EQUALITY

Normally, two strangers will avoid or cut short any accidental eye contact. Ordinary eye contact in conversation lasts but one or two seconds. When this gaze is intensified or prolonged it shows inordinate interest, frequently of a sexual nature.

A Nast
B Enoch Arden
C Endorsing
D Lassos
E Yearling
F Goosefoot
G Extort
H Nitty
I Drawn to
J Ersatz
K Ratios
L Mystical
M Yellow fever
N Tapioca
O Hottentots
P Over the hill
Q Frowned
R Entrance
S Queen Anne's lace
T Unicorn
U Accuracy
V Libidinous
W Intuit
X Tsarists
Y Yonder window

79

(KEVIN) NELSON
(THE) GREATEST GOLF SHOT EVER (MADE)

The function of a golf club is no different today than it was for those … sheepherders who … invented golf by hitting rocks into holes with sticks … Gussy it up as you will, golf is still basically a target game played on an improved cow pasture.

A Northampton
B Eelpout
C Lop off
D Scowl
E Outrageous
F Nightshade
G Gonif
H Rails
I Embraceable You
J Addict
K Twit
L Entails
M Swaddled
N Tipsy
O Gypsy
P Off-white
Q Lactic
R Flatten
S Sabu
T Holy Writ
U Of the Yukon
V Ti leaves
W Engrossing
X Visits
Y English horn
Z Rockfish

80

KENNETH ATCHITY
A WRITER'S TIME

The imagination functions like the feelers of an ocean-floor crustacean. As we make our way across the sea of life, the imagination helps us scout out where we're going to be before we actually go there. It's set up to do the advance work for us.

A Kennesaw Mountain
B Edna
C Negating
D Noetic
E Eerie
F The office
G Hoot owl
H Arrogate
I Trousseau
J Choose
K Haughtiest
L Ill will
M The cuff
N Yoknapatawpha
O Affect
P Wishes
Q Rode
R Insufferable
S Token
T Elevators
U Roues
V Sebaceous
W Tomorrow
X Icy
Y Mute
Z Escargot

81

RICHARD LEDERER
(THE) PLAY OF WORDS

We continue to ship goods, even when that shipping is done by truck, train, or plane. We compliment someone on "running a tight ship," even when that "ship" is an office or a classroom. And many things besides ships can be shipshape or sinking ships.

A Repentant
B Ichabod Crane
C Chemist
D Hunch
E Apophthegm
F Relapses
G Dissipate
H Lyons
I Enoch
J Dominion
K Emphasis
L Rowing
M Embosses
N Rottenstone
O Pakistan
P Lip service
Q Avon
R Yanks
S Obies
T Foppish
U Whining
V On the wing
W Running the show
X Dauphins
Y Sifting

82

RING LARDNER
A WORLD'S SERIOUS

It looks to me like as if the serious should ought to be well over by Sunday night and the little woman's new fur coat delivered to our little home some time Monday and maybe we will get invited out somewheres that night and they will be a blizzard.

A Rough out
B Intertwine
C Network
D Gandhi
E Lakewood
F Amman
G Rigidity
H Detested
I Niveous
J Eyelet
K Revival
L A thing
M Wizened
N Of the cloth
O Rialto
P Lilith
Q Dumb
R Shibboleth
S Sweetest way to me
T Emblazon
U Rolled
V Immodest
W Outlets
X Unhealthful
Y Somebody's always

83

PETER DEVRIES
PECKHAM'S MARBLES

Peckham eagerly awaited her report at home, where he was fixing beef Stroganoff for their dinner. He had always prepared many of his own meals and was now content to play chief cook and bottle washer as a small price to pay for keeping servants out of their little nest.

A Pay off
B Eyestrain
C Thorny
D Escapee
E Right-hand
F Doorway
G Epsom salt
H Vituperate
I Repelled
J Indifferent
K Effort
L Saw-whet owl
M Parsifal
N Ephod
O Cheap-o
P Know-Nothings
Q Hot water
R Axiomatic
S Mahatma
T Stranger
U Marsh hen
V Annie Oakley
W Rawboned
X Bellwether
Y Lacoste
Z Esker
Z₁ Scoffing

84

NORMAN COUSINS
HUMAN OPTIONS

A man comes to know himself through the pictures he takes. Just in the process of reviewing the hundreds of pictures I have taken over the years in many parts of the world, I learn some things about the texture of my own responses—conscious and subconscious.

A Never mind
B Operational
C Russell
D Move on
E Asafoetida
F No jesting
G Chunky
H Oxpecker
I Up in the air
J Sumter
K Incestuous sheets
L Nerves
M Scotches
N Hateth his brother
O Unheard-of
P McGrew
Q Acorn
R No whitewash
S Omit
T Prowess
U Tough it out
V In the buff
W Odyssey
X Nefast
Y Smocks

85
MIKE ROYKO
DR. KOOKIE, YOU'RE RIGHT!

Rock music. One reason nobody can understand rock lyrics, besides the deafening decibels, is that everybody is singing in some sort of southern or black drawl. You even hear English rockers howling. ''C'mawnn all you pee-puhhlll, let's git togayder.''

A Moody
B Icicles
C Kong
D Events
E Rabid
F Osric
G Youth and Art
H Knowledge
I Onerous
J Down in the dumps
K Regency
L Kills
M Oval Office
N On the board
O Knolls
P Isles
Q Enchant
R Yes, Sir
S Ocular
T Uriah Heep
U Redding
V Erratic
W Ruggles
X Incense
Y Glossy
Z Helen Brown
Z_1 That's My Baby

86
E.B. WHITE
(WRITINGS) FROM THE NEW YORKER

We need what crackpots we can muster for education in our ... world ... educators who believe that character is more precious than special knowledge, that vision is not ... just arrived at through a well-ground lens, and ... a child is the most hopeful property the Republic boasts.

A Euphuistic
B Bachelor's-button
C Watch out
D Hustings
E Impractical
F The shores of Trip-oli
G Espoused
H Fatalities
I Reject
J On a wild hunch
K Marrow
L Tapped
M Huddled
N Endeavor
O Nave
P Elephant's-ear
Q Wedged
R Young Lochinvar
S Otter shrew
T Rout
U Kowtow
V Electrical storm
W Rack one's brains

87
(HOWARD) FAST
THE BRIDGE BUILDER'S STORY

We ... went into the lounge to smoke our cigars, a habit I had inherited ... as a birthday gift from my grandfather. He had waited until I was a student at MIT before presenting me with my first box of cigars, remarking that it would at least keep me away from cigarettes.

A Flagged
B Awkward
C Steam Heat
D Two-bagger
E Teary
F Hair shirt
G Existentialism
H Best shots
I Rackets
J Imputation
K Damage
L Gaiter
M Earth Mother
N Bahadur
O Unfounded
P Immediacy
Q Legitimate
R Differ
S Emetic
T Rarity
U Skinflint
V Swing out
W The wit
X Off the bat
Y Renown
Z Yawn, or 'Pooh!'

88
PETER DEVRIES
THE PRICK OF NOON

Once my father gathered up spilled produce from an overturned truck ... and ... was mistaken for a thief ... At last he got a job as a landscape gardener in a cemetery, which he held until the day he died. Being caretaker of a cemetery is a grave responsibility.

A Photograph
B Eugene Field
C Tweed
D Emphatic
E Race
F Dada
G Erstwhile
H Venerable
I Ready
J Intriguing
K Eritrea
L Shank
M Taverns
N Hopalong Cassidy
O Eject
P Pariah
Q Rhea
R Intercede
S Charade
T Knack
U Of my mystery
V Free State
W Nibbled
X Old Faithful
Y Outcome
Z Nostradamus

89
SYDNEY (J.) HARRIS
(IN) DEFENSE OF (WORTHLESS) SLANG

No English teacher should be ''against'' slang, but only against speech that is tired, dull, and drained of vitality. The pompous and, proper, cadences of a banquet orator are a greater offense to the English tongue than any teen-ager's flip innovations.

A Schottische
B Yours truly
C Depot
D Number One
E Eelpout
F Yard-of-ale
G Hasten
H Airhead
I Robots
J Ravage
K Iraq
L Spatterdash
M Dressed up
N England to
O Fastening
P Evangeline
Q Naphtha
R Shattering
S Enable
T Openings
U Falling-out
V Sniff at
W Locate
X Antonio
Y Noetic
Z Gandhi

90
(RICHARD) ARMOUR
(THE) CLASSICS RECLASSIFIED

The Scarlet Letter ... is set in Boston, back in colonial times ... The Puritans are a gloomy lot, and by the time the reader gets to the second paragraph, in which the author dwells lovingly on jails and cemeteries, he knows this is no place to be looking for laughs.

A Atrocities
B Recalcitrant
C Malevolent
D Ottoman
E Uttar Pradesh
F Rakish
G Cheeky
H Lighten
I Apple towns
J Sleigh
K Snow job
L Italian hand
M Chesterton
N Shouted
O Reuben
P Elegy
Q Cinched
R Lobo
S Alley
T Snook
U Smothering
V Ishmael
W Freebooters
X In a tight spot
Y Eights
Z Disallow

91
WILLIAM ZINSSER
WRITING TO LEARN

English was Nabokov's fourth language, but no native-born writer of my native language dazzles me more with the precision of his imagery. ... Lolita is ... one of the most minutely observed travel books ever written about America and its tacky landscape of motels and burger huts.

A Works out
B Indefatigable
C Limping lump
D Lazarushian-leather
E Ingest
F Anchor
G Mouth off
H Zingers
I Immaculate
J Numbs
K Stowed
L Shivers
M Everett
N Rotten
O Welds
P Rocky
Q Innermost
R Tees
S If I Loved You
T Nova
U Gavotte
V The Sabbath day
W Over
X Lowboy
Y Elocution
Z Anger of men
Z_1 Rabbit ears
Z_2 Nagasaki

92
JERRY SEINFELD
SEINLANGUAGE

One of the most popular procedures today is the nose job. The technical term ... is rhinoplasty. Rhino? I mean do we really need to insult the person at this particular moment of their life? They know they have a big nose, that's why they're coming in.

A Jelly Roll Morton
B Establishment
C Rebounded
D Rattan
E Yorkshire
F Share the
G Epitaph
H Ithaca
I No way
J Foolish
K Encomiast
L Lennie
M Dish for the
N Shopworn
O Entity
P Impostor
Q Nymph
R Louche
S Arithmetic
T Natty
U Guttersnipe
V Udo
W Achieves
X Goethe
Y Eye of newt

93
CAROLYN SEE
DREAMING (HARD LUCK AND GOOD TIMES) IN AMERICA

No fancy cocktails for this crowd. Just bourbon and scotch, and water and sometimes soda. The ratio of liquor to water is about fifty-fifty. There's plenty of laughing and shouting, but nobody throws up. The whole idea is to hold your liquor.

A Chastity
B Autograph
C Ruthless
D Old fool
E Ladybug
F Yell out
G No joy
H Stood off
I Ethics
J Erskine
K Drift off
L Rowboat
M Espouse
N Anhydrous
O Mowat
P Into the woods
Q Nafud
R Gib
S Ibis
T Nadir
U Athwart
V Mirthful
W Equator
X Renown
Y Inch by inch
Z Cottoned to
Z_1 Acquits

94
BILL MOYERS
HEALING AND THE MIND

My parents talked about our friend... who "worried himself sick," and my Uncle Carl believed that laughter could ease what ailed you long before Norman Cousins published his story about how he coped with serious illness by watching Marx Brothers movies and... Candid Camera.

A Bowwows
B Imaginary
C Luckless
D Led
E Mobbed
F Out of this world
G Yerevan
H Eucalyptus
I Roundhouse
J Shipshape
K Hendrix
L Eclair
M Arrant knave
N Litchfield
O In cahoots
P Nailhead
Q Graybeard
R Ambulatory
S Norris
T Ditches
U The Shadow
V Hermes
W Embergoose
X Mimics
Y Inculcated
Z Newton
Z_1 Doubtful

95
J(ESSICA) MITFORD
(THE) AMERICAN WAY OF BIRTH

Alabama and Mississippi tend to run neck and neck in a perpetual race for which is the worst in national statistics in just about anything to do with public welfare: education, housing, mean annual income (and "mean" is the mot juste).

A Jam session
B Mobile
C Instant
D Talk about
E Fanatic
F On the phone
G Righteous
H Diminution
I Attract
J Muscle
K Ensprit
L Radical
M Impending
N Cowed
O Assurance
P Nitwit
Q Windup
R Allowance
S Yes-man
T On a junket
U Fishes
V Bunch
W Innate
X Rhoda
Y Tapa
Z Hiatus

96
(WILLARD R.) ESPY
AN ALMANAC OF WORDS AT PLAY

My brother Edwin used to say that I was so lazy I was bound to wind up as a minister. Ironically... Ed... devoted his life to religion, and Ed is one of the hardest-working men I know. But... few people are lazier than I. When I approach a revolving door, I wait for someone to give the first push.

A Element
B Suez, where the best
C Periodic
D Yea-forsooth knave
E Astride
F Novitiate
G Attitude
H Lawful
I Moot point
J Abie's Irish Rose
K Nowhere
L Astutely
M Chip in
N Of his wholesome bed
O Favor
P Wind sprint
Q Ozymandias
R Rakehell
S Downwind
T Swinging
U Ague-proof
V Toward
W Pardon
X Livid
Y Airing
Z Yahoo

97
(DAVID) DAVIES
(THE) CENTENARIANS OF THE ANDES

Most of the drink taken is a fresh form of rum, drawn off when sugar juice is being boiled;... It tastes like sweet water and looks like pale, milkless tea. However, this ferments inside the stomach in about one hour and one becomes intoxicated.

A Deep Throat
B Animation
C Vent
D Injudicious
E Emblem
F Switch
G Claw
H Esau
I New Bedford
J Tabs
K Edith
L Nether
M Ambiguous
N Rooks
O Inkhorn term
P Anklet
Q Net
R Shook off
S Oak Forest
T Fess
U Tossed
V Hearth
W Eiffel Tower
X Anorexia
Y Nemeses
Z Dislike
Z_1 Enigmatic
Z_2 Swill

98
A(NNE) MOIR, Ph.D. AND D(AVID) JESSEL
BRAIN SEX

In one study of nursery-school children many of the boys took toys apart; none of the girls did. This skill extends beyond mere destructiveness: boys were twice as fast as girls, and made half as many mistakes, in assembling jigsaws and other three-dimensional objects.

A Anonymity
B Marchbanks
C Okey-dokey
D In trust
E Riddles
F Passionate
G Hothead
H Dissemble
I Allworthy
J Nancy
K Dwindles
L Desserts
M John-o'Groat's
N Embarrasses
O Suggestive
P Stiffness
Q Elton John
R Led off
S Befitting
T Rabid
U Awesome
V Ichneumon
W Nast
X Starry-eyed
Y Essentials
Z Xochimilco

99
PETER SINGER
ANIMAL LIBERATION

Pork production is not yet dominated by huge indoor units... It is still possible to allow pigs to graze on pasture land... but the trend is toward intensive units and perhaps half of all pigs slaughtered never lived outside.

A Philistine
B Ezra Pound
C Tough
D Elaborate
E Rudest
F Shipping out
G Ill-advised
H Nippy
I Gavotte
J Edda
K Rowdies
L Andros
M Nous
N Idols
O Mongrels
P Andes
Q Lost
R Lush
S Ink Spots
T Brunt
U Rift
V Abode
W Tropical fish
X Intuit
Y Overtly
Z Newgate

100
(RICHARD) MITCHELL
LESS THAN WORDS CAN SAY

The bureaucrats who have produced most of our dismal official English will, at first, be instructed to fix it. They will try, but nihil ex nihilo. That English is the mess it is because they did it... They write that stuff because that is the kind of stuff they write.

A Mitigate
B In the buff
C Twitted
D Crutches
E Handiest
F Etiolate
G Lewisite
H Luxury
I Lottery
J Either-Or
K Stitch
L Shuffled off
M Twist
N Habits
O Ambition
P Navy
Q Whitefish
R Oilcloth
S Rubbed out
T Distasteful
U Sheepish
V Childish
W Aftermath
X Nashe
Y Sixty-four
Z Awestruck
Z_1 Yielding

101
HOWARD FAST
BEING RED—A MEMOIR

Wartime encourages neither truth nor good writing . . . the accounts of the process must be gussied up . . . to make the most lunatic of . . . institutions seem not only sane but reasonable. Tolstoy said . . . that every account of a battle is a lie, and I agree . . . War itself is a lie.

A Habitable
B Out of the blue
C Waifs
D Authority
E Rollicking
F Discount
G Footle
H Astound
I Statutes
J Tedious
K Bacchus
L Earthenware
M Impost
N Newgate
O Gracious
P Rattling
Q Eleemosynary
R Delicious
S Attentive
T Manassas
U Enforcement
V Moonshot
W Orates
X Interesting
Y Respite

102
WILLIAM ZINSSER
WRITING TO LEARN

It's astonishing how quickly . . . students can learn to write if they . . . need to compose an essay telling the admissions office why they are so desirable. All the aimlessness . . . the lazy thinking, the clogged passages—is for one shining moment made tidy. Motivation clears the head faster than a nasal spray.

A When Francis
   Dances
B In stitches
C Leatherstocking
D Lapwings
E Insanity
F All day long
G Miasma
H Zookeeper
I In the flesh
J Nathan
K Shasta
L Sides
M Eagle-eyed
N Ratty
O With Me
P Rooftops
Q Isolated
R Thomas
S If I Had You
T Nighties
U Gadfly
V Thistles
W Overcoming
X Lithe
Y Easy on the eyes
Z Assembled
Z₁ Resistant
Z₂ Norman Conquest

103
KURT VONNEGUT
(BRIEF ENCOUNTERS ON THE) INLAND WATERWAY

Women only pretend to like boats to hook a man who owns one . . . A boat to your average woman is just one more damn house to take care of, only it's more uncomfortable, and the man orders her around like Captain Bligh, and she doesn't trust the machinery or the plumbing.

A Knotty problem
B Under the gun
C Rhatany
D Teacher
E Valorous
F Ommateum
G Not so fast
H Namath
I Entries
J Geronimo
K Unities
L Too soon
M Ichabod
N Newfoundland
O Lookalike
P Anthem
Q Naphtha
R Dore
S Worms
T Amphitryon
U The Robe
V Eustace Diamonds
W Robert
X Woebegone
Y Arson
Z Yellow Jack

104
JACQUES BARZUN
SIMPLE AND DIRECT

In saying . . . that it is preferable to say nail, brad, or pin rather than thing, we were close to discussing the subject of technical words. Our civilization has required that many such words be taken into the common tongue. One cannot live or speak or write without using them.

A Jabberwocky
B Astronauts
C Cannery Row
D Quotation
E Unmitigated
F Envious
G Stock
H Blowfish
I Artists
J Rowboat
K Zorro
L Universal
M Neighs
N Sei whale
O Intuit
P Moored
Q Philanderer
R Loose
S Enigmatic
T Anne
U Nifty
V Destitute
W Dolphin
X Ipecac
Y Raises
Z Entrenchment
Z₁ Crwth
Z₂ Teach high
    thought

105
R(OBERT) L. SCHRAG
TAMING THE WILD TUBE

There are no television programs in the world today that should be given preference over holding your baby, talking to your baby, playing with your baby, or even changing your baby. People, not television screens, are the ideal companions for babies.

A Rattrap
B Leaves
C Shabby
D Creepy
E Hey, nonny nonny
F Reported
G Acharnians
H Groovy
I Topped off
J Althea Gibson
K Merriment
L Innocuous
M Nourisheth it
N Goober
O Took away
P Hobbledehoy
Q Ebullient
R Weave
S Illogical
T Lobbies
U Divers
V Trite
W Upbringing
X Borage
Y Everyday

106
GEORGE (F.) WILL
(STROM THURMOND:) THE GREAT NAY-SAYER

Thurmond's support of . . . Nixon's Southern strategy was so crucial to Nixon's . . . election that the White House was supposed to become "Uncle Strom's Cabin." But Thurmond knows an untrustworthy gang when he sees one and soon denounced Nixon's "ultraliberal advisers."

A Guns down
B Euchred out
C Overtax
D Rumble
E Goshen
F Extraction
G Windows
H Ill-founded
I Lemmon
J Lessons
K Tissot
L Hotchpotch
M Entrust
N Gossoon
O Rounds out
P Escutcheon
Q Annex
R Thews
S Nebbish
T Amphibians
U Yarrow
V Stunned
W Assertion
X Yoknapatawpha
Y Encrust
Z Russian roulette

107
E.B. WHITE
THE YEARS OF WONDER

There is a period near the beginning of every man's life when he has . . . nowhere to go but all over the place. . . . In those days, I kept a diary . . . I called it my journal; the word "journal," I felt, lent a literary and manly flavor to the thing. Diaries were what girls kept.

A Ejaculation
B Between the ears
C Walker
D Hadj
E In a big way
F Trivialities
G Everyman
H Toiled
I Horror
J Envision
K Youth-and-old-age
L Emphatically
M Arrangement
N Right and left
O Shelf
P Otter shrew
Q Frankly
R Wright
S Oliphant
T Nefarious
U Dollop
V Eyeteeth
W Replenished

108
DALTON TRUMBO
(THE) TIME OF THE TOAD

It has become an unfashionable cliche . . . that equal penalties for the rich and the poor are actually unequal, since the rich man's family eats while he is in jail and the poor man's family doesn't. We accept the inequality as a misfortune.

A Don Juan in Hell
B Arcane
C Loquacity
D Thomas Hardy
E Officially
F Nile
G Tantara
H Rematches
I U
J Mashie
K Beaten up
L Orcas
M Tapestry
N Impure
O Mechanic
P Enchants
Q Oblique
R Fit of pique
S Taine
T Half-wits
U Eaten
V The whales
W Oath
X Achilles' heel
Y Dimensions

109
N(EIL) POSTMAN
AMUSING OURSELVES (TO DEATH)

A student's freedom to read is not seriously injured by someone's banning a book on Long Island or in Anaheim or anyplace else. But . . . television or the student's freedom to read . . . it . . . does not ban books, it simply displaces them.

A Numbness
B Puns
C Open Door
D Snob
E Tomb
F Mystified
G Adjusted
H Nemesis
I Applications
J Mobile
K Untidy
L Stackable
M Whitewash
N Offshoot
O Millions
P Ashamed
Q Naphtha
R Showers
S Bobbles
T Likeliest
U Upper hand
V Ebullient
W Spilling

110
FUNNIEST VERSES OF OGDEN NASH

In this foolish world there is nothing more numerous / Than different people's senses of humorous. / And the difference between different senses of humors / Is as wide as the gap between shorts and bloomers. . . . / Humor depends on the point of view, / It's a question of what is happening to who.

A Finish
B Ushers
C Noninflammable
D No-no
E Insubordinate
F Ephedrine
G Shoot-the-chutes
H The houses
I Ventriloquism
J Effeminate
K Reese
L Soft-hearted
M Erewhon
N Sow one's wild oats
O Opprobrium
P Foofaraw
Q Offense
R Ghettoes
S Dipped its top
T Endows
U Newsprint
V Nights
W And set me down
X Suffers
Y Heigh-ho

111
IRENE SAX
LOVE TO HATE FRUITCAKE

There is a family in Michigan that owns an antique fruitcake. Every year they bring it out and put it on the table, then pack it away until the next Christmas. It's somewhere between an icon and a centerpiece, and the nice thing is that nobody ever has to eat it.

A Inattention
B Rainier
C Einstein
D Newman
E Ethnobotany
F Shaw
G Attenuant
H Xantippe
I Lien
J Ohio
K View
L Ether
M Testament
N Oath
O High-keyed
P Avid
Q Tete-beche
R Endophyte
S Fiat
T Rhumba
U Untarnished
V Incarcerate
W Toggle switch
X Chaise
Y Artsy-craftsy
Z Kit-Cat Club
Z₁ Equanimity

112
MEYER LIBEN
A NOTE ON CHIVALRY

Let us by no means forget the great middle ground of experience—the American Midwest, the Victorian novelists, Wednesday at three o'clock in the afternoon, the land lying between women's breasts, all the forgotten working hours.

A Menhir
B English are effete
C Yellow Rose
D Entr'acte
E Ripe
F Luxury
G Indent
H Blew
I Edict of Nantes
J Neglect
K Aggregated
L Newest
M Oblomov
N Theodor Mommsen
O Ethos
P Ostend
Q Net
R Cannon
S Howard Taft
T Insight
U Vathek
V Atheists
W Lured
X Rainbow
Y Yorick

113
ERICA JONG
ANY WOMAN'S BLUES

Waiting by the phone . . . has got to be of all distaff griefs the worst. It is the powerlessness, the sense of being out of control, that annihilates. Breathe on the phone. Make it jingle. Pull on the old umbilicus and make it pulse.

A Et tu, Brute
B Rooftops
C Intense
D Cheek
E Agitated
F Jetties
G Out of the night
H Nona
I Get off
J Allergies
K Notion
L Yachtsmen

114
GEORGE ELIOT
MIDDLEMARCH

Celia was not impulsive: What she had to say . . . came from her always with the same quiet, staccato evenness. . . . She never could understand how gentle, wellbred persons consented to sing and open their mouths in the ridiculous manner requisite for that vocal exercise.

A Gospel truth
B Eratosthenes
C Other-directed
D Ranch hands
E Glow-Worm
F Exultation
G Enceinte
H Leashes
I Imprecise
J Overthrust
K Towers of silence
L Midway
M Involute
N Dubuque
O Despatch
P La Chaise
Q Essay question
R Malevolent
S Ann Veronica
T Raw fish
U Chastisement
V Hand-me-downs

115
ANNE BAXTER
INTERMISSION

Nature runs around with her shoes off in Australia. Unkempt and unfettered, she's always pulling oddments out of her sock and tossing them about to see what'll happen. With that much space and so few people, she can experiment.

A Athens
B Not rash
C Newton
D Euhemerus
E Butterfingers
F Awkward Age
G Xanthippe
H Tiddlywinks
I Effluence
J Rat-a-tat-tat
K Impulses
L Nassau
M The Odd Couple
N Echo
O Raffles
P Mushmouth
Q Impost
R Snood
S Scrapple
T Innuendoes
U On the whole
V Naphtha

116
BARBARA QUICK
NORTHERN EDGE

The air is liquid and clear, like water seen through glass. As we stand there, the lavender sky breaks out into a sweat of color in three-hundred-and-sixty degrees around us. . . . The sun hovers golden and fat as an egg yolk above the horizon.

A Baffin
B Austerity
C Roughhouse
D Bewails
E Adherent
F Rotated
G Asseverate
H Quo Vadis?
I Undergrowth
J Inherent
K Console
L Kaddish
M Nashe
N Overalls
O Rostand
P The turkey
Q Headstrong
R Exhaustion
S Reynolds
T Narwhal
U Engaged
V Dickens
W Gloat
X Ezekiel

117
NORMAN W. SCHUR
ENGLISH ENGLISH

The British tip their refuse into a refuse tip. Americans dump their garbage into a garbage dump. A tip-truck is a dump truck. An American might well be mystified at the sight of a sign out in the open country reading NO TIPPING.

A Nightrider
B Obit
C Rub it in
D Mumps
E Airhead
F Niagara
G Whippet
H Sagacity
I Creating
J Hauptmann
K Upset
L Rusk
M Either-or
N Natation
O Greece
P Lite
Q Impart
R Simp
S Hit it off
T Eyesight
U Nutmegger
V Gutbucket
W Lamppost
X Indiana
Y Scoffer
Z Hidebound

118
(EDWARD) GIOBBI
ITALIAN FAMILY COOKING

I would ask the butcher in those days for bones for my dog, then I would make exquisite soup of those bones and I always had a pot steaming on the stove. It was several years before my butcher realized that I didn't have a dog.

A Gazebo
B Italia
C Odets
D Bower
E Breast-fed
F In Dutch
G Ionosphere
H Taxpayer
I Andy
J Laski
K Inquests
L Advised
M Navy blue
N Foster homes
O Aghast
P Miffed
Q Isthmus
R Lathered
S Yeomanry
T Chevalet
U Oath
V Other
W Kowtow
X Ibid
Y Nuthouse
Z Goose down

119
(Edited by Philip Handler)
BIOLOGY AND THE FUTURE OF MAN

The building blocks are nucleotides, . . . and . . . the same nucleotides are found in all known species. The genes of a man differ from those of, say, a horse only in the linear arrangements of nucleotides. . . . Despite all appearances, there is only one form of life on earth. Life need have originated only once.

A Beholden
B Inflame
C Orlop deck
D Lonely
E Of heart
F Gainsayers
G Yellow like ripe corn
H Adam's profession
I Negation
J Deafening
K Taffrail
L Handler
M Election Day
N Fantastic toe
O Usumbura
P Tips off
Q Undeserved
R Resonate
S Edam cheese
T On the loose
U French Indochina
V Mill on the Floss
W Arouse
X Nineteen eighteen

120
(SAM) LEVENSON
EVERYTHING BUT MONEY

Courageous teachers who raise their voices often end up having their loyalty questioned. Eventually they retreat to the three Rs, carefully omitting the mention of the fourth R—responsibility— personal and collective.

A Lewis
B Equality
C Vocation
D Etcher
E Niece
F Scholarly
G Outmatched
H Neither
I Effective
J Version
K Earthly
L Rather
M Yale
N Tenure
O Harvard
P Indisposition
Q Nuptial
R Genet
S Betel
T Upturn
U Thought to
V Motherly
W Others
X Noose
Y Effortless
Z Yogi

121
W. B. YEATS
A POET TO HIS BELOVED

I bring you with reverent hands / The books of my numberless dreams, / White woman that passion has worn / As the tide wears the dove-grey sands, / And with heart more old than the horn / That is brimmed from the pale fire of time: / White woman with numberless dreams, / I bring you my passionate rhyme.

A Wainwright
B Borrowed
C Yoknapatawpha
D Ethel Merman
E Amethyst
F Twister
G Somnambulist
H Arrhythmia
I Persimmon
J Out-of-the-way
K Emery boards
L Their shining nights
M The fiend
N On the way
O Humour
P I shot the albatross
Q Somme
R Befriend
S Embowered
T Lined
U Overhand smash
V Vision
W Esther Waters
X Defends

122
(THOMAS) HARRIS
THE SILENCE OF THE LAMBS

The moth was wonderful and terrible to see . . . on its wide furry back, the signature device that has struck fear in men . . . The domed skull, a skull that is both skull and face, watching from its dark eyes, the cheekbones, the zygomatic arch traced exquisitely beside the eyes.

A Hubbub
B Assessee
C Redheaded
D Runnymede
E Interest
F Swimming
G Tick-tock
H Helter-skelter
I Emaciate
J Saskatchewan
K Incaic
L Lasso
M Ersatz
N Nobility
O Chukker
P Excelsior
Q Oddity
R Fiddle-faddle
S Through the hawthorn
T Hearth
U Efface
V Lose
W Attentive
X My thoughts
Y Butterfly
Z Squawk

123
FRED LEWIS PATTEE
MARK TWAIN

Few authors are more adapted for anthology use than Mark Twain. His works, even his novels, are patchwork creations. His very lack of unity is his salvation. As a whole he is tedious stuff, but injudiciously chosen selections he is glorious.

A Furnished
B Ratification
C Enough
D Drooly
E Loves
F Eschars
G Wehrmacht
H Isodose
I Suspicious
J Phone
K Anyhow
L Taffy
M Trestlework
N Evasive
O Eucharist
P Mat
Q Assailing
R Roustabout
S Kersey
T Trashiness
U Who killed John Keats?
V Avow
W In-house
X Nullification

124
(JOHN) IRVING
A PRAYER FOR OWEN MEANY

Taking a seat in my grandmother's living room was never easy, because many of the available seats were not for sitting in—they were antiques, which my grandmother was preserving, for historical reasons; sitting in them was not good for them.

A Inhibitions
B Rooks
C Vanquish
D Immaculate
E Niches
F Gnawing
G Avowal
H Peony
I Rostov
J Ambergris
K Yachting
L Estrange
M Rattles on
N Fastens
O Otter shrew
P Referees
Q Oliver Hardy
R Whitman
S Emmet
T Noggin
U Mastiff
V Eastward Hoe
W Airtight
X New Moon
Y Yesterdays

125

**(WOODY) ALLEN:
THE (GREAT) COLORIZATION DEBATE**

If audiences who have grown up on mindless television were so desensitized that a movie like "It Happened One Night" . . . had to be viewed in color to be appreciated – then the task would be to cultivate the audience back to some level of maturity rather than to doctor the film.

A	Achilles' heel	N	Impetuous
B	Leaded	O	Zwieback
C	Leviticus	P	Anything Goes
D	Effluvium	Q	Teeter-totter
E	Netted	R	Immediate
F	The Dane	S	Out of whack
G	Hearth	T	Ninnies
H	Echo stop	U	Donated
I	Chow down	V	Embroider
J	Odds-on	W	Browbeat
K	Levitation	X	Appreciation
L	Oshkosh	Y	Titivate
M	Revolve	Z	Elephant

126

**B(ENJAMIN) NETANYAHU:
(TERRORISM) HOW THE WEST CAN WIN**

The terrorist is the self-appointed arbiter of what is just and necessary. If others do not quite see it that way, they will be forced to submit to the terrorist's will by a fearful violence that claims everyone as a legitimate target.

A	Bitters	N	Titular
B	Notables	O	Heartily
C	Toques	P	Eerily
D	Affective	Q	Wombat
E	Noodle	R	Ethos
F	Yeast	S	Sophomoric
G	Abjectly	T	Traipse
H	Hoisted	U	Calumets
I	Uttered	V	Affright
J	Horsehide	W	Nitwit
K	Overhang	X	Waffles
L	Wastrel	Y	Irritate
M		Z	Nastiest

127

**(DEAN) ACHESON:
PRESENT AT THE CREATION**

As in the case of Castlereagh and Metternich, a distinction was made between a nation and its leaders. As France was restored to an honored and responsible place in the earlier period, the same was done with Germany and Japan in the later one.

A	Arabian	O	Aeneas
B	Connotation	P	Twaddle
C	Henley	Q	Thwarts
D	Entente	R	Haw-Haw
E	Spooner	S	Enjoined
F	Offhanded	T	Catches
G	Nattiest	U	Remember
H	Pedestrians	V	Empirical
I	Roasted	W	Angels
J	Echidna	X	Tail end
K	Shawnees	Y	Imperial
L	Erase	Z	Oasis
M	Nodding	Z_1	Narrator
N	Tace		

128

**ALISTAIR COOKE:
THE AMERICANS**

When Britain really ruled the waves, in good King George V's glorious reign, . . . the Foreign Office . . . felt no call to bandy debating points with the press. The Foreign Office distributed handouts, no questions asked. It did not justify its policies. It announced them.

A	Apostrophe	N	Tootsie
B	Luftwaffe	O	Harquebus
C	Ivory Coast	P	Eights
D	Sighted	Q	Affenpinscher
E	Third World	R	Mafeking
F	Avignon	S	Engine
G	Ignoble	T	Redoubt
H	Rebutted	U	Illusionist
I	Chitterling	V	Conjunction
J	Offended	W	Agonistes
K	Otiose	X	Nineties
L	Katydid	Y	Slightly
M	Eiderdown		

**(LUDWIG) BEMELMANS:
FATHER, DEAR FATHER**

An emaciated, hatless man . . . held the lapels of his coat closed. Snowflakes stuck to his eyelids. . . . "Poppy," Barbara said earnestly after staring at him a long time, "I wonder, if Christ came back to earth, could he get a table at Twenty-One?"

A	Bowie	N	Eyewash
B	Enchiridion	O	Rattled
C	Mystic	P	Damask
D	Ecclesia	Q	Entrechat
E	Looped	R	Alhambra
F	Malmsey	S	Rapacity
G	Attacks	T	Floats
H	Newest	U	Attendant
I	Stafford	V	Tendentious
J	Folio	W	High-hat
K	Appaloosa	X	Eggshell
L	Tiles	Y	Rubberneck
M	Heats		

**LETTY (COTTIN) POGREBIN:
(HOW TO MAKE IT IN) A MAN'S WORLD**

In business you can switch trains mid-journey and never get derailed. You may start as a receptionist, move into the art department and end up as something crazily unrelated – like sales manager for the entire West Coast territory or the wife of the chairman of the board.

A	Lady Macbeth	M	Nutrition
B	Epsom Downs	N	Also-rans
C	Transistorized	O	Myriad
D	Tooth fairy	P	Ammunition
E	Young and Gay	Q	Niven
F	Patent Office	R	Sturdier
G	Our Hearts Were	S	Witchetty
H	Grenade	T	Orthoptera
I	Rajah	U	Rarefied
J	Ecclesiastes	V	Let them eat
K	Bunnies		cake
L	Irrelevant	W	Demosthenes

**(B.A.) BOTKIN:
NEW ENGLAND FOLKLORE**

There is a terrible pink mixture (with tomatoes in it, and herbs) called Manhattan Clam Chowder, that is only a vegetable soup, and not to be confused with New England Clam Chowder, nor spoken of in the same breath. Tomatoes and clams have no more affinity than ice cream and horse radish.

A	Brunhild	M	Lancashire hearth
B	Overshadow	N	Abecedarian
C	These fences	O	Nomothetic
D	Knight-errant	P	Defamed
E	Iconoclast	Q	Fifth wheel
F	Nosophobia	R	Ombudsman
G	Nestorianism	S	Lament
H	Evaporated	T	Knotty rhatany
I	Witwatersrand	U	Lomax
J	Epictetus	V	On hand
K	Niche	W	Roams
L	Golden wattle	X	Emblematic

**CYNTHIA HEIMEL:
SEX TIPS FOR GIRLS**

A date in Los Angeles often entails sushi bars. A date in Texas means crossing the border into Mexico and . . . later remembering nothing. A date in Philadelphia means falling asleep in front of the TV together. A date in San Francisco means wondering if your date has had a sex change.

A	Canons	O	Endangered
B	Yard-of-ale	P	Xanthin
C	Natural law	Q	Tosses
D	Terrified	R	Imbalance
E	Handiest	S	Paradoxes
F	Inhabitant	T	Scenario
G	Amanuensis	U	Fiends
H	Hedge	V	Orthogonal
I	Expatriate	W	Right hand
J	Indeterminate	X	Gesso
K	Magician	Y	In the flesh
L	Escape	Z	Rambling
M	Leave	Z_1	Long shot
N	Smote	Z_2	Sent off

133
MICKEY FRIEDMAN: THE FAULT TREE

In the early seventies, there were dozens of Indian saints, . . . yogis, bodhisattvas, Sufis, dervishes, you name it running around San Francisco and Berkeley establishing ashrams, temples, . . . giving lectures, classes, ... Everybody was seeking the Way and the Path.

A Mannerly
B Impressionable
C Cuba stout
D Knives
E Etherized
F Youth-and-old-
   age
G Frights
H Ridings
I Issuance
J Eagle-eyed
K Disadvantage
L Manning
M Assays
N Ninny
O Trashy
P Hock
Q Essenes
R Firsts
S Arrested
T Unenviable
U Liverish
V Twins
W The bow
X Ray of hope
Y Eschews
Z Estivates

134
TOM WOLFE: THE RIGHT STUFF

Perhaps that was what New York existed for, to celebrate those who had it, whatever it was, and there was nothing like the right stuff, for all responded to it, and all wanted to be near it and to feel the sizzle and to blink in the light. Oh, it was a primitive and profound thing!

A Two walk together
B Outfitting
C Mission control
D Will-o'-the-wisp
E Openhanded
F Lord Haw-Haw
G Firewater
H Exhibition
I Tenderizes
J Hard-Hearted
   Hannah
K Edwards
L Rabbity
M Invoke the fifth
N Galvanized
O Hottentot
P Take the "A"
   Train
Q Shallow
R The staple
S Upstanding
T Festered
U Flattops

135
ABRAHAM LINCOLN: AUTOBIOGRAPHY

If any personal description of me is thought desirable . . . I am, in height, six feet four inches; . . . lean in flesh, weighing on an average one hundred and eighty pounds; dark complexion, with coarse black hair and gray eyes. No other marks or brands recollected.

A Adhesive
B Boardwalk
C Rhodope
D Anachronism
E Hypotheses
F Andirons
G Mixologist
H Lingered
I Infringe
J Nightingale
K Charmed
L Off and on
M Lexicon
N Neuroses
O Achy
P Untied
Q Throng
R Obelisk
S Brawler
T Impunity
U Offered
V Garlic
W Rhea
X Accented
Y Parentheses
Z Haiku
Z₁ Yeast

136
MERLE MILLER: PLAIN SPEAKING

To . . . President Truman history was the men who made it, and he spoke of Marcus Aurelius or Henry of Navarre or old Tom Jefferson or old Andy Jackson as if they were friends and neighbors with whom he had only recently discussed the affairs of the day.

A Majority
B Echinoderm
C Raw fish
D Laydown
E Estuary
F Motherhood
G Infested
H Leathernecks
I Left-handed
J Everywhere
K Rhinoceros
L Projects
M Loaded
N Authority
O Isherwood
P Narrowness
Q Shuffleboard
R Payoffs
S Enthusiasm
T Affords
U Kant
V Intend
W Noah
X Gymnasium

137
(HOWARD) FAST: THE JEWS—STORY OF A PEOPLE

Yahweh was a . . . loving god. If he equated the universe with universal justice, it was inconceivable that he should love or honor war . . . to think that he used armies for his purpose was folly. Such was the preaching of the prophet Habakkuk.

A Forward view
B Acquisitive
C Sheiks
D Ticking
E The Thaw
F Hangdog
G Evanesce
H Jephthah
I Euphues
J Worthiest
K Swinburne
L Sketched
M To show
N Orlando
O Refresh
P Youthful
Q Ohthere
R Fallow
S Akimbo
T Panache
U Earthy
V Outhaul
W Privation
X Lavish
Y Espousal

138
BURPEE SEEDS (AND EVERYTHING FOR THE GARDEN): EARTHWORMS

Earthworms create channels around plant roots which improve soil structure and make it easy for roots to reach the minerals and moisture in the subsoil. Their castings in the soil provide ideal plant root food and when the gardener decides to go fishing his bait is ready.

A Birthright
B Under the Lilacs
C Raining
   pitchforks
D Pincushion
E Embattled farm-
   ers
F Echo and Narcis-
   sus
G Seeded
H Erle Stanley Gard-
   ner
I Eschalots
J Dogtooth violet
K Switch
L Elihu Root
M Aeration
N Rose fruit
O Topiaries
P Hoedown
Q Withe
R Onion domes
S Rotation
T Martha's Vine-
   yard
U Sam Spade

139
COLIN SIMPSON: THE LUSITANIA

Prior to the sailing, threatening statements were published in the American press, foretelling the sinking of the liner . . . making it plain that the intention to commit it was deliberately formed, and the crime itself planned, before the ship sailed.

A Coffin
B Okhotsk
C Ladder stitches
D Inferior
E Needy
F Swing Time
G Imminent
H Mandible
I Persephone
J Street Arab
K O'Higgins
L Nattered
M Tenet
N Healths
O Element
P Lattermost
Q Ulithi
R Sennacherib
S Implosion
T Treating
U At Philippi then
V New Deal
W Illiterate
X Affright

140
RICHARD MITCHELL: (THE) GIFT OF FIRE

Epictetus put it . . . that philosophy . . . was bounded by the skin. It had no power over the world. It could bring about tremendous changes, but only inside. . . . It is not for the persuasion of others that one studies to be better, but for the sake of being better.

A Rattletrap
B In short
C Cubbyhole
D Hoihow
E Attenborough
F Retribution
G Dubious
H Mobbed
I In the works
J Tightwad
K Cusp
L Hophead
M Entebbe
N Lookout
O Lets up
P Godspeed
Q Itty-bitty
R Fondest
S The front
T Oases
U Festive
V Fussed
W Incantation
X Rittenhouse
Y Enterprise

141
(JIM) TRELEASE
THE (NEW) READ-ALOUD HANDBOOK

If a plastic box in your living room can turn your child on to breakfast cereal or talking teddy bears, then you should be able to do ten times as much—because you are a sensitive, intelligent, and loving human being. (They've yet to invent the television or VCR that can hug a child.)

A Talent
B Rhone
C Earth almond
D Logical
E Entreaty
F Attraction
G Subtlety
H Engelbert
I Touchy
J Humperdinck
K Excavation
L Rabble in Arms
M Embellish
N Avaricious
O Donne
P Accident
Q Loosing
R Overactive
S Unsuited
T Diving
U Hugo
V Authority
W Naughty
X Devious
Y Bovine
Z Of the flesh
Z₁ Ostensibly
Z₂ Kenya

142
ROBERT ARDREY
AFRICAN GENESIS

We are a transitional species, without doubt. We are a pioneer creature testing the potentialities of the enlarged brain. The first species to be blessed by such a mutational marvel, we must be forgiven if sometimes we use it badly.

A Restful
B Otranto
C Bible belt
D Estimate
E Richelieu
F Twittery
G Aweather
H Reeve's Tale
I Dust-bin
J Rant
K Esteem
L Yoshida
M Auster
N Filament
O Rib cage
P Insight
Q Compost
R Amadis
S Novalis
T Goucher
U Etouffé
V Nipponese
W Epeios
X Sweeten
Y Iturbide
Z Sawbwa

143
WILLIAM F. ALLMAN
STAYING ALIVE (IN THE 20TH CENTURY)

A feeling of control can actually make a risky technology even more dangerous. That's because we often have inflated opinions of ourselves. We consider ourselves above-average drivers, more careful than most when using appliances and power tools. … Such overconfidence is dangerous.

A Wakeners
B It Can't Happen Here
C Leftover
D Loosens
E Inwardness
F Alcoholics
G Michaelmas Day
H Foreknowledge
I Accuracies
J London tuft
K Logographers
L Maccaboy
M Affective
N Neuroses
O Sever
P Thunderous
Q Afford
R Yaupon
S Imagination
T Newness
U Gloved
V Average
W Leverets
X Innocuous
Y Verbose
Z Evolution

144
W(ILLIAM) MANCHESTER
AMERICAN CAESAR

MacArthur was like Julius Caesar: bold, aloof, austere, egotistical, willful. The two generals surrounded themselves with servile aides-decamp: remained long abroad, one as proconsul and the other as shogun, leading captive peoples in unparalleled growth.

A Well-dressed
B Mapped out
C Anguished
D Nameless
E Catfacing
F He who refuses
G Ellsworth
H Scouts
I Tongues
J Ends up with
K Rajah
L All over
M Mistook
N Edouard
O Rough-hew
P Indelible
Q Calling on
R Appurtenant
S Noodle
T Casimir-Perier
U Australia
V Elevated
W Scagliola
X Arable
Y Revolt

145
HOWARD GARDNER
CREATING MINDS

Only in the past century … have artists, writers, and other creative persons shown … interest in the symbolic products of young children. … Einstein once declared that we know all the physics that we will ever need. … by the age of three.

A Helen of Troy
B Oaths
C Willy-nilly
D Akron, Ohio
E Recherche
F Dives
G Gulches
H Attic
I Rotten
J Dependent
K Nene
L Enthusiast
M Retrieves
N Cesta
O Rowdydow
P Earth
Q Albanese
R Two-bit
S Icily
T Newport News
U Gutta-percha
V Myths
W Infers
X Nerve
Y Depths
Z Snitch

146
EDWARD PHILLIPS
SUNDAY'S CHILD

It was that kind of party, full of people … Hummus turned down by the Canada Council. Hummus and guacamole and about five different colours of wine. Also sangria. It made one long for the days when one washed down onion soup and sour cream dips with rye and ginger ale.

A Edition
B Dandelion
C Warrens
D Attenuate
E Raggedy Anne
F Downspout
G Photon
H Humpback
I Indecorous
J Lift-off
K Locomotive
L Idealist
M Puffin
N Snow blower
O Samoyed
P Unanimously
Q Newfoundland
R Decoder
S Afghan
T Yarrow
U Scalawag
V Chartered
W Haifa
X Isthmus
Y Lounge
Z Daphne

147
CANDICE BERGEN
KNOCK WOOD

While we dated fourteen-year-old boys in white bucks and braces, making out in parking lots, angora fluff rising from our sweaters, we dreamed of screen stars of the moment. Invariably, for me, it was the tall blond blue-eyed ones, Aryan icons in khakis and crewnecks.

A Carries away
B Arriviste
C Numbers game
D Distaff side
E Interminably
F Commonwealth
G Endymion
H Band of brothers
I Ebb and flow
J Rakehells
K Grandiosity
L Egregiously
M Neater
N Krill
O Newspeak
P Ostentation
Q Chaffinches
R Knuckles down
S Weakens
T Out of funds
U Outerwear
V Draco

148
ROY BLOUNT
NOW, WHERE WERE WE?

I tend to pronate. I learned that from the salesman at Urban Hiker while trying on shoes. Pronating means turning your ankles in. That doesn't mean I need a special pronater's shoe. It just means I was sold shoes by someone who wasn't afraid to get into biomechanics.

A Raptor
B On one's high horse
C Yacka Hula Hickey Dula
D Bigamists
E Lambda
F Ordinary
G Up to no good
H No-man's-land
I Tantamount
J Nastiness
K Oat bran
L Weariest
M Witherspoon
N Hessian
O Estate
P Replete
Q Enmeshes
R Withstood
S Efficient
T Remiss
U Entertaining
V Walter Johnson
W Eminent

149
ALICE KAHN
THE BRIE GENERATION

A superficial impression ... might lead one to believe that the majority of readers in this country are preschool children, gay communists, or lobotomized housewives. At least, these seem to emerge as the big markets, judging from the number of titles being pitched to them.

A Affright the air
B Lighter
C Insightful
D Cobblestones
E Emboss
F Kermiss
G At Agincourt
H Hammer and tongs
I Nutmeg
J The ropes
K Horsehide
L Evocative
M Moralitee
N Rattlepate
O Implicit
P Enzymes
Q Good times
R Eyeful
S Nobody
T Easier
U Rejoice
V Ashamed
W The jitters
X Immersed
Y Outcome
Z Nephrolith

150
WILFRID SHEED
CLARE BOOTHE LUCE

"She was the best of dames, she was the worst of dames," my father suggested as an opener for this book. Just about everything I've read about Clare Boothe Luce so far has taken one view or the other, painting her as either an angel or a dragon lady.

(From Kahn: *My Life as a Gal*)

A Waste not, want not
B Iffy
C Loathes
D Fokker
E Rajah
F Inertia
G Dinosaurs
H Serendipity
I Hash
J Engages
K Eggy
L Doted
M Cuff
N Lasso
O Alabama
P Ragout
Q Evasive
R Behemoth
S Overwrote
T Others
U The stars are
V Hobbes
W Ephod
X Lowers
Y Underneath the bough
Z Cameo
Z₁ Earnest

151
ANONYMOUS
LIFE OF A TUGBOAT

I push, I pull— / I pant and chug— / I'm nothing but / A dirty tug. // I back and fill, / And turn and wheel— / And sometimes tip / Right off my keel. // But gently, gently / With little din, / I coax the bulgy / Ocean liners in. // A toot of my whistle, / A ring of my bell— / And I'm off like a regular / What-the-hell!

A At long last
B Night latch
C Other half
D Nils
E Yellow plum
F Millionth
G Officiant
H Underling
I Syllabify
J Lily-white
K Itty-bitty
L Fudge edge
M Egyptian gum
N Outside right
O From hand to hand
P American snow-ball
Q Tax in kind
R Unmindful
S Ghurkha
T Backbiter
U Outweep
V Ailment
W Teepee

152
ANDREW WEIL
THE NATURAL MIND

The history of science makes clear that the greatest advancements in man's understanding of the universe are made by intuitive leaps at the frontiers of knowledge, not by intellectual walks along well-traveled paths.

A Affective
B Nightingale
C Deftly
D Rapscallion
E Edo
F Wast Water
G Whacking
H Eventual
I Imminent
J Labyrinth
K Tones
L Hofstadter
M Esplanade
N Novelette
O Averts
P Throttle
Q Unrest
R Rakish
S Amassed
T Lather
U Mouse
V Ignoble
W Netsuke
X Decency

153
K(ENDALL) HAILEY
(THE DAY) I BECAME AN AUTODIDACT

I feel so emotional about Halloween. ... it's the one holiday that really changes as you grow up. No matter how old you get there'll always be Thanksgiving and Christmas presents and Valentines ... and Easter eggs ... but I'll never be a trick-or-treater again.

A Knock on Wood
B Hightail
C Alligator
D Into thy depths
E Leaves
F Elementary
G Yellow-belly
H Insolent
I Braes
J Erroneous
K Chasuble
L Angola
M Moralitee
N Essen
O Ashtabula
P Narrator
Q Avenger
R Unfit
S The sight
T Overeats
U Dawes
V Innings
W Dwight
X Amputate
Y Cadge
Z Treaty

154
(JOHN) KEEGAN
THE MASK OF COMMAND

The leader of men in warfare can show himself to his followers only through a mask, a mask that he must make for himself, but a mask made in such form as will mark him to men of his time and place as the leader they want and need.

A Khartoum
B Elsewhere
C Emanates
D Ghats
E Amethyst
F Nethermost
G Taffrail
H Half hams
I Embalm
J Monochrome
K Astrakhan
L Shame
M Kaffee klatsch
N Onion field
O Fossil
P Chiliasm
Q Ohio printer
R Mantua
S Misled
T Awkward
U Newly hewed
V Dumfound

155
THOMAS O'DONNELL
ON SARATOGA

Unlike Atlantic City, ... the town has retained its nineteenth century atmosphere. "Saratoga hasn't had a facelifting," says one frequent returnee. "She's like a successful madam. Proud of her sometimes notorious past and sure of her aging beauty."

A Territory
B Hatteras
C Occurrence
D Mastery
E Authenticity
F Saffard
G Ouphe
H Desists
I Oranges
J Newman
K Nauseate
L Equanimity
M Lohengrin
N Leashes
O Ophthalmologist
P Neutralise
Q Suffuse
R Affected
S Redoubt
T Ankh
U Temptation
V On the sand
W Genius
X Askance

156
WILFRID SHEED
THE GOOD WORD

At Madison Square Garden ... Kerouac read a poem to Harpo Marx ... "Harpo, I'll always love you / ... Oh, when last you powder-puffed your white face with a fish-barrel cover / Harpo, who is that lion I saw you with?" ... It was ... political man staring blankly at gypsy moth, each with half of his brain missing.

A Wistfully
B Infant phenome-non
C Looking up to
D Flew away
E Raw data
F Iberia
G Drowns the par-son's saw
H Showa
I Hollyhock
J Eerily
K Euphoria
L Disputatious
M This slave's offal
N Horse Feathers
O Excalibur
P Gravy train
Q Omophagia
R Obloquy
S Diagrammatic
T Whirlaway
U Oom-pah-pah
V Rhythmic
W Ditchwater

157
DANIEL DEFOE
MOLL FLANDERS

After ... five weeks I grew better, but was so weak, so melancholy, and recovered so slowly, that the physicians ... gave it as their opinion that my mind was oppressed, that something troubled me, and, in short, that I was in love.

A Dewy-eyed
B Aghast
C Ninotchka
D Inchoate
E Enthusiast
F Lewisite
G Dimity
H Esther Waters
I Foists
J Old Harry
K Evoe
L Moment
M Orphic
N Laps up
O Levite
P Fattest
Q Lovable
R Arrowsmith
S Negative
T Draws the long-
   bow
U Eastward Hoe
V Romps
W Skin and bones

158
(JOHN) CROMPTON
THE LIFE OF THE SPIDER

I have seen members of the Matabele tribe roasting and eating dishes of spiders. I pitied them at the time, thinking it indicated starvation, but I have changed my mind since. ... The time may come when spiders, like oysters, are one of our most expensive and fashionable dishes.

A Curds
B Ricardo Palma
C Out-Herod
D Met the enemy
E Parlor
F Testified
G Ossian
H Newsmen
I The Metamor-
   phosis
J Hives
K Engadine
L Lightheaded
M Initiative
N Fabre
O East Indies
P Oftentimes
Q Feminists
R Thanksgiving
S Hobby
T Ebb Tide
U Stichomythia
V Pensive
W Ike
X Death and taxes
Y Eminence
Z Ramose

159
THE RANDOM HOUSE DICTIONARY
(OF THE ENGLISH LANGUAGE)

J, the tenth letter of the English alphabet, developed as a variant form of I in Medieval Latin, and, except for the preference for the J as an initial letter, the two were used interchangeably, both serving to represent the vowel (i) and the consonant (y).

A Tattletale
B Hottentot
C Epping Forest
D Reefer
E Archbishop
F Newari
G Dejected
H Off-center
I Majorette
J Heath
K Old Wives' Tale
L Umteenth
M Syrinx
N Even-steven
O Daphne
P Inapt
Q Caboshed
R There Shall Be No
   Night
S Itinerate
T Offend
U Nairn
V Aaron
W Revival
X Yellow light

160
(JEAN) MALAURIE
THE LAST KINGS OF THULE

When adventure does not come to him, the Eskimo goes in search of it. ... A group ... taken aboard [Peary's] ship left it ... because they found ... its comforts upsetting. ... How can life be worth living if it offers no surprises, no adventures?

A Montespan
B Afford
C Lvov
D Adherent
E Ugsome
F Rapt
G Ivory tower
H Eosin
I Toupee
J Hoosier
K Erubescent
L Lynch
M Abacus
N Stowed
O Tooth
P Keswick
Q Initiates
R Night off
S Grampians
T Stuff
U Oenone
V Finds
W Thief
X Hired
Y Umber
Z Logistics
Z₁ Euphrates

161
(RICHARD) MITCHELL:
(THE) LEANING TOWER OF BABEL

The ... schools have one supreme, if unintended, virtue. They are such chaotic and Byzantine bureaucracies, ruled over by herds of inept and dull-witted functionaries, that some good teachers ... can often go undetected for years.

A Marzipan
B Inherent
C Tocsin
D Ceded
E Hideous
F Enhanced
G Love Nest
H Laced
I Loft
J Euchre
K Anchored
L Naysayer
M Inch by inch
N Nauseate
O Greece
P Taos
Q Overdone
R Witty
S Entrust
T Rufus
U Out of favor
V Fruits
W Booted
X Aghast
Y Butted
Z Ephemerid
Z₁ Lucid

162
M(ARK) TWAIN
THE DIARIES OF ADAM AND EVE

After all these years, I see that I was mistaken about Eve in the beginning; it is better to live outside the Garden with her than inside it without her. At first I thought she talked too much; but now I should be sorry to have that voice fall silent and pass out of my life.

A Malicious
B To every thing
C Wordsworth
D Attitude
E Inglenook
F Navigate
G There is a season
H Highfalutin
I Ethiop's
J Dubious
K In toto
L Attenuate
M Rhine
N Irate
O Elbert
P Sashimi
Q Off-white
R Febrile
S Athwart
T Dobby
U At the still
V Makeshift
W Adhesive
X Nuts
Y Dottles
Z Ethyl
Z₁ Vetch
Z₂ Enthuse

163
SUSAN ISAACS
SHINING THROUGH

Unless you were a sauerkraut tycoon there was no reason to like Hebel's. It was one of those phony gemütlichkeit places ... where waiters from Saxony ran around in Bavarian lederhosen. Their pale fat thighs looked like bratwurst.

A Skunkweed
B Ullapool
C Skokie
D At fault
E Narthex
F Icelander
G See It Now
H Amnesia
I Arrowroot
J Catastrophe
K Swarthy
L Swinburne
M Has-been
N Iolite
O Nestle
P Infests
Q Neb
R Gus Kahn
S To Sir With Love
T Hoofer
U Rhea
V Orrery
W Ulmaceous
X Gaea
Y Hydrophyte

164
DANIEL (T.) RODGERS:
CONTESTED TRUTHS

Church membership boomed in both Britain and the United States in the late eighteenth and early nineteenth centuries; ... reformers crisscrossed the Atlantic as ... church-going citizens grasped for the levers of politics at the front of assaults on slavery, prostitution ... and drunkenness.

A Dross
B Affectation
C Nebbish
D Impolitic
E Enterprising
F Louts
G Relentlessly
H Overbearing
I Don
J Gapes
K Estivate
L Riches
M Stringent
N Creche
O Oaths of office
P Ninotchka
Q Tundra
R Enchiridion
S Strumpeted
T Tubs
U Enthusiastic
V Death's-head
W Trysts
X Ranchers
Y Underneath
Z The Harlem
   Moon
Z₁ Hazel-nut
Z₂ Stentor

165
(JAMES) VILLAS
(THE) FRENCH COUNTRY KITCHEN

Alas, it's not true that all French country wines are charming and eminently drinkable; I've gulped my share of plonk over the years and wondered how my French tablemates had managed to survive so long without radical intestinal surgery.

A Valhalla
B Illusionary
C Luddite
D Larded
E Approach
F Strutted
G Frown
H Redolent
I Enlighten
J Nagurski
K Combat
L Heave-ho
M Crafty
N On the ball
O Unnerving
P Nose
Q Torrid
R Referred
S Yachtsman
T Knaves
U Immensity
V Towering
W Castaway
X Hedonism
Y Eyewash
Z Nutmeg

166
DAVID MCCULLOUGH
TRUMAN

As much as any president since Lincoln, he brought to the highest office the language and values of the common American people. He held to the old guidelines: work hard, do your best, speak the truth, assume no airs, trust in God, have no fear.

(In Memoriam John Edward Muhs)

A Dragonfly
B Awful
C Votress
D Inattention
E Dovetailed
F Misanthrope
G Cacophony
H Cottage cheese
I Unhorse
J Left-handed
K Leatherette
L Of manners
M Umbrage
N Garrulous
O Hitchhikes
P Thebes
Q Roughhoused
R Unlikelihood
S Mishmash
T Appendices
U Nougat

167
FRANK GRAHAM
CASEY STENGEL

Casey made his return to Brooklyn a memorable one. As he was about to step into the batter's box, Stengel turned and doffed his cap to the crowd. It was a spectacular gesture. A sparrow darted out of the cap and flew away over the infield.

A Fastidious
B Rationality
C Attractive
D Nomenclature
E Know-how
F Gawain
G Rubber plant
H Awesomeness
I Housecoat
J A peach
K Matted
L Crass
M Abbotsford
N Serrated
O Etched
P Yesterday
Q Snaffle
R To draw the bow
S Ephod
T North
U Guadeloupe
V Exported
W Left

168
WILL DURANT
CAESAR AND CHRIST

The Etruscans are among the irritating obscurities of history. They ruled Rome for a hundred years or more, and left ... so varied an influence that Rome can hardly be understood without them; yet Roman literature is as mute concerning them as a matron anxious to forget, publicly, the surrenders of her youth.

A Whets
B Inert
C Lyme
D Life of Riley
E Dromedary
F Unfasten
G Resonant
H Arnhem
I Nothing But the Truth
J The House of Atreus
K Categorical Imperative
L Assiduously
M Exhortation
N Soft-hearted
O Autocracy
P Romney
Q And threescore
R Northumberland
S Dudgeon
T Coriolanus
U Harbinger
V Rifts
W Intermediary
X Structure
Y Thomas Moore

169
(RICHARD) ARMOUR:
A SHORT HISTORY OF SEX

Louis XV, who came to the throne when he was only five ... was not at once given a mistress. "Play with these. ...," he was told, and for several years he had to get his kicks by pulling up the dresses of dolls and manikins ... to look at their fanikins.

A Awkward
B Recklessly
C Misfits
D On hand
E Unchaste
F Reawaken
G Atones
H Svelte
I Hovels
J Oilcloth
K Reeking tube
L Twists
M Healths
N Invidious
O Serenity
P Totters
Q Omphaloid
R Ran down
S Yataghan
T Oliphant
U Fishwives
V Shook off
W Enmeshed
X Xylophage

170
THORNTON WILDER
THEORY OF LIFE

I erase as I go along. I look forward so much I have only an imperfect memory for the past. When your eyes are directed to the future, you have no hurt feelings over the praise or criticism of the moment because moment by moment the present becomes the past.
From *The Los Angeles Times*, Dec. 8, 1975

A Termagants
B Hoorah's nest
C Obeah
D Repartee
E No motion
F Tergiversate
G Osteophyte
H Nose
I Wombat
J Impromptu
K Lecher
L Defamation
M Eschew
N Rhyme
O Thaumaturgy
P Hymenoptera
Q Embryonic
R Oeuvre
S Rockfish
T Yeti
U Odds
V Feuilleton
W Lurches
X Immense
Y Ferocious
Z Effective

171
J(AMES) A. MICHENER
THE FLOATING WORLD

Hokusai ... ran back and forth across the huge paper, outlining a portrait of Japan's best-loved saint, Daruma, who once sat so long in one position contemplating the nature of world and man that his arms withered away ... By dusk the portrait had taken form ... Daruma nearly sixty feet high.

A Jupiter
B Awkward
C Mein
D Inaugurated
E Cabaletta
F Humpty Dumpty
G Ensign
H Nights in the
I Exophthalmos
J Rat snake
K Tattoo
L Handout
M Effort
N Fafner
O Lookers
P Orchestra
Q And bay the moon
R Thirst
S Isaac Nathan
T Nabatea
U Gardens of Spain
V Work horse
W Oliphant
X Rhinoceros
Y Louis d'or
Z David ap Gwilym

172
RICHARD CURREY:
FATAL LIGHT

The recruiter said ... "Gentlemen, you are about to be reborn. You are about to become soldiers, like it or not. May I remind you that these are the last kind words you will ever hear. Best of fuck. ..." He stepped aside. We filed into the van.

A Ray Bradbury
B Intolerable
C Chemise
D Hoofers
E Astute
F Redeemed
G Dubious
H Cheese it
I Underwent
J Revisit
K Rumination
L Enderby Land
M Yakutsk
N Freaks
O Autotelic
P To boot
Q Athlete
R Looped
S Lewisite
T Interplay
U Goethe
V Heave-ho
W Tomorrow

173

S(TEPHANIE) BRUSH:
MEN: AN OWNER'S MANUAL

You should shop for men the way you shop for shoes or puppies or tomatoes. And it's not easy —you can't tell all the important things about a man just by sniffing him or squeezing him or walking him around the block.

A Shook up
B Brett
C Rooftops
D Unafraid
E Some joy
F Hotchkiss
G Mobbing
H Ezra Pound
I Naughty
J Ashley
K Noisome
L One old cat
M Whiten
N Naysay
O Eloquent
P Rim shot
Q Still
R Mouth-watering
S Affirm
T Nymphs
U Usual
V Apportion
W Lighthouse

174

(VICTOR) BORGE:
MY FAVORITE INTERMISSIONS

The Russians not only didn't invent opera, they practically disinvented it. Not that they had anything . . . against opera. . . . But . . . opera is a form of music, . . . something the peasants liked, and anything the peasants liked the Czars didn't, and when the Czars didn't like something, watch out.

A Bandits
B Outwitted
C Roasts
D Gods
E Entertainment
F Modern
G Yatters
H Fondest
I Attaché case
J Vend
K Otterhound
L Ravishing
M Izaak Walton
N Toddy
O Espial
P Intellect
Q Nantucket
R The Phantom
S Epiphany
T Rehashing
U Mythical
V India ink
W Saddening
X Sisyphus
Y In the night
Z Old chap
Z₁ Nazareth
Z₂ Shifty

175

DAVID BUTLER:
THE FALL OF SAIGON

Seldom, if ever, has a victorious army entered the enemy capital with the discipline shown by the forces that occupied Saigon that week. . . . No one has ever claimed . . . a single instance of theft, rape, or other mistreatment on the part of the occupying forces.

A Demote
B Apothegm
C Visor
D In the wink of an eye
E Demerit
F Beseech
G Ups and downs
H Tacit
I Luminous
J Empty heads
K Rapacity
L The priest
M Horatio
N Everyman
O Fetch
P African
Q Loftier
R Loathe
S Orange
T Forthwith
U Scotches
V Accept
W Intolerance
X Groves
Y On the shelf
Z Niceties

176

(CALVIN) TRILLIN:
UNCIVIL LIBERTIES

My research on the subject indicates that there is not a woman in America who can refrain from looking a bit surprised when her husband refers to her constantly in conversation with a hotel manager as "la principessa."

A Testament
B Rejoinder
C Iphigenia
D Laboratory
E Larch
F In touch with
G Namaste
H Unhitched
I Narrates
J Caress
K Inordinate
L Verges
M Inch by inch
N Lampoon
O Lassos
P Inchworm
Q Barman
R Efforts
S Renfrew
T Tenace
U Ishikawa
V Euphrates
W Snoot

177

(WALTER) KAUFMANN:
DISCOVERING THE MIND

Socrates, in Plato's *Symposium*, could take or . . . leave alcohol. . . . When the wine and . . . conversation were good, he went on talking and drinking until the last person had passed out, left at dawn, took a bath, and spent the day as if nothing had happened.

A Kingfisher
B Acknowledge
C Upsetting
D Fathead
E Maladroit
F Apple pan dowdy
G Nates
H Naphtha
I Dodo
J Induct
K Stanton
L Chews out
M Osier
N Venal
O Eyewash
P Ransack
Q In the shell
R Nat Turner
S Gladstone
T Tolls
U Henbane
V Epitaph
W Mistook
X Innovate
Y Nohow
Z Doodad

178

CHET HUNTLEY:
THE GENEROUS YEARS

Shep was an uncertain mixture of shepherd and collie, and I have no sure recollection just how handsome he really was. I recall that his nose was cold, his tongue was warm and friendly on my hands and face, and his fur was made for a small boy to grasp and cling to through romp and roughhouse.

A Cutaway coat
B Howard Hughes
C Effaced
D Tonto
E Hands off
F Unsightly
G Narcissus
H Trip-hammer
I Local
J Exponential
K Yod
L Thrall
M Hard-won
N Emphasis
O Gulls
P Edward Howard
Q Newfoundland
R Elias Howe
S Ram's horn
T Once in a blue moon
U Unavailing
V Sojourns
W Yields
X Escaped harm
Y Anthem
Z Rehash
Z₁ Sangre de Cristo

179

CONSTANCE M. GREIFF:
LOST AMERICA

We tend to denigrate the tastes of the generation or two immediately preceding our own, at the same time that we are attached to the life style of their predecessors—first, perhaps, as merely amusingly quaint, and then as the object of serious study and admiration.

A Cenotaph
B Ousted
C Nether
D Straiten
E Testament
F Adjudicated
G Nettlesome
H Cotter
I Erewhon
J Misfire
K Guelph
L Ramada
M Eddystone
N Inquest
O Fraise-des-bois
P Fishmonger
Q Lagniappe
R Outwardly
S Sweetheart
T Throaty
U Awesome
V Mithraist
W Effigy
X Rheostat
Y Iolanthe
Z Cited
Z₁ Attorney

180

T(HOMAS) HARDY:
THE RETURN OF THE NATIVE

A well-proportioned mind is one which shows no particular bias. One of which we may safely say that it will never cause its owner to be confined as a madman, tortured as a heretic, or crucified as a blasphemer. Also . . . that it will never cause him to be applauded as a prophet, revered as a priest, or exalted as a king.

A Taxonomies
B Halation
C Appalachians
D Rambunctiously
E Droopiness
F Young at Heart
G Tahitians
H Hippodrome
I Estival
J Redeem
K Effervesce
L Twin-screw
M Upbraid
N Racketeers
O Nowadays
P Oppenheimer
Q Flow chart
R The Little Prince
S Hollowware
T Eschew
U Nauseated
V As far as
W Theda Bara
X Idlewild
Y Victorious
Z Embassadorial

181

(HAROLD) ROSENTHAL
(I KNOW) IT'S HERE, SOMEWHERE

Pencils are always stacked . . . in old plastic ice-cream containers or souvenir beer glasses. . . . Don't expect that any pens from any of these containers will work since no one has used them in the last four years. Use the one in your shirt pocket.

FROM "The World & I," Jan. '87

A Reciprocity
B Occiput
C Seabees
D Euripides
E Nessus
F Tarpon
G Handout
H Allocate
I Lancets
J Innovation
K Tristram
L Shandy
M Hassock
N Erewhon
O Roles
P Echinate
Q Slanted
R Out of the money
S Marlin
T Essence
U Waxwings
V Hockey
W Enterprise
X Rank
Y Effortlessly

182

SATURDAY REVIEW
FRONTRUNNERS

An American living in France tells us that in Sam Peckinpah's war film "Cross of Iron," shown recently in Paris with French subtitles, a German soldier peers out of his bunker, spots an oncoming Russian armored column and shouts, "Tanks!" The subtitle reads, "Merci."

A Subcutaneous
B Ammann
C Trinkets
D Ulfilas
E Ramparts
F Dispassionate
G Ankh
H Yttrium
I Recoils
J Enlists
K Verbalist
L If
M Ellsworth
N Winchendon
O Fisherman's
P Reprint
Q Ossining
R Nalchik
S Tace
T Rimpfischhorn
U Umbrageous
V Nacogdoches
W Neutron
X Esclarmonde
Y Repin
Z Software

183

G(EORGE) F. WILL
WASHINGTON'S (LITTLE) MIRACLES

Many thinkers are ready . . . to explain badness . . . in terms of this or that correctable flaw in the social environment. Washington has a growth industry devoted to such explanations. There is less interest in goodness, perhaps because it is not a "problem."

FROM "Newsweek," Dec. 5, 1983

A Goethite
B Foxes
C Wanderer
D Inchcape
E Lemurs
F Loch Ness
G Woodhenge
H Anabasis
I Shrill
J Hard Times
K Intentions
L Nefertiti
M Gondwanaland
N Topsy-turvy
O Othonna
P Navarre
Q Spohr
R My heart is pure
S Ideate
T Rabbits
U Asterisk
V Contempt
W Little boots
X Essex
Y Stanchions

184

HENRY KISSINGER
OBSERVATIONS

If we do not act we face many risks including the loss of the relatively free international trading system that was the basis of post-war prosperity. Contrary to classical economic theory a free-trading system does not run itself. It requires a conscious act of political leadership.

A Half-crowns
B Ellipses
C Nepenthe
D Rattletraps
E Yurt
F Koalas
G Inroads
H Station
I Safflower
J Immediacy
K Nancy Drew
L Gethsemane
M Equality
N Reconstruction
O Office
P Bewildering
Q Satisfactorily
R Ecce homo
S Ralph Roister
   Doister
T Vicissitudes
U Attaints
V Tintoretto
W Ichor
X Offaly
Y Nosy
Z Scapegoats

185

BOOTH TARKINGTON
CLAIRE AMBLER

All her life—even when she was a child—she had seemed to be not one person but two. One was an honest person and the other appeared to be an artist. The honest person did the feeling and most of the thinking; but the artist directed her behaviour and cared about nothing except picturesque effects.

A Bathsheba
B Offends
C Otter shrew
D Thespis
E Henequen
F Tut
G Arthrobacter
H Redhorse
I Kettle of fish
J Isanthous
K Newcastle
L Graphite
M Taxonomic
N Open-handed
O Napped
P Cheesewood
Q Lading
R Appended
S Ishbosheth
T Rusticated
U Entente
V Attrahent
W Mud hen
X Bee-eater
Y Luncheonette
Z Easting down
Z_1 River of Oblivion

MAKE YOUR PUZZLE COLLECTION COMPLETE
with Simon & Schuster's Convenient Backlist Order Form

Now in its ninth decade of publication.

The Original Crossword Puzzle Series

____0-684-81473-0	#195	Feb. 97	Samson	$9.00
____0-684-86936-5	#218	Feb. 01	Samson	$9.00
____0-684-86937-3	#219	Apr. 01	Samson	$9.95
____0-684-86938-1	#220	Jun. 01	Samson	$9.95
____0-684-86941-1	#222	Oct. 01	Samson	$9.95
____0-7432-0537-5	#223	Dec. 01	Samson	$9.95
____0-7432-5096-6	#236	Feb. 04	Samson	$9.95
____0-7432-5111-3	#237	Apr. 04	Samson	$9.95
____0-7432-5112-1	#238	Jun. 04	Samson	$9.95
____0-7432-5121-0	#239	Aug. 04	Samson	$9.95
____0-7432-5122-9	#240	Oct. 04	Samson	$9.95
____0-7432-5123-7	#241	Dec. 04	Samson	$9.95
____0-7432-5124-5	#242	Feb. 05	Samson	$9.95
____0-7432-5125-3	#243	Apr. 05	Samson	$9.95
____0-7432-5126-1	#244	Jun. 05	Samson	$9.95
____0-7432-5127-X	#245	Aug. 05	Samson	$9.95
____0-7432-5128-8	#246	Oct. 05	Samson	$9.95
____0-7432-5129-6	#247	Dec. 05	Samson	$9.95

Simon & Schuster Crossword Treasuries

____0-684-84366-8	#40	Sept. 99	Samson	$9.00
____0-684-85637-9		S&S 75th Anniversary Vintage Crossword Treasury		
		Apr. 99	Farrar	$9.00
____0-7432-4795-7	#41	Nov. 03	Samson/Maleska	$10.00

Simon & Schuster Crostics

____0-671-87193-5	#111	July 94	Middleton	$8.00
____0-684-81380-7	#114	Nov. 95	Middleton	$8.00
____0-684-82963-0	#116	Nov. 96	Middleton	$8.00
____0-684-83652-1	#117	Aug. 97	Middleton	$8.00

Simon & Schuster Crostics Treasuries

____0-671-87221-4	#3	Mar. 94	Middleton	$8.00
____0-684-84354-4	#5	Mar. 98	Middleton	$9.00
____0-7432-0059-4	#6	Nov. 00	Middleton	$9.00

Simon & Schuster Fun with Crostics Series

____0-684-84277-7	#20	Jan. 98	Duerr	$8.00
____0-684-84361-7	#21	Jun. 98	Duerr	$8.00
____0-684-85942-4	#24	July 99	Duerr	$8.00

Simon & Schuster Super Crostics Books

____0-671-51132-7	#3	Mar. 95	Middleton	$10.00
____0-684-81340-8	#4	Mar. 97	Middleton	$10.00
____0-684-84364-1	#5	Mar. 99	Middleton	$10.00

Simon & Schuster Super Crossword Books

____0-671-79232-6	#7	Nov. 92	Maleska	$10.00
____0-671-89709-8	#8	Nov. 94	Maleska	$10.00
____0-684-82964-9	#9	Nov. 96	Maleska	$10.00
____0-684-84365-X	#10	Oct. 98	Samson	$10.00
____0-684-87186-6	#11	May 01	Samson	$10.00
____0-7432-5538-0	#12	Nov. 04	Samson/Maleska	$10.00

Simon & Schuster Large Type Crossword Puzzle Books

____0-684-81187-1	#1	Oct. 95	Maleska	$10.00
____0-684-84367-6	#3	Nov. 99	Maleska	$9.00

Savage Crossword Puzzle Series

____0-684-87195-5	#1	Jul. 00	Savage	$12.00
____0-684-87196-3	#2	Mar. 01	Savage	$12.00

S&S Super Crossword Puzzle Dictionary and Reference Book

____0-684-85696-4		Apr. 99	$15.00

SEND ORDERS TO:

Simon & Schuster Inc.
Order Processing
Department

100 Front Street
Riverside, NJ 08075
Customer Service:
1-800-223-2336
Fax: 1-800-943-9831

Total Cost of All Books Ordered _____

Add Applicable State Sales Tax _____

Check or Money Order Enclosed for _____

Please Charge VISA ____ MASTERCARD ____ AMEX ____

Card # _____ Exp. Date _____

Signature _____

Ship to:

Name _____

Address _____

City _____ State _____ Zip Code_____

FIRESIDE
A Division of Simon & Schuster
A VIACOM COMPANY

Printed in Great Britain
by Amazon

22084494R00128